REIMAGINING THE STATE

This book examines what value, if any, the state has for the pursuit of progressive politics; and how it might need to be reimagined and remade to deliver transformative change.

Is it possible to reimagine the state in ways that open up projects of political transformation? This interdisciplinary collection provides alternative perspectives to the 'antistatism' of much critical writing and contemporary political movement activism. Contributors explore ways of reimagining the state that attend critically to the capitalist, neoliberal, gendered and racist conditions of contemporary polities, yet seek to hold onto the state in the process. Drawing on postcolonial, poststructuralist, feminist, queer, Marxist and anarchist thinking, they consider how states might be reread and reclaimed for radical politics. At the heart of this book is state plasticity – the capacity of the state conceptually and materially to take different forms. This plasticity is central to transformational thinking and practice, and to the conditions and labour that allow it to take place. But what can reimagining do; and what difficulties does it confront?

This book will appeal to academics and research students concerned with critical and transformative approaches to state theory, particularly in governance studies, politics and political theory, socio-legal studies, international relations, geography, gender/sexuality, cultural studies and anthropology.

Davina Cooper is a Research Professor in Law and Political Theory, Dickson Poon School of Law, King's College London.

Nikita Dhawan is Professor of Political Science and Gender Studies at the University of Gießen, Germany.

Janet Newman is Professor Emeritus in the Faculty of Arts and Social Sciences at the Open University, UK.

Part of the SOCIAL JUSTICE Series

Series Editors

Sarah Keenan
Birkbeck College, University of London, UK

Davina Cooper
King's College, London, UK

Sarah Lamble
Birkbeck College, University of London, UK

For information about the series and details of previous and forthcoming titles, see
https://www.routledge.com/Social-Justice/book-series/RCSOCJ

REIMAGINING THE STATE

Theoretical Challenges and Transformative Possibilities

Edited by Davina Cooper, Nikita Dhawan and Janet Newman

Routledge
Taylor & Francis Group
a GlassHouse Book

First published 2020
by Routledge
2 Park Square, Milton Park, Abingdon, Oxon OX14 4RN

and by Routledge
52 Vanderbilt Avenue, New York, NY 10017

A GlassHouse book

Routledge is an imprint of the Taylor & Francis Group, an informa business

British Library Cataloguing-in-Publication Data
A catalogue record for this book is available from the British Library

Library of Congress Cataloging-in-Publication Data
Names: Cooper, Davina, editor. | Dhawan, Nikita, editor. | Newman, Janet, 1945– editor.
Title: Reimagining the state : theoretical challenges and transformative possibilities / edited by Davina Cooper, Nikita Dhawan and Janet Newman.
Description: Abingdon, Oxon ; New York, NY : Routledge, 2019. | Series: Social justice | Includes bibliographic references.
Identifiers: LCCN 2019012314 (print) | LCCN 2019980988 (ebook) | ISBN 9780815382157 (hbk.) | ISBN 9780815382195 (pbk.) | ISBN 9781351209113 (ebook)
Subjects: LCSH: State, The—Philosophy. | Radicalism—Philosophy. | Political geography—Philosophy.
Classification: LCC JC131 .R44 2019 (print) | LCC JC131 (ebook) | DDC 320.101—dc23
LC record available at https://lccn.loc.gov/2019012314
LC ebook record available at https://lccn.loc.gov/2019980988

ISBN: 978-0-8153-8215-7 (hbk)
ISBN: 978-0-8153-8219-5 (pbk)
ISBN: 978-1-351-20911-3 (ebk)

Typeset in Bembo
by Apex CoVantage, LLC

MIX
Paper from
responsible sources
FSC   FSC® C013985
www.fsc.org

Printed in the United Kingdom
by Henry Ling Limited

CONTENTS

ACKNOWLEDGEMENTS

This book would not have happened without the two seminars which facilitated its development. We are grateful for the funding received from the Socio-Legal Studies Association, *Social and Legal Studies* and Kent Law School. The research group at Kent Law School, Social Critiques of Law (SoCriL), provided crucial support and seed funding for this initiative. Thanks to Emilie Cloatre and Donatella Alessandrini for encouraging and financially supporting this idea through SoCriL and so making the two workshops possible.

We are grateful to the series editors, Sarah Keenan and Sarah Lamble, for their very helpful feedback on draft chapters, and to our commissioning editor Colin Perrin for his advice and input. Special thanks also go to Luisa Hoffmann for her support in preparing the manuscript.

CONTRIBUTORS

ACKNOWLEDGEMENTS

Sarah Browne is an artist based in Ireland. Her work is concerned with addressing non-verbal, bodily experiences of knowledge, labour and justice. This primarily sculptural practice also includes writing, publishing, performance and public projects. Recent solo exhibitions include *Report to an Academy* at Marabouparken, Stockholm (2017), *Hand to Mouth* at CCA Derry~Londonderry & IMA, Brisbane, and *The Invisible Limb*, basis, Frankfurt (both 2014). In 2016, she developed *In the Shadow of the State*, a major collaborative co-commission by Artangel and Create with Jesse Jones. This project involved close collaboration with women in the fields of law, music, material culture and midwifery, and addressed the regulation of the female body by the nation-state through a series of legal workshops and performances in Derry, Liverpool, Dublin and London. In 2009, Browne co-represented Ireland at the 53rd Venice Biennale with Gareth Kennedy and Kennedy Browne, their shared collaborative practice. She is associate artist at the UCD School of Law and Social Science.

María do Mar Castro Varela is Professor of Pedagogy and Social Work at the Alice Salomon University in Berlin and lectured at the University of Basel, Switzerland, the Zurich Academy of Arts, Switzerland, and the University of Innsbruck, Austria. Besides Postcolonial Theory, her research interests lie in Gender and Queer Studies, Critical Migration Studies, Critical (Adult-)Education and Trauma Studies. Recent Publications include *Postcolonial Theory. A Critical Introduction* (with Nikita Dhawan) and *The Demonization of Others* (ed., with Paul Mecheril) (both published in German).

John Clarke is an Emeritus Professor of Social Policy at the UK's Open University, where he worked for over 35 years before retiring in 2014. He is also a Recurrent Visiting Professor in the Department of Sociology and Social Anthropology at Central European University in Budapest. He undertook postgraduate work at the Birmingham Centre for Contemporary Cultural Studies in the 1970s before teaching and researching around a range of topics, including welfare states, citizenship, public service reform and the impacts of managerialism and consumerism. He has also been working on the politics and policies of Austerity and the strange political moment of 'Brexit', with articles on the former in *Critical Social Policy* (2012, with Janet Newman) and on the latter in *Critical Policy Studies* (2017, with Janet Newman). His most recent publications include *Critical Dialogues: Thinking Together in Turbulent* Times (2019); *Making Policy Move: Towards a Politics of Translation and Assemblage* (with Dave Bainton, Noémi Lendvai and Paul Stubbs, 2015) and *Disputing Citizenship* (with Kathy Coll, Evelina Dagnino and Catherine Neveu, 2014).

Davina Cooper is Research Professor at the Dickson Poon School of Law, KCL. Her interdisciplinary research approaches questions of transformative politics – their possibilities, limits and conflicts – and the ways in which experiments in living and governing can stimulate new progressive conceptual accounts. Her most recent book is *Feeling like a State: Desire, Denial, and the Recasting of Authority* (2019). Her earlier books include *Everyday Utopias: The Conceptual Life of Promising Spaces* (2014), *Challenging Diversity: Rethinking Equality and the Value of Difference* (2004) and *Governing Out of Order: Space, Law and the Politics of Belonging* (1998). From 1986 to 1990, she was a locally elected member of Haringey Council, London.

Chiara De Cesari is an anthropologist and associate professor in European Studies and Cultural Studies at the University of Amsterdam. Her research focuses on memory, heritage and broader cultural politics and the ways in which these change under conditions of globalisation, particularly the intersection of cultural memory, transnationalism and current transformations of the nation-state. She is also interested in the globalisation of contemporary art and forms of creative institutionalism and statecraft. She is co-editor of the book *Transnational Memories: Circulation, Articulation, Scales* (with Ann Rigney, 2014) and author of *Heritage and the Struggle for Palestine* (2019); she has published widely in journals such as *American Anthropologist, Museum Anthropology, Memory Studies* and the *International Journal of Middle East Studies*.

Nikita Dhawan is Professor of Political Science and Gender Studies at the University of Gießen, Germany. She received the Käthe Leichter Award in 2017 for outstanding achievements in the pursuit of women's and gender studies and in support of the women's movement and the achievement of gender equality. Her publications include *Impossible Speech: On the Politics of Silence and Violence* (2007), *Decolonizing Enlightenment: Transnational Justice, Human Rights and Democracy in a Postcolonial World* (ed., 2014), *Global Justice and Desire: Queering Economy* (co-ed., 2015), *Negotiating Normativity: Postcolonial Appropriations, Contestations and Transformations* (co-ed., 2016) and *Difference that Makes No Difference: The Non-Performativity of Intersectionality and Diversity* (ed., 2017).

Her articles have appeared in leading journals such as *Hypatia, boundary 2, Contemporary Political Theory* and *Feministische Studien.*

Nick Gill is Professor of Human Geography at the University of Exeter, UK. He is a political geographer whose work focuses on issues of justice and injustice, especially in the context of border control, mobility and its confiscation, incarceration and the law. His books include *Carceral Spaces: Mobility and Agency in Imprisonment and Migrant Detention* (ed., with Dominique Moran and Deirdre Conlon, 2013), *Nothing Personal? Geographies of Governing and Activism in the British Asylum System* (2016) and *Asylum Determination in Europe: Ethnographic Perspectives* (ed., with Anthony Good, 2018). His current research concerns court spaces and access to justice in the context of asylum seeking in Europe.

Didi Herman is Professor of Law and Social Change at the University of Kent. She is the author of *Rights of Passage: Struggles for Lesbian and Gay Legal Equality* (1994), *The Antigay Agenda: Orthodox Vision and the Christian Right* (1997), *Globalizing Family Values: The Christian Right's International Activism* (with Doris Buss, 2003), *An Unfortunate Coincidence: Jews and Jewishness in English Law* (2011) and numerous other publications.

Jesse Jones is a Dublin-based Irish artist. Her practice crosses the media of film, performance and installation. Often working through collaborative structures, she explores how historical instances of communal culture may hold resonance in our current social and political experiences. Her project and exhibition *NO MORE FUN AND GAMES* at Dublin City Municipal Gallery, the Hugh Lane, established a 'parasite' institutional structure within the museum space. This work explored how the politics of exclusion operates in relation to the role of women in the history and production of the artistic canon. She is concerned with how political movements and ideas might be expanded to institutional performative gestures. Jones questions how we may look not only through the lens of vast historical movements, but also through the incremental shifts in how we inhabit our everyday lives and experiences. Previous exhibitions include the Istanbul Biennale 2009, as well as solo exhibitions at Artsonje Centre Seoul and RedCat Los Angeles. Jones represented Ireland's pavilion at the 57th Venice Biennale 2017 and lectures at Technological University, Dublin.

Ruth Kinna has published a number of books and articles on anarchist political thought, most recently *Kropotkin: Reviewing the Classical Anarchist Tradition* (2016). She is currently working with Alex Prichard on an ESRC-funded project, 'Anarchy as a Constitutional Principle: Constitutionalising in Anarchist Politics'. The co-authored essay 'Anarchism and Non-Domination' is forthcoming in the *Journal of Political Ideologies.*

Anna Maria Krämer is a political scientist. She currently works for the NGO basa e.V. in the domain of *popular education.* In her doctoral thesis, she carried out a genealogical reconstruction of contemporary and historical representations of statehood in Euro-Western discourses on Africa. Her research interests include postcolonial theory, materialist state theory and African philosophy, as well as feminist and critical race theories. Additionally, she has been working on issues of migration and development in West Africa for medico international and Pro Asyl.

Morag McDermont is Professor of Socio-Legal Studies at the University of Bristol Law School. Her scholarship is informed by 16 years of working in the UK social housing sector in urban renewal, housing associations and cooperative housing. Her concern for inclusive systems of regulation and governing led her to research the role of the advice agencies in supporting citizens' rights and to running *Productive Margins: Regulating for Engagement,* a five-year programme of co-produced, multidisciplinary research with community organisations in Bristol and South Wales.

Janet Newman is Emeritus Professor at the Open University, UK. Her research brings feminist and cultural perspectives to analyses of governance, politics and power. Recent publications have focused on activist engagements with governance, the politics of austerity and approaches to understanding the politics of Brexit and the wider populist turn.

Shirin M. Rai is Professor in the Department of Politics and International Studies, University of Warwick. Her research interests are interdisciplinary: in feminist international political economy, gender and political institutions, and politics and performance. She has written extensively on issues of gender, governance and development. She has consulted with the United Nations' Division for the Advancement of Women and UNDP and was Director of the Leverhulme Trust programme on Gendered Ceremony and Ritual in Parliament. She is the co-editor of *Social Politics* and on the board of *International Feminist Journal of Politics, Politics and Gender, Global Ethics* and the *Indian Journal of Gender Studies.* She is the author of *The Gender Politics of Development* (2008) and co-editor of *The Grammar of Politics and Performance* (2015, Routledge). Her articles have appeared in leading journals such as *International Feminist Journal of Politics, Global Networks, New Political Economy, Hypatia, Political Studies, Social and Legal Studies* and *Signs.* She has just finished her latest book (with Carole Spary) *Performing Representation: Women MPs in the Indian Parliament* (2019) and is co-editing the *Oxford Handbook on Politics and Performance.*

INTRODUCTION

Davina Cooper

The chapters in this book are a response to an invitation that was also a provocation: what might it mean and entail to reimagine the state for transformative progressive politics? In other words, taking on board the many left critiques of the state, what else can be said and done with the state – as a material formation, as something imagined, and in the movement between the two? Asking this question foregrounds the radical and substantive changes more socially just, environmentally responsible worlds require. Inviting contributors to reimagine the state gave form to a seminar in May 2016, where many of these chapters were discussed.[1] A second seminar followed in the autumn of 2017. Contributors bore different fields, methodologies, places and perspectives with them as they took up the invitation to reimagine the state in diverse ways. Some focused on the thorny questions that taking up the state for a progressive politics entails. Others engaged with the challenging labour involved in reimagining; some critically questioned the utility and value of the state's recuperation. This introduction situates the project to reimagine the state within some wider conversations concerned with the challenges, implications and methodological issues this undertaking invokes. It focuses on three themes: the work of reimagining; what it is to be a state; and the contribution(s) states might make to transformative progressive politics.

The work of reimagining

In recent years, there has been renewed interest in the radical imagination as something to consider, but also to develop (e.g. Haiven and Khasnabish, 2014). This book

---

1 See blog post by Tom Kemp, "Can States be progressive? On reimagining the state", *Countercurrents* https://blogs.kent.ac.uk/countercurrents/2016/06/01/can-states-be-progressive-on-re-imagining-the-state/.

explores how practices of reimagining can be collectively and individually inflected, aligned with the right and left, institutionalised and informal. New imaginings can live in the mind, in texts, in social and political systems and things; and they can be enacted and staged through social and cultural innovations, experiments and conflict. But what different forms of reimagining share, in contrast to the naturalised, often beneath-conscious-awareness of mainstream and dominant imaginaries, is an articulated coming-into-presence. Whether virtual or material, reimagining involves deliberate practices of framing, interpreting, cutting and connection-drawing, as alternative histories and futures get posited (e.g., see Browne and Jones, this volume).

Reimagining, however, is not just about other times. While often associated with hopes and longings for better futures or nostalgic returns to romanticised pasts, imagining things otherwise is also anchored in the present. This has a tacit dimension, in the sense that the discourses, concerns, anxieties and fantasies expressed in and through reimagining belong to the contemporary moment. It also has a practical dimension, as the task of reimagining the state calls forth present-day action. This is addressed by Nick Gill in his chapter on border abolition. Gill's chapter provides a detailed engagement with the task of transitioning from our current world of state borders to one where people can move freely. He asks: what international challenges are raised; and what kinds of measures and reforms might be needed? Reimagining is simultaneously about what does and does not yet exist, as it explores, but also at times troubles and explodes, the border between the two.

If reimagining involves consciously and purposefully treating the affairs of this world as if they were, or could be, otherwise, why take up the task of reimagining the state? There is a tremendous body of critical work, as several chapters discuss, on the harms that states cause and participate in, from relations of capitalist exploitation, and neo-colonial domination, to environmental destruction, the oppression of people (at home and abroad) and the marginalisation or crushing of less powerful cultures. Given the central role states play in the production of injury and harm, many would argue that seeking to revalue the state, and so investing time in its reimagining, is politically misguided. Not only does it recuperate a political formation and concept saturated with violence and inequity, but it also invokes a form of idealism in which reimagining states does stuff – that if we think of the state as benign, at least in its potential, this can have transformative material consequences. This book does not seek to sanitise the state; to dismiss left state critiques as misleading or flawed; or to present the state's reimagining as a 'first step' to its more perfect realisation. At the same time, while the book recognises that more hopeful state imaginaries *can* cast a veil over the harms and oppressions states participate in, it also works from two other key premises.

First, the book treats the state as an important and productive concept for progressive transformative politics that cannot and should not be cast to one side – at least not too quickly or too easily.[2] Janet Newman (this volume) argues that states

---

2 I explore this more fully in Cooper (2019).

matter when it comes to tackling global problems, including social inequality; states are also important providers of education, welfare, rights and the management of collective independence. Shirin Rai (this volume) emphasises the importance of the state's political, legal and performative role in regulating production and social reproduction. Contributors' views overlap; but there is no easy consensus. Authors in this book take different positions on why and how the state, or particular states, matter, drawing on socialist, postcolonial, feminist and other left perspectives, including anarchist ones, with quite different interests and responses to the state. As discussed below, this book puts these different approaches into conversation with each other, without seeking a resolution. Second, it recognises that state imaginaries have effects. How the state is thought about and understood makes a difference. This point has been addressed by various scholars (e.g. Gill, 2010; Navaro-Yashin, 2002; Yang, 2005). Their work suggests that whether states are imagined as democratic or oppressive, legitimate or illegitimate, permeable or sealed-up, successful or failing, is consequential. It affects international relations, social movement activism, and the discourse, strategic conduct, and policy practices of officials and politicians.

Yet, how states are imagined, by which we mean those representations and understandings perceived as obvious, truthful or real, is not quite the same as deliberately and purposefully *reimagining* the state. At the heart of this book are the conscious efforts of academics, activists, artists, officials and others to imagine the state – both what it is and could become – *against the grain of prevailing accounts*. New imaginaries borrow, bury, divert, complicate and stand upon older ones (see Newman and Dhawan, this volume), but they do so for different reasons. In some cases, it is as a hopeful attempt to bring something new into being, including by acting as if it was already there. Chiara De Cesari's chapter explores this rationale in relation to museum and arts-based projects intended to provide an 'anticipatory representation' of Palestine by depicting, or more accurately 'performing', Palestine as a nation-state. Certainly, these projects had a critical dimension in the opposition they posed to the global order's refusal to support Palestine's national aspirations. However, staging Palestine, rendering it normal, also functioned as a performative act of experimental statecraft – acting as if something existed in order to usher it in (see also Browne and Jones, this volume).

Imagining states against the grain may focus on what particular states can become. Alternatively, they may focus on critically rereading states as they are (or seem to be), placing them within different discursive networks (see Aretxaga, 2003). Taking to task the dominant Eurocentric paradigm of statehood, Anna Krämer critically questions depictions of African states as failed or fragile. Didi Herman offers a rereading of Israel, challenging the taken-for-granted assumption that Israel is simply and narrowly a Jewish state. Reinterpreting particular states challenges the prevailing terms of critique. In so doing, it suggests other pathways and modes of resolution, as well as other placeholders for responsibility and culpability. Herman (this volume), for instance, suggests that Israel is not simply a product of Jewish nationalism (or zionism), but also of Christian-based antisemitism, premillennialism and colonialism. Paying attention to the networks that tie Christianity to

Israel reorients, at least in part, how to think about Israel's present and future. But reimagining can also move away from the aspirations and limitations of particular materially situated states and state projects and assume a more conceptual form (Cooper, this volume). Left scholarship has long engaged in rereading the capitalist state – rejecting its liberal characterisation as democratic, benign or merely self-interested in order to emphasise its structured and structuring relationship to dominant class, racialised, gendered and colonial relations (e.g. see Rai, this volume). Other contemporary rereadings focus on state form (discussed shortly) and affect, including the state's relationship to irrationality, passion and the erotic, challenging the assumption that states are rational, emotionless, non-erotic entities (see Newman, this volume; also Hunter, 2015; Jupp et al., 2016).

Embarking on the task of forging new conceptual imaginaries does different things. Refreshing the conceptual toolbox, positing a newly patterned conceptual landscape, reveals, revalues and makes sense of hopeful practices that have been ignored or neglected because they fail to fit prevailing paradigms. It provides new connections or articulations between activities and norms otherwise kept apart; and it gives recognition to the capacities and power of minor forces. Both John Clarke and Nick Gill (this volume) engage in a conceptual rereading of what statehood could come to mean and be in their discussions of state coercion and the dismantling of state borders respectively. The experimental quality of Gill's chapter, in particular, is echoed by Sarah Browne and Jesse Jones, who construct what they describe as an archive of the 'post-patriarchal state', signalling present-day practices and objects that will have become defunct, existing as little more than historical waste within a post-patriarchal future.

Academic research reveals that how the state is imagined matters; it also reveals the labour that goes into its reimagining through academic, activist, artistic, policy and official work (see Newman, this volume). National struggles for liberation and activist projects to remake particular states demonstrate the work that flows from reimagining, as well as the work involved in rethinking how statehood might be done. Practising the state imagination emerges in the course of prefigurative institutional initiatives that seek to actualise a preferred kind of state. This is a dual strategy: to bring such states into being – as De Cesari (this volume) describes in relation to Palestine; and second, to allow such states (or aspects of them) to be *practised* in the present. Fiona McConnell (2016) describes this process in relation to the Tibetan Government-in-Exile, with its extra-territorial rehearsing of statehood in India. Reimagining and re-enacting the state engages different registers of political feeling from gravity, determination and resistance to imagination, creative improvisation and play, recognising how these also combine (e.g. see McConnell, 2012). They also involve different scales. While geographers emphasise the contested, improvised and agentic character of scale-*making*, efforts to reimagine the state, including the nation-state, often involve compact spaces of prefigurative activity, whether through municipal government (Cooper, this volume; Russell, 2019), refugee settlements (Mundy, 2007) or protest camps (Routledge, 1997). Mundy's (2007: 278) account of Western Saharan refugee camps in Algeria provides one striking example of how a camp might undertake new national performances. He writes: 'Following an uneasy start, the refugee camps ... evolved into a kind of state in exile, a space where Western Saharans could practise the kind of citizenship and governance that they hoped to achieve upon independence.' There are also other scales to the work involved in redoing the state, including those of imagining – from the collective engagement with new nation-asserting practices that De Cesari describes, to the academic-NGO partnerships discussed in the chapter by Morag McDermont and the Productive Margins Collective on reimagining regulation, to María do Mar Castro Varela's account of the labour of Jewish theorist, Judith Butler, in developing a reflexive and ethical response to Israel/Palestine.

Investing labour in reimagining the state and taking up its terms, however, is not uncontentious. Anarchists oppose the state's recuperation, and pitch a very different imaginary of the state as an abstract symbol of domination and oppression that is, consequentially, not simply unnecessary, but politically damaging (see, for instance, Newman, 2001; Springer, 2012). Through their critique, anarchists contest the state's enduring psychic power as an idea and attachment, arguing for the need to break free from its hold in order to imagine and build worlds based on freely chosen, non-hierarchical, decentralised forms of organising (see Kinna, this volume). Yet, differentiating localised organisational forms and relations from those of the state suggests a clear distinction between the two, that we can know which forms are state forms, and which are not. If the state needs to be reimagined in order to have a place within a progressive transformative politics, might some anarchist forms of organising also come to be considered state forms, albeit micro-ones? Can voluntary membership and horizontal action have a place in certain kinds of reimagined states; or does this render the concept of the state so expansive as to be meaningless? We might then ask, as John Clarke does in his contribution, when are we *re*imagining the state or in fact imagining something else?

What is it to be a state?

Reimagining the state invokes a series of crucial questions about what it takes to be a state – recognising that states and state-thinking bear the baggage of different conceptual histories and geopolitical trajectories. The standard liberal answer, from the Global North, is that states involve institutional apparatuses with control over territory, populations and things, along with the organised deployment of legitimate force in conditions where this is recognised by other states. But if this is the definitional crux of what it is to be a state, the contribution states can make to progressive politics, even when norms of representative democracy are added, appears limited. Nation-states can govern territory and populations, and use coercive force, for equality-supporting as well as hierarchical ends. But if states are to be deliberative, democratic, responsible and socially just, new conceptions of what it means to be a state are also required (see Cooper, 2019). This raises questions about how such imaginaries can be enacted, as well as imagined. It also raises questions about state form. Should the state be understood as a material formation, an idea, as both or neither (see Hay, 2014)? Do states necessarily condense wider social relations; and does this mean they reflect, shape or coordinate dominant social interests? How do states relate to subordinate interests? These are questions that have received extensive discussion within state theory and scholarship as several contributors identify. They underscore the complex relationship between how the state is conceptualised and defined, on the one hand, and the different kinds of entities recognised as states, on the other. They also raise important questions for thinking about the state's reimagining. Undertaking to reimagine a material structure raises different issues to reimagining an idea; reimagining a formation that is, by definition or in practice, tightly structured is different to reimagining a formation that is already contradictory, porous and provisional. If states simply mirror wider social relations, the value of their radical reimagining seems slight. Other aspects of social life may be more pressing subjects for rethinking.

Contributors to this book take quite different approaches to the question of state form and its relationship to wider social life. In doing so, an important question is raised: how can we know if the state is worth reimagining if we cannot agree on what it means to be a state?

Paralleling accounts of 'essentially contested concepts' (Gallie, 1955) and different 'language games' (Wittgenstein, 2009 [1953]; see also Haugaard (2010)), this book starts from the premise that conceptual plurality is not only inevitable, but also valuable, in conditions where a full and nuanced account of the state comes from the combination of different perspectives (rather than from their ranking). Approaching the state as a polysemic concept, no single, right or best mode of conceptualising exists in abstraction. The question is, what do different interpretive cuts and frames reveal and generate when it comes to organised political life? What alternative perspectives are made available on shared questions and concerns? And how do different ways of imagining (or reimagining) the state engage with, stimulate and enrich each other, recognising that these imaginaries have material lives and do not just exist as disembodied floating images.

Conceptual plurality unsettles taken-for-granted notions of what counts as a state, making it possible to identify states in new, innovative ways. But, even if we treat the state as a socio-material formation, to the extent that states are not just nation-states and can incorporate other organisational forms that engage in practices of governing, what if anything is distinctive about states? There are several risks in defining the state too expansively. For our purposes, two stand out. The first is the risk of muddying the work done by a sharper critical definition, attuned to inequalities, domination and the changing social relations that states are shaped by. The second is losing the specificity of state practice and responsibility. Certainly, many of the attributes that progressives associate politically with the state, such as democratic accountability, 'public things' (Honig, 2017) and social provision (Newman and Clarke, 2014), might also be expected of other forms of governance. However, the risk is that those market rationalities associated with non-state governance become ever more hegemonic if the specifically social and political forms of justification associated with states become watered down or diffused.

Ruth Kinna (this volume) explores one way of giving the state distinctiveness, by placing the state's institutional formation in relation to an "undergirding" political theory, which, in her critical account of liberal states of the Global North, is contract theory. Approaching the concept of the state in this way emphasises the broader cultural, normative and ideational constellations in which state formations and their justifications are embedded, and which they in turn carry. It means reading states as more than practical apparatuses of governance; central to their conceptualisation is a political account of their place and purpose. This is a helpful framing. However, as Kinna's chapter explores, this approach raises questions about how states should be understood when the undergirding political theory is contested or deemed to 'mask' reality (witnessed in critical responses to liberal notions of state democracy or the rule of law). It also raises important questions about the political ideas that might undergird radically reimagined states. If we reimagine states as formations with the *capacity* to subvert social relations of power, advance the interests and needs of the dissident and powerless, and take shape as micro-states or local states (as well as national and global ones), what kinds of ideational constellations might these states be embedded within and carry? Or is it better to think of 'states' that significantly trouble a more conventional account in other terms – as shadow states, make-believe states, counter-states, even para-states, claiming an authorised status they cannot meaningfully or fully access?

This book explores some of the narratives, cultures, ideas and historical memories that subversive states and attempted states carry. At the same time, the book does not seek to conclusively answer ontological questions regarding the state's 'real' form (see Hay, 2014; Jessop, 2016). Approaching the concept of the state as necessarily plural, contextual and purposive, the book opens space for exploring the work different state conceptions (might) do, while paying attention to the tasks and conditions out of, and through, which these conceptions arise.

What states offer progressive politics?

This takes me to the third question of this book: what do states offer (and what can they offer) progressive and transformative political projects? This question, of course, is intricately tangled up with the conception of the state adopted. As a consequence, it has been a site of considerable, often ferocious, contestation on the Marxist and feminist left. Wider discussion often focuses on whether state advancement of welfare and social justice agendas (to the extent states are deemed to advance these agendas) constitute 'real' gains wrought by political struggle or deliberate state forms of mystification and appeasement. This discussion is an important, if often overly polarising, one. However, our focus here is less on exposing the cynical agendas driving 'progressive' policies or, conversely, on arguing that such policies demonstrate real meaningful benefits, than on exploring the presence of progressive possibility in ways that attend to states' contradictory character. The capacity of states to simultaneously be progressive and regressive, authoritarian and enabling, remains whether the state is understood as an assemblage, terrain, idea or institutional effect (e.g. see Dhawan, Newman, Rai, this volume). However, much of the writing on states' progressive value approaches states as socio-material formations of governance.

Public goods, planning, care, education, coordination, environmental sustainability and forging a commons are some of the benefits attributed to state-based forms of governance. While discussion typically focuses on liberal types in the Global North, related arguments have also been made about other states, including postcolonial states in the Global South. Newman and Dhawan explore this further in their concluding remarks to this book. According to Dhawan and Randeria (2013), these postcolonial states have the potential to advance rights and justice for subaltern groups. Despite their own political vulnerability, and often unjust practices, Dhawan and Randeria (2013) suggest such states remain essential in containing, mediating and countering the global reach of more powerful transnational forces. This argument is picked up by Anna Krämer (this volume) in her discussion of postcolonial Africa.

In reimagining the state, we might, then, approach states as formations able (although they may refuse) to hold responsibility for social and environmental well-being (Cooper, 2019). This is a responsibility that is not predefined, zero-sum and limited, but capable of being open, reflexive and in development (see Noxolo et al., 2012; Trnka and Trundle, 2014). In practice, state responsibility is often rejected, curtailed or aligned with powerful interests and right-wing agendas. Nevertheless, the possibility for state formations to hold and exercise a more egalitarian, environmentally sustainable responsibility is crucial. Political responsibility is often linked to what states bring into being; however, it can also involve states in practices of abolition. At times, these involve decriminalisation – abolishing the regulatory frameworks that make particular practices, such as gay sex, sex work or drug-use, illegal. Abolition, however, can target (newly) stigmatised practices as well as proscriptive laws. Drawing on states' symbolic and coercive weight, Gill (this volume) considers the role that states might play in undoing national borders (on imagining nations without territory, see also Castro Varela, this volume). In other words, he suggests, states could become key players in creating a world without national frontiers. Of course, some might argue, progressive state action to ameliorate economic and social inequality, whether it involves abolishing borders or proscribing slavery, simply has states undoing (or reducing) harms they have caused or for which they are otherwise responsible. Acute economic inequality, for instance, is sustained by private property and corporate power, which depend on protection and recognition from state law. Thus, states produce distinctions and divisions, which they subsequently unsettle or re-tone: the state as *pharmakon* (see Dhawan, this volume). Yet, the argument that states should participate in reforming social life, on social justice grounds, does not depend on a saviour narrative in which states (from the Global North) sweep in to save the day, a figure evoked by Sarah Keenan (2015: 1–5) in her discussion of asylum law. Rather, to the extent recognised states have power and presence across a wide range of activities and fields – from the legal classification of gender to property relations, language usage and geopolitical divisions – they constitute important terrains and assemblages of action in pursuit of political change.

State capacity to criminalise harms also raises important questions about the place of coercion and regulation in reimagining progressive statecraft. Neither coercion nor regulation is exclusive to the state; but to the extent states perform (and should perform) such functions, can they do so in ways that advance a transformative progressive politics? Several contributors take up the question of the coercive and command-based powers of states. John Clarke explores what place coercive social control might have within a transformative state account. His analysis sits within wider debates where those arguing for the thorough-going dismantling of states' coercive and penal infrastructures – worried about the easy turn to state force to deal with harms such as hate-speech (see also Dhawan, this volume) – meet others adopting a more pragmatic approach, attentive to the contribution state-managed social control might make to protecting and supporting exposed communities. Coercive social control also raises other issues. Debate often focuses on the question of what to do about interpersonal annoyances, the terrain of anti-social behaviour and nuisance law with its attunement to unwanted sounds, smells, sights and bothersome forms of touch. However, a more thorough reimagining, as Clarke identifies, foregrounds the politically contested question of what constitutes harm and so is rightfully subject to regulation; the democratic mechanisms and relations of accountability that would need to be put into place; and the modes of regulation that might displace a vertical top-down state model.

Today, new forms of regulatory practice are emerging as some states, in some areas of life, try to govern at a distance, shaping and guiding (rather than determining) the conduct of others. Julia Black (2001) has explored these more indirect forms of public governing in terms of 'decentred regulation' as actors and fields are enabled to govern themselves. Legal pluralists also emphasise the work done by non-state forms of normative ordering (Cooper, this volume), forms that variously borrow, interact, mirror and diverge from state ones. The relationship between state and non-state forms of legal and normative ordering emerge in relation to speech that is deemed provocative or hateful (see Dhawan, this volume). How should speech that stigmatises, excludes or hurts others be treated? Is it better for community norms to structure the management of painful public speech, as in a university setting, for instance; or should governments participate; and if so, how? Kinna's account of contract theory in relation to "free agreement" poses similar questions about the value of normative community frameworks in contrast to state ones. But the relationship between different regulatory orders (whether state or non-state) is not just one of distribution and competitive coexistence. It is also about how they combine, a process that takes place across a wide array of spaces, from courts, police stations and adoption cases to public sex sites, university disciplinary procedures and cooked food.

One model of regulatory combination, identified by Clarke (this volume), involves a composite network of state and non-state bodies, within a 'pyramid' approach to social control and enforcement (see Braithwaite, 2002; Hepple, 2011).

Here, the question is less whether states should act coercively (or whether coercion is better performed by other bodies) than how coercive and non-coercive modes of regulation might work together, as non-state bodies and informal regulatory structures become enlaced with state-based and coercive ones. A different form of co-regulation is offered by Morag McDermont and the Productive Margins Collective in their chapter, which addresses the possibilities and challenges regulatory co-production faces. Reimagining regulation in a more fundamental way, as this chapter seeks to do, means unpacking regulatory systems to explore how control, resources, laws, policies, things, ideas and authority combine, in order to address how those excluded from participation in regulatory systems, and particularly those subject to such systems, can play a different role. One issue raised by this chapter is the importance of process (echoing the wider discussion of prefigurative initiatives in this book). The authors argue regulatory thinking and processes need to pay attention to the involvement of citizens as participants rather than just as targets and objects. They also need to grapple with different modes of 'seeing and knowing'. Both are regulatory imperatives that foreground the importance of how the translation and brokering of regulation are performed for communities at the margins. McDermont and the Productive Margins Collective's argument, alongside Newman's (this volume), asks us to consider the methods we deploy in accessing and knowing the state, and the stakes involved in knowing the state through other means. For instance, how might we comprehend what it is and could mean to be a state if we paid more attention to knowing the state through, for instance, registers of touch (or even taste and smell), as well as sight – the more common focus of academic work?

Finally, let me briefly introduce the chapters that follow. The book is arranged in four parts. The first part, 'The politics of reimagination', consists of three chapters which, in different ways, consider the struggles involved in reimagining the state – from the varied and situated labour of its pursuit, to the state harms that reimagining has to counter, and the challenges that engaging with a multifaceted formation, able to undo as well as cause injustice, can generate. Janet Newman's chapter opens this section, taking up the claim that states matter. Approaching the state as an unstable ensemble of forces, tendencies and antagonisms, she explores a series of propositions that offer productive resources for rethinking states' relationships to plurality, nationhood, feeling and publicity. Central to Newman's account is the embodied political labour that goes into reimagining the state. Importantly, here, imagining is not simply a mental process or one materialising only on our computer screens or in print. Instead, it involves a range of sites – activist and arts-based, as well as institutional – where new forms of political 'stitching', policy development and experimenting occur.

The complexity and difficulty of rethinking the state also provides the starting-point for Shirin Rai's discussion. Arguing for the urgency of reimagining, and the need for a feminist postcolonial perspective that stresses the place and being-ness of humans in the world, Rai's analysis focuses on the relationship between the state and the gendered household given relations of capitalist production and social reproduction, questions of political form, and the vital need for new forms of solidarity underpinned by an intersectional approach to social relations. A refusal to treat the state as straightforwardly beneficial or harmful for a transformative progressive politics also underpins Nikita Dhawan's chapter. Her discussion centres on the place of the state in relation to hate-speech debates. Dhawan traces some of the difficult issues, which arise for critics of legal intervention in relation to the challenge of responding to and regulating violent and racist speech, including as political satire. From within state theory, she argues that the state's ability to intervene in and regulate social power-conflicts, including hate-speech disputes, should be recognised even as the state also contributes to such conflicts' structure, force and genesis. At the heart of Dhawan's account is a refusal to romanticise non-state life as radically other to the state, as well as a refusal to celebrate the withdrawal of the state from everyday social conflicts.

Part II of the book offers a series of rereadings of the state, focusing on individual and regional states, as well as the concept of the state itself. These rereadings challenge dominant understandings and narratives, for instance on Israel or African forms of statehood, as well as the stories that get told about state legitimacy and what underpins it. In 'Why Africa's "Weak States" matter', Anna Krämer critically addresses the dilemmas facing African states. To be recognised and heard, African states have had to subject themselves to the global order of states. But while claiming statehood may be pragmatically necessary in order to be intelligible within international politics, it measures and assesses states against norms emanating from the Global North. This leads to depictions of African states as 'weak', 'failed' or 'fragile' – safe havens for transnational terrorists, and so as regional and global security threats. It also undermines the basis on which a more democratic global order could be constructed. Krämer concludes by arguing for the need to reimagine statehood in Africa – to replace currently hegemonic concepts with transnational approaches that take as their starting point the postcolonial condition of the continent's political formations.

María do Mar Castro Varela's chapter offers a reading of Judith Butler's book *Parting Ways: Jewishness and the Critique of Zionism* (2012), in which she places Butler's pursuit of an ethical state imaginary in conversation with Marxist, feminist and postcolonial state theories. This critical work offers tools for approaching the state as dynamic, relational and heterogeneous, a formation that condenses different political projects, rationalities and interests. Such an approach to the state informs Castro Varela's discussion of belonging, nationhood and ethical responsibility. What also emerges from her chapter is the emotional labour involved in taking an ethical stand. In ways that resonate with Newman's earlier discussion, Castro Varela reflects on Butler's undertaking in reflexively criticising Israel as a Jewish American feminist and the wider intellectual, ethical and communal Jewish sources that support this process.

Didi Herman's chapter, on rereading Israel, combines two rarely connected fields – the critical study of Christianity and critical scholarship on Israel. The aim of her chapter is to complicate taken-for-granted accounts of Israel as a Jewish state by exploring the different ways in which Christianity and Christendom have also contributed to Israel's formation. Her analysis focuses on four key strands: histories of antisemitism, Christian empire building, the role of Christian evangelicals and evangelical thought, and Israel's place as a Christ-like messiah. Engaging with wider critical discourse on Israel, not least its depiction as a settler colony, Herman argues for a multi-faceted account that can make room for different (including contradictory) approaches. In concluding, she considers what her account means for thinking about a Jewish state.

Ruth Kinna's chapter moves away from Israel/Palestine to offer a rereading of the liberal state in relation to political contract theory. It contrasts the work of two leading critics of contract, Charles Mills and Carole Pateman, and considers the implications of their critiques for political analysis and action. Kinna's account focuses on the question of whether contract constitutes a 'tool' of the 'master' (or state) causing it to be constrained in its radical application. Drawing on anarchist political thought, Kinna develops Pateman's approach, which substitutes the concept of free agreement for that of contract. Imagining citizens negotiating their own justice claims through direct action, Kinna challenges the notion that 'tools' such as rights belong to the state. Instead, she argues, they constitute grass-roots resources for community-driven action.

Prefiguration provides the focus of the third part of this book. This is a theme that runs through many of the book's chapters, including those of Newman and Kinna. This section, however, foregrounds diverse practical attempts to prefigure, anticipate or otherwise practice more democratic or just forms of statecraft, including by means of the regulatory practices with which the state is associated. Chiara De Cesari's chapter illuminates the ways in which artists and cultural producers contribute to performing the nation-state in conditions where it does not yet exist, by acting as if it did. Her discussion focuses on experimental cultural practices in relation to a Palestinian national museum, and Palestinian art biennials, by a Palestinian non-governmental organisation in 2007 and 2009. She argues that these experiments do not just represent or imitate the social world; they also aim to be performative in the sense of advancing a new polity under conditions of current statelessness.

My chapter similarly explores a form of experimental practice; in this instance the municipal prefiguring of socialist government in Britain. My aim in taking up an episode of imaginative progressive governance is to explore not only what prefiguring the state, as a practical experiment in governing, might entail, but also what it means to prefigure the state as a concept – that is, to act as if the state could now mean something different from the neoliberal accounts that currently prevail. Central to this discussion is the plural state. However, while plural state thinking makes room for different kinds and scales of statehood, it does not necessarily foreground progressive ones. I therefore turn to 1980s British municipal radicalism to help consider what an imaginary of the state as horizontal, everyday, activist and stewardly might involve, and what a prefigurative conception of the state might accomplish. Practising institutional life differently likewise anchors the chapter by

Morag McDermont and the Productive Margins Collective, which offers a form of prefigurative conceptualising in relation to regulation. McDermont and colleagues explore the challenge of practising regulation (as both an idea and a mode of operating) in ways that engage communities at the margins of state decision-making. Their account is critical of recent developments that frame regulatory participation too narrowly, excluding in particular those with little power or formal credentialised knowledge, but who are yet still affected. Exploring a different, collaborative approach to regulation, the authors focus on four themes: expertise, experience, deliberation and creativity. They conclude by arguing for the importance of reimagining politics and for the need to secure a different political infrastructure that can support marginalised communities.

The final part of the book continues with the challenge of how to reimagine the state. While the chapters in the previous section explore practical attempts to anticipate a more progressive state or to actualise new regulatory forms, these final three chapters offer thought-experiments, which, in different ways, confront some of the most politically troubling qualities associated with states. In a wide-ranging discussion, John Clarke examines certain problems that arise when principles and practices of coercion are mobilised in relation to progressive statehood. Taking the question of social control's place in relation to progressive political transitioning as his starting point, Clarke's discussion focuses on three sets of issues: can existing powers and agencies be reimagined; the role of coercion and the matters that might legitimately give rise to it; and the institutional arrangements that should be sought, and made subject to democratic forms of control. Nick Gill takes up a parallel set of concerns in his discussion of state borders. Like Clarke, he is concerned with the question of what state power can be used to do. Both he and Clarke pay particular attention to questions of process and transition, something Gill explores in some detail in relation to border abolition. In an ambitious thought experiment, Gill traces a gradual process of cooperative abolition of state controls over migration through international treaty. Anchored in the right to free international movement, he explores some of the principles and provisions that might be needed for free movement to function as part of an internationalist, progressive agenda rather than a neoliberal market one.

Gill's chapter is a thought-experiment that, by discussing some of the practical issues posed by border abolition, makes its advancement thinkable and more plausible. Sarah Browne and Jesse Jones's photographic essay takes a different approach. What they offer is a 'post-patriarchal archive', identifying objects obsolete once patriarchy has fallen. Like the Palestinian arts initiatives, discussed by De Cesari, their aim is a performative one – to represent a desired future as already present – or at least imaginable, in order to support its accomplishment. Browne and Jones's written essay in this book provides an alternative medium to the workshop demonstration they have created in which everyday objects are stamped, in turn, to indicate their hazardous character to women within the terms of 'late-capitalist oppression'. In a political act of bold prediction, the essay (and performance) place things proleptically stamped with their future redundancy back into present-day circulation.

Finally, we close with a concluding chapter by Janet Newman and Nikita Dhawan where they reflect on the discussion of the state evoked by the invitation to reimagine. Their account follows four threads drawn from the preceding chapters: the challenge of thinking differently, the politics of representation, transformative progressive change, and on living politically with ambivalence.

Acknowledgements

I am grateful to the two book editors, Janet Newman and Nikita Dhawan, for their feedback on earlier drafts, and also for the comments of the series editors, Sarah Keenan and Sarah Lamble.

References

Aretxaga, B. (2003) 'Maddening States', *Annual Review of Anthropology*, 32(1), pp. 393–410.
Black, J. (2001) 'Decentring Regulation: Understanding the Role of Regulation and Self-Regulation in a "Post-Regulatory" World', *Current Legal Problems*, 54(1), pp. 103–146.
Braithwaite, J. (2002) *Restorative Justice and Responsive Regulation*. New York and Oxford: Oxford University Press.
Cooper, D. (2019) *Feeling Like a State: Desire, Denial, and the Recasting of Authority*. Durham, NC: Duke University Press.
Dhawan, N. and Randeria, S. (2013) 'Perspectives on Globalization and Subalternity' in Huggan, G. (ed.), *The Oxford Handbook of Postcolonial Studies*. Oxford: Oxford University Press, pp. 559–86.
Gallie, W. B. (1955) 'Essentially Contested Concepts', *Proceedings of the Aristotelian Society*, 56, pp. 167–98.
Gill, N. (2010) 'Tracing Imaginations of the State: The Spatial Consequences of Different State Concepts among Asylum Activist Organisations', *Antipode*, 42(5), pp. 1048–70.
Haiven, M. and Khasnabish, A. (2014) *The Radical Imagination: Social Movement Research in the Age of Austerity*. London: Zed Books.
Haugaard, M. (2010) 'Power: A "Family Resemblance" Concept', *European Journal of Cultural Studies*, 13(4), pp. 419–38.
Hay, C. (2014) 'Neither Real nor Fictitious but "as if Real"? A Political Ontology of the State', *British Journal of Sociology*, 65(3), pp. 459–80.
Hepple, B. (2011) 'Enforcing Equality Law: Two Steps Forward and Two Steps Backwards for Reflexive Regulation', *Industrial Law Journal*, 40(4), pp. 315–35.
Honig, B. (2017) *Public Things: Democracy in Disrepair*. Oxford: Oxford University Press.
Hunter, S. (2015) *Power, Politics and the Emotions: Impossible Governance?* London: Routledge.
Jessop, B. (2016) *The State: Past, Present, Future*. Cambridge: Polity.
Jupp, E., Pykett, J. and Smith, F. M. (2016) *Emotional States: Sites and Spaces of Affective Governance*. Oxford and New York: Routledge.
Keenan, S. (2015) *Subversive Property: Law and the Production of Spaces of Belonging*. London: Routledge.
McConnell, F. (2016) *Rehearsing the State: The Political Practices of the Tibetan Government-in-Exile*. Chichester, UK: John Wiley & Sons.
McConnell, F., Moreau, T. and Dittmer, J. (2012) 'Mimicking State Diplomacy: The Legitimizing Strategies of Unofficial Diplomacies', *Geoforum*, 43(4), pp. 804–14.

Mundy, J. A. (2007) 'Performing the Nation, Pre-figuring the State: The Western Saharan Refugees, Thirty Years Later', *Journal of Modern African Studies*, 45(2), pp. 275–97.

Navaro-Yashin, Y. (2002) *Faces of the State: Secularism and Public Life in Turkey*. Princeton, NJ: Princeton University Press.

Newman, J. and Clarke, J. (2014) 'States of Imagination', *Soundings*, 57(1), pp. 153–69.

Newman, S. (2001) 'War on the State: Stirner's and Deleuze's Anarchism', *Anarchist Studies*, 9(2), pp. 147–64.

Noxolo, P., Raghuram, P. and Madge, C. (2012) 'Unsettling Responsibility: Postcolonial Interventions', *Transactions of the Institute of British Geographers*, 37(3), pp. 418–29.

Routledge, P. (1997) 'The Imagineering of Resistance: Pollok Free State and the Practice of Postmodern Politics', *Transactions of the Institute of British Geographers*, 22(3), pp. 359–76.

Russell, B. (2019) 'Beyond the Local Trap: New Municipalism and the Rise of the Fearless Cities', *Antipode,* 51(3), pp. 989–1010.

Springer, S. (2012) 'Anarchism! What Geography Still Ought to Be', *Antipode*, 44(5), pp. 1605–24.

Trnka, S. and Trundle, C. (2014) 'Competing Responsibilities: Moving beyond Neoliberal Responsibilisation', *Anthropological Forum*, 24(2), pp. 136–53.

Wittgenstein, L. (2009 [1953]) *Philosophical Investigations*. 4th edn. Chichester, UK: John Wiley & Sons.

Yang, S.-Y. (2005) 'Imagining the State: An Ethnographic Study', *Ethnography*, 6(4), pp. 487–516.

PART I

The politics of reimagination

PART I

The politics of reimagination

1

THE POLITICAL WORK
OF REIMAGINATION

Janet Newman

Introduction

Any project of reimagination cannot begin with a blank slate. As authors, academics and activists, our thinking is already marked by personal and political histories. I, like many others contributing to this volume, have engaged in long-running critiques of the state and its practices. I have been excited by attempts at reimagination, and helped to shape new paradigms with practitioners and activists, working for social change in spaces I imagined offered alternatives to state-centric ways of doing things: collective projects of housing, education, culture, childcare, health and so on. Later, as an academic, my intellectual efforts have tended to focus on critiques of the state: its patriarchal and paternalistic institutions, its undemocratic regimes of power, its unresponsiveness to the needs and voices of citizens and its entanglement with neoliberalism. But such critiques tend to resonate uncomfortably with would-be hegemonic projects of the political right that demonise the institutions of the state and pillory its 'experts' (Clarke and Newman, 2017a).

Once states have been identified as the agents of neoliberal rule, there seems little left to say. But in the current climate of neoliberal projects of rolling back the state, coupled with populist disdain for governing elites and professional expertise, I have come to realise the importance of re-engaging with a politics of the state. Citizens look to states to protect rights and deliver justice, and to 'do something' about common problems and anxieties. States are able – if not willing – to regulate the excessive power of corporations. They can collaborate to address global problems of climate change, migration and health. They have the resource power that might enable them to address inequality, both within and between nations. They can provide services to promote the education and welfare of citizens. They embody the legal and regulatory powers that can bestow rights, mitigate injustice and protect citizens from abuse. They are fundamental to contemporary struggles for independence and sovereignty. And they have the capacity to defend vestiges of public culture, public space and public institutions – as well as to eviscerate them (Newman and Clarke, 2008). States, it seems, still matter.

My engagements with projects of reimagination were inspired by concurrent experiences as an activist in the emerging social movements of the 1970s and 1980s, and as a local government worker. As such, I experienced the state both as object (distant, impersonal, oppressive) and as constitutive of my personal and professional identities as a state worker. These contradictory experiences have shaped the approach of this chapter. I do not, then, imagine the state as strongly bounded from its others (civil society, community, market). Nor do I view it as a coherent and singular entity. Rather, I follow Mitchell (2006), Painter (2006) and others in their concern with the 'state effects' produced through the interaction of multiple actors in a plurality of institutions and sites. I also focus on the importance of cultural and representational practices through which the state is imagined and enacted. Such practices, I argue, shape the kinds of politics that are possible.

And the kinds of politics that are possible depend both on how states are imagined, and on how such imaginings are realised – or not. In what follows, then, I want to avoid normative proposals; instead, I set out a series of propositions that I hope will offer productive resources for reimagining states. These draw on a range of disciplinary perspectives, from developments in human geography to cultural theory; from feminist perspectives to conjunctural analysis. I do not, then, want to imply that if added together they might offer a coherent programme or political platform. Rather, they trace different ways of conceptualising politics, power and agency, each of which has the potential to unsettle dominant formations of power. The propositions I offer are 'imaginaries' in that each requires a suspension of embedded pathways of thinking. But imaginaries do more than offer visions or ideals; while these are necessary, transformation relies on reimagination as political labour. Later in the chapter, I show how such labour is not only conceptual (building new forms of theory, fostering new imaginaries), but also material (creating new things), cultural (developing new symbols, telling new stories) and embodied (working in contested and often precarious spaces). The chapter explores the significance of such labour in crafting connections between idealised hopes and aspirations and the material and ideological work of bringing them to life (what Cooper, 2013, depicts as oscillations between imagining and actualisation).

Proposition 1: Imagining states beyond nations

My purpose here is not to offer normative prescriptions for 'global governance' or the empowerment of transnational institutions as a means of addressing contemporary problems. Rather, I ask how far it might be possible to reimagine states for progressive purposes given the rise of new nationalisms that promote regressive nostalgias and xenophobic exclusions. Is it only possible to imagine a 'progressive' state by discarding national imaginaries?

One productive resource is offered by Gupta (1998), who shows how the hyphen in the concept 'nation-state' works to mask the paradoxical entanglement of state and nation. He points to the provisional quality of their relationship, and the struggles to forge – and maintain – alignments between them. This helpfully opens up questions about the particular ways in which they are aligned in specific global contexts. In postcolonial nations, states remain the focus of movements by subaltern populations for self-determination. Contemporary struggles arise from the political aspirations of peoples denied sovereignty and legitimacy in the redrawing of national boundaries at different points of the twentieth century (Palestine, Kurdistan). Some are associated with the rise of right-wing nationalisms in the twenty-first century (the Lega Nord). Others offer initial hope followed by despair (the so-called Arab Spring). Prefigurative forms of the state sometimes emerge from such struggles: for example, the Syrian region of Rijava, at the front line of fighting both Assad and ISIS, was described as a democratic experiment enabling Arabs, Christians and Kurds to work together (Ross, 2017). Territorial sovereignty and independent statehood remain fundamental mobilising imaginaries. But at the same time, such states are increasingly subject to the demands of neoliberal globalisation on the one hand and the critiques of transnational justice and human rights activists on the other.

These different examples might be read as underscoring the significance of context: the particular dynamics associated with postcolonialism, or of nations traversed by historical divisions that remain unsettled. In postcolonial nations, progressive politics are fundamental to projects of state-making and to the mobilisation of resistance to colonial and 'development' projects (Hansen and Stepputat, 2001). But across much of Europe, the nation has forcefully returned as a key signifier:

> In a political landscape marked by austerity and uneven and exclusionary responses to ongoing migration flows, divisive geographical imaginaries have acquired centre stage (Featherstone and Karaliotas, 2018, pp. 286–7).

However, rather than simply referring to different geographical contexts, I want to emphasise the *contested* alignments between different notions of state and nation. For example, independence movements (in Barcelona, Scotland, the Lega Nord and other would-be nations within nations) can be viewed as contesting established formations of statehood as well as nation – and not always in progressive ways.

The rise of new nationalisms is taking place at a political moment in which, it is often assumed, the nation-state has been hollowed out, bypassed and rendered powerless by the rise of 'globalisation'. The thesis of globalisation is at the core of national narratives of nostalgia (for a golden past) and blame (of the other), and is fundamental to the legitimation strategies of austerity and retrenchment. But globalisation is a contested concept: Sassen (2006) argues that, rather than diminishing the importance of nation-states, it serves to reassemble them for new purposes. States are fundamental to the management of neoliberalism, seeking out sites of innovation, opening up new markets and installing new logics of work, education and consumption. The material and psychic harms that result have paved the way for the rise of populist political movements of the extreme right, as well as the left populisms of Syrizia in Greece and Podemos in Spain and other nations seeking political responses to economic and political crises. Such struggles show that the apparently settled alignments between state and nation are contested and provisional, opening up the possibility of new institutional forms, new democratic channels, new imaginaries of citizenship and identity that might – in some cases – transcend national borders. And, as Featherstone and Karaliotas (2018) argue, they also offer resources for reimagining politics – particularly forms of politics that challenge social and spatial divisions.

The paradoxical juxtaposition of new nationalisms and seemingly powerless nations is mirrored in many of the new social movements and activist struggles that have emerged in the late twentieth and early twenty-first centuries. There is a tendency to bypass nation-states in order to focus on more cosmopolitan sensibilities and the exciting potential of global activist networks, from the Occupy protests to new forms of feminist politics. Action on human rights, migration, climate change and other issues necessarily transcend – or seek to dissolve – borders (Gill, this volume). Alongside such global imaginaries, progressive politics also tend to reassert the significance of the 'local' as the focus of political renewal (see Featherstone et al., 2012, on 'progressive localism'). While governments tend to construct the local as the domain of civic entrepreneurship and social responsibility, activists often view it as a locus for fostering enhanced forms of democratic participation and of creating progressive alternatives to the state.

But following Massey (2005, 2007), the transnational and local cannot be imagined as free-floating spaces above and below nations. Her work on the relational constitution of space and scale challenges binary distinctions between 'local' and 'global' or 'centre' and 'periphery': each only exists because of the imagined other. Imagining European nations as relationally constituted, for example, brings into view the colonial and neocolonial relations whose echoes inform contemporary politics, as well as the construction of ideas of Europe through its imagined relationships with the US or Russia. A relational perspective implies a more porous conception of states, offering ways of understanding how ideas and actions flow across social and spatial divisions, being remade as they travel. Such movements are mobilised through networks that, rather than dissolving the specificities of place, are embedded in and generative of local actions and protests.

A focus on the relational constitution of space and scale does not, however, mean abandoning the state as a source of progressive action. But it does require a shift away from the dominant conception of states as simply the passive pawns of neoliberal globalisation and towards a more positive role. Part of such a role is potentially delineated in state policies (on borders, migration, support for international institutions and so on). Part is legal – the potential role of states in addressing xenophobia, hatred and abuse of 'the other'. But fundamental to both is a focus on the cultural role of states – the subject of proposition 4, below.

Proposition 2: Imagining the multi-ness of states

The notion of a unitary, coherent state can be viewed as an ideological trope that obscures the fragile and fragmentary workings of state power (Abrams, 1988). This renders problematic progressive attempts to capture or transform the state around a single cohesive imaginary (a participative state, a relational state, a decentralised state). Challenging this ideological trope means moving towards different conceptions of the multi-ness of states, brining into view potential spaces of power, of agency, in which alternative imaginaries might flourish and that might be mobilised by counter-hegemonic movements.

But if not as coherent entities, how are states to be imagined? One conception of the 'multi-ness' of states foregrounds different scalar 'levels' (transnational, national, regional, local) with policies flowing 'downwards' through clear-cut implementation plans, and (perhaps) projects developing power and responsibility to subordinate tiers of governance. This offers a rather mechanistic spatial imaginary. What is at stake here is not an interaction between 'levels' of governance, but rather the contested alignment of multiple, and often antagonistic, forces. Foucauldian concepts of governmentality illuminate how power is not devolved, but is *dispersed* to multiple actors and agents, coordinated through disciplinary logics that simultaneously empower and constrain their action (Clarke and Newman, 1997). The dispersal of power serves to weaken formal democratic accountability, but paradoxically also generates spaces of agency as multiple actors (many espousing progressive politics) are (selectively) drawn into governing practices. For example, some regions or cities may be the source of progressive experiments (see Cooper, this volume, on 'municipal socialism' in some local authorities in the 1980s), while others can be viewed as crucibles of neoliberal development. Such experiments are not, however, spatially bounded. Following Massey's arguments discussed earlier, they are relationally constituted. Progressive ideas and experiments can, it follows, flourish within the seemingly hegemonic dictates of neoliberalism; indeed, such experiments, it is argued, are necessary for the continued expansion of neoliberal rationalities into new sites of exploitation and appropriation.

But the idea of dispersal is not the only sense of multi-ness I want to explore. What is at stake, rather, is an unstable ensemble of multiple forces, tendencies and antagonisms. I want to develop this form of analysis by proposing an understanding of states as a field of relationships traversed by different, and not necessarily compatible, *political projects*. Political projects can be viewed as more or less coherent efforts to bring ideas, interests, people and power together (Newman and Clarke, 2008; Sharma, 2008). They transcend party allegiances and help shape major shifts in social and political settlements; the development of welfare states, anti-colonial struggles, the formation of the EU, the rise of equality and human rights discourses (with their association with 'modern' statehood) and of course the projects that sustain neoliberal rule.

This form of analysis points not to the power of 'the' (reified, singular) state, but to the alignment (or not) between the multiple projects through which state power is constituted and legitimised. It offers the possibility of seemingly settled settlements becoming unstuck as a plurality of actors, institutions, technologies, ideologies, political parties and movements are assembled in novel ways, producing new formations of power and agency. Some may offer hope for progressive movements, unshackling agency from the dead hand of past assumptions about the permanence of inhospitable state forms. However, the projects that result may become subject to processes of co-optation, incorporation or erasure. For example, projects of community mobilisation and activism may lose their radical meaning as they become aligned with governmental projects that seek to 'responsibilise' community, or with development projects that seek to mobilise non-state resources. In the UK, the contemporary emphasis on the 'coproduction' of services, developed to 'empower' service users, has been adapted to new purposes as services have faced successive rounds of cuts and the capacity of state institutions has been eviscerated. The alignment of would-be progressive projects of transformations and governmental projects of austerity is not a happy one. Yet, processes of erasure or incorporation may not be complete: what is at stake are antagonisms between multiple forces rather than the simple roll-out of dominant forms (Newman, 2014).

Rather than unified consolidations of power, this opens up the possibility of transformation. The alignment of diverse projects is always temporary and unstable, and political projects constantly bend and borrow from projects incubated in other parties or movements. For example, Edgar (2017) describes the emergence of a new fault line in the settlements of social democracy that had characterised the dominant politics of many European states in the twentieth and early twenty-first centuries. Parties of the political right, he suggests, had won power by appropriating the economic justice elements of social democracy (broadening their appeal to working voters), but separating these from the forms of social liberalism that had underpinned moves towards gender equality, gay marriage, open borders and 'cosmopolitan' values. This helps explain the rise of Trump and other populist leaders, as well as the outcome of the Brexit referendum in the UK; although it might be argued that Brexit worked across multiple antagonisms rather than a single fault line (Watkins, 2016; Clarke and Newman, 2017a, b).

Such forms of cultural theory puncture grand and generalising theories of the state as unambiguously populist or neoliberal, strong or weak, 'modern' or 'postcolonial'. At stake are potentially unstable articulations of multiple forces and tendencies. This imagery is drawn from a Gramscian conception of conjunctural analysis (Gramsci, 1971). Grossberg explains:

> A conjunctural story seeks to understand the specificity of what is going on by identifying as carefully as possible what is new and what is old, what is part of a longer history and what has been introduced into the current context, and then, how these multiple elements shape each other so that the old can take on new characteristics and effects, and the new can take up residual forms and resonances (Grossberg, 2018: 34).

In foregrounding multiplicity, then, I do not want to imply that all that is needed is to 'let a thousand flowers bloom' in a flat political landscape, taking comfort in the proliferation of new activisms. Rather, I want to emphasise the necessity of analysing multiple dimensions of power, how these are ordered in spatial and temporal relationships, where contradictions are played out, and where fractures might appear. Conjunctural analysis rests on the analysis of multiple social forces and their shifting alignments (as in the Edgar example above). Finally, and most critically, it pays attention to struggles for consent – a point I return to later in the chapter.

Proposition 3: Imagining a 'feeling' state

I want to develop the arguments of the previous section by considering the significance of feminist movements in shaping particular political projects. Feminism has an ambivalent relationship to states, regarding them as both patriarchal and oppressive, and as a source of equality, rights and justice. Feminist work has generated a series of challenges to and critiques of state forms, as well as offered a rich source of alternative imaginaries (Rai, this volume). Feminism is not, of course, a single body of theory nor source of activism. While other chapters in this volume draw out the contribution of feminist poststructuralism in decentring established theory, my focus here is on the uneven and contested impact of feminism on state forms and practice. Feminism has helped unlock the power-knowledge hierarchies of the state, inspiring new discourses of personal life, relational concepts of welfare, and an emphasis on participative decision-making. Feminist activists – inside policy circles as well as in social movements – have worked to expand policy rationales of care: care for those experiencing violence or domestic abuse, care for those in poverty or poor housing, care for LGBTQ prisoners, asylum seekers and other groups. In such work, notions of care, activism and transformative change are deeply entangled. As my own research shows, there is a tendency for 'the feminism to come off' as soon as transformative ideas became inscribed in policy (Newman, 2012). For example, feminist calls for equality and inclusion have informed governmental projects in which women have been constituted as agents of economic development or as 'responsible' citizens. But feminism nevertheless changed the landscape of state policy and practice, bringing considerations of the 'personal' – bodies, care, relationships – into public policymaking and public life.

Feminism has also offered new conceptual repertoires for analysing and transforming states. In the twentieth century, feminist work highlighted the emotional labour of staff as they engage in 'feeling work', while in the twenty-first, new work emerged on the affective registers of state practice. Cooper (2014) writes of the possibility of 'emotionally contactful' states that are themselves touched by wider events and that seek to touch others, reaching out and engaging in 'attentive understanding' in order to embrace subjects (2014: 62). Jupp et al. propose an 'emotionally attuned' approach to governance, which sees emotions as 'constitutive of the very workings of government and policy' (2017: 1). Such work suggests that a concern with the emotions might offer the foundation for a 'more humane' state (Nussbaum, 2013), opening up the possibility of 'care' – for others, here or 'elsewhere', for the environment, for the generations to come – moving from the neglected periphery to the centre of public policy.

Indeed, policy streams that seem to support the idea of an 'emotionally contactful' state are proliferating as welfare states look beyond traditional forms of service provision. The emphases on personalisation and coproduction (Hunter, 2007), well-being or happiness (Dolan, 2014) on finding solutions to 'troubled' families or family breakdown (Jupp, 2017), preventing racial hatred and urban conflict (Jones, 2015), all build on prefigurative practices in social movements, the therapeutic professions and social enterprises. But all are readily aligned with projects of summoning the post-welfare subject. Issues of personhood and ethics, and what Williams terms a 'moral grammar of welfare from below' (1999: 668), become incorporated as state discourses in ways that both challenge traditional welfare regimes and enable the retrenchment of welfare states.

Does this mean that the turn to a consideration of emotional governance is necessarily compromised? The outcomes are rooted in the politics of alignment discussed above: strategies of emotional governance cannot be divorced from the contradictory imperatives of the political projects in which they are embedded. Austerity governance, in particular, has attempted to call on sentiments of responsibility, morality and self-sufficiency that speak to traditional values rather than progressive ideals (Forkert, 2017). The moves towards promoting well-being and happiness by some organs of the state take place alongside the rolling back of welfare benefits and services, and the impoverishment of public space and public life. But the idea of a 'feeling' state also deflects attention from structural inequalities and from the institutions that both produce them (states pursuing neoliberal policies) and have the capacity to mitigate them (through policies of redistribution, regulation and the law). And feeling states may be malign. The success of populist leaders of the political right has been built on eliciting feelings of exclusion and marginalisation, expressed through hatred of 'the other' (variously migrants, experts, judges). Mishra (2017) argues that what we are witnessing is a new 'age of anger', while Müller (2016) notes the rise of a visceral politics that privileges authenticity (of feeling) rather than authority (of evidence).

There is, then, a 'dark side' of reimaging states as feeling, as emotionally contactful. As the democratic legitimacy of many states is declining, governing rationalities are becoming increasingly entangled with projects of identity production. The consumerist revolution in public services in the UK in the 1990s was designed to overcome the presumed unresponsiveness of service organisations to their users (Clarke et al., 2006), but it also helped inculcate forms of individualism and served to expand neoliberal rationalities into personal lives. States, then, can be understood as *constitutive* of affective dispositions through economic and social policies, through cultural practices and through exemplary forms of action. They are infused with and constitutive of the 'structures of feeling' (Williams, 1977) that characterise a particular social/cultural moment in a particular place. I develop this idea below by exploring how far states are – and could be – constitutive of public identities and solidarities.

Proposition 4: Imagining states as public things

Much of my past intellectual work has centred on the evisceration of public institutions and public values in the face of neoliberal market individualism. The public/market dynamic differs widely between nations, as does the dynamic interface between secular and religious norms of publicness (see Herman, De Cesari, both this volume). A dominant trend, however, is neoliberal marketisation and consumerist imaginaries of governing, both further eroding the idea of states – settled or emergent, national or municipal – as public entities, with dire consequences for the legitimacy of public regulation, public services and public culture (Brown, 2015; Randeria, 2007). Critiquing this trend is, however, problematic. Poststructuralist and postcolonial critiques have challenged liberal public ideals such as equality, openness and tolerance. They rightly contest idealised images of a Habermasean public sphere, and view notions of the public as falsely universalistic, colonial and statist. How, then, is it possible to envisage more productive sites and manifestations of publicness?

Honig (2017) offers a productive resolution to this dilemma by focusing on the 'thingness' of publics. She asks whether democracy is possible in the absence of the common ownership of public things: infrastructure, spaces, services, monuments, buildings and other objects. These all carry, she suggests, the integrative powers necessary for the renewal of democratic collectivity. Drawing, in different ways, on Arendt (1998) and Winnicott (2007), she proposes that such things form the basis of attachments and adhesions to something beyond the self, and offer a sense of durability and permanence in a world of flux and contingency. However, Honig emphasises that public things cannot be equated with state sovereignty: many actors contribute to their making and renewal. She shows how public things are political rather than neutral objects: 'policed, restrictively controlled in an asymmetrical way' (2017: 25). The making of some apparently public things – streets, parks, buildings, reservoirs – often rest on appropriating land and resources from those with little power. And the public things that constitute the demos exclude some and privilege others. But 'even when they are divisive, they provide a basis around which to organise, contest, mobilise, defend or reimagine various modes of collective being together in a democracy' (2017: 24).

Public things, then, help crystallise imaginary belongings and act as an anchor for democratic politics. In the UK, the extent of public protest and dissent that arises when some public things are threatened – the hospital, the public library, the public open space – attests to their significance. My own activism has been reduced to working to save a public library from closure by transferring the service to a community-based charity (a frequent process in the UK: Forkert, 2017: ch. 5). Here, paradoxically, we are required to perform like a state (in order to demonstrate our probity and business skills), while at the same moment we are organising to oppose its actions (convening angry public meetings and performing dissent in stealthy ways). And even should we 'win', the *public* status of the library – part of the public infrastructure that aligns people, places and resources – would be precarious. But while the dominant trend is towards further cycles of privatisation, moves to reclaim privatised goods and services are proliferating. There are many projects to 'remunici-palise' water supplies across the globe (www.remunicipalisation.org), and there have been numerous attempts to take privatised railways and other elements of infrastruc-ture back into public control. Public things, then, are not static, but are realised and altered through being mediated, assembled and represented in new ways.

Honig's focus on objects might be considered part of the 'material turn' in social theory; but rather than the object relations theory of Winnicott the material turn is more closely associated with Actor Network Theory, with its emphasis on objects, spaces, instruments, technologies, artefacts, bodies and the networks that assemble matters of concern:

> Each object – each issue – generates a different pattern of emotions and disruptions, of agreements and disagreements . . . Each object gathers around itself a different assembly of relevant parties. Each object triggers new occa-sions to passionately differ and dispute. Each object may also offer new ways of achieving closure without having to agree on much else. In other words matters of dispute . . . bound us all in ways that map out public space pro-foundly different from what is usually recognised under the label of 'the political' (Latour, 2005).

The law, regulation, parliaments and the technologies of policymaking can all be viewed as devices for making things public (alongside many other ways of pro-ducing connections). Each supports the resilience and renewal of public things and attachments, and, at the same time, generates change. For example, the law offers technologies through which public claims on the state – for security, for rights, for redress – are enacted and contested. But it also delineates shifts in the proper bound-ary between public and private matters: of public space (what activities are permit-ted where), of persons (who is to be considered child or adult, male or female) and people (who can be part of a national public – and who is to be excluded). The law offers instruments – the public inquiry, mechanisms of public accountability – that support democratic challenges, however imperfectly; and is itself open to chal-lenge as particular publics contest the way in which accountability is exercised (see Clarke, this volume). For example, there was considerable conflict around whose voices and experiences should be represented in the public enquiry set up follow-ing the Grenfell Tower fire in London in June 2017 (Hagen, 2018). Regulation, in turn, offers a means of ensuring the resilience of public things: food safety, water purity, air quality, housing standards, the safety of workers, the payment of taxes. The Grenfell fire disaster was particularly poignant given the discovery that warn-ings by the residents group about fire safety hazards had been ignored. After decades of regulation being viewed as a hindrance to the free workings of the market, there seems to be an emerging public mood for more stringent controls of corporate and governmental power.

Both parliaments and the policies they enact are crucial representations of the publicness of states, and the means through which states are reproduced – and diminished. States can be viewed as devices through which the border between public and private things, between democratic and market relationships, is demarcated. But viewing things and relationships as objects in various assemblages enables them to be imagined as mutable: the objects shift position, are juxtaposed with new objects and brought into new (public/private/personal) relationships. As such, the relationship between public things and democratic practice is ambiguous. If, like Latour, we regard 'matters of concern' as public things, then this broadens the scope of democratic mobilisation. As new matters of concern generate new clusters of interests and actors, so they may give rise to alternative conceptions of democratic practice. As Randeria notes:

> Whereas the right to vote . . . remains tied to a world of territorial nation-states, the right to inspect, judge, exercise surveillance, the right to evaluate or denounce have not merely gained significance but are also being exercised both within and beyond state borders (2007: 2).

Investigative reporting, hacking and blogging are publicising the consequences of unfettered markets, environmental degradation and corporate greed, and activist projects are offering new imaginaries of citizen-led or co-produced regulation (McDermont, this volume). These prefigurative publics and states are both mutually entangled and mutually constitutive (Cooper, 2016).

Reimagination as political labour

Thinking of the state in such public terms means going beyond an interest in relationships between states and citizens to imagine the complex network of things, ideas, institutions, places and people through which the state (that strange abstract notion) is brought to life.

The four propositions I have outlined offer different resources for projects of *reimagining* states – as spatially ambiguous, politically plural, affective and cultural bodies. These resources draw on different literatures and offer different conceptual framings. As such, they cannot be aggregated into a single coherent picture of a progressive state: to propose such an image would be to misread my arguments. Each of the propositions is the site of contestation, paradox and contradiction. Political labour, then, is fundamental not only to generating, but also to sustaining progressive actions in the face of processes of erasure, colonisation and appropriation. Political labour cannot adequately be represented through traditional images of party building, bargaining and negotiation: it is performative (generating new worlds) and creative (based on imaginings and actions). It is relational (not 'owned' by one actor, but constituted through interactive processes). It is symbolic (constituting new repertoires of meaning and action) and embodied (taking place in precarious and often exploitative economic spaces).

I want to conclude, then, by trying to draw out some wider understandings about the political labour of reimagination. I draw, in part, on earlier research on how women attempted to align progressive ideas with state practice in the UK from the mid-twentieth century to the first decade of the twenty-first (Newman, 2012, 2013a, b, 2014, 2017). The participants in the research were involved in community politics and campaign groups; government and local government; policy groups and the professions; the voluntary sector and NGOs; higher education, think tanks and research organisations. However, these categories were fluid; most participants had fractured working lives that traversed different sectors and spheres of action, taking their skills and experience with them. The research shows how their labour was simultaneously antagonistic to the state and contributed to the remaking of state policies and practices.

Their work offered a form of political praxis in which actions and ideas were closely enmeshed. This was at the core of what I term *generative labour*: the work of making new things. The research subjects fostered a rich array of prefigurative forms that challenged and enlarged state practice: that is, critique (of established formations of power) was entangled with developing what participants hoped would be a more inclusive, equitable, responsive and engaging state, while fostering alternative projects and resources. They generated concepts and ideas that served to shape wider projects of transformation, from 'partnership working' to 'participative leadership', from 'democratic renewal' to 'coproduction'. They also translated feminist, antiracist and community-based politics into governmental innovation, both in policy development and by appropriating the technologies of audit and monitoring. All encountered (and challenged) embedded forms of state practice, negotiating resources and mediating relationships with citizens. All were also crucial resources on which states draw in projects of development.

This research, together with more recent work, inspired the propositions outlined earlier in this chapter. In proposition 1, I argued for a relational conception of space and scale. The labour of linking different spatial imaginaries and working different scalar embodiments of state practice can be understood as one form of *relational labour*: working between familiarity and strangeness, and forging networks and generative possibilities. The political imaginations of most participants had flourished by learning from experience 'elsewhere', whether through networks of municipalities or through attempting to replicate apparently successful political experiments in other nations/regions. Their skills were acquired both through embodied mobilities (many of those I interviewed were migrants, others had experience of working overseas or in transnational NGOs); but such skills were also acquired through political activism. Such forms of relational labour are the backbone of contemporary projects such as transition towns, regional assemblies, urban projects, environmental initiatives, local/global democratic innovations and many others. All constitute networks of expertise and ideas and serve as crucibles of innovation, enabling progressive ideas and experiments to flow horizontally across borders and connect different scalar 'levels' – taking on new forms as they travel (Clarke et al., 2015). Organisations such as Médecins Sans Frontieres, Reporters without Borders, Lawyers without Borders, NGOs and relief agencies perform acts of citizenship beyond the nation (Isin, 2015), in the process constituting alternative formations of welfare, expertise and professional practice. Across the globe, transnational movements and emergent actions offer new grammars of politics that excite the imagination and inspire new generations of activists (Gill, this volume).

In proposition 2, I discussed the transformative possibilities offered by conceptualising the multiplicity of state forms, projects, sites and relationships. I argued that it was in the imperfect and contested alignments between different political projects that spaces of agency and transformation were possible. Such transformation, however, relies on the *work of articulation*. All the women I interviewed were 'border workers' managing the tensions between multiple – and often incompatible – political projects. They moved into and out of policy networks, think tanks, research organisations and education programmes, helping to link critical theory building to embedded political action. They spoke of 'stitching things together', managing conflicts, working across boundaries and making new productive associations. And they did not do so alone: forming productive alliances was crucial. They generated new forms of partnership, participation, research, policy and project work, each of which served as an incubator for 'progressive' innovation, as well as a platform for state retrenchment (Newman, 2001).

In doing so, they confronted some of the contradictions of statehood. So called 'modern' states strive to present themselves as offering rational, scientific governance, non-partisan institutions and dispassionate judgments: an image against which postcolonial and so-called 'weak' states are judged deficient. But the supposed rationality of state action is, of course, a well-rehearsed performance. States are suffused with affect, whose registers range from paranoia to persecution, from expansive tolerance to defensive aggression (Hunter, 2015). It follows that the borders worked by participants in the research were not comfortable places to be: it was there that the contradictions between an expansive neoliberal state and progressive politics were most sharply felt. The processes of co-optation, appropriation and residualisation of progressive ideas were personal and embodied, with significant consequences for individual and collective health. Throughout the period covered by the research, market imperatives were crowding out the public solidarities to which participants were committed, as well as taking (or transforming) their jobs. Some took on policy roles managing processes of contracting out and outsourcing, attempting to mitigate their effects on public services as far as possible, although their successes were eroded as legislation repeatedly changed the rule of the game. Others appropriated the technologies of audit and contract in efforts to enlarge the impact of equality policies. In the later era of cuts and downsizing, some remained within the state in attempts to lessen the consequences of austerity, while others worked in community projects or social enterprises to fill the gaps left by the retreating welfare state. Across different periods and scales, participants actively sought to appropriate emerging governance rationales – of partnership working, active citizenship, consumerism, community engagement – and to align these with alternative forms of public politics. Looking back to Grossberg's conception of conjunctural analysis, we can see how they worked to both defend and transform the 'old' (however ambiguously), while also promoting new emergent forms. The entanglement of embedded and emergent forces, institutional form and political praxis has important implications for projects of reimagination.

The progressive imaginaries that activists brought to their work enabled an expanded social and political field, characterised by *transformative ethical labour* oriented towards constituting a future world. Proposition 3 explored the impact of feminism on transformative state projects, and on the conceptual vocabularies of critique. Certainly, the forms of relational labour and border work I have described involve high levels of emotional labour; but there are dangers here of reducing the analysis to individualised transactions or personal ethical choices. Instead, I want to try to capture the wider sense of ethics of care that seemed to characterise the labour of participants in the research. These included new vocabularies of intergenerational care and new formations of publicness based on an imagined 'commons' that extend beyond, and perhaps subvert, entrenched public institutions and established norms.

Such forms of ethical labour resonate with Beasley and Bacchi's (2007) concept of 'social flesh', viewing care not simply as a personal moral quality, but as a political ethic for both current and future practice. Rather than the neoliberal emphasis on atomistic individuals, social flesh offers an alternative political rationale for conceptualising human embodied interdependence – including mutual reliance for access to global social space, infrastructure and resources. Such an ethic of care is not simply concerned with the importance of effective welfare provision: it offers a relational conception of justice and other normative ideals. As such, it opens up a much wider set of responsibilities towards the other as the basis of social justice and sustainability (Tronto, 2015; Williams, 2001). Such ideals came through in the research, offering both solace for the difficulties of the present and hope for the future. They offered different temporal understandings of how policies should be made and outcomes assessed, privileging notions of sustainability and intergenerational interdependence. Such notions are closely aligned with environmental politics and the challenge to economic growth as the primary indicator of progress (Raworth, 2017).

Such future imaginaries sit uneasily with the sense of decline and destruction of public resources, institutions and solidarities. Revalorising 'public' discourse appears to be a marginal concern in these neoliberal times; yet, new publics and forms of pubic action can be discerned in embodied encounters (and contestations) across disciplinary, professional and activist borders. The labour of *public making* traverses political (public/private, state/civil society, national/transnational) categories. It is evident in recent movements such as *Occupy*, the *No Borders* campaign, feminist events and performances, community initiatives, crowd sourcing, environmental actions and a myriad of alternative economic forms. And it is concerned with generating new (and prefigurative) public things: ethical food networks that connect

producers and consumers, cooperative schemes promoting environmental sustainability, projects fostering support for migrants and asylum seekers, new models of
transport and housing, and in local 'takeovers' of formerly public assets (from post
offices to libraries, from banks to bus routes). These help constitute what Gibson-
Graham and Roelvink (2011) term 'community economies' that link economic
change to the pursuit of environmental and social justice, offering ecological ways
of bringing into being 'post-capitalist' forms of the ownership of land, money and
other resources in the present rather than in some fantasy future.

The examples cited here are not centred on the state (understood as a bounded
set of institutions) – indeed, it is their distance from the state that enables them to
be productive. Nor are they oriented to traditional forms of political participation
(parties, trade unions and so on) out of which past projects of state reform emerged.
But they offer both conceptual resources for reimagination (that can be translated
for other sites and contexts) and symbolic resources (that can inspire hope and help
to shape prefigurative political actions). This is part of Gramsci's struggle for consent. It is not about manipulation and persuasion, but about the work of creating
articulations between fragments of popular 'common sense' (e.g. the importance
of social justice) and alternative political imaginaries (that challenge the dominant
orthodoxies of market individualism).

This is *cultural work*. It includes what Jackson (2011) terms the 'social work'
of culture industries seeking transformative change through the performing and
visual arts. Film and documentary producers, writers, cartoonists, vloggers, journalists and broadcasters all offer forms of creative labour through which new political narratives and images are produced. Cultural and artistic projects offer public
imaginaries of belonging (De Cesari, this volume), and performative repertoires
that invoke involvement and agency (Browne and Jones, this volume; McDermont,
this volume). However, creative interventions are not simply the domain of artists.
At the time of writing, movements combating racism and sexism are offering powerful visual images – the bended knee of Black football players in the US, the 'Me
too' hash tag used by women to reveal past episodes of sexual abuse, or the pink
hats worn by women mobilising against the Trump administration. It is through
stories, images, representations and performances that affective – and potentially
politicising – responses are summoned. Such labour can challenge the racism and
xenophobia of populist movements, show the value of public solidarities and public
things, and generate hope. It is work that offers alternative imaginaries of how states
might think and act – and feel – as public entities.

Cultural work is not, of course, necessarily progressive. States themselves are crucial actors in the promulgation of symbols and images: flags, uniforms, ceremonies,
parliaments, elections are all public things that offer images of solidity and permanence, although their struggle for hegemony may not be successful. They also tell
stories – about what makes a good citizen, why austerity is needed, why the nation
must be protected from encroachments by alien others and so on. And despite the
efforts of states to win support for their policies and actions, most governmental
narratives tend to be negative: the state is spending too much, is overburdened, out

of touch, too big, weighed down by bureaucracy and red tape, overstaffed and in need of transformation.

The problem is, however, that progressive actors also tend to tell highly negative stories about states – as oppressive, coercive, unresponsive – and move on to what are viewed as more promising sites of action. This takes me back to where I began: with the contested alignments between political activism and progressive imaginaries of the state. It is possible to trace projects of reimagining on which future forms of the state might draw, whether in cooperative experiments in Italy and Spain, in new economic and political models offered by some emerging political parties, or in experiments in mutuality or sustainability in some parts of the Global South. These may be fragile and short lived. But, like the feminist movement with which I began, they generate alternative models of justice, well-being, welfare and democracy in the present – rather than in a hypothetical future when the state is transformed.

References

Abrams, P. (1988) 'Notes on the Difficulty of Studying the State', *Historical Sociology*, 1(1), pp. 58–89.

Arendt, H. (1998) *The Human Condition*. Chicago: Chicago University Press.

Beasley, C. and Bacchi, C. (2007) 'Encouraging a New Politics for an Ethical Future', *Feminist Theory*, 8(3), pp. 279–98.

Brown, W. (2015) *Undoing the Demos: Neoliberalism's Stealth Revolution*. New York: Zone Books.

Clarke, J., Bainton, D., Lendvai, N. and Stubbs, P. (2015) *Making Policy Move: Towards a Politics of Translation and Assemblage*. Bristol: Policy Press.

Clarke, J., Newman, J., Smith, N. et al. (2006) *Creating Citizen-Consumers: Changing Publics and Changing Public Services*. London: Sage.

Clarke, J. and Newman, J. (1997) *The Managerial State: Power, Politics and Ideology in the Remaking of Social Welfare*. London: Sage.

Clarke, J. and Newman, J. (2017a) '"People in this Country Have Had Enough of Experts": Brexit and the Paradoxes of Populism', *Critical Policy Studies*, 11(1), pp. 101–16.

Clarke, J. and Newman, J. (2017b) 'The Instabilities of Expertise: Remaking Knowledge, Power and Politics in Unsettled Times', *Innovation: The European Journal of Social Science Research*, 39(1), pp. 40–54.

Cooper, D. (2014) *Everyday Utopias: The Conceptual Life of Promising Spaces*. Durham, NC: Duke University Press.

Cooper, D. (2016) 'Transformative State Publics', *New Political Science*, 38(3), pp. 315–34.

Dolan, P. (2014) *Happiness by Design*. London: Penguin.

Edgar, D. (2017) *Cosmopolitans, Communitarians and the New Fault Line: How to Renew the Traditional Labour Alliance*. Compass Think Piece 87. London, Compass.

Featherstone, D., Ince, A., Mackinnon, D. et al. (2012) 'Progressive Localism and the Construction of Alternatives', *Transactions of British Geographers*, 37, pp. 177–82.

Featherstone, D. and Karaliotas, L. (2018) 'Challenging the Spatial Politics of the European Crisis: Nationed Narratives and Trans-Local Solidarities in Post-Crisis Conjuncture', *Cultural Studies*, 32(2), pp. 286–307.

Forkert, K. (2017) *Austerity as Public Mood*. London, Rowan & Littlefield.

Gibson-Graham, J. K. and Roelvink, G. (2011) 'The Nitty-Gritty of Creating Alternative Economies', *Social Alternatives*, 30(1), pp. 29–33.

Gramsci, A. (1971) *Selections from the Prison Notebooks*. New York: International Publishers.

Grossberg, L. (2018) *Under the Cover of Chaos: Trump and the Battle for the American Right*. London, Pluto Press.

Gupta, A. (1998) *Postcolonial Developments*. Durham, NC: Duke University Press.

Hagen, A. (2018) 'Grenfell Tower', *London Review of Books*, 40(11), pp. 3–43.

Hansen, T. B. and Stepputat, F. (eds.) (2001) *States of Imagination: Ethnographic Explorations of the Postcolonial State*. Durham, NC: Duke University Press.

Honig, B. (2017) *Public Things: Democracy in Disrepair*. New York: Fordham University Press.

Hunter, S. (ed.) (2007) *Coproduction and Personalisation in Social Care*. London: Jessica Kingsley.

Hunter, S. (2015) *Power, Politics, Emotions: Impossible Governance?* London, Routledge.

Isin, E. (2015) *Citizenship without Frontiers*: London, Bloomsbury.

Jackson, S. (2011) *Social Works: Performing Art, Supporting Publics*. London, Routledge.

Jones, H. (2015) *Negotiating Cohesion, Inequality and Change: Uncomfortable Positions in Local Government*. Bristol: Policy Press.

Jupp, E. (2017) 'Troubling Feelings in Family Policy and Interventions' in Jupp, E., Pykett, J. and Smith, F. (eds.), *Emotional States: Sites and Spaces of Affective Governance*. London: Routledge.

Jupp, E., Pykett, J. and Smith, F. M. (2017) *Emotional States: Sites and Spaces of Affective Governance*. London: Routledge.

Latour, B. (2005) 'From Realpolitik to Dingpolitik, or How to Make Things Public', *Pavilion; Journal for Politics and Culture*, 15 [online]. Available at http://pavilionmagazine.org/bruno-latour-from-realpolitik-to-dingpolitik-or-how-to-make-things-public/ (accessed 3 March 2019).

Massey, D. (2005) *For Space*. London: Sage Publications.

Massey, D. (2007) *World City*. Cambridge: Polity Press.

Mishra, P. (2017) *The Age of Anger: A History of the Present*. London, Allen Lane.

Mitchell, T. (2006) 'Society, Economy and the State Effect' in Sharma, A. and Gupta, A. (eds.), *The Anthropology of the State*. Oxford, Blackwell, pp. 169–86.

Müller, J.-W. (2016) *What is Populism?* Philadelphia, PA: University of Pennsylvania Press.

Newman, J. (2001) *Modernising Governance: New Labour, Policy and Society*. London: Sage.

Newman, J. (2012) *Working the Spaces of Power: Activism, Neoliberalism and Gendered Labour*. London: Bloomsbury Academic.

Newman, J. (2013a) 'Spaces of Power: Feminism, Neoliberalism and Gendered Labour', *Social Politics*, 20(2), pp. 200–21.

Newman, J. (2013b) 'Performing New Worlds: Policy, Politics and Creative Labour in Hard Times', *Policy and Politics*, 41(4), pp. 515–32.

Newman, J. (2014) 'Landscapes of Antagonism: Local Government, Neoliberalism and Austerity', *Urban Studies*, 51(15), pp. 3290–3305.

Newman, J. (2017) 'The Politics of Expertise: Neo-Liberalism, Governance and the Practice of Politics' in Higgins, V. and Larner, W. (eds.), *Assembling Neo-Liberalism: Expertise, Practices, Subjects*. New York: Palgrave Macmillan.

Newman, J. and Clarke, J. (2008) *Publics, Politics and Power: Remaking the Public in Public Services*. London, Sage.

Newman, J. and Clarke, J. (2014) 'States of Imagination', *Soundings*, 57, pp. 153–69.

Nussbaum, M. C. (2013) *Political Emotions: Why Love Matters for Justice*. Cambridge, MA: Harvard University Press.

Painter, J. (2006) 'Prosaic Geographies of Stateness', *Political Geography*, 25, pp. 752–74.

Pickerill, J. and Krinsky, J. (2012) 'Why Does Occupy Matter?', *Social Movement Studies*, June, pp. 279–87.

Randeria, S. (2007) 'The Depoliticisation of Democracy and the Judicialistion of Publics', *Theory, Culture and Society*, 24(4), pp. 38–64.

Raworth, K. (2017) *Doughnut Economics*. Random House.

Ross, D. (2017) *Accidental Anarchist: Life without Government*, BBC 4, 23 July 2017 [online]. Available at https://www.youtube.com/watch?v=XudWK8ua2WA (accessed 3 March 2019).

Sassen, S. (2006) *Territory, Authority, Rights: From Mediaeval to Global Assemblages*. Princeton, NJ: Princeton University Press.

Sharma, A. (2008) *Logics of Empowerment: Development, Gender and Governance in Neoliberal India*. Minneapolis, MN: University of Minnesota Press.

Tronto, J. (2015) *Who Cares? How to Reshape a Democratic Politics*. New York: Cornell University Press.

Watkins, S. (2016). 'Editorial: Casting Off?', *New Left Review*, 100, pp. 5–31.

Williams, F. (1999) 'Good Enough Principles for Welfare', *Journal of Social Policy*, 28(4), pp. 667–87.

Williams, F. (2001) 'In and Beyond New Labour: Towards a New Political Ethics of Care', *Critical Social Policy*, 21(4), pp. 467–93.

Williams, R. (1977) *Marxism and Literature*. Oxford: Oxford University Press.

Winnicott, D. W. (2007) *The Maturation Process and the Facilitating Environment: Studies in the Theory of Emotional Development*. New York: Carnac.

2

REIMAGINING THE STATE

Marxism, feminism, postcolonialism

Shirin M. Rai

> 'A map of the world which does not include Utopia is not even worth glancing
> at, for it leaves out the one country at which Humanity is always arriving.'
>
> *Oscar Wilde*

Reimagining the state in a political climate of neoliberal populism is a brave and some would say foolish enterprise. We are, it seems, in the vicious embrace of populist masculinist right-wing leaders who perform the politics of hate – from Duterte in the Philippines to Modi in India and Trump in the US. And yet, the dangers that we face today also make the task of reimagining the state an imperative one. I outline four reasons why we must reimagine the state (Rai, 2018): First, without reimaginings we could become complicit in the reproduction of the dominant norms and values, our unjust worlds. Unless we are able to challenge the lives we live through reimagining these in a new register, we are also not able to make judgements about right and wrong, good and bad, about how we can live a good life when so much is bad around us (see Adorno, 1974; Butler, 2012). Contemporary work on feminist utopias (Cooper, 2014; Gornick and Meyers, 2009) may be one such way of reimagining life, but needs to be situated in the unequal worlds that we occupy (Hassim, 2009). Second, such reimaginings, 'necessary utopia' as Panitch and Gindin (1999) have called it, reassures us that 'other worlds are possible' – that there are (different) routes out of our individual or collective conditions. Take, for example, Buddhism: as the Buddha learned, behind the curtain of happiness drawn around him by his adoring parents lay a world that was marked by pain, illness and death, as well as education, meditation and renunciation. For the Buddha, a utopic life was one where everyone followed the *Dharma* – the laws of social good – and where this 'right path' led to *Nirvana*, or the freedom from the cycle of rebirth. The difference, as between the *Hinayana* (small vehicle) and *Mahayana* Buddhism (big vehicle) is important: while the former is focused on self-realisation through detachment, the latter promotes enlightenment for all, welfare for the collectivity. Individual self-realisation can, of course, lead to collective action.[1] Third, imagining another world also makes us struggle over resources we might need to bring it into being. Rights to material goods as well as public political goods, individual as well as collective capabilities that are honed and those that wither, discourses of what we collectively recognise as important socially, are all to be struggled over for a fairer distribution of these resources. Fourth, an alternative imaginary provides us with a sense of belonging, and of solidarity. Utopia thus challenges the paralysis of pessimism, to quote Ernst Bloch: 'the most dogged enemy of socialism is not only . . . great capital, but equally the load of indifference, hopelessness; otherwise great capital would stand alone' (in Panitch and Gindin, 1999: 2).

However, in reimagining the state, how far should we allow our imagination to flow? Too far and we risk untethering the state from any sources of power or histories; too close and we bind the reimagining to banal reforms that wither on the vine. This is a difficult but important issue; Ruth Levitas has argued for, building on Ernst Bloch's work, concrete utopias, which are characterised by 'a praxis oriented category' underlined by 'militant optimism' (1995: 70). Here, utopia is a method of analysis of contemporary society, which shows how utopic norms – 'meritocracy', for example – can be used as justification for social inequalities. For Levitas, then, the process matters – moving towards an alternative, 'a better way of being' (2010: 9). Erik Olin Wright, building on and challenging Marxism, however, writes of 'real utopias', which, he notes, exist in our social contexts and which if scaled up could lead to an emancipatory life for all (2010). As Cooper has argued, contemporary utopic thinking does not mean seeking new macro blueprints for reworked societal norms, but as 'an ethos of complex process whose failure and struggles are as important as success' (2014: 4). Whilst there are differences among them, what unites these approaches is that all seem to be aware of both – the possibilities and the limits of utopia. This means that state policy then becomes a legitimate arena for contestation if we are to move towards a better life – a good life – collectively. In Andre Gorz's words: 'it is the function of utopias . . . to provide us with the distance from the existing state of affairs which allows us to judge what we *are* doing in the light of what we *could* or *should* do' (Gorz, 1999: 113, original emphasis).

Then, there is the question of whose imagination? I have most often felt this when at big conferences where feminism and postcolonialism flow in different, discrete and separate channels of thought. I go to a feminist panel on the state and in all the sophisticated and rigorous debates wonder where the politics of difference disappears; it irritates me and saddens me, just as it annoys me when I go to postcolonial panels and hear little about gendered regimes of power, which the state

1 This led Ambedkar – Chair of the Indian Constituent Assembly and leader of India's Dalits – to urge Dalits to leave their oppressive existence within Hinduism for the more equal spaces of Buddhism (2014). Even though this strategy of 'moving out' did not produce the results Ambedkar hoped for, it allowed for conversations about the place of Dalits in Indian (not just Hindu) society.

reproduces and regulates. Instead of a solidarity of the marginalised, I worry about parallel universes, which prevent dialogue and the building of intersectional modes of politics. And yet, to bring the two literatures, theoretical arguments, concepts and experiences together is not easy. They constantly slip away, escape, hide, so that before you know it, your attempt to let your imagination loose is subsumed by the weight of the familiar ways of talking, listening, reading and writing.

What I want to do is not to develop new frameworks or provide a grand theory that reimagines the state; after all, as Bob Jessop has quite correctly pointed out, '[t]he state is such a complex theoretical object and so complicated an empirical one that no single theoretical approach can fully capture and explain its complexities' (2008: 132). The question of the state – what is it, strategies of reforming it, challenging it and overcoming it – has formed the substance of political debates for a long while. I do not have the space to rehearse these debates on the state here; only to underline that I hold that the state takes many political forms – clearly recognisable and often overlooked – and as an aggregate of modes of power continues to play a crucial role in managing the market – labour as well as money – through different modes – policy, violence, aesthetics and ideology. So, my aim here is to examine the state from a feminist and postcolonial perspective and to raise questions about the state in a globalised world – how we reimagine it foregrounding these arguments. In order to learn we must acquire new modes of reading and thinking cross generationally, in gendered and raced regimes of knowledge. Not all debates and writing are called 'classics' – the presentism of our world, its insistence on the instantaneous and the immediate means that not all voices are heard; but hear these we must, even as new historical periods bring up new challenges for us in understanding the political forces surrounding us. Whose imagination then becomes a relevant question to ask as we critique the present modes of power and rethink the state.

The third issue that puzzles me is how can we, who are interested in transformative politics, write at such levels of abstraction that human beings disappear from our analyses? In asking this question, I take my inspiration from the group of Indian historians who saw history as the work of sentient, feeling and struggling subaltern individual and collective subjects (the Subaltern Studies group). This, to my mind, raises two different problems: one is that the absence of the human form is also an absence of a gendered, sexed and raced human being; if we overlook the embodied form of social relations that we write about, it is no wonder that we neglect the place of colour and sex/gender in our work. Second, the abstraction gets in the way, I feel, of communication: how can we change the world if we cannot change our vocabulary to engage people out there; if our vocabularies become so enmeshed in our rather particular modes of thinking that we cannot translate the work of others to understand their standpoint?

I have tried to go back to some old/new debates about the state in raising some questions. There are three in total: (1) the relationship between the state and the gendered household: how does the state continue to reproduce and re-form the household and social reproduction through law and social policy to respond to capitalism's needs and crises? (2) Does the political form of the state matter? And if it does, then (3) how should we engage with and challenge the state in its fractions to bring about change making through our own political solidarity? What I am hesitant to do is 'reimagine' the state for the readers; rather, through my discussion of feminist and postcolonial literatures I tease out how we might pose better questions about the state, and address the differences that undermine our efforts to change it.

Regulating the form of the household and social reproduction

The issue I have been most concerned with in my own work is that of social reproductive work and its framing by the state and market. Nancy Fraser has quite correctly pointed out the need for looking 'behind' Marx's abode to connect an expanded understanding of social relations – including gender, ecology and political power – to understand capitalism and its contradictions (2014). And yet, she pays rather less attention to the global relations of care and power than she does to gender and political power in her analysis. The question for me is how we theorise social reproduction, the state in both a feminist and postcolonial frame.

Fraser succinctly outlines Marx's definition of capitalism: (1) private property and class divisions in terms of its ownership; (2) free labour – in terms of legal status and in terms of access to means of production; (3) accumulation of capital: 'capital itself becomes the Subject. Human beings are its pawns, reduced to figuring out how they can get what they need in the interstices, by feeding the beast' (2014: 58); (4) markets that serve to allocate resources for commodity production by means of commodification and 'they determine how society's surplus will be invested' (2014: 57–8). Looking behind Marx's abode, and reflecting a long history of Marxist feminist thought, Fraser expressed the long-held Marxist feminist position on capitalism: 'Marx's account of capitalist production only makes sense when we start to fill in its background conditions of possibility' (2014: 60).

The argument that many feminist Marxist political economists have made is that the separation of production and social reproduction is one important element necessary for the continuance of capitalism. And the state is an important node of power in ensuring and regulating this separation. Accumulation through commodification and annexation of social reproduction, while at the same time denying its value, is at the heart of capitalism's development and takes different forms in different periods. This appropriation without recognition is made possible through – what feminist legal and political scholars have pointed to – a 'reliance on public powers to establish and enforce its constitutive norms' (Fraser, 2014). Marriage and its regulation have been one of the powerful modes of such exercise of state power. So, from the start, both commodity production and social reproduction are important in capital accumulation; poor households derive a great deal of sustenance from self-provisioning (Fraser 2014: 59), community support and increasing and decreasing state transfers and through dispossession of millions in one form or other. Core countries also accumulate through promoting mass consumerism, which depends on the cheap labour of peripheral societies. Colonialism was, of course, a regime of what Harvey has called accumulation as dispossession, and has left its imprint in the regimes of dependency and divisions between core and periphery that continue to play out in global markets of production and exchange (Harvey, 2004).

But these regimes are regulated not by something called 'capitalism', but by the different fractions of the state. When the Reagan/Thatcher duo, in the afterglow of the fall of the Soviet Union, tried to argue for doing away with the state's regulatory role, the negative consequences of the withdrawal of the state in terms of both the market and administration of capital became all too clearly visible. As would be clear from this outlining of capitalism, the state as an institution legitimises and reinforces the gendered division of labour attributed to social reproduction and through its laws and social policies does this in different ways in different periods and contexts of capitalism. One insight of feminist debates on social reproduction is that the exclusion of women from the public sphere is not dependent upon capitalism, but in fact capitalism has gained from this pre-capitalist form of gender relations. The issue is, as Engels pointed out, the regulation of property, in which the state is critically involved. The state is interested in the form of household – law and policy support that. As Veena Das points out, 'the law is the sign of a distant but over-whelming power that is brought into the framework of everyday life by the representation and performance of its rules in modes of rumor, gossip, mockery, and mimetic representation' (2007: 162); it is also a sign of immanent violence and control. As we shall see below, law forms part of state's governance in different registers: the governance of politics and the governance of communities, which makes for multiple sovereignties and in the specific context of the law, of legal pluralism. The critical question for me here is also how the particular forms of bourgeois family and of social reproduction itself are not just gendered, but racialised, and whether and how this affects our theorisation of the state.

Silvia Federici draws attention to the primacy of women's unpaid domestic work, sexuality and procreation as practices indispensable to capitalism, describing it as 'unfree labour, revealing the umbilical connection between the devaluation of reproductive work and the devaluation of women's social position' (Federici, 2012: 97). Social reproductive work within the household is largely perceived as women's work. This preconception influences not just women's labour market participation (supply side), but also labour recruitment (demand-side) decisions; markets are, after all, gendered institutions (Fraser, 2014). Therefore, even within the framework of a monetised economy, which privileges economic growth, prevailing gendered norms of the labour market mean not just a loss of realising human capital worth, but also the neglect of social reproductive work. Social reproduction was traditionally used as a descriptive category and set against production as a way of describing the known world and all the activities within it. Since the emphasis on production as the central productive activity, social reproduction has become a 'second-level' activity and is either undervalued or not valued at all (Rai and Hoskyns 2016: 394). Social reproduction can be defined in the following way: (1) it includes biological reproduction, which includes the reproduction of labour, the provision of sexual, emotional and affective services that are required to maintain households; (2) production in the home, of both goods and services as well as social provisioning and voluntary work (Rai and Hoskyns 2016; see also Bakker, 2007; Dalla Costa and James, 1971; Humphries, 1977; Mies, 2014); (3) reproduction of culture and ideology, which stabilises and (sometimes challenges) dominant social relations (Laslett and Brenner, 1989). As Bhattacharya has noted, social reproduction allows for a more commodious approach to what constitutes the economy and treats questions of gender inequality as structurally reproduced through capitalist social relations (2017: 2–3). Such outlining of social reproduction has led feminist economists to view the home not just as a node of altruism and/or consumption, but for multiple gendered transfers between individuals, the market and the state (Folbre, 2001).

In her path-breaking analysis, Maria Mies has attributed the gender division of labour to the legacy of 'housewifisation', understood as an ideological process that produces new, gendered subjectivities and relations of production under capitalism. In the West, from the nineteenth century onwards, the belief in a monogamous, nuclear family became institutionalised, and the image of the 'good, Christian woman' carved out a new, private arena of the household where, as a mother and wife to the male 'breadwinner', she would be tasked with responsibility for the family, born out of 'love' and requiring new forms of consumption to fulfil her womanly duties. Consequently, women's labour was 'externalised and ex-territorialised', considered 'supplementary' to formalised, paid work and leaving them atomised and disorganised, with an attendant decline in the possibilities of political and bargaining power. This model of women's labour and subjectivity was rolled out as the 'norm' in the colonies, and Mies pays particular attention to the subsequent devaluing of women's labour in these spaces through 'self-help' development interventions and poverty eradication programmes:

> Women are the optimal labour force because they are now being universally defined as 'housewives', not as workers; this means their work, whether in use value or commodity production, is obscured, does not appear as 'free wage labour', is defined as an 'income-generating activity', and can hence be bought at a much cheaper price than male labour (Mies, 2014: 110ff).

The recognition and non-recognition of this work – largely through paid and unpaid elements of this work, but also through the state-supported ideology of motherhood – is a critical element of not only the form the household takes, but also how it is inserted into the labour market and is vulnerable to being mobilised by the state in the interest of the market. The current phase of labour mobilisation – of the female proletariat worldwide – in the context of, as in India, jobless growth is one such example of the market state imbrication. However, one thing that we can note is that social reproductive labour has always been classed, raced and affected by relations of power between nations. Attention to the global flows of labour also alert us to the ways in which the state regulates migration in the interest of capital needs; the fact that the ideologies of culture and the nation often undermine an economist analysis of migration is important for us to study.

If the state regulates the family form and the social reproductive labour associated with it, we can also see how social reproduction itself becomes part of the crisis of capitalism. In Europe today, there is a palpable concern about the 'crisis of care' as the population ages and needs of the labour market lead to the increased mobilisation of women globally. As Fraser puts it:

> Without [social reproduction] there could be no culture, no economy, no political organization. No society that systematically undermines social reproduction can endure for long. Today, however, a new form of capitalist society is doing just that (2016: 99).

However, the state steps in here as well. For example, the withdrawal of state welfare provision in the aftermath of economic crises (and the lack of this provision at any time in many countries) leads to the increased reliance on unpaid work as a coping strategy, creating additional burdens that tend to be borne by women (Himmelweit, 2017; Hoskyns and Rai, 2007; see also Levitas, 2001).

The crisis of care or social reproduction can be characterised as depletion through social reproduction. Depletion is interwoven with regimes of the state and the market, as well as 'historically specific, culturally contested' social relations (Rai et al., 2014: 90). Crucially, we consider the multiple forms of harm that can arise from depletion – to individuals (adversely affecting their physical and mental health), to households (adversely affecting the relationships and material fabric of the home) and to the community (through erosion of public spaces accessed by all, as well as of solidarity relations). It also harms by generating a very different politics of citizenship where those not recognised as workers (in the home) are also not recognised as citizens with entitlements against the state; rather, they are constructed as recipients of welfare (ibid.), recognising the diverse and varied manifestations of depletion in a world where work is increasingly precarious and insecure (Standing, 1997; Standing, 2012). Depletion increases, we argue, with neoliberal restructuring and changing labour markets, with women's unpaid work subsidising the withdrawal or reduction of public services (Rai et al., 2014).

This depletion needs to be mitigated to protect the reproduction of life and labour.[2] However, the neoliberal state is unwilling to invest in social infrastructure – still holding on to the 'male breadwinner' model of employment, even as this

---

2 The governmentalisation of populations can be seen in state policies that are both pro- and anti-natalist and in Foucauldian terms include state, non-state and individual actors who govern others and themselves in regulating growth rates and health. While China remains the most obvious example of the latter, countries like France and Italy have pro-natalist policies that focus on producing the right mix of citizens through a racialised mode of pro-natalism (Greenhalgh and Winckler, 2005; Inhorn, 2007).

crumbles around us with the increased mobilisation of women into the labour market; ideology matters. As Sauer and Wohl have argued:

> The new border regimes are usually gender selective and racist, because they construct subjects that are 'useful' and 'useable' in the local or national labour market and subjects that are 'of no value' to the national economy (2011: 118).

One way in which the state facilitates care work is through privatisation – migration policies have enabled care labour to be imported. So, now we not only witness the extension of global production chains that allow for post-Fordist modes of production, but also global care chains that keep our hospitals and care homes running although often in very narrow time frames, which means that the idea of care itself is squeezed into 15-minute slots of basic physical necessities, not allowing time for conversations that address issues of loneliness and fear. Middle-class women are able to join the labour market as the commodification of many aspects of social reproductive work become possible through employing cheap and informal labour. The histories of colonialism and peripheral capitalism live and work in our homes every day. Rich migrants bring their servants with them to Europe; as Kalayan, a small organisation helping informal domestic labour, says:

> informal nature of work in a private home where the worker is dependent on their employers for housing and immigration status as well as employment and where hours are often seen to be flexible means that many workers are often seriously exploited.[3]

In this context, I would argue with Janet Bair that in the absence of any overarching analysis of 'how gender, as a set of context-specific meanings and practices, intersects with the structure of global capitalism and its systemic logic of value extraction and capital accumulation' (Bair, 2010: 205; see also Bakker, 2007; Federici, 2004; Fraser, 2013; Hewamanne, 2008; Lynch, 2007; Werner, 2016), we will fail to effectively counter gendered forms of exploitation within global labour regimes.

But, of course, gender intersects with global practices in particular forms; it is here that we begin to open up the issue of how different identities and structural positionalities are mobilised by the state and how we need to disaggregate these practices in order to challenge this critically important governance move. In a robustly argued paper on 'Marxism, and Class, Gender, and Race', Gimenez takes feminists to task for conflating social locations and subjective identities, which then, she argues, leads to an individual-level analysis of oppression (2001). This is a classical Marxist position, which is not without merit. The argument goes that the reason why certain forms of difference – race, gender and sexuality, for example – can be shown to be easier to fold into capitalist regimes of accumulation as well

3 See http://www.kalayaan.org.uk/ (accessed 23 April 2019).

as distribution, is that class does not lend itself to such expropriation. However, as outlined in the discussion on social reproduction above, the subsidy provided by those engaged in this labour – and it is deeply gendered – is essential to the continuance of regimes of accumulation. Also, while I have some sympathy with Gimenez's argument, it is also, I would argue, important to take seriously feminism's and postcolonial theory's epistemic challenge to Marxism – that experience matters; that the processes of accumulation take different forms, and this is reflected in who experiences these in what ways and how these different experiences affect the responses of those affected. The question that remains, however, surely is what weight do we give to experience and how do we answer the question regarding whose experience? As I have suggested above, class is an important vector in mitigating gender-based inclusions into the labour market – the buying in of labour power of those who have travelled far away from their homes poses not only questions of individual racialised experience of employment and of being an employer, it also raises structural issues of routes of Empire, of capitalism's backwaters and of expulsions of labour as much as of regimes of migration. In his book, *The Intimate Enemy*, Ashis Nandy, like Franz Fanon before him, has argued that the reach of colonialism encompasses both the political economy of the colony and the mappings of its culture and its selfhood as expressed by its political elites (Nandy, 1983: 2). The subjectivity of the male breadwinner, at least in the West, has also been that of a white male breadwinner. Asserting this in neoliberal times takes particular forms, which the struggles of black and ethnic minority men to gain access to better paid jobs and of black and ethnic minority women to fight the injustice of a racist society and of a gendered community regime evidences. Intersectional analysis, then, is a challenge for all of us – how not to weigh down class analysis, but to complexify it. Without this, the building of solidarity in challenge to the state would remain fractured and weak.

The political, legal and performative form of the state

Under neoliberalism and globalisation, the state's regulatory role has changed. As under colonialism, the neoliberal mode of capitalism has revealed more clearly than ever the necessary mobilisation of labour in the periphery to undercut labour price in the core countries. At the same time, this has provided the postcolonial state to reconstitute the labour market – through Export Processing Zones (EPZs), migration/remittances and urbanisation. In the UK Empire, Windrush remains an iconic ship that brought Caribbean people 'home' to the UK, at a time of war-based deprivation and also the urgent need for labour to rebuild a devastated economy. As Stuart Hall as has argued:

> questions [of culture and identity] are not in any sense separate or removed
> from the problems of political mobilization, of cultural development, of eco-
> nomic development and so on. The more we know and see of the struggles
> of the societies of the periphery to make something of the slender resources

available to them, the more important we understand the questions and problems of cultural identity to be in that process (1995: 3).

At the same time, in order to resolve questions of political and economic mobilisation, the state also deploys culture and identity – to shape the labour market; responses to imperfect information of the labour market often result in, as it did in the 1950s and as we are seeing today in Europe, a political response of racism and cultural violence which is both classed (H1 visas) and gendered (the burka). Nationalism has been an important trope for the state; indeed, in the postcolonial world the state was often called the nation-state and the politics of self-determination played out in very particular ways. As Hobsbawm points out, '[n]ationalism thus acquired a strong association with the left during the anti-fascist period, an association which was subsequently reinforced by the experience of anti-imperialist struggles in colonial countries' (1990: 148). In many postcolonial countries, a developmental state was the outcome of these struggles – in the context of the Cold War – which allowed different strategies of managing class tensions through creative discourses of redistribution and democracy. Take, for example, India – a state that chose to follow a 'mixed-economy' model: as Vivek Chibber has argued, the Indian state under Nehru attempted to show that 'planning need not presuppose the abolition of property, but could, in fact, be harnessed to the engine of capitalist accumulation' (2004: 3, 85). That its development was blocked, however, by 'the widespread and organized resistance of the business class' is another story; as is the rise of the neoliberal state that is in operation today.

But, as we are seeing in the Global North today, capitalism's tensions and contradictions played out to a point of crisis for these states – the pain that is being felt in the West today was felt long ago in the Global South through structural adjustment policies (SAPs). Austerity, residualisation of the state, the focus on fiscal budgets rather than investment in social infrastructure and the dependence on the double burden of women's labour – all these were experienced by countries under the SAPs regime; we can also note the enduring legacies of colonisation and Empire operative here – in the gendered and racialised regimes of assembly lines, rural food production and care provisions (Rai et al., forthcoming; Beneria et al., 2012; De Schutter, 2013; Hothschild, 2002; Ong, 2006; Ruwanpura and Hughes, 2016; Safri and Graham, 2010; Standing, 1999). The emergence of export-processing enclaves that include factory work as well as home-based production, subcontracting firms (Beneria and Feldman, 1992), have resulted in increasingly elongated and diffuse chains of accountability, enhancing precariousness and leading to a decline of collective bargaining under the guise of 'flexibilisation' (Standing, 1999; see also Ong, 2006). While a new vocabulary has been mobilised to discuss the state of the economy in the West, the discourses are familiar in the context of the Global South and the experience of SAPs.

This affects our politics, of course; the welfare state has become, in the current context, the line we are defending in the Global North. This is a significant change in the way in which we understand the feminist politics of engagement with the state. In the 1970s and 1980s, Marxist feminists in Europe saw the welfare state as an actor ensuring the stability of unequal gender relations, male breadwinner model of employment and supporting through education and religion the ideology that underpins patriarchy, as well as its enactment in social relations. In contemporary neoliberal times, however, the struggles against the residualisation of the state and social provisioning are uniting women in broad alliances against the state. In the Global South, however, most postcolonial states do not provide much of a welfare net anyway. And the histories of nationalist struggles have meant that the feminist movement and women's groups did participate in, however marginalised, bringing the nation-state into being. In both locations, however, the engagement with the state has not been straightforward – fractions of the state both reproduce and main- tain the gendered hierarchies of difference, while at the same time other fractions mediate these. So, the battles are different and yet the same in the Global South and the Global North. Difference also attaches itself to different visions of change – despite many debates, we continue to think if not speak and write of feminists without making explicit their political frameworks. This allows for the narrative of feminist expropriation – rather than challenging liberal feminist forms of political engagements. In the Global South, this has led to the discourse of 'NGOisation' of the women's movement. The shift from the vocabulary of the state and government to that of governance also allowed these political erasures as we became used to thinking of power relations as more diffuse than before.

The question of governance is complicated – on the one hand, the underpin- ning narrative was about the leaking of state sovereignty and making visible the insertion of non-state actors in the globalising political decision-making; on the other, governance literature unpacked how new forms of governmentality con- struct the social. Partha Chatterjee argues, for example, that:

> the classical idea of popular sovereignty, expressed in the legal-political fact of equal citizenship, produced the homogeneous construct of the nation, whereas the activities of governmentality required multiple, cross-cutting and shifting classifications of the population as the targets of multiple policies, producing necessarily a heterogeneous construct of the social (Chatterjee, 2004: 35–6).

This heterogeneous social is, I argue, also gendered.

In considering the relations between state and non-state modes of regulation and disciplining in the context of India and Pakistan, Baxi et al. showed how the fractured modernity of postcolonial states under pressures of globalisation also refract its responses – cultural heritage is fetishised, when, at the same time, the lib- eralisation of the economy creates new bridges to the 'modern' political economy. Elsewhere I have argued, with Baxi and Sardar Ali (2006), that:

> Two axes might allow us to explore this complex nature of the interaction between modernity and tradition at the local, national and global levels of

governance. The first is that of governance of polities (state statutory governance bodies such as panchayats, courts and the police). The second axis is the
governance of communities (caste panchayats and jirgahs). The regulatory
power of both is limited as well as complex. This power comes to be articulated at the intersection of disciplinary power of caste or community discourses of honour with sovereign, or as Foucault would say politico-juridical,
discourses of crime and adulthood. The translation of caste or community
transgressions into crimes shows us how the politics of honour captures state
law, while the suspension of legal action against forced marriages allows the
familial to escape legal intervention. The claims to citizenship in the realm of
the domestic sphere must be understood in the interstices of the relationship
between law, violence and governance (Baxi et al., 2006: 1241).

Governance of communities by caste panchayats has allowed the development
of non-state parallel systems of adjudication, which are performed publicly, with
authority that builds on the community's consent and sense of belonging, in a
context of changes to the local economies and demographies. Racism and sexism – every day and in concert with state/governmentality practices – ensure that
governance of communities works to segregate, separate and enclose some lives
everywhere, just as others access positions, roles and repertoires of power.

An important political question for me today is: Does the form of the state
matter?[4] Obviously, I am not asking this question in the post-Cold War triumph of
capitalism mode! Does it matter that the state takes a form that is democratic/non-
democratic, overtly racist and Islamophobic or not so, overtly sexist in the way that
it restricts the life choices of women, segregates populations? Does it matter that it
mobilises dominant prejudices that are then backed up by state violence? Finally,
the question of the form of the state also brings us to the vocabulary of governance – is the state one of many administrative and regulatory organisations? The
answer to the first set of questions for me is – yes; I would rather live in a bourgeois
democracy than in a bourgeois or religious dictatorship. As Fraser has argued, and
we can quarrel with her about the context in which she says this:

> the most general meaning of justice is parity of participation . . . Overcom-
> ing injustice means dismantling institutionalized obstacles that prevent some
> people from participating on a par with others as full partners in social inter-
> action (2007: 20).

---

4 This is a different question from the Poulantzean debate on the 'relative autonomy' of the state or of
fractions of capitalist classes within the state. As the post-2008 global financial crisis has shown, at least
in the EU, financial interests materialise themselves within states in specific ways, perhaps not directly,
but through certain actors who support certain fractions of capital. Take, for example, the continuing
non-regulation of taxes on speculation by the European Commission or the reluctance of the British
state to plug tax loopholes. This suggests that certain fractions of corporate and financial capital gained
access to the state directly, leaving Poulantzas's 'relative autonomy' an issue to revisit.

However limited, a bourgeois democracy generates spaces to challenge it, to mobilise dissent and to generate new solidarities – the struggle is to expand this space and to remove the obstacles that prevent some from accessing it. This is not to accept, as Miliband suggested of the Labour Party, that devotion to the parliamentary system becomes the be all and end all of political action (Wetherly et al., 2008), or a Gramscian analysis of the state that points to the importance of democratic institutions as one way to achieve hegemony. Indeed, these democratic spaces also allow 'the other side' to mobilise – electorally, but also through social mobilisations; so, these spaces have to be occupied, fought over and used to hold democratic institutions accountable. Gender is an axis of inequality, as well as a lens to make visible such inequalities. The role of the state in maintaining as well as mediating these inequalities has been an important element of the feminist scholarship on the state. It urges us to recognise the splintered complexity of the state and a multiplicity of the strategies of struggle needed by women to confront and/or mobilise state fractions in their own interests (Sangari and Vaid, 1990; Rai, 1995; Sunder Rajan, 2003). Das and Poole have argued that 'margins are a necessary entailment of the state, much as the exception is a necessary component of the rule' (2004: 4). I have argued elsewhere that given their class as well as gender positioning, women often operate, economically and politically, in the margins and interstices of the system, only occasionally moving on to the formal legal terrain (1996). Further, that because of the role that state structures play in the everyday lives of women and men, we cannot but engage with its institutions even as we are aware of the limitations of these strategies of engagement (see also Wöhl, 2014: 7). I concluded by arguing for an understanding of the state informed by issues of a relative autonomy of state fractions from the existing social relations on the one hand, and state embeddedness in social relations and the consequences of such embeddedness for women, on the other.

In the context of settled democracies, we have to also think about the political boundary drawing quite differently from where democratic institutions are fragile or largely absent. As Goetz has pointed out:

> Still, liberalism's respect for equal rights has offered a crucial entry-point for women to politics, has required democracies to create institutions defending minorities against the majority, and has created institutions to hold leaders to account (2018: 214).

Issues of representation become important here. Take, for example, India – it prides itself as the largest democracy in the world, and yet it scores badly in gender empowerment indices and remains at the bottom of the league where women's representation in parliament is concerned (IPU, 2019). Where we can agree perhaps is that we need to mobilise to maximise spaces of contestation by engaging the state through its different institutions – in the interstices of the state. The key point that Miliband raised in his critique of the Labour Party was its vulnerability to being appropriated by the system so to speak. The Labour Party and indeed the labour movement became focused on pushing forward and trying to meet the demands of organised labour, which, as we have seen already, were framed by the male breadwinner model. Trade unions were slow to acknowledge and incorporate the concerns of women, and omitted recognition of how waged work was effectively subsidised by the un- and underpaid work of social reproduction (Rai et al., forthcoming). This has been a fundamental concern of the feminist movement too. Michelle Barrett notes that 'there is an underlying fear in many sections of the movement that direct engagement with state policy and constitutional politics would lead to liberal reformism' (Barrett, 1986: 228). This liberal reformism then has led Janet Halley to call out 'governance feminism' (2018) and for Fraser to excoriate it as 'capitalism's handmaiden' (2013). Chibber's (2004) critique of postcolonial theory also similarly critiques the limited nature of the subaltern challenge to capitalism and therefore to structures of inequality.

And yet . . . we cannot let go of existing political institutions as outside of the purview of our political struggles. This is for a simple reason: laws and policies matter. As Michelle Barrett argued, '[t]he law itself encodes fundamental assumptions about gender division and it is salutary to consider how recently it is that women have been recognized as legal subjects in their own rights' (1986: 236). And in the words of Martin Luther King:

> . . . it may be true that morality cannot be legislated, but behaviour can be regulated. It may be true that the law cannot change the heart, but it can restrain the heartless. It maybe true that the law cannot make a man love me; but it can restrain him from lynching me; and I think that is pretty important also. And so, while the law may not change the hearts of men it does change the habits of men if it is vigorously enforced and through changes in habits, pretty soon attitudinal changes will take place and even the heart may be changed (speech at Newcastle University, 1967).

Contesting the systematic exclusion of a group of people then also matters.

Engaging the state: solidarity

Marx's dictum that our analysis of social relations should lead to the transformation of society is, of course, apposite here. And yet, as J. K. Gibson-Graham has noted:

> My feminism reshapes the terrain of my social existence on a daily basis. 'Why can't my Marxism have as its object something that I am involved in (re)constructing every day? Where is my lived project of socialist construction?' They further argue that

> 'If we can divorce our ideas of class from systemic social conceptions, and simultaneously divorce our ideas of class transformation from projects of system transformation, we may be able to envision local and proximate socialisms' (2006: 264).

I do not necessarily agree with this formulation; rather, as I have argued elsewhere:

> if we see successful transformation not as a single revolutionary event but as a
> bundle of changes that may add up to transformation in the longer term, then
> we may find some elements of that bundle emerging through these struggles
> for gender equality (Rai et al., 2014: 15).

This also perhaps helps us go past the issue of change as universally recognised form: while it might be correct to critique postcolonial theory as confusing universality with homogeneity and underlining that struggles over material needs are, in fact, the universal condition of conflict between elites and the poor (Brennan, 2014), the resolution of this conflict might take different forms – incrementally as well as contradictorily. So, two things need to be addressed: the *form* that this conflict takes and *how* we may universalise rather than homogenise these struggles.

The other question concerns the immediacy of change – how to balance the urgency of policy mitigation with the long-term effects of a social transformation. In terms of social policy, Orloff asks 'who will be entitled to . . . new social protections and services?' (2009: 141). The International Domestic Workers Federation (IDWF), an alliance of over 500,000 workers organising in 50 countries worldwide, hailed a breakthrough moment in the struggle for recognition by homeworkers, care-workers and others engaged in informal labour when the C189 – Domestic Workers Convention, 2011 was ratified. It extended rights to an estimated 67 million domestic workers worldwide (ILO, 2011). And yet, it did not challenge the premise of the bifurcation of paid and unpaid domestic work. Similarly, the parliamentary battle today between the politics of austerity and those who oppose it is not inconsequential for those affected. So, the question for me is about how to tether political pragmatism to progressive politics?

For Marx, solidarity was class reflexivity translated into political action against exploitation; however, historically, trade unions as organisations mobilising class interests have been castigated as 'bastions of male privilege', limited to articulating the interests of men in the formal sector (McIntyre, 2008; Padmanabhan, 2011; Ruwanpura, 2004). Increasingly, labour activism is organised through cross-boundary strategising and transnational networks operating at multiple scales, linking actors at different nodes of supply chains to articulate claims in different arenas of power (Bronfenbrenner, 2007; McIntyre, 2008; Zajak et al., 2017). Feminists have seen solidarity at times as 'global sisterhood' and at others solidarity in difference. Reflexive analysis of the erasures of race and culture in the stories of feminist theory, however, are made possible through a series of ontological and epistemological manoeuvres, which structure the emergence of a 'common sense' regarding the boundaries of the known and knowable and make alliances across these boundaries difficult (Hemmings, 2011).

Our task going forward could be thinking through how through reimagining social reproduction, and stabilising this reimagined process through the law, we can engage in transformative politics by mobilising in solidarity. On this, the insights of anti-racist and postcolonial theory might provoke us into working to answer this question of difference, even as we develop new forms of collective politics. One materialist approach to solidarity that also builds on the feminist critique of the economy and the state is that of Silvia Federici's chapter on 'Feminism and the Politics of the Common' in her book *Ground Zero* (2012). Here, she calls for the 'reconstruction of our everyday life' through collective forms of living, where reproductive work is carried out in common: 'if "commoning" has any meaning, it must be the production of ourselves as a common subject' (145). This will help recombine, she argues, 'what the social division of labor in capitalism has separated' (144). While this is an important intervention in the politics of change, it does not answer the questions that inevitably are raised when we take into account different forms of social reproduction; the politics of commonising seems to assume a solidarity not generate it.

So, what new forms of solidarity – universalist but not homogenising – can we work towards?[5] This reimagining solidarity is an important question to raise in the current climate of economic fragility, the rise of a politics of hate and the attack upon democratic opposition with the continuing strengthening of the executive branch of the state. This political landscape makes the need for an ampler understanding of the forms of capitalist exploitation and resistance to these urgent. Solidarity – in such a capacious form – militates against, what Giroux calls, 'the sheer weight of apocalypse' (1986: 247). According to Sharon D. Welch, solidarity is the opposite of indifference: 'To remember the reality of oppression in the lives of people and to value those lives is to be saved from the luxury of hopelessness' (1985: 90). But this can only come about if there is a more symmetrical relationship among those whose visions of change coalesce around similar forms of politics – we often get into political hot water with our potential allies if we are not in tune with issues of representation, for example. Solidarity is reflexive: it illuminates practices of power at work within different discursive and institutional relations of domination, but it also remains vigilant about its own practices. In these acts of solidarity, we can also see how Marx thought (in unfeminist vocabulary) of the 'species being' – that each human being must, by virtue of being human, imagine 'himself'/herself as the example of being human. Multiple imaginings of society and the state require modes of working together towards these new horizons.

Whilst I might not have more to say about a reimagined state, as intellectuals, educators, we can participate in developing this solidarity – we can do this through reflecting on our curricula, our pedagogy, our writing and the spaces we are ready to occupy. bell hooks called for 'renewal and rejuvenation in our teaching practices ... so that we can create new visions, [through] a movement which makes education the practice of freedom' (1994: 12). Acts of everyday solidarity – marching

---

5 Some of the ideas in this section are based on my work (Rai, 2018).

together in protest, standing on picket lines, giving refuge to those in need, teaching differently – help bridge the private and public, the individual and the collective, and challenge the dichotomies of knowledge/power, by:

> uncovering forms of historical and subjugated knowledges that point to experiences of suffering, conflict, and collective struggle, social re-enactment and counter conduct teachers as intellectuals can begin to link the notion of historical understanding to elements of critique and hope (Giroux, 1986: 254).

As I have argued elsewhere, '[i]n doing so, we place ourselves in relation to the social that we critique, the individual that we nurture in our classrooms, and the political that we seek to change' (Rai, 2018: 15–16).

Acknowledgements

I would like to thank Nikita Dhawan, Davina Cooper, Janet Newman and colleagues who participated in the Reimagining the State workshop at the University of Kent for comments on this paper. I would also like to thank Stephanie Woehl for her close reading of this work and for her robust and thoughtful comments.

References

Adorno, T. W. (1974) *Minima Moralia, Reflections on a Damaged Life*. London: Verso Books.

Bair, J. (2010) 'On Difference and Capital: Gender and the Globalization of Production', Signs: Journal of Women in Culture and Society, 36(1), pp. 203–26.

Bakker, I. (2007) 'Social Reproduction and the Constitution of a Gendered Political Economy', *New Political Economy*, 12(4), pp. 541–56.

Barrett, M. (1986) *Women's Oppression Today*. London: Verso.

Baxi, P., Rai, S. M. and Ali, S. S. (2006) 'Legacies of Common Law: "Crimes of Honour" in India and Pakistan', Third World Quarterly, 27(7), pp. 1239–53.

Benería, L., Deere, C. D. and Kabeer, N. (2012) 'Gender and International Migration: Globalization, Development, and Governance', *Feminist Economics*, 18(2), pp. 1–33.

Beneria, L. and Feldman, S. (1992) *Unequal Burden: Economic Crises, Persistent Poverty, and Women's Work*. Oxford: Westview Press.

Bhattacharya, T. (ed.) (2017) *Social Reproduction Theory: Remapping Class, Recentering Oppression*. London: Pluto Press.

Bloch, E. (1995) *The Principle of Hope*. Cambridge, MA: MIT Press.

Brennan, T. (2014) 'Subaltern Stakes', New Left Review, 89, pp. 67–87.

Bronfenbrenner, K. (2007) *Global Unions: Challenging Transnational Capital through Cross-Border Campaigns*. Ithaca, NY: Cornell University Press.

Butler, J. (2012) 'Can One Lead a Good Life in a Bad Life?', *Radical Philosophy*, 176 [online]. Available at https://www.radicalphilosophy.com/article/can-one-lead-a-good-life-in-a-bad-life (accessed 1 January 2018).

Chatterjee, P. (2004) *The Politics of the Governed*. New York: Columbia University Press.

Chibber, V. (2004) *Locked in Place State-Building and Late Industrialization in India*. Princeton, NJ: Princeton University Press.

Cooper, D. (2014) *Everyday Utopias*. London: Duke University Press.

Dalla Costa, M. and James, S. (1971) *Women and the Subversion of Community*. Brooklyn: Pétroleuse Press.

Das, V. (2007) *Life and Words*. Berkeley, CA: University of California Press.

Das, V. and Poole, D. (2004) 'The Signature of the State: The Paradox of Illegibility' in Das, V. (ed.), *Anthropology in the Margins of the State*. Delhi: Oxford University Press, pp. 3–35.

De Schutter, O. (2013) 'The Agrarian Transition and the "Feminization" of Agriculture', Conference Paper #37. Food Sovereignty: A Critical Dialogue International Conference, 14–15 September.

Federici, S. (2004) *Caliban and the Witch: Women, the Body and Primitive Accumulation*. New York: Autonomedia.

Federici, S. (2012) *Revolution at Point Zero: Housework, Reproduction, and Feminist Struggle*. Oakland, CA: PM Press.

Folbre, N. (2001) *The Invisible Heart: Economics and Family Values*. New. York: New Press.

Fraser, N. (2007) 'Feminist Politics in the Age of Recognition: A Two-Dimensional Approach to Gender Justice', Studies in Social Justice, 1(1), pp. 23–35.

Fraser, N. (2013) 'How Feminism Became Capitalism's Handmaiden – and How to Reclaim It', *The Guardian*, 14 October [online]. Available at https://www.theguardian.com/com mentisfree/2013/oct/14/feminism-capitalist-handmaiden-neoliberal (accessed 3 March 2019).

Fraser, N. (2014) 'Behind Marx's Hidden Abode', *New Left Review*, 86, March–April.

Fraser, N. (2016) 'Contradictions of Capital and Care', *New Left Review*, 100, pp. 99–117.

Gibson-Graham, J. K. (2006) *The End of Capitalism (As We Knew It): A Feminist Critique of Political Economy*. Minneapolis, MN: University of Minnesota Press.

Gimenez, M. E. (2001) 'Marxism, and Class, Gender, and Race: Rethinking the Trilogy Race, Gender & Class', *New Orleans*, 8(2), p. 23.

Giroux, H. A. (1986) 'Solidarity, Struggle, and the Discourse of Hope: Theory, Practice, and Experience in Radical Education, Part II', *The Review of Education*, 12(4), pp. 247–55.

Goetz, A. M. (2018) 'Has Democracy Failed Women?', *Gender and Development*, 26(1), pp. 214–216. Available at http://www.genderanddevelopment.org/issues/261-sexuali ties/book-review-has-democracy-failed-women/ (accessed 3 March 2019).

Gornick, J. C. and Meyers, M. K. (2009) 'An Institutional Proposal' in Gornick, J. C. and Meyers, M. K. (eds.) *Gender Equality: Transforming Family Divisions of Labour*. London: Verso Books.

Gorz, A. (1999) *Reclaiming Work: Beyond the Wage-Based Society*. Cambridge: Polity Press.

Greenhalgh, S. E. and Winckler, A. (2005) *Governing China's Population: From Leninist to Neoliberal Biopolitics*. Stanford, CA: Stanford University Press.

Hall, S. (1995) 'Negotiating Caribbean Identities', *New Left Review*, January–February, pp. 3–14.

Halley, J., Kotiswaran, P., Rebouché, R. and Shamir, H. (2018) *Governance Feminism: An Introduction*. Minneapolis, MN: University of Minnesota Press.

Harvey, D. (2004) 'The "New" Imperialism: Accumulation by Dispossession', *Socialist Register*, 40, pp. 63–87.

Hassim, S. (2009) 'Whose Utopia' in Gornick, J. and Meyers, M. K. (eds.), *Gender Equality: Transforming Family Divisions of Labour*. London, New York: Verso Books.

Hemmings, C. (2011) *Why Stories Matter: The Political Grammar of Feminist Theory*. Durham, NC: Duke University Press.

Hewamanne, S. (2008) *Stitching Identities in a Free Trade Zone: Gender and Politics in Sri Lanka*. Philadelphia, PA: University of Pennsylvania Press.

Himmelweit, S. (2017) *Changing Norms of Social Reproduction in an Age of Austerity* [online]. Available at http://iippe.org/wp/wp-content/uploads/2017/01/suegender.pdf (accessed 3 March 2019).

Hobsbawm, E. (1990) *Nations and Nationalism Since 1780, Second Edition: Programme, Myth, Reality*. Cambridge: Cambridge University Press.

hooks, b. (1994) *Teaching to Transgress: Education as the Practice of Freedom*. London: Routledge.

Hoskyns, C. and Rai, S. (2007) 'Recasting the Global Political Economy: Counting Women's Unpaid Work', *New Political Economy*, 12(3), pp. 297–317.

Hothschild, A. (2002) 'Love and Gold' in Erenreich, B. and Hoschchild, A. (eds.), *Global Woman: Nannies, Maids and Sex Workers in the New Economy*. New York: Henry Holt, pp. 15–30.

Humphries, J. (1977) 'Class Struggle and the Persistence of the Working-Class Family', *Cambridge Journal of Economics*, 1, pp. 241–58.

Inhorn, M. C. (2007) *Reproductive Disruptions: Gender, Technology, and Biopolitics in the New Millenium*. New York: Berghahn Books.

International Labour Organization (2011) C189 – Domestic Workers Convention, 2011 (No. 189). Available at http://ilo.org/dyn/normlex/en/f? p=NORMLEXPUB:12100:0 ::NO::P12100_ILO_CODE:C189 (retrieved 27–08–17).

Inter-Parliamentary Union (IPU) (2019) 'Women in Politics: 2019'. Available at http://archive.ipu.org/wmn-e/classif.htm (accessed 23 April 2019).

Jessop, B. (2008) 'Dialogue of the Deaf: Some Reflections on the Poulantzas-Miliband Debate' in Wetherly, P., Barrow, C. and Burnham, P. (eds.), *Class, Power and the State in Capitalist Society*. Basingstoke, UK: Palgrave Macmillan.

King, M. L. (1967) Speech on Receipt of Honorary Doctorate in Civil Law, 13 November 1967, University of Newcastle upon Tyne [online]. Available at http://www.ncl.ac.uk/media/wwwnclacuk/congregations/files/Transcript%20of%20Dr%20Martin%20Luther%20King%20Jr%20speech%2013th%20November%201967.pdf (accessed 3 March 2019).

Laslett, B. and Brenner, J. (1989) 'Gender and Social Reproduction: Historical Perspectives', *Annual Review of Sociology*, 15, pp. 381–404.

Levitas, R. (2001) 'Against Work: A Utopian Incursion into Social Policy', *Critical Social Policy*, 21(4), pp. 449–65.

Levitas, R. (2010) *Utopia as Method: The Imaginary Reconstitution of Society*. Basingstoke, UK: Palgrave Macmillan.

Lynch, C. (2007) *Juki Girls, Good Girls: Gender and Cultural Politics in Sri Lanka's Global Garment Industry*. Ithaca, NY: Cornell University Press.

McIntyre, R. P. (2008) *Are Workers' Rights Human Rights?* Ann Arbor, MI: University of Michigan Press.

Mies, M. (2014) *Patriarchy and Accumulation on a World Scale: Women in the International Division of Labour*. London: Zed Books.

Nandy, A. (1983) *The Intimate Enemy*. New Delhi: Oxford University Press.

Ong, A. (2006) *Neoliberalism as Exception: Mutations in Citizenship and Sovereignty*. Durham NC and London: Duke University Press.

Orloff, A. S. (2009) 'Should Feminists Aim for Gender Symmetry?' in Gornick, J. C. and Meyers, M. K. (eds.), *Gender Equality: Transforming Family Divisions of Labour*. London and New York: Verso Books.

Padmanabhan, N. (2011) 'Globalisation Lived Locally: A Labour Geography Perspective on Control, Conflict and Response among Workers in Kerala', Antipode, 44(3), pp. 971–92.

Panitch, L. and Gindin, S. (1999). 'Transcending Pessimism: Rekindling Socialist Imagination' in Panitch, L. and Gindin, S. (eds.), *Necessary and Unnecessary Utopias*. New York: Monthly Review Press, pp. 1–29.

Rai, S. M. (1995) 'Women Negotiating Boundaries: Gender, Law and the Indian State', *Social & Legal Studies*, 4, pp. 391–410.

Rai, S. M. (1996) 'Women and the State in the Third World: Some Issues for Debate' in Rai, S. M. and Lievesley, G. (eds.), *Women and the State: International Perspectives*. London: Taylor & Francis.

Rai, S. M. (2018) 'The Good Life and the Bad: Dialectics of Solidarity', *Social Politics*, 25(1), pp. 1–19.

Rai, S. M., Brown, B. and Ruwanpura, K. (2019) 'SDG 8: Decent Work and Economic Growth – A Gendered Analysis', World Development, 113, pp. 368–80.

Rai, S. M., Hoskyns, C. and Thomas, D. (2014) 'Depletion: The Cost of Social Reproduction', *International Feminist Journal of Politics*, 16(1), pp. 86–105.

Rai, S. M. and Hoskyns, C. (2016) *Social Reproduction – the Achilles Heel of Feminist Transformation? Handbook of Gender and World Politics*. London: Edward Elgar.

Ruwanpura, K. N. (2004) 'Quality of Women's Employment: A Focus on the South', IIL Discussion Paper Series, no. 151.

Ruwanpura, K. N. and Hughes, A. (2016) 'Empowered Spaces? Management Articulations of Gendered Spaces in Apparel Factories in Karachi', *Gender, Place and Culture*, 23(9), pp. 1270–85.

Safri, M. and Graham, J. (2010) 'The Global Household: Toward a Feminist Post-Capitalist International Political Economy', *Signs: Journal of Women in Culture and Society*, 36(1), pp. 99–125.

Sangari, K. and Vaid, S. (eds.) (1990) *Recasting Women: Essays in Colonial History*. New Delhi: Kali for Women.

Sauer, B. and Wöhl, S. (2011) 'Feminist Perspectives on the Internationalization of the State', Antipode, 43(1), pp. 108–28.

Standing, G. (1997) 'Globalization, Labour Flexibility and Insecurity: The Era of Market Regulation', European Journal of Industrial Relations, 3(1), pp. 7–37.

Standing, G. (1999) 'Global Feminization through Flexible Labour: A Theme Revisited', *World Development*, 27(3), pp. 583–602.

Standing, G. (2012) 'The Precariat: From Denizens to Citizens?', Polity, 44(4), pp. 588–608.

Sunder Rajan, R. (2003) *The Scandal of the State*. New Delhi: Permanent Black.

Welch, S. D. (1985) *Communities of Resistance and Solidarity: A Feminist Theology of Liberation*. Ossining, NY: Orbis Books.

Werner, M. (2016) *Global Displacements: The Making of Uneven Development in the Caribbean*. Sussex: Wiley-Blackwell.

Wetherly, P., Barrow, C. W. and Burnham, P. (eds.) (2008) *Class, Power and the State in Capitalist Society: Essays on Ralph Miliband*. Basingstoke: Palgrave Macmillan.

Wöhl, S. (2014) 'The State and Gender Relations in International Political Economy: A State-Theoretical Approach to Varieties of Capitalism in Crisis', *Capital & Class,* 38(1), pp. 87–99.

Wright, E. O. (2010) *Envisioning Real Utopias*. London: Verso.

Zajak, S., Egels-Zandén, N. and Piper, N. (2017) 'Networks of Labour Activism: Collective Action across Asia and beyond. An Introduction to the Debate', Development and Change, 48(5), pp. 899–921.

3

STATE AS *PHARMAKON*

Nikita Dhawan

The Marxist state theorist Bob Jessop describes an encounter he had on the way to a conference. Jessop noticed that the person sitting next to him was going to the same event, so he introduced himself: 'I am Bob Jessop and I am a state theorist'. The person turned to Jessop and responded, 'I am Niklas Luhmann and the state does not exist'.[1] Jessop suggests that it was a very prophetic remark as even after 30 years it is still unclear to him if the comment means that parts of the government are not functioning as they ought to, or implies that the state as such does not exist, but is merely a fictional 'non-entity' that may nonetheless have power effects. On the other hand, if the state does exist, how might one define it and does one desire that it wither away? Jessop shares that Luhmann's comment provoked a positive irritation, which kept him coming back to the question of the state. Jessop explains that the most difficult question that is ever posed to a state theorist, the question he dreads, is 'What is the state?'

Like Jessop, I too am perplexed and intrigued by the question of the state, particularly from a postcolonial-queer-feminist perspective: Given the state monopoly on violence and its patriarchal, racist, imperialist proclivities, should feminists, queers, religious and racial minorities be wary of engaging with the state and devote their progressive political labour (see Newman in this volume) to extra state initiatives? Given the valid anxieties about the state's coercive powers, can the state be interpellated as a site of redress? Or should progressive politics focus on mastering the art of not being governed, as recommended by James Scott (2010), who proposes state evasion as a survival strategy for the subaltern classes? Rejecting state-making as a form of 'internal colonialism', Scott suggests that stateless peoples of Zomia highlands of Southeast Asia explore alternate forms of self-determination by fleeing the projects of the nation-state society that surround them. Scott argues

1 https://www.youtube.com/watch?v=ohh4qLHV7LY (accessed 6 March 2019).

that people remain deliberately and reactively stateless and invent tactics to discourage states to annex them to their territories. However, in an interview, Scott later clarifies that not to be incorporated into the state as a consciously evasive political choice is limited and remarks: 'The only alternative today is somehow taming this nation-state, because it can't be held at bay . . . the movie Avatar, which pretends you can burn bridges and keep "modernity" away is simply utopian'.[2]

It seems that progressive political projects are caught in a double-bind vis-à-vis the state and its coercive powers. In this chapter, I will outline the risks of disregarding the enabling role of the state, particularly the consequences of anti-statism for disenfranchised groups. Instead of an ideal theory of the state, the effort here is to rethink our understanding of the state. To this end, I will show that in approaching the state, two insights might be helpful. First, one should be careful of substituting an effect for a cause or metalepsis (Spivak, 1987: 205). Thus, instead of seeing the state as the origin of 'will-to-violence', it should be understood as an effect of multiple, contradictory and incoherent forces. Second, the temptation to juxtapose state versus non-state realms should be resisted: social norms, through their institutionalisation, cement the state power effects and are not disentangled from it.

In what follows, I will attempt to rethink the role of state in the context of debates surrounding racist hate speech. I will do so by juxtaposing contrary positions that envision differing expectations vis-à-vis the state. While some reject state censorship, others advocate that the state is responsible for protecting historically discriminated individuals and groups from injurious speech acts. These contrary positions reveal the impossibility of taking any unequivocal for or against position vis-à-vis the coercive powers of the state, which is like *pharmakon* (Derrida, 1981), namely, both poison and medicine. As Derrida explains:

> If the pharmakon is ambivalent, it is because it constitutes the medium in which opposites are opposed, the movement and the play that links them among themselves, reverses them or makes one side cross over into the other (soul/body, good/evil, inside/outside, memory/forgetfulness, speech/writing, etc.) (1981: 127).

The state can function as an instrument of hegemonic groups to protect their interests or a weapon of the weak in order to enfranchise them. In what follows, I will share my own ethical and political dilemmas regarding the state in the hope that this will contribute to the vexed project of reimagining the state and our difficult relation to it.

Words that wound

How light power would be, and easy to dismantle no doubt, if all it did was to observe, spy, detect, prohibit and punish; but it incites, provokes, produces. *It is not simply eye and ear: it makes people act and speak* (Foucault, 1994: 172).

2 http://www.theory-talks.org/2010/05/theory-talk-38.html (accessed 6 March 2019).

The right to freedom of speech is guaranteed and protected by most constitutions as one of the cornerstones of liberal democracy (Heinze, 2016). However, increasingly it is being debated whether hate speech, such as anti-Semitism, sexism, racism, homophobia, transphobia or ableism, that aims at degrading and slandering certain individuals or groups of people, should be protected as free speech? The 'Unite the Right' in Charlottesville, Virginia and 'Free speech rally' in Boston, which were held in August 2017 and included Neo-nazis, Ku Klux Clan members and other white supremacists, are notable examples of racist speech being protected by the first amendment of the US Constitution as free speech.[3] In an effort to counter the violence of hate speech, many private institutions, for instance, universities, have issued speech codes to regulate hate speech (Shiell, 2009). For example, 'No Platform' is a policy of the National Union of Students (NUS) of the United Kingdom,[4] which refuses to provide forums for individuals and groups holding racist and fascist views to propagate their violent ideologies. However, these speech codes have time and again been deemed unconstitutional as they are found to violate the right to freedom of expression. In contrast, in 16 European countries, an important restriction to right to free speech is the law against Holocaust denial, which criminalises genocide denial as well as banning expression of Nazi symbols (Herz, 2012). Interestingly, the denial of colonialism is not illegal. It is important to note that while Germany underwent post-war de-Nazification[5] with most physical relics of the Nazi regime being banished from public view, in contrast, in the American South, new monuments of Confederate veterans and martyrs that pay homage to men who fought to preserve chattel slavery were erected in the wake of the Civil War. These are being defended by white supremacists in cities like Charlottesville in the name of free speech. In the wake of the events in Charlottesville, technology companies refused to provide service to the neo-Nazi site Daily Stormer, which sought refuge in the so-called 'dark web',[6] which is impervious to conventional internet censorship. This controversial technology, while providing protection for dissidents in oppressive regimes, stands accused of harbouring hate groups and child abuse rings. Initially used to protect persecuted journalists and activists, the 'dark web' does not allow censorship of any form, thereby making it a controversial topic for anti-racist and feminist activists. Some argue that rather than repress it and drive it underground, it is better to allow hate speech publicly so that it may be contested

3 In a press conference, the American President Donald Trump remarked that the counter-protestors did not have permit, but the white supremacists had permission for their rally, thereby providing legitimacy to racist speech. Trump has announced his intent to issue an executive order that would make federal research funding contingent on whether the academic institution adequately protects free speech: https://edition.cnn.com/2019/03/05/opinions/trump-cpac-attack-free-speech-college-campus-kanefield/index.html (accessed 6 March 2019).
4 https://www.nusconnect.org.uk/resources/nus-no-platform-policy-f22f (accessed 6 March 2019).
5 This included persecuting former Nazis (the Nuremberg war crime trials), removing Nazi books and periodicals from libraries, discontinuing fascist newspapers and banning the display of swastikas and other Nazi iconography. In addition, political re-education was implemented to confront Germans with their Nazi legacy.
6 https://www.theguardian.com/technology/2017/aug/23/dark-web-neo-nazis-tor-dissidents-white-supremacists-criminals-paedophile-rings (accessed 6 March 2019).

through robust counter-speech, while others contend that there are limits to tolera-
tion of racist, homophobic and sexist hate speech. It is pointed out that defamation,
invasion of privacy and fraud are exempt from free-speech guarantees, whereas racist and sexist speech remains protected (Lawrence et al., 1993). Furthermore, there
is a controversial discussion whether hate speech is 'merely' offensive and those
targeted should 'simply' be less 'sensitive' about discriminatory speech acts, or do
these entail violent criminal conduct and thereby justify censorship and penalty. It
is warned that equating 'offensive' views with assault risks outlawing 'provocative'
and 'objectionable' ideas in general that have far-reaching repercussions for democracy. Moreover, it is unclear whether criminalisation is efficacious, as hate groups
stage themselves as 'victims' of censorship and, ironically, gain more audibility and
visibility. Thus, instead of criminalisation of hate speech, alternate mechanisms, like
protests, advocacy or diversity trainings, are recommended to counter 'unpopular'
and 'unwelcome' views. This would safeguard robust public spheres, where citizens
and non-citizens could participate in deliberative democracy. This position ignores
that not all subjects have the possibility of 'talking back' or equal access and parity
of participation in these debates, and their equality, dignity and safety are not always
ensured in such encounters.

These diverse examples from different regional contexts highlight the difficult
debates surrounding liberal, anarchist, Marxist, feminist, anti-racist, queer, postcolonial perspectives on the question of free speech. Drawing on these disputes, the text
seeks to engage with the following questions: How central is free speech to politics?
Should one set limits to free speech and who should have the power to do so? If
free speech should not be encumbered by legal, moral or commercial[7] imperatives,
how should vulnerable groups like racial, sexual and religious minorities respond to
the injuries and power inequalities produced through hate speech? Should the state
intervene or should extra state actors negotiate the violent effects of hate speech?

Beginning with a brief engagement with the philosophical principle of free
speech, the text outlines the duplicity of free speech advocates by focusing on the
controversial debate surrounding Charlie Hebdo and addresses the following questions: When is it legitimate to censor injurious speech acts? Who should determine
and enforce this? The focus is then on Judith Butler's rejection of state intervention and the limits of this position. Finally, the role of the state and civil society is
discussed.

Speech, agency, politics

The fundamental right of free speech forms one of the most important accom-
plishments of the European enlightenment. Arguing against censorship, in particular religious censorship, Immanuel Kant proclaims: 'Enlightenment is a man's

---

7 Certain forms of free speech are commercially protected by law and state from violations like trade-
marked, copyrighted speech.

emergence from his self-imposed immaturity' (1784). Kant equates immaturity, which includes absence of political voice (the German word *Stimme* is both voice and vote), with laziness, cowardice and lack of autonomy. This importance of freedom of speech is codified in democratic states as a constitutionally guaranteed right. In his canonical text *On Liberty*, John Stuart Mill describes the advantages of the Socratic dialogue and the dialectic of speech and counter-speech for democracy (Mill, 2005 [1859]: 45). In this context, speech functions as a driving force for the realisation of freedom rather than a transparent medium to communicate ideas (ibid.: 49). Speech is primarily awarded the function of political empowerment within liberal democratic tradition. However, Mill states that power can be rightfully exercised over speakers to prevent harm to others. Thus, despite being a radical advocate of free speech, Mill's 'harm principle' foresees the necessity of interfering with freedom when it causes injury.

In contrast to Mill, Hannah Arendt excludes violence from the sphere of speech: In her view, it is either something external to it or something threatening it as an obstacle for the exercise of free political speech. She argues in *On Revolution*:

> Where violence rules absolutely, as in concentration camps of totalitarian regimes, not only the laws . . . but everything and everyone must fall silent. It is because of this silence that violence is a marginal phenomenon in the political realm; for man, to the extent that he is a political being, is endowed with the power of speech . . . The point here is that violence itself is incapable of speech, and not merely that speech is helpless when confronted with violence (Arendt 1990 [1963]: 18).

Most liberal conceptions of free speech stress the performative enactment of political power in and through speech, so that censorship is seen as suppression of speech (Dhawan, 2007: 231–2). This has been severely contested by, amongst others, critical race theorists and radical feminists, who focus on the close links between speech and violence. They juxtapose the potential clash between one person's free speech and another's potential injury through violent hate speech (Lawrence et al., 1993). Along similar lines, the poststructuralist critique of discursive violence challenges the foundational premises of liberal definitions of political speech (Foucault, 1984: 85). In questioning liberalism's instrumental, referential and freedom-producing understanding of speech, poststructuralism disturbs one of the foundational underpinnings of the humanist tradition laid down in Aristotle's definition that humans are political (*zōon politikon*) and speaking beings (*zōon logon ekhon*). Within liberal political theory, the absence of political speech is synonymous with the absence of political agency. Thus, right to free speech is foregrounded within political struggles. Moving away from the understanding of free speech as a means to emancipation and freedom, the poststructuralists draw attention to the intricate relation between language/speech, power and violence. Foucault suggests that the speaking subject is a warrior in discursive struggles over power and is hence 'a subject who is fighting a war' (2003: 54). The poststructuralists juxtapose the claims of speech being invested with rationalist, freedom-producing powers with the idea of an originary violence that inhabits language *as such*. Here, the focus is on those forms of violence that are exercised 'discursively' and 'epistemically' (Dhawan, 2007: 249), so that the right to free speech conflicts with forms of hate speech that exert violence on minority groups. While some argue that minority groups can 'speak back' so that free speech is a tool to combat harm, others highlight that due to uneven distribution of agency not everyone has the possibility of speaking truth to power. This raises difficult questions about the unlimited right to free speech and the urgency of curtailing speech that is libellous, incites imminent violence or whips up racial hatred. Another good example of this is the debate around the controversial Network Enforcement Act, which came into full effect on 1 January 2018 in Germany.[8] Under the law, known in Germany as 'NetzDG', online platforms face fines of up to €50 million if they do not remove hate speech and other postings within the stipulated time after receiving a notification. A New Year's Eve tweet by the right-wing AfD (Alternative for Germany) politician Beatrix von Storch accusing Cologne police of appeasing 'barbaric, gang-raping Muslim hordes of men' appeared to be the first post to have violated the law.[9] Developed by the Social Democrat-run justice ministry, the law has been critiqued by left, liberal and right political parties. While the AfD complains of 'Stasi methods' and paints itself as a 'free speech martyr', left critics accuse the state of outsourcing work to private companies that should be carried out by judicial bodies. The justice minister, Heiko Maas, who initiated the law, defended himself against the criticism. 'Incitement to murder, threats, insults and incitement of the masses or Auschwitz lies are not an expression of freedom of opinion but rather attacks on the freedom of opinion of others', he said.[10] This seems to resonate with Mill's harm principle.

The right to provoke

Since the terrorist attacks on Charlie Hebdo's editorial office on 7 January 2015, the French satirical magazine has been celebrated as a symbol of free speech. After the attack, people all over the world demonstrated holding banners of solidarity such as *Je suis Charlie* ('I am Charlie'). Subsequent to the attacks, Charlie Hebdo made a profit of millions of Euros through newspaper sales. There have been discussions about using the money to establish a foundation for freedom of speech.[11]

Defending the publication of the Mohammed caricatures, the chief editor Stéphane Charbonnie[12] stated:

8 https://www.theguardian.com/world/2018/jan/05/tough-new-german-law-puts-tech-firms-and-free-speech-in-spotlight (accessed 6 March 2019).

9 Ibid.

10 Ibid.

11 https://www.welt.de/debatte/kommentare/article136986645/Muslime-traut-euch-doch-ueber-Mohammed-zu-lachen.html (accessed 6 March 2019).

12 http://www.nachrichten.at/nachrichten/weltspiegel/Charlie-Hebdo-Satireblatt-mit-Skandal-Tradition;art17,1595508 (accessed 6 March 2019).

We publish caricatures every week on everybody and everything. But when it is about the prophet, it is called a provocation. First one will not be allowed to represent Mohammed, then a radical Muslim and every time it will be said: This is a provocation for a Muslim. Is freedom of press a provocation? Just as I do not go to a mosque to listen to a discourse that contradicts my convictions, I do not expect an orthodox Muslim to read Charlie Hebdo. We are following the laws of the Republic and the Constitutional State.

In defence of the right to free speech, the German-Jewish publicist Kurt Tucholsky, who was one of the most important journalists of the Weimar Republic and whose books were banned and burned by the Nazis, is cited repeatedly. When asked what satire was permitted to do, Tucholsky answered succinctly with the word 'Everything!' (1975: 42).

A few months later, Charlie Hebdo's caricature on the sexual assaults in Cologne on New Year's Eve 2015/2016 stirred a huge controversy. The satirical magazine triggered intense discussions on the 'right to provoke' with its caricature of Alan Kurdi, the refugee child, whose image made global headlines after he drowned in the Mediterranean Sea. The caricature shows two pig-faced men chasing two women. The headline reads: 'What would little Alan have become had he grown up?' The answer is 'Arse-groper in Germany'. Critics argue that Charlie Hebdo has violated limits of satire with this cynical image.[13] This had nothing to do with freedom of speech, but is simply distasteful, racist and repulsive. Defenders argue that the caricaturist is mocking the current media discourse,[14] which instrumentalised Alan into a symbol of all refugees. Then, suddenly, the Cologne gropers became the symbol of all refugees, so that compassion was replaced by racism and Islamophobia. By outlining the link between these two aspects, the caricaturist Sourisseau is hoping to reveal the double standards of those insinuating that all refugees are criminals, which would include little Alan. According to his defenders, Sourisseau is not a racist, but a humanist.[15] Although the cartoon was sharply condemned, there were no legal consequences for the cartoonist or Charlie Hebdo.

In contrast, the most prominent and most senior cartoonist and columnist of the newspaper, 79-year-old Maurice Albert Siné, was sacked in 2008 for a caricature that was accused of being anti-Semitic.[16] Siné, who was renowned for provocative comments on politics, military and religion, targeted Nicholas Sarkozy's son in his column. Commenting on Jean Sarkozy's rumoured conversion to Judaism, so he could marry Jessica Sebaoun-Darty, an heiress of the reputed Jewish Darty

13 http://www.spiegel.de/kultur/gesellschaft/charlie-hebdo-empoert-mit-karikatur-zu-totem-flue
    chtlingskind-alan-kurdi-a-1071922.html; https://www.welt.de/politik/ausland/article151029361/
    Charlie-Hebdo-zeigt-Aylan-als-Pograpscher-in-Koeln.html (accessed 6 March 2019).
14 http://www.stern.de/panorama/weltgeschehen/charlie-hebdo—darum-ist-die-karikatur-von-
    aylan-kurdi-nicht-rassistisch-6650436.html (accessed 6 March 2019).
15 Ibid.
16 http://www.telegraph.co.uk/news/worldnews/europe/france/4351672/French-cartoonist-Sine-
    on-trial-on-charges-of-anti-Semitism-over-Sarkozy-jibe.html (accessed 6 March 2019).

family, Siné wrote: 'He'll go a long way in life, this lad!'[17] The journalist Claude Askolovitch attacked the comments as anti-Semitic[18] and triggered a controversy that divided the media and the Parisian intelligentsia: While Siné's critics accused him of reproducing stereotypes about Judaism, his defenders countered: 'Siné does not like idiots. He's an anarchist.'[19] The magazine's editor Philippe Val demanded a letter of apology from Siné as he feared being sued by the Sarkozy family. Siné responded that he would rather 'cut off his balls'[20] than bow before the Sarkozys. He was, however, willing to apologise to those who might have misunderstood his words as anti-Semitic and therefore were hurt.[21]

Siné's supporters accused Charlie Hebdo of double standards. The caricaturist Plantu from the newspaper *Le Monde* argued that Charlie Hebdo had committed a grave mistake by firing Siné, for a newspaper like Charlie Hebdo 'needs provocations and this includes accepting slip-ups'.[22] The feminist lawyer Gisèle Halimi, who repeatedly critiqued Siné's sexist style, announced that she would no longer read the newspaper.[23] Rejecting the accusation of anti-Semitism, Siné claimed: 'I critiqued the Sarkozys' opportunism and greed for money. Had junior wanted to convert to Islam, I would have written about Islam.'[24] Siné pressed charges against Askolovitch for defamation and was also granted compensation for wrongful termination.[25]

This example illustrates the difficulties of determining the limits of freedom of speech. Satire and humour raise challenging questions of who may legitimately make fun of others and how certain issues and groups are protected from offence. In the following section, I will address the challenging question of censorship by focusing on Judith Butler's rejection of state intervention.

Speaking truth to power?

Contradicting those who advocate regulation of hate speech for violating rights of vulnerable citizens, Butler rejects the alleged efficacy of hate speech and questions the mechanical and predictable reproduction of power through hate speech. She recommends delinking words from their power to injure and suggests recontextualising them, so as to open up the possibility for counter-speech. Those who fix the inevitable relation between certain speech acts and their injurious effects foreclose the possibility of a kind of talking back that disrupts and subverts the

17 https://www.theguardian.com/world/2008/aug/03/france.pressandpublishing (accessed 6 March 2019).
18 https://www.theguardian.com/world/2008/aug/03/france.pressandpublishing (accessed 6 March 2019).
19 http://www.taz.de/!5177081/ (accessed 6 March 2019).
20 Ibid.
21 Ibid.
22 Ibid.
23 Ibid.
24 Ibid.
25 http://en.rfi.fr/culture/20160505-former-charlie-hebdo-cartoonist-sine-dies-after-controversial-career (accessed 6 March 2019).

effects produced by hate speech (Butler, 1997: 15). In contrast, Butler focuses on the gap between speech and conduct that offers possibilities of non-juridical forms of political opposition that go beyond legal prosecution. Butler argues that strategies devised by, for example, critical legal theorists and anti-discrimination politics to include speech as discriminatory conduct tend to enhance state regulation and reinstate state monopoly on violence (ibid.: 24). Butler proposes that the category 'hate speech' exists retrospectively; only after certain speech acts are declared 'criminal' by state authorities. In this way, the state reserves for itself the power to define hate speech and, conversely, the limits of acceptable discourse. Butler explains that the proposals to regulate hate speech extensively cite such speech, so that the censor is compelled to repeat the speech that it seeks to prohibit (ibid.: 39). Unfolding this 'performative contradiction' (ibid.: 134), she warns that keeping injurious terms unsaid and unsayable can also work to freeze them, thereby preserving their power to injure. This inhibits the possibility of a reconfiguration that might shift their context and purpose (ibid.: 40). According to Butler, censorship cannot purify language of its 'traumatic residue' (ibid.), whereby there is no circumventing the difficult task of resignification. The 'reduction' of the scene of racism to a single speaker and his or her audience risks casting the political problem only in terms of tracing the harm as it travels from the speaker to the addressee (ibid.: 81–2). This limits the complex institutional structures of racism, homophobia and sexism to the scene of utterance, which is over-determined (ibid.: 82). Locating the cause of injury and accountability in a culpable speaking subject clears the way to seek recourse to the law, which is granted a certain neutrality. The power of judicial language to establish and maintain the domain of the permissible speech implies that the state demarcates the line between speakable and the unspeakable (ibid.: 143). Butler is not only concerned about protecting 'civil liberties against the incursion of the state', but also about the '*discursive power* given over to the state through the process of legal redress' (ibid.: 79, emphasis in the original). Even those who are otherwise wary of state power pronounce faith in the capacities of legal discourse in the service of progressive politics. It is argued that racist speech conflicts with the commitments to universal equality that are fundamental to the Constitution and thus forfeit its right to 'protection'. In an incisive analysis, Butler points out that accepting such a view would effectively imply that any speech that actively contests the founding premise of the Constitution should not be protected (ibid.: 90), so that only speech that qualifies to be protected falls in the domain of speakability. This line of argument goes beyond the question of hate speech and enters the domain of laying down the criteria of distinguishing legally and legitimately acceptable from unprotected speech (ibid.).

Instead of state-sponsored censorship, Butler argues for a social and cultural struggle of language, whereby 'agency is derived from injury and injury countered through that very derivation' (ibid.: 43). The 'breakdown' between saying and doing deprives hate speech of its 'projected performative power', so that the one who is addressed can 'speak back', thereby dislodging the power to injure (ibid.: 95). Such a strategy affirms that hate speech does not destroy the agency of vulnerable individuals and groups, even as it dislocates state censorship (ibid.: 43).

Butler points out how hate speech arguments have been invoked by the state against minority groups, whereby, in the name of abolishing racism and sexism, free speech of sexual and racial minorities is censored (ibid.: 99). One of the most notorious examples of censorship was the banning of Fanon's posthumously published *The Wretched of the Earth*, which was censored in France as soon as it came out and copies were seized from bookstores on the grounds of inciting violence. The racist and sexist side-effects of hate speech legislation that turns victims into perpetrators and strengthens a criminal justice system needs to be urgently addressed. Hate speech debate can disproportionately criminalise minorities and disadvantaged groups for supposed hate crimes against structurally privileged groups. The current weaponisation of hate crime legislation in countries like Germany that stigmatises Muslim migrants, mostly young male-assigned people, as anti-Semitic and homophobic as well as pushes for gentrification of previously poor migrant neighbourhoods as settings for hate crimes to make them safe for habitation for respectable citizens, highlights the difficulties of expecting justice from law and risks of the 'punitive turn' (Haritaworn, 2015: 8, 32, 125). Instead of protecting those vulnerable to violence, racialised and orientalised bodies end up being stereotyped as 'hateful' even as they are pathologised as paranoid when they complain of being discriminated against (ibid.: 130). This intersects with Butler's arguments that hate crime activism is undergirded by carceral and biomedical paradigms (ibid.: 140). In Butler's view, censorship is not primarily about speech; rather, it operates to make certain kinds of citizens possible and others impossible and is thereby a necessary part of the process of nation-building (Butler, 1997: 136). Here, censorship can be used to build consensus about national identity and memory, as is the case in Germany with laws against Holocaust denial (ibid.).

To summarise Butler's position: When the state determines what counts as hate speech and what does not and forbids specific words, it deprives the feminist and anti-racist movement of the possibility to subversively appropriate hate speech. Handing over the power of definition to the state constitutes a restriction of the political field by regulating the freedom of re-contextualisation and resignification. Following Butler, this does not always lead to the advantage of progressive political projects.

State as *pharmakon*

The above-mentioned examples raise difficult questions about the role of state and non-state forces, especially when it concerns the question of vulnerability and agency of non-hegemonic groups in the face of hate speech. Can the demand for equality through law enable changing the state's relation to vulnerable citizens and non-citizens? Can one use the coercive powers of the state for progressive politics (John Clarke; Nick Gill in this volume)? Or can special protections hurt minorities by constructing them as per se vulnerable, thereby undermining their agency while consolidating state's coercive power?

Anti-state positions that reject state censorship are based on a specific ontology of state power. As Jessop (2014) explains, the state is a 'heterogeneous institutional ensemble (comprising, minimally, a territory, apparatus, and population) that has no agency *per se* but does have various capacities and action-relevant biases inscribed in itself when considered as a strategic terrain'. In his view, ideas about nature and purposes of state power and state projects create the appearance that the state acts *as if* it were a unitary subject. The state seems to provide a fitting foil, onto which virulent and ugly problems confronting communities and societies may be projected. One has the impression that if the state did not exist, anti-state positions would have to invent it (see Hay, 2014). It might perhaps help democratic politics if it were to reject the temptation to ontologise the state, and instead would draw on the heuristic power of the state 'as-if' it can be potentially mobilised as a motor of justice to mitigate discrimination, inequality and disenfranchisement. As Clarke asks (in this volume), do non-state forms of power differ from the state power? And if the state would no longer exist, how would progressive politics be non-stately?

If group-differentiated vulnerability is produced and sanctioned by the state, then the question is whether the state should be held accountable to undo this or does this pave the way for more violence, so that extra-state spaces should become repositories for abolitionist politics? Foregrounding negotiations between non-state actors as the key to countering hate speech and protecting free speech ignores that one of the most important functions of the state is to mediate between citizens. Why should the negotiations between non-state actors be necessarily less violent than between state and citizens as implied by those who reject state intervention? Just as the state is never neutral in its mediations, extra-state mechanisms of negotiations too are not uncoercive.

Critical race theorists, feminist and postcolonial scholars and activists rightly argue that it is not sufficient to solely place faith in the subversive resignification of hate speech and forgo recourse to legal redress. In the US context, while 'first amendment revisionists' are accused of acting like 'thought police' who are allegedly protecting the over-sensitive 'snowflake generation' by advocating censorship, 'first amendment fundamentalists' are charged with weaponising liberal values of free speech (Lawrence et al., 1993: 15). Given that there are already instances in which protection of intellectual property, privacy and individual reputation justifies infringements on speech, Lawrence questions whether first amendment fundamentalists' resistance against regulations of hate speech is due to 'unconscious racism' (1993: 81).

In Lawrence's view, racism is simultaneously speech and conduct, such that the concept of 'race' is not a noun, but a verb. The cultural meaning of race is promulgated through millions of contemporaneous speech/acts. The social construction of race is an ongoing process, such that 'we are raced' (Thomas cit. in Lawrence 1993: 62) and every racial slur shapes this 'racing'. Ironically, many civil libertarians seem to be more concerned about possible infringement of the assailants' liberties than violations of the constitutional rights of the assailed (ibid.). Against liberal defence of marketplace of ideas where the best argument prevails, critical race theorists highlight that racist speech decreases the total amount of speech that reaches the market by coercively silencing members of those groups who are its targets (ibid.: 79). Lawrence questions the strategy of rejecting all government regulation of speech by those who believe that the best cure for bad speech is good speech, which by virtue of being more compelling will ultimately prevail over racist, sexist, homophobic and anti-Semitic hate speech (ibid.: 82–3).

In response to the challenge of who should determine the parameters for censorship, Matsuda (1993) suggests that by relying on testimonies of victim groups, one could distinguish between 'benign' and 'hateful' speech. This victim-based theory of harm is, however, inadequate, as the 'victim groups' are not homogenous and have disagreements over what is harmful. This consensus-oriented approach assumes that all members of a 'victim group' recognise hate speech at once, thereby disregarding possibilities of differences in responses to speech acts.

In his landmark book, *The Signifying Monkey* (1988: 22), Henry Louis Gates, Jr. explains how 'Signifying' in black vernacular alludes to the ambiguous relation to language and speech based on a certain suspicion and mistrust of words. Consequently, even the most literal utterance allows room for multiple interpretations. Language is both verbal play, but also hazardous, such that it can liberate, but also terrorise. The double bind is understandable given that ideas, concepts and discourses were weaponised by Europeans to justify slavery and to dehumanise the colonised, but were also mobilised as tools for emancipation. Gates's theory offers a counterpoint to censorship because it asserts that the signifying techniques employed by the African-American literary, vernacular and artistic traditions operate by 'the obscuring of apparent meaning' (1988: 53), thereby enabling subversion.

Of the many memorable figures that appear in black vernacular tales, perhaps only Tar Baby is as enigmatic and compelling as the oxymoronic, the Signifying Monkey. The ironic reversal of a received racist image of the black as simianlike, the Signifying Monkey dwells at the margins of discourse, embodying the ambiguities of language, simultaneously repeating and reversing established tropes (ibid.: 52). Gates argues that the undecidability of language necessitates careful attention to play of differences and techniques of decoding. 'Never can this interpretation be definitive, given the ambiguity at work in its rhetorical structures' (ibid.: 53). Gates explains that misinterpretation frequently arises because non-blacks do not realise that black speakers reverse the apparent meanings of their words 'as a mode of encoding for self-preservation' (ibid.: 67). The vulnerable speaker, by virtue of his or her position of vulnerability to hate speech, cannot afford to speak literally. Rather, he or she must proceed subtly, by reversal and subversion; he or she must speak in code, if his or her message is to prevail. And even as he or she is heard as having spoken 'literally', in fact he or she speaks 'figuratively' (ibid.: 40). Gates suggests that words do not have only one meaning and at times hurtful assertions can have unintended consequences. One can only claim to offer stringent criteria to differentiate between coercive and non-coercive statements if one ignores the indeterminacy of language.

In contrast, against the claim that more speech, not less, is the proper cure for offensive speech, Matsuda and Lawrence argue: 'The first amendment goal of maximizing public discourse is not attained in a marketplace of ideas distorted by coercion and privilege. Burning crosses do not bring to the table more ideas for discussion . . .' (Matsuda and Lawrence, 1993: 136). Given that first amendment coexisted with slavery, the promise that it will protect minorities to the same extent that it protects whites has proven to be empty, although it is claimed that minorities have benefited greatly from first amendment protection (Lawrence, 1993: 76). It is questionable that fighting to protect free speech of racists will ensure the dignity of minorities (ibid.).

When racist hate speech is tolerated in the name of larger good, it is invariably subordinated groups who pay the price for protecting democracy and freedom. Lawrence calls this 'taxation without representation', as these minorities do not necessarily consent to this arrangement. Thus, it is imperative that the individuals who bear the burden have the opportunity to participate and be heard in social, political and legal deliberations (Lawrence, 1993: 80). At the same time, subordinated groups must also have the option of receiving compensation for verbal injuries even as those who exert verbal assault must be sanctioned (Matsuda, 1993: 48). Here, the state becomes indispensable.

Following Althusser, most scholars who reject the progressive use of state's coercive powers believe that the core of the state is its repressive apparatus that must be resisted. However, this disregards an important criticism of Marxist and anarchist state theory – namely, even if the state were to become obsolete and disappear, politics will not simply comprise of non-violent struggles between non-state actors. The vision that society will no longer require coercion to induce hegemonic groups to behave in a non-sexist, non-racist, non-homophobic way and belief that bureaucratic and coercive functions of the state can be replaced by collective and decentralised negotiations between non-state actors disregards that social conflicts and antagonisms in non-state spaces are not non-violent, even if the coercion manifests itself differently. This is not to draw false equivalences between state and non-state violence, but to focus on their entanglements.

Foucault (2008) warns against 'state phobia' as a strategy of neoliberal rationality that is parasitical on dismantling state power, while guaranteeing individual freedom. In the context of our discussion, the neoliberal subject is assured that speech is 'free' and should not have any limits and each individual has an inalienable right to offend. In a Darwinist move, it is claimed that ultimately the best argument will prevail in the marketplace of ideas. Those who plead against any form of state intervention propose that the state be placed in a position of passivity in the legal domain, which echoes the neoliberal demand of state passivity in relation to the economy (Foucault, 2008: 284 ff). The antidote offered against the repressive state is to withdraw from its scope and abdicate state power to create alternative spaces beyond its control. This narrative renders non-state spaces beyond the repressive state apparatus. However, as argued by Dean and Villadsen (2016: 19), the state is not only something to be resisted, but also the condition that enables individual and collective capacities that make civil struggles possible. In valorising the creative agency of non-state actors, positions rejecting state intervention simply assume the infrastructural supports necessary for the exercise of these practices and capacities that are provided by the state (ibid.: 177). State-phobic discourses overlook how social rights, welfare, public education and health care are all entitlements secured through establishing a stable political order in the form of a state with territorial jurisdiction (ibid.: 5).[26] The demonisation of the state and the romanticisation of non-state spaces and actors locates their uncontaminated political agency in structures like family, community or marketplace that are all linked to the state (ibid.: 30). The promise of civil society to free individuals from the domination of the state obscures that it is part of the state and not just oppositional to it, even as civil society shapes and frames how state institutions exercise power. Without the regulation of conflicts between civil society actors and groups by the sovereign state power, there can be no exercise of agency in the civil society (ibid.: 36), as witnessed in Charlottesville.

A good historical example that illustrates the entanglements between state and non-state violence are the *lettres de cachet*. The letters contained orders directly from the king, often to enforce arbitrary actions and judgments that could not be appealed. While undertaking archival work, Foucault came across a dossier of *lettres de cachet* that were submitted by ordinary people to restrict the freedom of an immediate family member, by way of house arrest, exile or incarceration (Farge and Foucault, 2012: 178). What was earlier the prerogative of religious authorities was now orchestrated bottom-up, wherein those who were censured as 'sinful' or 'deviant' were monitored and penalised by ordinary people (Dean and Villadsen, 2016: 61–2). The king's sovereign exercise of power was in fact in response to requests from the masses, who mutually regulated intimate social practices and behaviours. Foucault engages in-depth with the 'poison-pen letters' as well as with responses given by the official institutions (Rocha, 2012: 189). His engagement with these numerous letters changed his thinking about power, about how ordinary people's private family affairs intersected and flowed into the workings of political institutions and state authorities (ibid.). Instead of a top-down model of power, Foucault explores how the social body, which included neighbours, priests and tenants, served as a site from which denunciation was operationalised (ibid.: 184). By convincing the king to issue the letter to punish one's relative, the *lettre de cachet* made private repression legal by circumventing the public system of justice.

For Foucault (1994: 167–8), the *lettres de cachet* system enabled the interpenetration of political sovereignty with the most elementary dimension of the social body and the fabric of everyday life. The masses solicit sovereign intervention and mobilise the coercive powers of the sovereign against the vulnerable and the marginalised. The everyday practices of denunciation, surveillance and control that

---

26 Anti-colonial struggles were often accompanied by aspirations of establishing sovereignty and self-determination in the form of postcolonial states.

were part of the social body formed the basis of the tactics of governing of the ruler-monarch and eventually the modern state institutions like schools, prisons and hospitals (Dean and Villadsen, 2016: 63). Instead of being paragons of non-violence and tolerance, these social groups were pioneers in parajudicial policing mechanisms and surveillance through enforcement of local norms. Subsequent state-administered biopolitics drew on these micro technologies and tactics that emerged 'from below' (ibid.). The expansive reach of dispositifs of legal and disciplinary power had humble beginnings in the family, community and social body. Here, Foucault seems to resonate materialist state theory's understanding of state power as the

> form-determined (institutionally mediated) condensation of a shifting balance of forces oriented to the exercise of capacities and powers associated with particular political forms and institutions as these are embedded in the wider social formation (Jessop, 2014: 485).

As diagnosed by Foucault, instead of being a singular domain of ethical relations and democratic deliberations, the civil society is a site permeated with mutual surveillance, strategies of control and tactics of normalisation (ibid.: 64). Instead of being imbued with lofty ideals of conviviality and social cohesion, civil society is marked by unrelenting struggles for power and domination. This is what Foucault's renowned inversion of Clausewitz's dictum that 'politics is the continuation of war by other means' succinctly summarises (Foucault, 2003: 16). The state, on the other hand, as Foucault explains (2008: 4), is not a coherent and centralised locus of power; rather it is an effect of multiple and contradictory strategies and tactics. For instance, the modern state is not only a law-making, but also a law-governed, entity (Dean and Villadsen, 2016: 174). The state is inflected by institutional contingencies and diverse rationalities and thus capable of both coercion and protection.

To conclude, let us return to the Enlightenment promise of free speech as a sign of robust deliberative democracy and mature citizenry. The West prides itself on its deliberative tradition nurtured by rituals of free speech. The freedom to criticise is coded as a right as well as duty of every modern individual, whose relentless pursuit of truth and freedom is the signature of his or her political agency. In fact, in the US, the state saw it as its fundamental responsibility to enable free speech as part of state policy. From the nineteenth century, the US postal service facilitated political conversation by subsidising the transportation of newspapers and magazines (Grantham and Miller, 2017: 226).

From this perspective, censorship is anti-Enlightenment and societies that regulate speech are caught in a stage of 'civilizational infantilism' (Mehta, 1999: 70). While Muslim humourists and cartoonists all over the world routinely engage in religious satire and are subject to *fatwas*, as with the infamous case of Salman Rushdie, this is often weaponised in the West as evidence of Islamic intolerance. Concomitantly, humour and satire are read as political virtues, as signs of self-reflection and self-critique, a form of speaking truth to power. In the current political climate,

Muslim societies are stereotyped as lacking sense of humour, of not being able to laugh it off, of not getting the joke and are marked as 'backward' and intolerant. If critique's primary function is to enable 'maturity', turning men into adults who reject external authority and can think for themselves, Talal Asad (2009) questions how the Global North coerces the Global South to assume what they regard as a mature critical attitude. The Charlie Hebdo attacks were mobilised to consolidate nationalist narratives about the French Republic and its self-staging as the guardian of the universal principles of free expression and democracy against assaults from humourless and bigoted 'barbaric' forces (Khiabany, 2017: 114). Ironically, subsequent to the attacks, the state of emergency and state racism was justified in the name of 'protecting' democracy, free speech and tolerant values (Khiabany, 2017: 115). An instructive example of 'performative contradiction'! Additionally, 'draw the Prophet' competitions (Titley, 2017: 24) were held all over Europe to coerce Enlightenment upon those who resist it. In April 2015, the small extreme-right Pro-NRW party in Nordrhein-Westfalen successfully organised a competition entitled 'Freedom instead of Islam', with the winning entries posted on the 'free speech website' *Politically Incorrect* (ibid.: 25). On 24 June 2015, in the Netherlands, Geert Wilders exhibited the winning cartoons on live television, proclaiming:

> I do not broadcast the cartoons to provoke; I do it because we have to show that we stand for freedom of speech and that we will never surrender to violence. Freedom is our birth right. Freedom of speech must always prevail over terror and violence (cit. in Titley 2017: 25).

Against accusations of racism, defenders of Charlie Hebdo argue that the satirists are 'equal opportunity' provocateurs, who spare no one (Grantham and Miller, 2017: 234). However, in the face of uneven distribution of vulnerability that results in 'targets' of offence occupying unequal positions in society, it is disingenuous to claim that the power effects of these speech acts can be resisted and contested by all. Moreover, considering that Donald Trump is notorious for his push-back against journalists and satirists and allegedly defended the Saudi Regime in the Jamal Khashoggi murder, Western posturings as bastions of free speech are farcical. As Ghassan Hage remarks:

> ...'democracy', 'tolerance' and 'freedom of speech' all can become – and are increasingly becoming in the Western world – *fin d'empire* colonial, racialised strategies of phallic distinction. They are what Westerners 'flash' to the racialised Muslims to say: 'Look what we have and you haven't got. At best, yours is very small compared to ours.' And this is at the very same time as Western societies are becoming less democratic, tolerant, and committed to freedom of speech (2017: 260).

As argued in this chapter, satire can also be an exercise of colonialist, racist, sexist, homophobic, anti-Semitic verbal assault. In *Jokes and their Relation to the Unconscious*

(1905), Freud proposes that satire is inseparable from hostile impulse; the joke is always at someone's expense. Wit (*der Witz*) is a means by which we experience pleasure by overcoming inhibitions against expression of hostility. These hindrances may be due to 'external' factors like the risk involved in attacking powerful authorities or 'internal' prohibitions due to being socialised in a 'highly developed aesthetic culture' (Freud, cit. in Griffins, 1994: 162). The pleasure is not just experienced because we can ventilate our aggressions; rather, the 'secret' source of the pleasure of jokes is because the effort expended in regulating hostility and aggression is reduced. European societies pride themselves on being tolerant, democratic and free, so the Freudian insight is extremely instructive in understanding the 'forbidden pleasure' Europeans can enjoy via jokes about Islam and Muslims that would obfuscate aggressive racist and Islamophobic hostilities. Freud asserts: 'By making our enemy small, inferior, despicable or comic, we achieve in a roundabout way the enjoyment of overcoming him' (cit. in Griffins, 1994: 163). There is something very gratifying in satire's power to wound, especially when the abasement of the victim is done indirectly so as to absolve us of any responsibility of violence and coercion (ibid.: 164).

In April 2015, a group of reputed writers objected to the award by PEN of its Freedom of Expression Courage Award to Charlie Hebdo, arguing that 'there is a critical difference between staunchly supporting expression that violates the acceptable, and enthusiastically rewarding such expression' (cit. in Titley, 2017: 20). Satirists as fearless defenders of liberty are excused for trafficking in orientalist caricatures, colonial tropes and dehumanising imagery (ibid.: 22). Withdrawal of state institutional support when it comes to combating hate speech works in the favour of hegemonic groups, whose right to be racist is constitutionally protected by liberal values of free speech. It is no wonder that Steve Bannon, the mastermind behind Trump's nationalist ideology and the former executive chairman of Breitbart News, a platform for the alt-right to champion their racist, anti-Semitic and sexist points of view, explained that the goal was an unending battle for 'deconstruction of the administrative state'.[27] Foucault foresaw the dovetailing of left- and right-wing anti-statism when he warned of state phobia.

It is interesting to note that, in an interview, even Butler admits:

> Of course, I want legal protections for certain kinds of freedoms ... The point is not to be against all law, nor is it to live without any laws. The point, in my view, is to develop a critical relation to law which is, after all, a field of power, one that is differentially applied and supported (2012: 94 ff).

This indicates the contradictory, double-bind relation we have to the state as *pharmakon*. This requires acknowledgement of the ambivalences in the formation of states and the inconsistent functions of its institutions and apparatus.

27 https://www.washingtonpost.com/politics/top-wh-strategist-vows-a-daily-fight-for-deconstruc tion-of-the-administrative-state/2017/02/23/03f6b8da-f9ea-11e6-bf01-d47f8cf9b643_story. html?noredirect=on&utm_term=.9ac12dc0c4d4 (accessed 06 March 2019).

Three quick examples to illustrate this: Trump's Muslim ban was overturned by the courts with one organ of the state working against another. Shahidul Alam, an award-winning and internationally recognised photojournalist, was accused of allegedly making 'provocative' comments in an Al Jazeera interview and was arrested under section 57 of Bangladesh's infamous Information and Communications Technology Act, which authorises 'the prosecution of any person who publishes, in electronic form, material that is fake and obscene; defamatory; tends to deprave and corrupt its audience; causes or may cause deterioration in law and order; prejudices the image of the state or a person; or causes or may cause hurt to religious belief'.[28] Alam was subsequently granted bail, but if convicted could face life imprisonment.[29] In India, politician Raja Singh of the right-wing political party BJP was charged on 30 July 2016 of hate speech for a Facebook post against *Dalits*. A case was registered against him under IPC section 153A (promoting enmity between different groups on grounds of religion, race, place of birth, residence, language, etc., and doing acts prejudicial to maintenance of harmony).[30] These examples show how the state as *pharmakon* has no stable essence and is marked by contradictions: violence and justice, ideology and emancipation, law and repression. The undecidability, contingency and doubleness of the state as *pharmakon* implies that it already bears its own opposite within itself, the possibility of the transmutation of poison into remedy, curse into cure. The sole focus on the negative aspects of *pharmakon*, namely, death and destruction, neutralises and ignores the enabling and empowering possibilities. Following Derrida, to transform poison into counter-poison, it is imperative to envisage a critique of the state beyond state-phobic rhetoric and politics.

Acknowledgements

The author thanks Davina Cooper, Janet Newman, Ruth Kinna, Anna Krämer and Antke Engel for their helpful suggestions.

References

Arendt, H. (1990 [1963]) *On Revolution*. London: Penguin.
Asad, T. (2009) 'Free Speech, Blasphemy and Secular Criticism' in *Is Critique Secular? Blasphemy, Injury, and Free Speech*. California: The Townsend Papers in the Humanities.
Butler, J. (1997) *Excitable Speech*. London: Routledge.

---

28 https://www.aljazeera.com/indepth/opinion/bangladesh-arrest-shahidul-alam-180809112820231.html (accessed 6 March 2019).
29 https://www.aljazeera.com/news/2018/11/photographer-shahidul-alam-released-bail-bangladesh-jail-181120192606577.html (accessed 6 March 2019).
30 'Una Dalit Attack: BJP MLA Raja Singh Who Defended Gau Rakshaks Booked for "Hate Speech"' in *Indian Express*, https://indianexpress.com/article/india/india-news-india/una-dalit-flogging-telangana-bjp-mla-raja-singh-booked-for-hate-speech-for-defending-una-attack-by-gau-rakshak-2953863/ (accessed 30 August 2018).

Butler, J. (2012) 'On Anarchism: An Interview with Judith Butler' in Heckert, J. and Cleminson, R. (eds.), *Anarchism & Sexuality: Ethics, Relationships and Power.* London and New York: Routledge, pp. 93–100.

Dean, M. and Villadsen, K. (2016) *State Phobia and Civil Society: The Political Legacy of Michel Foucault.* Stanford, CA: Stanford University Press.

Derrida, J. (1981) *Dissemination.* London: The Athlone Press.

Dhawan, N. (2007) *Impossible speech: On the Politics of Silence and Violence.* Sankt Augustin: Academia.

Farge, A. and Foucault, M. (2012) '"Présentation", *Le Désordre des familles: Lettres de cachet des Archives de la Bastille au XVIIIe siècle* (1982)' in Duschinsky, R. and Rocha, L. A. (eds.), *Foucault, the Family and Politics.* London: Palgrave Macmillan, pp. 178–88.

Foucault, M. (1984) *The Foucault Reader,* Paul Rabinow (ed.). New York: Pantheon.

Foucault, M. (1994) 'Lives of Infamous Men' in Faubion, J. (ed), *Michel Foucault: Power, The Essential Works 3,* New York: The New Press, pp. 157–75.

Foucault, M. (2003) *Society Must Be Defended.* New York: Picador.

Foucault, M. (2008) *The Birth of Biopolitics: Lectures at the Collège de France, 1978–1979.* London: Palgrave Macmillan.

Gates Jr., H. L. (1988) *The Signifying Monkey: A Theory of Afro-American Literary Criticism.* New York: Oxford University Press.

Grantham, B. and Miller, T. (2017) 'We Hate to Quote Stanley Fish, but: "There's No Such Thing as Free Speech, and It's a Good Thing, Too." Or Is It?' in Titley, G., Freedman, D., Khiabany, G. and Mondon, A. (eds.), *After Charlie Hebdo: Terror, Racism and Free Speech.* London: Zed Books, pp. 223–38.

Griffins, D. H. (1994) *Satire: A Critical Reintroduction.* Lexington, KY: University of Kentucky Press.

Hage, G. (2017) 'Not Afraid' in Titley, G., Freedman, D., Khiabany, G. and Mondon, A. (eds.), *After Charlie Hebdo: Terror, Racism and Free Speech.* London: Zed Books, pp. 259–61.

Haritaworn, J. (2015) *Queer Lovers and Hateful Others: Regenerating Violent Times and Places.* London: Pluto Press.

Hay, C. (2014) 'If It Didn't Exist We'd Have to Invent It . . . Further Reflections on the Ontological Status of the State', *British Journal of Sociology,* 65(3), pp. 487–91.

Heinze, E. (2016) *Hate Speech and Democratic Citizenship.* Oxford: Oxford University Press.

Herz, M. (2012) *The Content and Context of Hate Speech: Rethinking Regulation and Responses.* Cambridge: Cambridge University Press.

Jessop, B. (2014) 'Towards a Political Ontology of State Power: A Comment on Colin Hay's Article', *British Journal of Sociology,* 65(3), pp. 481–6.

Kant, I. (1784) 'Beantwortung der Frage: Was ist Aufklärung?', *Berlinische Monatsschrift,* 4, pp. 481–94.

Khiabany, G. (2017) 'The Visible Hand of the State' in Titley, G., Freedman, D., Khiabany, G. and Mondon, A. (eds.), *After Charlie Hebdo: Terror, Racism and Free Speech.* London: Zed Books, pp. 114–28.

Matsuda, M. J., Lawrence, R. L. III, Delgado, R. and Williams Krenshaw, K. (1993) 'Introduction' in ibid. (eds.), *Words that Wound: Critical Race Theory, Assaultive Speech, and the First Amendment.* Boulder, CO: Westview Press, pp. 1–16.

Lawrence, C. R. (1993) 'If He Hollers Let Him Go: Regulating Racist Speech on Campus' in Matsuda, M. J., Lawrence, R. L. III, Delgado, R. and Williams Krenshaw, K. (eds.), *Words that Wound: Critical Race Theory, Assaultive Speech, and the First Amendment.* Boulder, CO: Westview Press, pp. 53–88.

Matsuda, M. J. (1993) 'Public Response to Racist Speech: Considering the Victim' in Matsuda, M. J., Lawrence, R. L. III, Delgado, R. and Williams Krenshaw, K. (eds.), *Words that*

Wound: Critical Race Theory, Assaultive Speech, and the First Amendment. Boulder, CO: Westview Press, pp. 17–52.

Matsuda M. J. and Lawrence C. R. (1993) 'Epilogue: Burning Crosses and the R.A.V. Case' in Matsuda, M. J., Lawrence, R. L. III, Delgado, R. and Williams Krenshaw, K. (eds.), *Words that Wound: Critical Race Theory, Assaultive Speech, and the First Amendment.* Boulder, CO: Westview Press, pp. 133–6.

Mehta, U. (1999) *Liberalism and Empire: A Study in Nineteenth-Century British Liberal Thought.* Chicago, IL: University of Chicago Press.

Mill, J. S. (2005 [1859]) *On Liberty and Other Writings.* Cambridge: Cambridge University Press.

Rocha, L. A. (2012) '"That Dazzling, Momentary Wake" of the *lettre de cachet*: The Problem of Experience in Foucault's Practice of History' in Duschinsky, R. and Rocha, L. A. (eds.), *Foucault, the Family and Politics.* London: Palgrave Macmillan, pp. 189–219.

Scott, J. C. (2010) *The Art of Not Being Governed: An Anarchist History of Upland Southeast Asia.* New Haven, CT and London: Yale University Press.

Shiell, T. (2009) *Campus Hate Speech on Trial.* Lawrence, KS: University Press of Kansas.

Spivak, G. C. (1987) *In Other Worlds.* New York: Routledge.

Titley, G. (2017) 'Introduction: Becoming Symbolic: From *Charlie Hebdo* to "Charlie Hebdo"' in Titley, G., Freedman, D., Khiabany, G. and Mondon, A. (eds.), *After Charlie Hebdo: Terror, Racism and Free Speech.* London: Zed Books, pp. 1–30.

Tucholsky, K. (1975) *Gesammelte Werke in 10 Bänden.* Gerold-Tucholsky, M. & Raddatz, F. J. (Hrsg.). Hamburg: Rowohlt. Band 2: 1919–1920, pp. 42–4.

PART II

Performing re-readings

4

WHY AFRICA'S 'WEAK STATES' MATTER

A postcolonial critique of Euro-Western discourse on African statehood and sovereignty

Anna Maria Krämer

In 1982, International Relations scholars Robert Jackson and Carl Rosberg published an article on the question of 'Why Africa's Weak States Persist' (1982a). Here, they set out the argument that most of the African states hardly showed any sign of empirical statehood, but could only survive because of their juridical recognition as formal states by the international community. Their sovereign existence would thus solely depend on the goodwill of the global community of states. As I will develop further in this chapter, this argument rendered possible a renegotiation of state sovereignty in the African context, which had been considered taboo since the anti-colonial independencies.

Today, African states are mainly represented as 'failed', 'weak' or 'fragile states', being described as safe havens for transnational terrorists and as a security threat for their citizens and neighbouring states, and also for the Global North. By linking state failure to transnational terrorism, the discourse on state in Africa inscribes itself into the debate on the concept of 'new wars', which lead to a shift in the perception of security from the idea of security as absence of war to the concept of 'human security'. With the emerging idea that states could be held responsible for the 'human security' of their citizens, sovereignty became a conditional right. At the same time, a 'responsibility to protect' was ascribed to the international community, which allows it to intervene in states not being able to fulfil their duty towards their populations. In this narrative, the international community is represented as benevolent saviour and African states are forced to remain in a subjected and dependent position.

I therefore argue that the hegemonic representation of African statehood as failed or fragile re-establishes – at least provisionally – colonial power relations. Furthermore, by paying barely any attention to colonialism and emphasising the contemporary relevance of so-called traditional modes of government ascribed to pre-colonial times, the colonial experience is literally written out of the hegemonic narratives of African statehood.

In a more general approach, I discuss the idea that this discourse represents a new version of the claimed historical right of the Global North to decide who is to be considered sovereign and who is not. This reminds us of colonial jurisdictions such as the 'Treaty of Tordesillas' or the 'General Act of the Berlin Conference' (see Fisch, 1988: 348). This undermines the basis on which a more democratic global order could be constructed, thereby deepening global inequalities.

In my view – despite acute problems – Africa's states should matter insofar as statehood is the only internationally recognised form of institutionalisation currently available. And this recognition, I argue, is crucial for those states in order to get an intelligible position in international politics. However, it appears to be necessary to reimagine statehood in Africa. The current hegemonic concepts must be replaced with approaches which take as a starting point the postcolonial condition of the continent's political formations.

I am going to substantiate my argument by first outlining the hegemonic representations of statehood in contemporary Western-European discourse on Africa. These can be subsumed under the concepts of 'state failure' and 'neopatrimonialism'. In doing so, I will reflect on their context, highlighting the imagination of African states they produce. In the second section, I will locate the hegemonic representations of African statehood in the currently ongoing debates on sovereignty, derived from the concepts of '(human) security' and the 'responsibility to protect-claim' (hereinafter referred to as r2p). The analysis of the contemporary discourse on statehood in Africa will be contrasted in the third section with historical representations. Here, I mainly draw on Kant's thoughts on colonialism and on the debates around the Berlin Conference in 1884/85 to which the principle of state sovereignty was central. In the final section, I debate the issue from a postcolonial perspective. By picking up on controversial discussions within postcolonial scholarship, I will reflect on the question of whether the concept of statehood should be abandoned as an integral part of colonial heritage, thereby integrating the African continent in a new and more democratic global world order, or whether sovereign statehood should be seen as an anti-colonial achievement in itself, which should therefore be defended (at least for now).[1, 2]

On 'African statehood'

The hegemonic concepts used to represent African states today can be subsumed under the terms of 'state failure' and 'neopatrimonialism' (Wai, 2012: 28). The *state failure* paradigm, on the one hand, constructs African states under the labels of

---

1 My argument here draws on the outcomes of my doctoral theses. In my research project, I undertook a critical, genealogical reconstruction of hegemonic representations of statehood in Euro-Western discourse on 'Africa', with the goal of making colonial continuities visible and destabilising fixating narratives of the continent's political formations (Krämer, 2019).

2 I would like to thank David McGettrick and David Schommer for proofreading this chapter and Nikita Dhawan for her encouraging and inspirational support.

weakness, fragility and failure as 'unable or unwilling' (see inter alia: Rotberg, 2003: 18; UK-DFID, 2005: 3; Patrick, 2006: 29) to guarantee its populations a certain set of self-defined fundamental state services. Whereas the concept of *neopatrimonialism*, on the other hand, constitutes an analytical category of the political, creating a universal understanding of an unchanging rationality of African states (Grimm et al., 2014: 199; Wai, 2012: 30–1).

The concepts of 'state', 'failure', 'fragility', weakness, etc. emerged in the course of the 1980s and 1990s simultaneously within academia and in the domains of international development and security politics (Helman and Ratner, 1992; Jackson and Rosberg, 1982a; Jackson and Rosberg, 1982b; Migdal, 1988; see also Hill, 2005: 146). By the end of the 1990s, they were commonly used in international policy reports and they became central for foreign policy and security strategies (e.g. OECD, 2005; US National Security Guidelines, 2002; World Bank, 1997; see also Grimm et al., 2014: 199). The attention given to the concepts of 'state failure' and 'fragility' within the domains of security and development grew even further after the terrorist attacks of 9/11. Experts from the various fields agreed on the assumption that the lack of state capacities of some states in the Global South represented a global security threat, which had to be countered by direct interventions (Grimm *et al.*, 2014: 200; Rotberg, 2003: 1; Wesley, 2008: 372). Although the literature on 'state failure' is vast and complex, these concepts primarily define a certain set of normative criteria, which a functioning state should embody. When attention is subsequently turned to the analysis of political formations on the African continent, these are found to be absent (see inter alia Migdal, 1988; Rotberg, 2004; Zartman, 1995).

The concept of 'neopatrimonialism', on the other hand, owes its wide international resonance to a strong francophone influence, being used by authors such as Jean-François Médard, Jean-François Bayart, Beatrice Hibou and Jean-Pascal Daloz. Médard locates its proponents in a third wave of political Africanist research, distinguishing it critically from both modernisation and dependency theory (Médard, 1991: 323). The main reference for the development of the neopatrimonialism concept is Shmuel Eisenstadt's *Traditional Patrimonialism and Modern Neo-Patrimonialism* (1973). The neopatrimonial state is derived from Max Weber's ideal type of the patrimonial state, integrating in its contemporary form elements of tradition and modernity (Médard, 1991: 332). It is thus conceived as a hybrid state form, as we can also see in Christopher Clapham's widely shared definition of neopatrimonialism as:

> ... a form of organisation in which relationships of a broadly patrimonial type pervade a political and administrative system which is formally constructed on rational legal lines. Officials hold positions in bureaucratic organisations with powers which are formally defined, but exercise those powers, so far as they can, as a form not of public service but of private property (Clapham, 1985: 48).

The two discursive strands are intertwined as the concept of 'neopatrimonialism' is often used in 'state failure' literature to explain the deviances of the states under examination (see inter alia Rotberg, 2004: 27). Furthermore, they both share a normative understanding of functioning states. The underlying state theories are derived from liberal social contract theory on the one hand, and from the Weberian ideal types of statehood on the other.

African states play a crucial role within both concepts because according to its representatives they are found particularly often on the continent (see inter alia Bertocchi and Guerzoni, 2012: 769–70; Jackson and Rosberg, 1982a: 1; Herbst, 2004: 302; Hutchison and Johnson, 2011: 738). In return, the *African experience* is frequently used to define the characteristics of the concepts themselves. In this perception, Africa becomes a research object and a negative model, or as William Zartman puts it: 'Even in its misfortunes and malfunctions, Africa has much to teach the world' (Zartman, 1995: 2).

Apparently, due to its historical and discursive predisposition, Africa is available to these scholars as a single unit, which they can treat as a homogeneous entity, as we can see in Robert Bates's *When Things Fell Apart* (2008).[3] Bates, who explicitly refuses to use 'cross-national data' from all around the globe, explains his focus on Africa as a whole with the argument that 'he does so . . . because Africa provides an unsettling range of opportunities to explore state failure and because political disorder is so important a determinant of the welfare of the continent' (Bates, 2008: 7). In this setting, Africa remains a centre of attraction for 'adventurers' and 'explorers' – this time personified by social science and international relations scholars.

More generally, we realise that the representations of statehood on the continent converge to a solely negative definition in contrast to an underlying ideal of modern statehood, which reaffirms an abstract idea of Euro-Western statehood. In his observations on the state of the art of Africanist state research, published in 1996, Goran Hyden persuasively demonstrates how the concepts of state failure and neopatrimonialism converge into the underlying assumption that statehood, as a research concept, had become merely irrelevant to the analysis of African countries. He writes:

'. . . with the state literally vanishing in much of Africa, scholarly interest is likely to be elsewhere, if not on regimes at least on institutions and the many informal ways in which cultural phenomena in Africa influence formal institutions' (Hyden, 1996: 34).

Consequently, he observes that there had been a shift in Africanist research from the focus on the political economy of states to political culture more generally, with the concept of state being increasingly replaced by notions such as 'regime'

---

3 Robert Bates uses this title explicitly as a reference to Chinua Achebe's *Things Fall Apart* (2000 [1958]), although he does only mention it in the sixth chapter, which also bears the same title. Here, he names the reference, but without further explanation. It has to be noted, however, that by using the title of a novel, which critically narrates the destruction of an Igbo village's historical structures by colonialism, and by simultaneously defending the position that colonialism is merely irrelevant for the contemporary situation of Africa's states, Bates overwrites Achebe's anticolonial critique with his argument.

or '(good) governance' (Hyden, 1996: 34). In the same vein, postcolonial authors have stated that in Western discourse African statehood is mainly labelled with words such as 'nullity', 'lack', 'absence' and 'nothingness' (Miller, 1985: 17; Mbembe, 2001: 4). Thus, the contemporary hegemonic representations of statehood in Africa constitute not only a form of 'othering', but they discursively construct them as non-existent. The normative models, which are at the basis of this binary argumentation, and which are derived from Western state theory, are reaffirmed through their comparison with the apparently deficient African states. In contrast, the modern capitalist state of the North is imagined as the 'normal' and 'superior' form of statehood.

The production of an *African difference* within Euro-Western discourse on statehood on the continent furthermore relies on the prevalent external perspective in the field, appearing in three crucial forms of 'othering': First, the concepts draw on the construction of a benevolent (external) research and development community – 'we'. Second, apart from a few exceptions, the external influences are seen as solely positive, from which a new (civilising) mission for the international community is deduced. And third, in compliance with the underlying modernist approach, the difficult situation faced by Africa's postcolonial states are explained exclusively on the basis of internal factors (Hill, 2005: 149; Nay, 2014: 219–20).

The historical narratives inherent to these approaches reinforce the focus on internal factors by barely considering external interventions. European colonialism is mainly seen as irrelevant to the contemporary situation of African states or it is even perceived as a positive factor for the creation of stable modern statehood (see inter alia Bates, 2008; Bertocchi and Guerzoni, 2012; Chabal and Daloz, 1999; Clapham, 1996; Rotberg, 2003; Herbst, 2000). The short existence of the independent African states is ignored or even wrongly dated back to 1960.[4] Meanwhile, by giving barely any attention to the colonial period and emphasising the contemporary relevance of so-called traditional modes of government ascribed to pre-colonial times, the colonial experience is literally written out of the historical narratives on African statehood.

While the hegemonic representations of statehood in Africa on the one hand convey an impression of homogeneous *African values*, the assumption of cultural and ethnical fragmentation is, however, central to the perception of problems within the discourse. We can observe this in the following generalisation by Jackson and Rosberg: '*African politics* are most often a personal or factional struggle to control the national government or to influence it' (1982b: 1, my emphasis). This argument directly links the field of 'state failure' literature to the concept of 'neopatrimonialism', which defines personal and factional struggles, as well as patronage and clientelism, as the main features of the 'hybrid African states' (Bratton and van de Walle, 1997: 62, 269). According to Zubairu Wai, this leads to the allegation of a universal logic of an African way of social organisation, combining a set of

---

4 As an example, see the cases of Namibia, Zimbabwe, Angola and Mozambique in Bates (2008: 33).

modern institutions with traditionalised and culturalised practices of government (Wai, 2012: 31; see also Médard, 1991: 330).

Finally, I would like to point to a strong tendency within much of the literature on both 'failed states' and 'neopatrimonialism', to construct the independencies of the former colonies as the main problem of contemporary African states. This discursive strand is, for example, represented by Helman and Ratner when they claim that 'the current collapse of states has its roots in the vast proliferation of nation-states, especially in Africa and Asia, since the end of World War II' (1992: 3). Subsequently, the historical error of the international community would not have been colonialism itself, but the premature dismissal of the colonies into independence and the recognition of those dysfunctional states as sovereign.[5]

As normative categories, 'state failure' and 'neopatrimonialism' have an effect on the perception of problems and on the assessment of possible strategies against them (Nay, 2014: 216). Becoming increasingly normalised in the last decades, they have defined a standard of government, resulting in specific 'state' and 'peace building' programmes (see inter alia Ellis, 2005; Herbst, 2000, 2004; Kaplan, 2008).

Human security and R2P: Debating sovereignty

As mentioned above, due to the concepts of 'state failure' and 'neopatrimonialism', Africa's states are mainly represented today as a local and regional security threat. Furthermore, being associated with transnational terrorism, they came to be perceived as a cause for global instability.[6] Against the backdrop of this imagination of African states, the debate on sovereignty in Africa was taken up within political science and international law from the 1990s onwards. With the emergence of the concept of 'human security', it is claimed by scholars and political practitioners alike that statehood should only be accorded to those states which are 'able and willing' to guarantee a certain degree of security to their citizens. At the same time, a 'responsibility to protect' was ascribed to the international community, raising anew the debate on the possibilities of intervention in formally sovereign but apparently failed or fragile states. Proposals here rank from UN trusteeships and conservatorships to a complete decertification. In this section, I explore the current debate on the sovereignty of so-called failed African states, contextualising it within the framework of the recent securitisation of development.

Helman and Ratner outline the core areas of the argument of global security, which allows for a renewed sense of mission, when they write:

5 The restriction of certain sovereign rights through the independence treaties remains untold in this story. E.g. the French Government negotiated so-called contracts of cooperation with nearly all of its former African colonies, which remained in force up until the 1970s and continue to exist to this day with modifications (see Joseph, 1978: 16f; Krämer, 2008: 62f).

6 Especially after the so-called 'refugee crisis' in Europe, these states are also regarded as an international threat because they do not have control over the perceived *exodus* of their populations and are partly held responsible for it.

... a disturbing new phenomenon is emerging: the failed nation-state, utterly incapable of sustaining itself as a member of the international community ... As those states descend into violence and anarchy – imperilling their own citizens and threatening their neighbors through refugee flows, political instability, and random warfare – *it is becoming clear that something must be done* (1992: 3, my emphasis).

As these states seem to be no longer capable of sustaining themselves and of guaranteeing internal law and order, various forms of external intervention are claimed to be, as Robert Rotberg puts it a decade later, 'the critical, all-consuming, strategic and moral imperatives of our terrorized time' (2003: 24). The argument for a moral need for intervention has to be seen within the context of the discourse on global security and 'new wars'.[7] From the early 1990s onwards, the perception of global security and global threats has changed, bringing the paradigm of 'new wars' to the forefront of the debate. The area of concern of security policies thereby shifted from national governments to the social level and to populations themselves, which had been until then the traditional political domain of developmental policies (Duffield, 2001: 36–7). In this sense, critical scholars such as Mark Duffield and Ole Wæver highlight the expansion of the concept of security beyond the idea of security as absence of war, adding an individual human level to it (Duffield, 2010: 53ff; Wæver, 1995: 47). By introducing the concept of 'human security' into the debate from the 1990s onwards and creating a Commission on Human Security in 2001, the UN Development Programme became a central actor in the promotion of this broader idea of security (Chandler, 2007: 367). With the concept of 'human security', the focus of development and security policies altered from the governmental level to the level of managing human life. This gave rise to the idea that sovereignty should only be granted to those states which are able to guarantee 'human security' to the population within their respective national borders (Neethling, 2005: 38). Being formerly conceived as an absolute right in international law, state sovereignty became conditional. As we can see below, this was crucial for the emergence of another related international law concept – the 'responsibility to protect':

It is acknowledged that sovereignty implies a dual responsibility: externally – to respect the sovereignty of other states, and internally, to respect the dignity and basic rights of all the people within the state (ICISS, 2001: 8).

As a reaction to the acknowledgement that wars were nowadays fought mainly within states and not between them and that the number of civilian war victims

---

7 In contrast to 'old wars', 'new wars' go beyond the classical interstate form of violent conflict where national armies stand against each other. 'New wars' are conceived as complex and diffuse violent constellations, in which various state and non-state actors, such as national armies, mercenaries, terrorist organisations, militias, paramilitary groups, etc. are involved. For a (critical) overview, see Duffield, 2001; Kaldor, 2013.

was rising, it was claimed that sovereignty could no longer be seen exclusively as an external legal form, but that it should imply a responsibility for the protection and the common welfare of its population. This led to a renegotiation of state sovereignty and created the possibility to intervene legally in formally sovereign states. The 'r2p' was subsequently established as a concept of international law, legitimising interventions in sovereign states.[8]

In political science, however, the disappointment over the economically stagnating independent African states and the rise of conflicts on the continent led to a debate on the sovereignty of these young states and on the need for external intervention already from the 1980s onwards. Here, the debate oscillates between two poles: first, the joint principles of sovereignty and of non-interference, which, together, form the basis of the current global political order (see inter alia UN Charter, Art. 2); and, second, the recent assumption that in order to prevent the risks allegedly posed by so-called failed states to their citizens and to other states, external intervention is needed and justified.

Furthermore, Jackson and Rosberg's distinction between juridical and empirical statehood provides the argument that the premature dismissal of the former colonised states into independence is at the heart of the problem with a theoretical fundament (1982a, 1982b; Jackson, 1992; Jackson, 1999; Jackson, 2000). They claim that based on a Weberian sociological definition of state, most African states have to be seen as non-existent. This, however, contradicts their legal existence through the recognition by the international community (Jackson and Rosberg, 1982a: 3). In order to add the perspective of international law to Weber's approach, Jackson and Rosberg took up Ian Brownlie's juridical approach to statehood. Brownlie defines those states as legal entities, which show a 'defined territory', a 'permanent population', an 'effective government' and 'independence' (ibid.: 3). Dividing Brownlie's approach into a juridical and an empirical aspect, it became possible to explain the international recognition of political formations, which allegedly showed no sign of empirical statehood. According to the authors, juridical statehood came to Africa as a new and arbitrary concept through colonialism (ibid.: 14). In their view, many of the African states became independent without showing the necessary economic and geographical conditions, and they only continue to exist because of the recognition by 'a benevolent international community' (ibid.: 16). With their approach, Jackson and Rosberg deny African states any form of political project, neglecting at the same time the existence of pre-colonial political formations.

---

8 There is an ongoing debate on the 'r2p' in international law and political science. The 'r2p' received a first institutional basis in 2005, being mentioned in a UN report. It then became legally binding with Resolution 1674 of the UN Security Council in 2006. In 2009, UN Secretary-General Ban Ki-moon published a report on the implementation of the concept. It came up again in Resolutions 1971 and 1973 of the UN Security Council, in which the Libyan state is reminded of its responsibility towards its population. The intervention in Libya in 2011 is also regarded as a precedent for the use of the 'r2p'. However, the impression that the 'r2p' is a Western invention is disproved by the fact that the African Union (AU) already included a right for intervention in its sovereign member states under certain conditions in its constitution from 2000. Regarding the relevance of the 'r2p' in the African context, see inter alia Kuwali and Viljoen, 2014; Mamdani, 2011; Rutazibwa, 2013.

Based on this argument, sovereignty itself as a guarantee for local autonomy and international security became negotiable (see inter alia Clapham, 1996: 267). Furthermore, the recognition of the phenomenon of state failure led to the claim to conceive those states differently in international law (see inter alia Herbst, 2004: 308). Taking this argumentative strand even further, some scholars propose that international community should consider the decertification or recolonisation of certain African states in order to help them cope with their fundamental problems (ibid.: 309; Ganahl, 2013: 254–5; Gilley, 2017: 2).[9]

The international law debate on the 'r2p' and the political science debate on sovereignty are, in certain respects, contradictory to each other. Whereas the former results in the definition of new normative standards of statehood, justifying thereby interventions against the principle of sovereignty, the latter puts sovereignty itself as an absolute right into question. However, both discursive strands contribute to a destabilisation of the principle of sovereignty itself, revealing a formally invisible global hierarchy of states. According to Olivia Rutazibwa, the partitioning of the world population into those who have capacities and therefore agency and those who have to be 'capacity-built' is particularly visible in this discourse (2013: 92, 102). Hence, the states of the Global North are represented as 'ethical intervenors' (Rutazibwa, 2010) and discursively constructed as the only actors able to prioritise humanist values over their own interests (Herbst, 2000). The proponents of this discourse also seem to share the assumption that they are, as a matter of course, in a position to decide which states are to be considered sovereign and which are not, thereby reaffirming the colonial argument for protection. Asking if this matter-of-fact attitude could be explained by way of historical debates on the continent's sovereignty, I now turn to the colonial discourse on Africa.

A note on colonial representations of 'African statehood'

It is certainly a difficult endeavour to talk about historical continuities in this context because the comparison between current developments and colonial conquest can lead to a relativisation of colonial power and violence. However, it seems obvious that the current renegotiation of state sovereignty shares certain traits with historical discourses. With modern statehood, the idea of sovereignty as a principle of international law emerged. As the modern nation-states in Europe developed parallel to increasing colonial activities, European debates on statehood and sovereignty also entered colonial discourse. Drawing on my genealogical reconstruction of hegemonic representations of statehood in Euro-Western discourse on Africa, I propose that the term of 'antithesis' is crucial to characterise the continual traits

9 Gilley explicitly urges the Western countries to assume their civilisational responsibility by recolonising certain countries (2017). Gilley's article only appeared online and was then withdrawn by the publishers Taylor & Francis a short time later because of alleged threats against the journal editor. It has been widely critiqued as a clickbait that backfired at the journal, provoking several board members to leave. Other authors, such as Sultana (2018), state that Gilley's article, however, represents a new trend of colonial nostalgia.

of this discourse (Krämer, 2019). This, I argue, is compelling insofar as the hegemonic representations through the centuries always implicitly or explicitly include an imagined ideal of statehood, against which the representations of *African statehood* are defined (Curran, 2006; Miller, 1985; Gates, 1987).

The antithetical aspect is especially visible in the narratives on African states and societies in the 'long eighteenth century' (Anghie, 2005: 1–2) and in the writings of central Enlightenment thinkers. Africa, which remained more or less unknown to the eighteenth-century European writers, is either utopia or dystopia. It represents a locus for the intellectual fight within European philosophical debates over the question of what should be considered *good* government. It is an imaginary and at the same time familiar place, serving as a setting for the authors to act out their vision of the state of nature of humankind.

The ambivalent character of the Enlightenment discourse on state sovereignty can be found in the tension in Kant's writings between his race theory on the one hand and his vision of cosmopolitanism on the other, which implies a critique of colonialism. He opposed colonial conquest based on his legal and moral conception of cosmopolitan right, which he derived from the assumption that all humans stood in an 'original Community of the soil' (Kant, 1887 [1797]: 70[10]). Therefore, his essay on 'Perpetual Peace' (1917 [1795]) is seen as a fundamental text for the enforcement of the principle of sovereignty. At the same time, his Eurocentric ideal of a democratic republicanism driven by reason, together with his race theory and his devaluating view on the human state of nature (Eberl, 2016: 289), express 'a new phase of imperialism' (Dhawan, 2016: 3). His colonial worldview is revealed inasmuch as his representations of African societies show that he took no interest at all in their various social structures. Although the references he draws on in his texts on African societies show that he knew about the complex political structures (e.g. of the Kingdom of Dahomey and of the Ashanti Empire), he chose to represent African societies and rulers in a pre-rational state of nature, mentioning the most absurd stories, such as the myth of the 'cannibal society' of Ansico (Kant, 1968 [1802]: 412). The imperialist moment and the normative violence in Kant's writings are most visible in his teleological concept of human development when seen in contrast to his negative imagination of the human state of nature. His critique of the 'inhospitable behaviour of the civilized nations' (Kant, 1917 [1795]: 139) can thereby merely be interpreted as a self-referential commentary aiming at a further improvement of Western humanism, than a real appreciation of non-Western cultures and societies (Dhawan, 2016: 3).

Even though he was opposed to violent colonisation, he still thought that modern European statehood would be universalised because it was the most rational institutional form to secure a peaceful cohabitation of the different societies (Kant, 1968 [1784]: 24). He adds that most certainly Europe would be providing legislation for the rest of the world in the future (ibid.: 29). Thus, against the argument

---

10 Origin: 'ursprüngliche Gemeinschaft des Bodens' (Kant, 1914 [1797]: 352).

of Kant's antiracial turn in his later writing (see inter alia Flikschuh and Ypi, 2014; Kleingeld, 2012), his racism is reaffirmed in the universalisation of his vision of a European-enlightened teleology and the explanation of European development and successful expansionism on the basis of his race theory (see Eberl, 2016: 341, 338). From this, I draw the conclusion that Kant's concepts of progress and development already express the Eurocentric perception of its rational and thus civilisational superiority, which still inhabits Western developmental policies.

I now turn to the Berlin Conference of 1884/85 as an important discursive event in the context of colonial representations of statehood in Africa in the late nineteenth century. Although it is widely acknowledged today that the colonial borders were not traced on that occasion, the conference had important material effects on the colonisation of the continent. Additionally, its symbolic role for both colonial legitimation as well as anti-colonial resistance cannot be ignored (see inter alia Bley, 2005: 14–15; Katzenellenbogen, 1996: 21–2; M'Bokolo, 2010: 19). Furthermore, the conference was relevant in the context of the enforcement of territorial administrative states as a universal model for statehood on the continent (Anghie, 2005: 96; Eckert, 2009: 1). In the conference documents, the debate on sovereignty remains ambivalent due to its oscillation between recognition and negation of sovereign entities on the continent. While the existence of sovereign governments was recognised through the signing of protectorate treaties, the interior of the continent was discursively and legally constructed as *terra nullius* (Anghie, 2005: 99; Fisch, 1988: 356). The colonial imaginary of African states shows the same ambivalence describing them on the one hand as structures of rational government which have to be taken seriously and denying them on the other hand a legitimate status due to the representation of their statesmen as drunken and lazy despots. The antithetical aspect is revealed in stories of despotism, immoral sexual behaviour and idolatry. Slavery and arbitrary rule are represented in this narrative as part of an *African nature*, whereas European actors are again constructed as saviours (see inter alia Brazza, 1984 [1887]; Cameron, 1877 III and IV; Stanley, 1878 I and II).

This contradiction is not only the expression of individual positions, but is also evident in the simultaneous use of two forms of colonial conquest in the General Act of the Berlin Conference: 'protectorate' and 'occupation' (see inter alia Arts. 34. and 35). At this time, the European continent was already dominantly structured by territorial nation-states and the relation between them was organised on the basis of the principles of sovereignty and non-interference. It is crucial to take a closer look at the concept of 'occupation' to understand why these principles were not applied to the African context. 'Occupation' juridically describes a form of primary acquisition of land, implying that the land in question is uninhabited. The only reason for the differing application of the term of occupation to European and African territories can be found in the distinction between *civilized* and *uncivilised* states, with only the former being recognised as legal subject. Thus, any territory not belonging to a legal subject could be declared as unoccupied (Fisch, 1988: 356).

In the same vein, the moral arguments of help and of civilisational progress are clearly prioritised over African sovereignty in the debates around the Berlin

Conference.[11] On the basis of the then prevalent race theories and the presumed duty of the self-proclaimed civilised nations to bring progress to *others*, a global hierarchy was reaffirmed, defining the terrain on which the right of political self-determination was negotiated (Burbank and Cooper, 2010: 364; Wariboko, 2011: 16). The self-representation of the conference participants as *white*, superior and civilised is best shown when the American representative John A. Kasson defends the international administration of the Congo basin with the argument that this would show 'blacks' that only *white* civilisation and government could bring them peace and freedom (cit. in Gatter, 1984 [1884]: 132). Slavery is thereby constructed as an inner African problem, whereas an external civilisational intervention is attributed to Europe, constituting it as an instance of moral *ratio* and international law (Eckert, 2009: 2).[12]

Why Africa's weak states matter: A postcolonial debate

The proximity between colonial claims (see inter alia Protocols of the Berlin Conference, in Gatter, 1984 [1884]: 221–2; Leroy-Beaulieu, 1902 [1874]: XXII) and current debates on external administration can hardly be neglected (see inter alia Helman and Ratner, 1992: 12). The justification of external intervention seen as moral duty and thus as a matter of course seems to be closely linked to the therein constructed subject positions of a 'benevolent international community' on the one hand and 'incapable or unwilling despots' on the other. Through the partitioning of humans into those who can help and those who are at the receiving end of help, the discourse on statehood in Africa inscribes itself on a social Darwinist agenda, which is part of what Gayatri Spivak calls the 'imperial axiomatic' (1999: 26, 2004: 425; see also Morton, 2003: 116).

This observation can lead to the claim that statehood as such should be overcome as being a colonial relic. Noah Bassil, in his postcolonial take on the issue of sovereignty in the African context, concludes that it would be necessary for the African states to accept their failure in order to free themselves from colonial heritage (2004: 29). This seems to be a coherent decolonial claim insofar as it puts the concept of state itself and the global hierarchical world order as a result of colonialism into jeopardy.

Bassil's argument could even be taken further by acknowledging that the discussion of alternative forms of statehood and the critique of the European model were at the core of anti-colonial debates on the African continent. Frantz Fanon, for instance, argued, based on his experience of an extremely violent form of colonialism in Algeria, that the formation of a nation was an important step towards

---

11 Article 6 of the Berlin General Act states that the signatories guarantee to watch over the conservation of the indigenous population, to improve their moral and physic condition, and to suppress slavery in order to make them understand the advantages of civilisation.

12 Reading the conference documents very carefully, it becomes clear, however, that the argument of protection first and foremost aims at the protection of Euro-American commercial interests.

independence (2002 [1961]: 234). But at the same time, he opposed an imitation of Europe, which in his eyes would have been an honour to European statehood (ibid.: 304). For Kwame Nkrumah, national liberation also represented only a first step in the direction of a Pan-African unity government (1963: 135). The Pan-African constellation, accompanied by economic integration, was supposed to also protect the continent against neo-colonial exploitative strategies (ibid.: 218). The European nation-states served him as a warning, as they were only trying to come to a unity after two world wars and against the threat of a re-strengthening German economy (ibid.: 216–17). Furthermore, Frederick Cooper reminds us that within all the anti-colonial movements in francophone West Africa, only one Cameroonian party fought for independence in the form of an independent nation-state until the end of the 1950s. The others were debating on a form of international sovereignty within the framework of a francophone federation, which had already begun to take shape with the foundation of the French Union after the Second World War. Due to colonial exploitation and a lack of resources, these movements feared the individual formations would be weak and poor as nation-states (Cooper 2014: 68–9).

However, in the African postcolonial context, an anti-state attitude tends to ignore the fact that – if we agree that the colonised people could not go back in history – the nation-state was the only form the independent African political formations could take on in order to be internationally recognised. Thus, the independent postcolonial states could only gain agency and an intelligible position to be heard by subjecting themselves to the global order of states, thereby becoming legal subjects – a status they had mostly been denied in their precolonial condition. Drawing on the analogy of subjectivation in Homi Bhabha's concept of 'mimicry' (1983; 2004 [1994]), the postcolonial state takes on a mimetic form of the colonial metropole. This does not necessarily lead to a positive development, but still can be read as a form of appropriation and anti-colonial empowerment. By solely regarding the postcolonial states as part of colonial heritage, the political projects, which were at the basis of those states, are ignored.

Thus, in conclusion, I argue with Mahmood Mamdani that the currently hegemonic representations of African statehood have to be seen as a serious threat against a major anti-colonial achievement. According to Mamdani, we are about to lose the political moment within the concept of sovereignty on behalf of a paternalistic narrative of help. The global humanist order, based on principles such as 'human security' and the 'r2p', ignores political civil rights, but deals only with fundamental rights for human survival (2011: 126). The concerned persons are not active bearers of rights, but passive recipients of protection; an assumption that articulates a potential need for external government. The paternalistic narrative of protection, however, is not new in the African context; rather, it was central to colonial legitimation (ibid.: 127). Against this backdrop, it seems imperative to engage with the political project of the postcolonial African states and to reimagine them from within their historical constitution, rather than abandoning the concept of statehood.

Drawing on Pal Ahluwalia, I suggest that the emergence of the contemporary African states must be analysed as a process of radical and violent transculturation, which does not allow for a simple recourse to precolonial forms of government (2001: 66–7, 72). Thus, the reimagination of statehood in the African context requires, first, conceiving of colonial rule as a fundamental episode in the historical development of the postcolonial African states. By doing so, as we can see in various historical analysis by postcolonial scholars, it becomes obvious that instead of universalising a democratic state model, the colonial state always only addressed the colonial elites, and that this elitist model was often reproduced after the countries' independencies (see inter alia Comaroff and Comaroff, 2012: 5; Guha, 1997: 4, 68; Chatterjee, 2010 [1993]: 15, 21; Mamdani, 1996: 19). Furthermore, a postcolonial approach to African statehood requires that we refrain from comparing it to a normative imagined ideal type of Western modern statehood. With authors such as Guha or Chatterjee, I therefore suggest to draw on actor-centred concepts of statehood, such as Gramsci's 'integral state' or Foucault's concept of 'governmentality', which analyse the state as expression of social power relations and practices (Guha, 1988, 1997; Chatterjee, 2004). Finally, by regarding colonialism as a fundamental organising principle of the modern global world order (Serequeberhan, 1997: 142–3), I propose to conceive of the postcolonial state as a genuinely transnational state. In doing so, internal as well as external actors in their reciprocal relationship come into the focus of analysis.

References

Achebe, C. (2000 [1958]) *Things Fall Apart*. Oxford: Heinemann.

Ahluwalia, P. (2001) *Politics and Post-Colonial Theory: African Inflections*. London and New York: Routledge.

Anghie, A. (2005) *Imperialism, Sovereignty and the Making of International Law*. Cambridge: Cambridge University Press.

Bassil, N. (2004) 'The Failure of the State in Africa: The Case of Dafur', *Australian Quarterly*, 76(4), pp. 23–9.

Bates, R. (2008) *When Things Fell Apart: State Failure in Late-Century Africa*. New York and Cambridge: Cambridge University Press.

Bertocchi, G. and Guerzoni, A. (2012) 'Growth, History, or Institutions: What Explains State Fragility in Sub-Saharan Africa?', *Journal of Peace Research*, 49(6), pp. 769–83.

Bhabha, H. (1983) 'The Other Question . . . Homi K. Bhabha Reconsiders the Stereotype and Colonial Discourse', *Screen*, 24(6), pp. 18–36.

Bhabha, H. (2004 [1994]) *The Location of Culture*. London and New York: Routledge.

Bley, H. (2005) 'Künstliche Grenzen, natürliches Afrika? Um die Berliner Kongokonferenz von 1884–1885 ranken sich allerhand Mythen', *iz3w*, 282, pp. 14–17.

Bratton, M. and van de Walle, N. (1997) *Democratic Experiments in Africa: Regime Transitions in Comparative Perspective*. Cambridge: Cambridge University Press.

Brazza, P. S. de (1984 [1887]) *Conférences et lettres de P. Savorgnan de Brazza sur ses trois explorations dans l'ouest Africain de 1875 à 1886*. Brazzaville: Kivouvou.

Burbank, J. and Cooper, F. (2010) *Imperien der Weltgeschichte: Das Repertoire der Macht vom alten Rom und China bis heute*. Frankfurt, Main and New York: Campus.

Cameron, V. (1877) *Across Africa*. 4th edn., vols. I–IV. London: Daldy, Isbister & Co.

Chabal, P. and Daloz, J.-P. (1999) *Africa Works: Disorder as Political Instrument*. Bloomington, IN: Indiana University Press.

Chandler, D. (2007) 'The Security–Development Nexus and the Rise of "Anti-Foreign Policy"', *Journal of International Relations and Development*, 10(4), pp. 362–86.

Chatterjee, P. (2004) *The Politics of the Governed: Reflections on Popular Politics in Most of the World*. New York: Columbia University Press.

Chatterjee, P. (2010 [1993]) 'The Nation and its Fragments. Colonial and Postcolonial Histories', in ibid., *The Partha Chatterjee Omnibus*. New York and Oxford: Oxford University Press.

Clapham, C. (1985) *Third World Politics: An Introduction*. Madison, WI: Wisconsin University Press.

Clapham, C. (1996) *Africa and the International System: The Politics of State Survival*. Cambridge: Cambridge University Press.

Comaroff, J. and Comaroff, J. (2012) *Theory from the South: Or, How Euro-America Is Evolving Toward Africa*. Boulder, CO: Paradigm Publishers.

Cooper, F. (2014) *Africa in the World. Capitalism, Empire, Nation-State*. Cambridge, MA: Harvard University Press.

Curran, A. (2006) 'Imaginer l'Afrique au siècle des lumières' in Abbattista, G. and Minuti, R. (eds.), *Le problème de l'altérité dans la culture européenne: Anthropologie politique et religion aux XVIII et XIX siècle*, pp. 101–27.

Dhawan, N. (2016) 'The Canary Who Sings in a Predictable Monotone: Kant and Colonialism', *Journal of Postcolonial Studies,* doi: 10.1080/13688790.2016.1262203, pp. 1–5.

Duffield, M. (2001) *Global Governance and the New Wars: The Merging of Development and Security*. New York and London: Zed Books.

Duffield, M. (2010) 'The Liberal Way of Development-Security Impasse: Exploring the Global Life-Chance Divide', *Security Dialogue*, 41(1), pp. 53–76.

Eberl, O. (2016) *Naturzustand und 'Barbarei': Begründung und Kritik staatlicher Ordnung im Zeichen des Kolonialismus*. Postdoctoral thesis presented to the department of social science and history at Technische Universität Darmstadt.

Eckert, A. (2009) '125 Jahre Berliner Afrika-Konferenz: Bedeutung für Geschichte und Gegenwart', *GIGA Focus*, No. 12 [online]. Available at http://www.giga-hamburg.de/de/system/files/publications/gf_afrika_0912.pdf (accessed 6 August 2014), pp. 1–8.

Eisenstadt, S. (1973) *Traditional Patrimonialism and Modern Neo-Patrimonialism*. London, Thousand Oaks, CA and New Delhi: Sage.

Ellis, S. (2005) 'How to Rebuild Africa', *Foreign Affairs*, 84(5), pp. 135–48.

Fanon, F. (2002 [1961]) *Les damnés de la terre*. Paris: La découverte.

Fisch, J. (1988) 'Africa as Terra Nullius: The Berlin Conference and International Law' in Förster, S., Mommsen, W. and Robinsons, R. (eds.), *Bismarck, Europe, and Africa: The Berlin Africa Conference 1884–1885 and the Onset of Partition*. New York and Oxford: Oxford University Press, pp. 347–75.

Flikschuh, K. and Ypi, L. (eds.) (2014) *Kant and Colonialism: Historical and Critical Perspectives*. New York and Oxford: Oxford University Press.

Ganahl, J. (2013) *Corruption, Good Governance, and the African State: A Critical Analysis of the Political-Economic Foundations of Corruption in Sub-Saharan Africa*. Potsdam: Potsdam University Press.

Gates, H. (1987) *Figures in Black: Words, Signs, and the 'Racial' Self*. New York and Oxford: Oxford University Press.

Gatter, F. (eds.) (1984 [1884f]) *Protokolle und Generalakte der Berliner Afrika-Konferenz: 1884–1885*. Bremen: Übersee-Museum.

Gilley, B. (2017) 'The Case for Colonialism', *Third World Quarterly*, doi: 10.1080/01436597.2017.1369037, pp. 1–17.

Grimm, S., Lemay-Hébert, N. and Nay, O. (2014) '"Fragile States": Introducing a Political Concept', *Third World Quarterly*, 35(2), pp. 197–209.

Guha, R. (1997) *Dominance without Hegemony: History and Power in Colonial India*. Cambridge, MA: Harvard University Press.

Guha, R. (ed.) (1988) *Selected Subaltern Studies*. New York and Oxford: Oxford University Press.

Helman, G. and Ratner, S. (1992) 'Saving Failed States', *Foreign Policy*, 89, pp. 3–20.

Herbst, J. (2000) 'African Peacekeepers and State Failure' in Rotberg, R. (ed.), *Peacekeeping and Peace Enforcement in Africa: Methods of Conflict Prevention*. Washington, DC: Brookings Institution Press, pp. 16–33.

Herbst, J. (2004) 'Let Them Fail: State Failure in Theory and Practice: Implications for Policy' in Rotberg, R. (ed.), *When States Fail: Causes and Consequences*. Princeton, NJ: Princeton University Press, pp. 302–18.

Hill, J. (2005) 'Beyond the Other? A Postcolonial Critique of the Failed State Thesis', *African Identities*, 3(2), pp. 139–54.

Hutchison, M. and Johnson, K. (2011) 'Capacity or Trust? Institutional Capacity, Conflict, and Political Trust in Africa, 2000–2005', *Journal of Peace Research*, 48(6), pp. 737–52.

Hyden, G. (1996) 'Rethinking Theories of the State: An Africanist Perspective', *Africa Insight*, 26(1), pp. 26–35.

ICISS (2001) 'The Responsibility to Protect' [online]. Available at http://responsibilityto protect.org/ICISS%20Report.pdf (accessed 23 March 2015).

Jackson, R. (1992) 'Juridical Statehood in Sub-Saharan Africa', *Journal of International Affairs*, 46(1), pp. 1–16.

Jackson, R. (1999) 'Sovereignty in World Politics: A Glance at the Conceptual and Historical Landscape', *Political Studies*, 47(3), pp. 431–56.

Jackson, R. (2000) *The Global Covenant: Human Conduct in a World of States*. New York and Oxford: Oxford University Press.

Jackson, R. and Rosberg, C. (1982a) 'Why Africa's Weak States Persist: The Empirical and the Juridical Statehood', *World Politics*, 35(1), pp. 1–24.

Jackson, R. and Rosberg, C. (1982b) *Personal Rule in Black Africa: Prince, Autocrat, Prophet, Tyrant*. Berkeley, CA: University of California Press.

Joseph, R. (1978) *Gaullist Africa: Cameroon under Ahmadou Ahidjo*. Enugu: Fourth Dimension Publications.

Kaldor, M. (2013) 'In Defence of New Wars', *Stability: International Journal of Security and Development*, 2(1) [online]. Available at http://dx.doi.org/10.5334/sta.at (accessed 21 March 2016), pp. 1–16.

Kant, I. (1917 [1795]) 'Perpetual Peace: A Philosophical Essay. Translated from German by Campbell Smith, M. (1968 1795) Zum ewigen Frieden', *Akademie Ausgabe*, 8. Berlin: De Gruyter, pp. 341–86 [online]. Available at http://oll.libertyfund.org/titles/kant-perpet ual-peace-a-philosophical-essay-1917-ed (accessed 22 March 2018).

Kant, I. (1968 [1784]) 'Idee zu einer allgemeinen Geschichte in Weltbürgerlicher Absicht', *Akademie Ausgabe*, 8. Berlin: De Gruyter, pp. 15–31.

Kant, I. (1968 [1802]) '"Physische Geographie" by Friedrich Theodor Rink based on Kant's Lecture Notes', *Akademie Ausgabe*, vol. 9. Berlin: De Gruyter, pp. 151–436.

Kant. I (1887 [1797]) *The Philosophy of Law: An Exposition of the Fundamental Principles of Jurisprudence as the Science of Right*. Translated from German by Hastie, W. origin. (1914 [1797]) 'Die Metaphysik der Sitten'. *Akademie Ausgabe*. 6. Berlin: Georg Reimer, pp. 203–493] [online]. Available at http://oll.libertyfund.org/titles/kant-the-philosophy-of-law (accessed 22 March 2018).

Kaplan, S. (2008) *Fixing Fragile States: A New Paradigm for Development*. Westport, CT: Praeger Security International.

Katzenellenbogen, S. (1996) 'It Didn't Happen at Berlin: Politics, Economics and Ignorance in the Setting of Africa's Colonial Boundaries' in Asiwaju, A. and Nugent, P. (eds.), *African Boundaries: Barriers, Conduits and Opportunities*. London: Pinter, pp. 21–34.

Kleingeld, P. (2012) *Kant and Cosmopolitanism: The Philosophical Ideal of World Citizenship*. Cambridge and New York: Cambridge University Press.

Krämer, A. (2008) *Grundgedanken für ein Konzept peripherer Staatlichkeit entwickelt am Fallbeispiel Kamerun*. Magister thesis, presented at Goethe-University Frankfurt/Main.

Krämer, A. (2019): *Repräsentationen von Staat in Afrika: Postkoloniale Kritik eines Diskurses*. Baden-Baden: Nomos.

Kuwali, D. and Viljoen, F. (2014) *Africa and the Responsibility to Protect: Article 4(h) of the African Union Constitutive Act*. London and New York: Routledge.

Leroy-Beaulieu, P. (1902 [1874]) *De la colonisation chez les peuples modernes*, vols. 1 and 2, 5th rev. edn. (including the 'Préfaces' of all editions 1874, 1882, 1885, 1891). Paris: Guillaumin et cie.

M'Bokolo, E. (2010) 'The Berlin Conference, Myth and Reality' in Arndt, L., Kruemmel, C., Schmidt, D., Schmutz, H., Stoller, D. and Wuggenig, U. (eds.), *The Division of the Earth: Tableaux on the Legal Synopses of the Berlin Africa Conference*. Cologne: Walther König, pp. 16–19.

Mamdani, M. (1996) *Citizen and Subject: Contemporary Africa and the Legacy of Late Colonialism*. Princeton, NJ: Princeton University Press.

Mamdani, M. (2011) 'Responsibility to Protect or Right to Punish?' in Cunliffe, P. (ed.), *Critical Perspectives on the Responsibility to Protect: Interrogating Theory and Practice*. London and New York: Routledge, pp. 125–39.

Mbembe, A. (2001) *On the Postcolony*. Berkeley, CA: University of California Press.

Médard, J.-F. (ed.) (1991) *Etats d'Afrique noire: formation, mécanismes et crise*. Paris: Ed. Karthala.

Migdal, J. (1988) *Strong Societies and Weak States: State-Society Relations and State Capabilities in the Third World*. Princeton, NJ: Princeton University Press.

Miller, C. (1985) *Blank Darkness: Africanist Discourse in French*. Chicago and London: University of Chicago Press.

Morton, S. (2003) *Gayatri Chakravorty Spivak*. London and New York: Routledge.

Nay, O. (2014) 'International Organisations and the Production of Hegemonic Knowledge: How the World Bank and the OECD Helped to Invent the Fragile State Concept', *Third World Quarterly*, 35(2), pp. 210–31.

Neethling, T. (2005) 'The Security-Development Nexus and the Imperative of Peacebuilding with Special Reference to the African Context', *African Journal of Conflict Resolution*, 5(1), pp. 33–60.

Nkrumah, K. (1963) *Africa Must Unite*. London: Heinemann.

OECD (2005) 'Fragile States Report' [online]. Available at http://www.oecd.org/dac/conflict-fragility-resilience/docs/Monitoring-resource-flows-to-fragile-states-2005.pdf (accessed 9 April 2019).

Patrick, S. (2006) 'Weak States and Global Threats: Fact or Fiction', *Washington Quarterly*, 29(2), pp. 27–53.

Rotberg, R. (2003) 'Failed States, Collapsed States, Weak States: Causes and Indicators' in ibid. (ed.), *State Failure and State Weakness in a Time of Terror*. Cambridge, MA: World Peace Foundation, pp. 1–25.

Rotberg, R. (2004) 'The Failure and Collapse of Nation-States: Breakdown, Prevention, and Repair' in ibid. (ed.), *When States Fail: Causes and Consequences*. Princeton, NJ: Princeton University Press, pp. 1–45.

Rutazibwa, O. (2010) 'The Problematics of the EU's Ethical (Self)Image in Africa: The EU as an "Ethical Intervener" and the 2007 Joint Africa–EU Strategy', *Journal of Contemporary European Studies*, 18(2), pp. 209–28.

Rutazibwa, O. (2013) 'What If We Took Autonomous Recovery Seriously? A Democratic Critique of Contemporary Western Ethical Foreign Policy', *Ethical Perspectives*, 20(1), pp. 81–108.

Serequeberhan, T. (1997) 'The Critique of Eurocentrism and the Practice of African Philosophy' in Eze, E. (ed.), *Postcolonial African Philosophy: A Critical Reader*. Oxford: Blackwell Publishers, pp. 141–61.

Spivak, G. (1999) *A Critique of Postcolonial Reason: Toward a History of the Vanishing Present*. Cambridge, MA: Harvard University Press.

Spivak, G. (2004) 'Righting Wrongs', *The South Atlantic Quarterly*, 103(2/3), pp. 523–81.

Stanley, H. (1878) *Through the Dark Continent*, vols. I–III. Hamburg: Karl Grädener.

Sultana, F. (2018) 'The False Equivalence of Academic Freedom and Free Speech: Defending Academic Integrity in the Age of White Supremacy, Colonial Nostalgia, and Anti-Intellectualism', *ACME: An International Journal for Critical Geographies*, 17(2), pp. 228–57.

UK-DFID (2005) 'Why We Need to Work More Effectively in Fragile States', London: Department for International Development [online]. Available at http://www.jica.go.jp/cdstudy/library/pdf/20071101_11.pdf (accessed 18 December 2014).

US National Security Guidelines (2002) 'The National Security Strategy of the United States of America' [online]. Available at https://www.state.gov/documents/organization/63562.pdf (accessed 4 March 2018).

Wæver, O. (1995) 'Securitization and Desecuritization' in Lipschutz, R. (ed.), *On Security*. New York: Colombia University Press, pp. 46–86.

Wai, Z. (2012) 'Neo-Patrimonialism and the Discourse of State Failure in Africa', *Review of African Political Economy*, 39(131), pp. 27–43.

Wariboko, W. (2011) *Race and the Civilizing Mission: Their Implications for the Framing of Blackness and African Personhood 1800–1960. An Inaugural Presentation*. Asmara: Africa World Press.

Wesley, M. (2008) 'The State of the Art of State Building', *Global Governance*, 14(3), pp. 369–85.

World Bank (1997) 'World Development Report: The State in a Changing World' [online]. Available at https://openknowledge.worldbank.org/handle/10986/5980 (accessed 18 December 2014).

Zartman, W. (1995) 'Introduction: Posing the Problem of State Collapse' in ibid. (ed.), *Collapsed States: The Disintegration and Restoration of Legitimate Authority*. London: Lynne Riener Publishers, pp. 1–11.

5

THE ETHICAL STATE?

María do Mar Castro Varela

Introduction

> If I succeed in showing that there are Jewish resources for the criticism of
> state violence, the colonial subjugation of populations, expulsion and dispos-
> session, then I will have managed to show that a critique of Israeli state vio-
> lence is at least possible, if not ethically obligatory (Butler, 2012: 1).

Is it possible to think about the state without concomitantly engaging with ethics?
If the main concern of ethics is questions about the good and bad life, rights and
responsibility, how can the ethical dimensions of the state be disregarded when
considering issues of equality, parity of participation and inclusion? In addressing
these crucial questions, my contribution engages in a broad sense with the complex
dynamics between the state and its ethical imperatives. The point of departure for
this chapter are reflections on Judith Butler's book *Parting Ways: Jewishness and
the Critique of Zionism* (2012). Although, an assessment of the political situation of
Israel/Palestine is beyond the scope of this chapter, Butler's critical engagement
with Zionism and the State of Israel are instructive in thinking about the larger
question of how theories about the state can profit from drawing on ethical considerations. My reading of Butler's contribution on the state aims to highlight her
argumentative strategies and supplement them with previous discussions of Marxist
state-theorists like Nicos Poulantzas and Antonio Gramsci.

Although Butler in no way claims to be a state theorist, nevertheless, her critical reflections on Zionism (2012) deal with the relationship between ethics, state,
citizenship and belonging. The aim of this text is not only to outline Butler's ethical
understanding of the state, but to do this through a postcolonial lens. This would
require, first and foremost, an exposition of what postcolonial state theoretical considerations do or should do, regardless of which theoretical framework they draw

on, whether Marxist, feminist, post-structuralist or liberal. It is important to note here that to speak of *the* postcolonial understanding of the state is erroneous. To homogenise or even to harmonise the different experiences and ideas of postcolonial state formations, though tempting, is deeply problematic, since the colonial states were very diverse in their operations, which led to very different processes and outcomes of decolonisation. In addressing issues of historical violence, justice and citizenship, Butler's writings become fruitful for postcolonial theory, even as her work is in turn inspired by insights from postcolonial scholarship. This mutually productive exchange is brought into dialogue with Marxist and feminist perspectives in this chapter. After a brief overview of some critical state-theoretical considerations, a short summary of approaches to the (post-)colonial state and its relation to decolonisation movements will be presented. Finally, Butler's critical observations on the state are outlined with particular focus on the Israeli–Palestinian conflict.

State power: Gramsci, Poulantzas and Foucault

The neo-Marxist theorist Nicos Poulantzas defines the state as a *condensation of the social relations of forces*, arguing that the question of its relative autonomy is a function of class struggle. For the Greek-French legal philosopher, the state is a field of forces that is configured by social conflicts. In his book *State, Power, Socialism* (1978), Poulantzas critically examines the writings of numerous scholars, including Antonio Gramsci and Louis Althusser, who have directly influenced his reading of the state that is based on three theoretical pillars: First, the state is not regarded as a static object, but as a material condensation of power relations. For Poulantzas, it is class struggle that brings about the specific formation of the state apparatus. Second, the state consists of three spheres: the ideological, the political and the economic. Although they are intertwined, they are nevertheless also autonomous from each other. And finally, the state produces the establishment of specific conditions of power and governing, which enables the state to rule through coercion and consensus – as argued by Gramsci. Poulantzas's state theory shows the importance of ideology and, in contrast to Althusser, also the significance of economic interventions.[1] The state is described as a dynamic structure rather than a static block of violence and repression, even though, as Poulantzas remarks, the state saturates all forms of power relations through its actions.

Inspired by Michel Foucault, who in turn seems to draw on Gramsci and Poulantzas, Governmentality Studies focus on biopolitics and the production of 'docile citizens' who, without the mobilisation of the coercive apparatus of the state, are interpellated to act in the interests of the state. The population, which is the focus of governmental action, begins to govern itself by internalising the 'hegemonic'

---

1 Poulantzas's theory, unlike other neo-Marxist theories, devotes attention to the importance of state-led economic interventions and is certainly one reason for its increasing popularity among state theorists (see Demirović et al., 2010).

ideals (see, for example, Foucault, 2011). The state regulates the population primarily through direct and indirect interventions into the subject formation of its citizens or what Foucault describes as the 'conduct of conduct' (*conduire des conduits*, Foucault, 1994: 237). This not only explains the processes of subjection, but also outlines issues of agency and self-responsibilisation of citizens.

Long before Foucault, Gramsci notably discusses in the *Prison Notebooks* how consensus formation stabilises hegemonic structures. The famous Gramscian definition of state reads as follows: 'State = political society + civil society, in other words hegemony protected by the armour of coercion' (Gramsci, 1971: 263). Gramsci understands the state as double-layered: the 'civil society' and the 'political society' (ibid.). The latter is the state in the narrow sense, which is the arena of political institutions and legal, constitutional control. Gramsci stresses, however, that the twofold division is purely conceptual and that, in fact, the two dimensions overlap and interact.

In contrast to anti-state positions (for a critique, see Dhawan, 2015: 45ff; Foucault, 2011), Gramsci and Poulantzas, as well as Foucault, focus on the ethics of rule, insofar as they emphasise how citizens are governed and made governable through discourses of responsibility and accountability. While the state can promote equality and even facilitate freedom, and thus claim legitimacy through its enabling interventions, it also produces subalternity and exclusion. In a conversation with Gayatri C. Spivak, Butler points out:

> If the state is what 'binds', it is also clearly what can and does unbind. And if the state binds in the name of the nation, conjuring certain versions of the nation forcibly, if not powerfully, then it also unbinds, releases, expels, banishes (Butler and Spivak, 2007: 4–5).

Butler's understanding of the state explicitly, and occasionally implicitly, resonates with critical insights propounded by Gramsci, Poulantzas and Foucault, even as they are more forthright about their ethical concerns of how to prevent violence in the form of exclusion, stigmatisation and even genocide. Drawing on Foucault, Butler understands *raison d'état* as a 'regime of truth', a 'historically instituted order of ontology maintained through coercive effects' (Butler, 2005: 109), which organises the means, the recognition and thus the conditions of subjectivation. 'Who is normatively human: what counts as a livable life?' are the central questions that concern Butler (2006). Thus, a merely biologically functioning body is not automatically included in the category 'human'; rather to count as human, one must be recognised, addressed and defended as one. The *raison d'état* regulates who counts as human and who is excluded from this normative category. According to Butler, this leads to a collective interdependence and need for recognition, which ultimately brings with it a fundamental social vulnerability. The shared condition of human vulnerability is distinct to the historical, socio-political and economic precarity that particular subjects and groups experience when they do not receive recognition and, as such, are excluded from being legitimate political subjects and are consequently subjugated by the state. What then is the ethical responsibility, Butler asks, of the state towards its most vulnerable citizens? Why should citizens rebel against (state) oppression? When is unlimited state power unlawful and must be subjected to vehement criticism?[2] What possibly less violent ways of living together exist beyond the nation-state? Butler raises these pertinent questions, which makes her reflections on the state fruitful for postcolonial theory. However, instead of an exhaustive theory of state, she highlights the consequences of what it entails to be made vulnerable and precarious by the state, rather than being protected by it.

Feminist state theory

If Gramsci's, Poulantzas's and Foucault's approaches are not anti-state, their models can neither be described as statist nor as anarchist. Instead, they all view the state as a field of ethico-political intervention. Along similar lines, various feminist state theories, which do not necessarily see the state in opposition to feminist concerns, are not automatically statist, even as what is expected of the state varies considerably. While some feminist scholars and activists call for autonomous structures 'uncontaminated' by state interests or influence, others argue for an overhaul of institutions and policies. Without focusing on the diverse feminist positions, I will briefly devote attention to state-critical positions. One such example is the materialistic-feminist state theory propounded by Birgit Sauer, which builds on Poulantzas's ideas by particularly foregrounding the role of the (European) state in inflecting gender relations and struggles (see Sauer, 2001; Ludwig and Sauer, 2010). Here, again, the state is not only brute power and violent actor, but more of a cunning hegemon, which maintains a heteronormative gender order through, for example, tax and family policies that legitimise unequal and discriminatory intimate and social relations. The state protects patriarchal interests and favours male citizens, who benefit from a heteronormative political order.[3] It constructs white, heterosexual and Christian nuclear families in Europe, who, as the 'norm', have access to civic rights, and function as a benchmark of 'good' citizenship. Here, the (European) state becomes the enabler that grants protection and defends its citizens from 'undeserving' subjects like migrants, welfare recipients or refugees. State action is therefore ethically problematic, insofar as it provides institutional support for some of its citizens, while denying it to others.[4] This reading of the state not

---

2 In this context, arguments about 'civil disobedience' and 'boycott policy' are compelling, for which Butler has been heavily critiqued, especially for her support of the Boycott, Divestment and Sanctions (BDS) movement. Not all supporters of left-wing politics see the strategy of boycott as an appropriate and effective form of state criticism.

3 For example, as pointed out by queer feminists, pro-natalist measures introduced by the conservative ministry for family affairs in Germany primarily benefit middle-class families with children, even as these policies are welcomed and perceived to be 'women-friendly' by the heteronormative feminist politics.

4 These include measures to fund 'family-friendly' universities or the demand for female quotas in the management structures of corporations.

only endeavours to highlight the omission of gender in policies and institutions, but also to make visible the centrality of it for state action (see Seemann, 1996; also Rai, this volume). Already Carole Pateman (1988) brilliantly demonstrated how and why the liberal social contract must be understood as a gender contract that determines hierarchical gender relations and, thus, upholds patriarchal structures (for more on Pateman, see Kinna, this volume). In addition, feminist state theories centrally consider the emergence and effect of the separation of 'public' and 'private' (see Ludwig et al., 2010), as well as issues of subject formation with particular focus on gendered and sexualised citizenship, which also plays an important role in postcolonial reflections on the state (see Castro Varela and Dhawan, 2006). In my view, the subversion of the hegemonic heteronormative order, which is produced by state institutions, sometimes paradoxically requires other hegemonic structures to be mobilised against the state. For instance, through the promotion of anti-discrimination policies and protection of women's human rights, the state can be made to act against the interests of the dominant citizens. This counters the characterisation of the state as an insurmountable monster to which vulnerable citizens are helplessly subjected.

The postcolonial state and the question of sovereignty

Despite decades of postcolonial critique, Western state-theoretical considerations, even feminist approaches, continue to be plagued by Eurocentrism. For instance, the emergence of nation-states, whether European or non-European state formations, are rarely considered against the backdrop of colonial history, even in feminist debates (see Anghie, 2007; Castro Varela and Dhawan, 2015b; Krämer, this volume). On the other hand, critical perspectives such as those of Gramsci, Poulantzas and Foucault have inspired postcolonial theorists to examine the colonial and post-colonial state in light of the interdependence of state-building and imperial rule. Such an approach understands the formation of states as complex, contradictory and ambivalent. Accordingly, the emergence of the postcolonial state is not just an effect of colonial domination, as argued by Aníbal Quijano (2008), but also of anti-colonial struggles and is thereby also a symbol of liberation. Thus, Quijano's idea of 'coloniality of power', which outlines the continuity of colonial regimes in the neo-colonial constitution of the world, must be supplemented with the histories and experiences of resistance, hopes and aspirations that inflect the formation of the postcolonial states. As argued by Dhawan (this volume), postcolonial states are like *pharmakon*, in that they can be both medicine and poison.

Another important concept for postcolonial debates is sovereignty, which is also of significance in Butler's writings. Instead of locating the emergence of the sovereignty doctrine in the 1648 Treaty of Westphalia, the postcolonial legal theorist Anghie (2007) presents an alternative history of international law by tracing its colonial origins and the constitutive role played by colonialism in establishing a Eurocentric understanding of sovereignty. While the Westphalian definition codified the autonomy and thus equality of all European states, the non-European world was not granted the same status. Anghie explores the continuity of this Euro-centrism in contemporary international law, which, though claiming universal-ity, has never overcome this fundamental asymmetry between the former colonial powers and the postcolonial world. The strategy of legitimising colonialism as a civilising mission and the dualism between 'civilized' and 'uncivilized' is repeated in current international discourses through categories such as 'developed' and 'under-developed' economies and legal systems (see Castro Varela and Dhawan 2015b). Without the instrument of international law and the concomitant idea of private property, the subsequent expropriation of land and resources in the colonies could not have been legitimised as legal. Along similar lines, current humanitarian and military interventions by Euro-American countries in the former colonies vio-late the sovereignty of postcolonial states in the name of upholding international law and order (see Anghie and Chimni, 2003). Postcolonial scholars highlight the asymmetry between the state of the Global North and those of the Global South as a tragic legacy of colonialism (see Krämer, this volume).

Judith Butler's perspective on state (criticism)

Butler, especially in her later writings, such as *Frames of War: When is Life Grievable?* (2009) and *Parting Ways: Jewishness and the Critique of Zionism* (2012), addresses the ethical responsibilities of the state and focuses on questions such as: Why is the support of the so-called 'war on terror' ethically untenable? Or why is the politics of the State of Israel problematic? Butler takes her subject position as a 'US citizen' and as a 'Jewish intellectual' as a significant challenge for her self-critical reflections:

> If, however, the question of the ethical relation to the non-Jew has become definitive of what is Jewish, then we cannot capture or consolidate what is Jewish in this relation. Relationality displaces ontology, and it is a good thing, too. The point is not to stabilize the ontology of the Jew or of Jewishness, but rather to understand the ethical and political implications of a relation to alterity that is irreversible and defining and without which we cannot make sense of such fundamental terms as equality or justice. Such a relation, which is surely not singular, will be the obligatory passage beyond identity and nation as defining frameworks (Butler, 2012: 5).

She outlines how being interpellated as 'Jewish' or 'US citizen', while offering membership to a political, religious, cultural and ethnic collectivity, brings with it a special ethical responsibility towards those who are considered to be non-affiliated to these groups. Ultimately, belonging always rests parasitically on non-belonging. As opposed to the claims of her critics, Butler does not evade positioning herself; instead, she uses this as a site from which she situates her critical and ethical delib-erations. This involves persistent questioning, scrutiny and interruption of speaking 'in the name of' (see Butler, 2012: 117). She does not claim to write as a 'Jew', but instead examines what it means to be 'Jewish'. Rather than disowning her US citizenship, she sees herself called upon to contest the hegemonic Western rhetoric of representation. To position oneself vis-á-vis the state is for her 'the precondition of any effort to think about territory, property, sovereignty, and cohabitation' (Butler 2012: 11). If the state, as Poulantzas argued, is a dynamic structure rather than a static block of violence and repression, then it is disingenuous to simply dismiss the state as straightforwardly coercive and thus unethical, even when it favours some citizens over others. It is important to focus on the historical dynamics as well as the changing intersections of power that create differing matrixes of agency and vulnerability and the ramifications for understandings of 'citizenship', 'belonging' and 'cohabitation'. These are critical terms that bring together postcolonial, feminist, Marxist and poststructuralist concerns in Butler's writings. What does sovereignty mean in the face of occupation and dominance legitimised through the constitution and institutions of the state? How is a global coexistence in the face of differences conceivable? Butler's effort is to seek ways of criticising the state, without being punished or sanctioned for it, although the danger of being 'exiled' from one's community is ever present. Butler takes upon herself the responsibility of criticising the Israeli state as a Jewish intellectual, like many other Jewish critics of the State of Israel, despite the risk of being labelled 'anti-Semitic' and 'a self-hating Jew'.[5] She notes that the only way to counter the accusation of anti-Semitism when critiquing the State of Israel is to point out time and again, with collective support, that critiquing Israeli state violence is justified and necessary, even as anti-Semitism against the Jewish people is absolutely unacceptable (Butler, 2012: 20).

It is in this context that Butler also thinks about the function of the diasporic intellectual, which bears close resemblance to Edward Said's concept of the 'secular intellectual' (see Said, 2000).[6] According to Said, the critique of a community, to which one belongs or wishes to belong to, is best achieved from the place of exile, namely, from the 'outside'. The process of exclusion inadvertently allows the critic a 'double perspective' (ibid.: 44) that enables the thinker to view the supposed 'homeland' from a distance and to examine how the state performs itself. In doing this, the intellectual undertakes the difficult journey from the centre to the margin. For Said, exile is a necessity and a source of despair for the critical worldliness of intellectual practice. The critic is not merely a translator or even reporter of a random series of events it witnesses, but biographically connected with the world in which he or she dwells. Said's concept of secular criticism is self-reflexive, yet sceptical, and is always aware of its shortcomings and failings (see Said, 1983: 26). Likewise, it emphasises the necessary condition of a real or metaphorical exile, which, according to Said, enables the pluralisation and diversifications of perspectives as an essential facet for the exercise of critique. Accordingly, Butler, who is not an Israeli citizen, but who identifies herself as a Jewish intellectual, claims responsibility for the actions of the Israeli state, particularly because Israel understands

5 A fate that she sadly shares with prominent Jewish intellectuals like Hannah Arendt and Walter Benjamin.
6 In *Reflections on Exile* (2000: 171–3), Said states unequivocally that one of the responsibilities of the intellectual is to speak for those who have been expelled and dispossessed from their homelands.

itself as a *Jewish* state (for a critical reading, see Herman, this volume). Butler could be understood as speaking from a position of exile, from a site of critical distance, which perhaps allows her a more nuanced view on Israel and her position as a quasi-member of the same. Nevertheless, as she points out: 'The opposition to Zionism requires the departure from Jewishness as an exclusionary framework for thinking both ethics and politics' (Butler, 2012: 2). Butler's postcolonial understanding of the state is not limited to the question of Israel/Palestine. In her writings and lectures, she critically highlights the production of non-citizens in the US, especially with regard to immigrants from Mexico who are denied citizenship rights (Butler and Spivak, 2007). Furthermore, she focuses on the consequences of the so-called 'war on terror' in the aftermath of 9/11. Butler draws attention to the unlawful, indefinite detention of those accused of terrorism in Guantanamo, the torture scandals in Abu Ghraib, Iraq, the drone bombings in Afghanistan, Pakistan and Iraq. She points to the 'embedded war coverage' which reports 'nameless deaths' that we only encounter as mere numbers, in contrast to the 'heroically deceased' US-American soldiers, who have names and faces and whose deaths are mourned and grieved (see Butler, 2006, 2009; Carver and Chambers, 2008). Her texts on Israel/Palestine are of particular interest here because Butler explores in them, more explicitly than in her other writings, alternatives to a situation that seems to suggest that the only two ethical options facing the state are either to destroy or to be destroyed (Butler, 2012: 98).

Jewish criticism of Zionism

> Only by dissolving colonial subjugation will coexistence become thinkable (Butler, 2012: 50).

The State of Israel, as we know it today, is just as unimaginable without a Zionist movement as it is without the *Shoah*. The creation of the Israeli state in 1948 was the fulfillment of the promise that diasporic Jewish people from all over the world would find a 'home', where they could live free from persecution and in peace. For Palestinians living in the same territory, however, the realisation of the promise of 'Israel' resulted in expulsion and subjugation. Butler remarks: 'Israel claims to represent the Jewish people, and popular opinion tends to assume that Jews "support" Israel without taking into account Jewish traditions of anti-Zionism and the presence of Jews in coalitions that oppose the Israeli colonial subjugation of Palestinians' (ibid.: 2).

While for some, the emergence of Israel is a blessing after centuries of persecution and expulsion from different places and the horrors experienced under the Nazi regime, for others it is a catastrophe (*Naqba*). For Butler, these different views and experiences of the same political event form the central focus of her ethical reflections.

In *Parting Ways*, Butler emphasises that her ethical disagreements with the aims and aspirations of the Zionist movement and their understanding of the Israel/

Palestine conflict is embedded in a tradition of Jewish thought. Butler's inspiration includes the writings of Hannah Arendt, Martin Buber, Walter Benjamin, Franz Kafka, Primo Levi and Emmanuel Lévinas. She explains, however, that concepts provided by a specific tradition – in this case the Jewish one – can only have a wider impact if they are disseminated through a process of translation (Butler, 2012: 7). It is important, Butler points out, that the intent of the concepts is exceeded through transgression, hybridisation and contamination. In outlining the numerous Jewish positions vis-à-vis Zionist perspectives, she states that 'equality', 'justice' and 'cohabitation', as well as 'criticism of state power', can only represent 'Jewish values' if they are not claimed to be exclusively Jewish (ibid.: 5). Thus, even as she links these norms to Jewish thinkers who proclaimed universal validity of these ideas, at the same time, she rejects their monopolisation as exclusively Jewish (ibid.: 2). Furthermore, she views the 'Jewish-ethical tradition' to be larger than the question of Zionism. Taking 'Jewish thinking' as the point of departure of her critique of Zionism is an ingenious move by Butler in delineating the limitations of the latter. It is important to note that Butler insists on the urgency of criticism of the State of Israel without in any way questioning its right to exist.

The influence of postcolonial thought on Butler's analysis of the conflict in this highly contested region (both militarily as well as ideologically) is also significant. She traces the multiple experiences of historical violence that inflect the region. To add to the complexity, she foregrounds the religious struggles between Christians, Muslims and Jews, the legacies of the *Shoah*, the influence of Zionism, and the ongoing war that persists despite countless diplomatic, political and educational attempts to bring peace to the region.

Butler has been massively attacked for her critique of Israeli state violence. But she is not the first Jewish intellectual to have been accused of being 'a self-hating Jew' and anti-Semitic for having engaged with anti-Zionist positions: Arendt, for example, was also reproached for her position on the Eichmann trial (Arendt, 2006; also Neiman, 2015) and her 'being Jewish' was repeatedly called into question. Gershom Scholem described Arendt as 'heartless' (Butler, 2012: 132). Along similar lines, Butler has been accused of being unpatriotic for her critique of the US intervention in Afghanistan and Iraq, while her politics vis-à-vis the Israeli state have earned her the charge of anti-Semitism. Despite these challenges, Butler continues to pursue a resilient and robust critical stance instead of intellectual surrender.[7] In an interview given in 2010 to the Israeli journal *Haaretz*, she points out: 'So how can I fulfill my obligation as a Jew to speak out against an injustice when, in speaking out against Israeli state and military injustice, I am accused of not being a good enough Jew or of being a self-hating Jew? This is the bind of my current situation.'[8]

---

7 One of the low points was certainly the protests of the Central Council of Jews in September 2012 in Germany against the Adorno Prize being awarded to Butler in Frankfurt am Main. Despite receiving the prize, Butler was vilified as 'anti-Semitic' and 'Israel hater' in the media.

8 See full interview: https://www.haaretz.com/1.5052023 (accessed 6 March 2019).

Drawing on Buber's position on cultural Zionism, Butler insists on the possibility and urgency of cohabitation and binationalism (Butler, 2012: 36). She concurs with Arendt that political Zionism can never be democratic. Arendt, who was initially pro-Zionist, later changed her position and was critical of Zionism. Arendt argued that the plurality of the demos is in a sense the precondition for political life. According to Arendt, a state that seeks to limit this plurality – and Butler agrees with her – is not only racist, but potentially genocidal (ibid.: 100). This is a valuable lesson from the postcolonial world, where, for example in Rwanda, the legacies of colonial racial rule tragically ended in genocide. The belief that a nation-state must be homogeneous when it comes to religion or ethnicity determines who may live within the borders and consequently easily justifies illegitimate state violence and civil wars. Although many non-Jews live in Israel, the definition of Israel as a Jewish state determines who has the possibility to access all the rights as citizens. Against this ideology, Butler argues: 'To cohabit the earth is prior to any possible community or nation or neighbourhood. We might sometimes choose where to live, and who to live by or with, but we cannot choose with whom to cohabit the earth' (ibid.: 125). This resonates with Arendt, who, as Butler reminds us, recommended 'nation without territory' (ibid.: 137) and opposed any form of assimilation of difference. This was an important lesson that Arendt learned from her own biographical experience of being persecuted during the Nazi regime (ibid.: 152). The 'nation' as outlined in Arendt's 'Jewish Writings' reads like a non-territorial community and suggests the possibility of an ethical imagination of belonging that would go against the very idea of a terrritorialised nation-state.

Limits of the ethical

> It is not easy to defend a notion of ethics, including key notions such as freedom and responsibility, in the face of their discursive appropriation
> *(Butler, 2015: 14).*

In all her writings, Butler deals with issues of identity, affiliation and subjectification, as well as with the question of responsible action in the face of global violence and injustice. In the introduction of *Parting Ways*, she emphasises that her biography certainly plays an important role in her engagement with these issues (see Butler, 2012: 20), but that there were five points that informed her arguments on 'militarism', '(state-)power' and 'Israel/Palestine'. She explains why she turns to Jewish authors in particular, in order to find answers to current political challenges. For Butler, certain Jewish values have always been an important inspiration to her in formulating a critique of militarism and nationalism. In addition, her ethical relationship with non-Jewish groups is central to her understanding of non-identitarian ethical approaches that include a focus on 'global democracy' and 'global cohabitation'. Third, she emphasises that the critique of unjustified coercive state power is central to the history of radical democratic social movements to which Jewish (female) activists have made significant contributions. These include protests against economic exploitation and systematic impoverishment induced by government action. Furthermore, according to Butler, the plight of refugees and stateless persons has strongly influenced her thinking, which is also why she has turned to Arendt's writings in recent years. And finally, the Jewish practice of shared mourning (the Jewish tradition of observing Shiva and reciting Kaddish in a supportive community) reminded her of the importance of collective recognition of human life. This is why she believes that ethical relationships give us an insight into whom we mourn collectively, whose death we take note of as a community and who is not deemed worthy of mourning (ibid.: 21).

Lévinas occupies a prominent place in Butler's writings. Like him, she repeatedly emphasises that responsibility towards those who are not recognised as affiliated to one's community is imperative. 'What might be done', she wonders, 'to shift the very terms of recognizability in order to produce more radically democratic results?' (Butler, 2009: 6). Drawing on Lévinas, whose ethical writings are as influenced by the reading of the Talmud as by Western philosophy, Butler develops radical ethical imperatives and proposes a form of non-violence: 'Indeed, responsibility is not a matter of cultivating a will (as it is for the Kantians), but of recognising unwilling susceptibility as a resource for becoming responsive to the Other' (Butler, 2012: 43). In Lévinas's ethical reflections, the Other is not distanced, rather the Other not only constitutes the Self in a fundamental way, but interrupts it and is thus fundamentally entangled with it (ibid.: 60). Lévinas's ethics is a persistent call to respond to the suffering of others.

However, Butler also deals critically with Lévinas's work, whose ethical-philosophical considerations she underwrites, but also questions. Although Lévinas speaks of the 'responsibility of the persecuted', he also describes Palestinians as 'faceless' and Asians as 'underdeveloped people' to whom the Jewish and Christian community are not ethically committed (cit. in Caygill, 2002: 182–3). According to Lévinas, ethics cannot be based on 'exotic cultures' (Butler, 2012: 46ff).[9] Butler argues: 'The fact that Palestinians remain faceless for him (or that they are the paradigm for the faceless) produces a rather stark quandary, since Levinas gives us so many reasons to extrapolate politically on the prohibition against killing' (Butler, 2012: 39).

In a move that Butler calls 'Lévinas v. Lévinas' (ibid.: 54), she tries to use his ethical ideas – in the spirit of Spivak's 'affirmative sabotage' (2012) – to reject his claim of impossibility of understanding Arabs and the Orient. Butler wonders why it is not possible for Lévinas to recognise 'the face' of the Palestinians? Why are ethical principles being denied to those who were disenfranchised, displaced, murdered and oppressed? Butler questions whether persecuted Jews have more rights than persecuted Palestinians (2012: 29)?

9 This is a disheartening example of the failure of ethical thinking, for Lévinas, as member of the French army, was prisoner of war in 1940, while his parents and brothers were murdered by the Nazis. The Lithuanian-French philosopher, who studied with Husserl and Heidegger, never again set foot on German soil.

Lévinas's arguments seem to echo the reasoning of the Enlightenment philosophers, who in their ethical promulgations excluded the colonised from the category of the human, so that liberal principles of equality and emancipation could be upheld for the Europeans, while legitimising colonial subjugation of the natives. A notable example is Immanuel Kant, whose infamous racist writings seem difficult to reconcile with his ethical principles.[10] Even Arendt, who eventually distanced herself from political Zionism, reproduces racial stereotypes (ibid.: 139; and Castro Varela 2014b). Butler bemoans that such a thoughtful scholar exerts normative violence, but instead of rejecting Arendt's writings, she mobilises Arendt's critical interventions against political Zionism to bolster her own arguments.[11]

Here, it seems instructive to turn attention to Said's essay, 'Zionism from the Standpoints of its Victims' (1997: 30), first published in 1979, wherein he outlines the similarities between the reasoning of the Zionist movement and European colonial discourses insofar as both characterise the territory to be populated as 'empty'. According to Said, Zionism is supported by a 'colonial vision' (ibid.: 24) that makes it impossible for Jewish settlers to grasp the injustice that is done to the Palestinians. 'The dehumanization of the Arab, which began with the view that Palestinians were either not there or savages, or both, saturates everything in Israeli society' (ibid.: 34). While Zionist ideology empowers Jewish women, according to Said, it simultaneously disempowers Palestinian women (see ibid.). Butler does not mention this important and much-discussed argument in *Parting Ways*,[12] but does argue that although the Jewish intellectual tradition is deeply influenced by Zionist ideas (see ibid.: 37), it is still possible to use Jewish thought to critique Zionism.

At the same time, Said calls for a critique of the deniers of the Holocaust in the Arab world. He calls on the Arabs to recognise the tragedy of the Holocaust as a sign of their humanity and their recognition of Jewish suffering, without letting the Israeli state use this as a blank check to subjugate the Palestinians. If the Palestinians expect the world to hear and see their suffering, according to Said, they, too, must acknowledge the sufferings of others, even their own oppressors. Said refutes simplistic ideas of *bien-pensants* intellectuals who disavow the relationship between the Holocaust and Israel (see Said, 2001: 285). Butler's own ethical considerations are inspired by similar reasoning that rejects ideas of states that are

10 One could name innumerable examples – such as of John Stuart Mill or Karl Marx, who limited their ideas of freedom and humanism to the Western world (see Said, 1997: 22). Even the defender of the colonised 'indigenous people', the humanist Dominican monk Bartolomé de las Casas, who accused the Spanish colonisers of cruelty, did not view all indigenous people as human and categorised them as barbarians (see Castro Varela and Dhawan 2015a: 25–6).

11 One could fault Butler for still using Arendt; however, in my view, instead of censorship and denunciation, it seems more fruitful to explore the aporias and contradictions in the text, as suggested by Derridean deconstruction, to read it against the grain (see also Castro Varela 2014a).

12 Ella Shohat's essay 'Sephardim in Israel: Zionism from the Standpoint of Its Jewish Victims' (1988), which supplements Said's analysis and focuses on the disenfranchisement of the so-called 'Oriental Jews', is also not discussed in Butler's reflections on Israel/Palestine. For Shohat, Zionism is essentially a European-Jewish project. Mizrahi Jews have always been represented as culturally inferior in Zionist discourse, and face socio-economic disadvantages in Israel.

based on notions of 'purity' and 'homogeneity' of one's own group, while denying the history and experiences of violence and suffering of other groups. For Butler, democracy is always plural and involves cohabitating with people and communities that we cannot choose in advance. In Arendt's writings, she finds inspiration against pseudo-democratic nation-states that view plurality as a threat and justify regulation of who should (not) be permitted to live in which territory (see Butler 2012: 100).

Utopias of peaceful coexistence

> Although it is commonly said that a one-state-solution and an ideal of binationalism are impracticable goals . . . it is doubtless equally true that a world in which no one held out for a one-state solution and no one thought anymore about binationalism would be a radically impoverished world (Butler, 2012: 28).

Butler claims that critique must also come from Jewish people outside Israel, who for ethical reasons must question Israeli state violence that is justified in their name. In Butler's view, the State of Israel is a colony and she vehemently distances herself from political Zionism that asserts the historical right of Jewish people in the occupied territories and the disenfranchisement of Palestinians. In her view, the territories which are now part of 'Israel' (including the occupied territories) were expropriated by means of military action from the population living there previously and declared to be Jewish 'home'.[13] Paradoxically, the moral legitimacy of this subjugation and expropriation is achieved by denying humanity to dispossessed Palestinian subjects. For Butler, it is beyond question that the territories that make up the State of Israel today were illegally occupied and, accordingly, repeatedly speaks of the expropriation, expulsion and subjugation of the Palestinians. In her critical examination of the nation-state of Israel, Butler explores the possibilities of critique of the colonial state.

Another important aspect is the question of belonging, which frames the nation-state. If, as Benedict Anderson (1983) argues, this represents an 'imagined community', then it is crucial to examine who has the right to determine the criteria of belonging. Following Tariq Modood, Butler (2009: 139) states that belonging to a nation-state entails full citizenship rights, which not only includes recognition as citizens, but also, as Modood argues, the ability to influence the conditions of recognition. Butler (ibid.: 149) outlines how state action is framed by powerful modes of intelligibility that transcend the domain of the state. The state works within an ontological horizon that precedes and surpasses state power. By way of example, Butler takes the normative idea asserted by the Zionist political movement, which determines who as a citizen of Israel finds recognition and who does not. Land and

---

13 The classic cases of settler colonies are the US, New Zealand, Australia and Canada, where the vast majority of indigenous peoples were victims of gruesome genocide, and the surviving generations were forced to live in reservations.

body, as well as identity, history and religion, form a powerful alliance here, making certain citizens of Israel legible as legitimate, while Muslim Palestinians – and to some extent also Christian Israeli Arabs – become the constitutive inside/outside of the demos (see Shohat, 1988).

Here, Arendt's writings, particularly on the plight of the stateless, are very instructive. Millions of people lost the protection of the state under the Nazi regime, and many more millions suffered as a consequence of the First and Second World Wars. Since then, despite efforts of the international community and the ratification of the UDHR (universal declaration of human rights) by the majority of states, individual states remain the main addressees and guarantors of the rights of citizens. At the same time, the national state produces statelessness through its normative framing of civic norms and marginalises those who are designated as non-citizens (see Arendt, 1994, 1943). Arendt, who in Butler's view was largely misunderstood, did not want to defend the nation-state; rather, Arendt outlined the limitations of both universal human rights and nation-states in protecting vulnerable subjects. Drawing lessons from historical experiences, Butler argues that she is in favour of a binational State of Israel/Palestine that enables cohabitation in the face of difference and wonders whether binationalism can translate into deconstruction of nationalism (Butler, 2012: 110). Arendt proposed the idea of a federal state, wherein small, local communities of Jews and Arabs could live together under the mandate of the United Nations (ibid.: 146). According to Butler, the goal was not to share sovereignty, but to undermine the idea of sovereignty altogether (ibid.). Arendt's and Butler's arguments echo postcolonial critique of state-formation and sovereignty, which always disadvantages vulnerable people.

Although Butler's ideas of cohabitation and binationalism may not seem plausible for politicians and policy-makers, and might be dismissed as yet another attempt by a US-American scholar to solve the problems of the Middle East, her criticism of Israeli state violence in particular and ethical-philosophical reflections on the coercive power of the state in general are instructive for anyone interested in imagining a post-imperial world order.

Although diplomatic attempts to find a peaceful solution in this region have hitherto failed, utopian thinking remains an important resource to imagine non-dominant futures. Frantz Fanon, for instance, on the one hand spoke of the 'purifying power' of anti-colonial struggle, but also hoped for 'another humanism' in the aftermath of decolonisation, which would usher in another world (Fanon, 2004 [1961]). Like Fanon and Said, Butler's ideas, too, push the imagination beyond pragmatic *realpolitik* and her analysis tries to give Lévinas's 'faceless' a 'face'.[14]

---

14 In addition to his academic career, Said was a frequent talk-show guest for the autonomous Palestinian government in exile, contributing not only to newspapers, but also appearing in popular media. In his work, Said particularly focused on the (mis)representation of the so-called 'Orient', of Palestine, the Arab world and the Arab Diaspora.

Conclusion

Butler's understanding of the state can only be understood through an ethical examination of notions of belonging, sovereignty, cohabitation and binationalism. In her writings, she explores possibilities of a critique of the state such that it addresses the plight of those particularly vulnerable to coercive state power. Her engagement with vulnerability is strongly influenced by her own experience of precarity and exposure to normative violence.

In light of these considerations, Butler is concerned with how the state withholds elementary rights and protections from those classed as 'illegal' and 'undeserving'. Her critique of the state, in my view, is driven by the effort to undo vulnerability by ensuring that justice is also guaranteed to those who are excluded from the demos and not just limited to those constituted as 'legitimate' bearers of citizenship rights.

Butler's critique of Zionism and Israeli state violence has earned her the ire of many, who threaten to exclude her from the Jewish community. Ironically, given that there is no such thing as a single Jewish community, this seems an empty threat. In turn, Butler argues that she particularly draws inspiration from the Jewish tradition and sees herself called upon to critique both Zionism and Israeli state violence as long as they deny the rights of the Palestinians and other vulnerable groups. Her larger project is to counteract dominant normative theories and practices and to envisage a global, anti-identitarian democracy.

In addition to politics and ethics, Butler also highlights the aesthetic aspects of critical thinking and concludes her book, *Parting Ways*, with a passage written by the Palestinian poet Mahmoud Darwish to emphasise the need to imagine other worlds and other ways of cohabitation through literature, poetry, music and art that enable us to transcend boundaries and expand our imagination (see also Spivak, 2004):

> Darwish invokes Said in his contrapuntal ode: 'He says: I am from there, I am from here,/But I am neither there nor here.' Who can say these lines? The ones who are within the State of Israel: surely. The Palestinians in the West Bank or Gaza: surely. In refugee camps in southern Lebanon: yes. Exile is the name of separation, but alliance is found precisely there, not yet in a place, in a place that was and is and in the impossible place of the not yet, happening now (Butler, 2012: 224).

In order to countervail state violence, Butler, drawing on Arendt and Benjamin, seeks multiple ways of resistance:

> It may well be . . . that we must oppose law, act against it, even engage in provisional anarchism when law becomes unjust. But there is no reason to think that the only way to oppose or suspend law is through recourse to an extralegal sovereignty (Butler, 2012: 173).

According to Butler, extra-legal forms of resistance are necessary in extreme cases when other forms of resistance are rendered ineffective. Imagining a world in which peaceful coexistence of difference is possible seems merely utopian and yet it is necessary. As Butler points out, we should 'try to think for a moment not only about whether all nationalisms are the same (they surely are not), but what we might mean by "nation"'. Citizens that are able to intervene in existing *social relations of forces*, to use Poulantza's terms, can function as agents of resistance by breaking with the hegemonic consensus. An ethical state can only emerge when it has fearless-thinking citizens, who challenge it persistently. Interestingly, the state has an obligation to provide the necessary educational opportunities and open spaces from which the civil society might intercede into state power and hold the state accountable. The politics of the governed makes the state ethical (see Dhawan in this volume).

References

Anderson, B. (1983) *Imagined Communities: Reflections on the Origin and Spread of Nationalism.* New York: Verso.

Anghie, A. (2007) *Imperialism, Sovereignty, and the Making of International Law.* Cambridge: Cambridge University Press.

Anghie, A. and Chimni, B. S. (2003) 'Third World Approaches to International Law and Individual Responsibility in Internal Conflicts', *Chinese Journal of International Law*, 2(1), pp. 77–103.

Arendt, A. (1943) 'We Refugees', Menorah Journal, 31(1), pp. 69–77.

Arendt, H. (1994) 'We Refugees' in Robinson, M. (ed.), *Altogether Elsewhere: Writers on Exile*, Boston: Faber & Faber, pp. 110–19.

Arendt, H. (2006) *Eichmann in Jerusalem: A Report on the Banality of Evil.* New York: Penguin Books.

Butler, J. (2005) *Giving an Account of Oneself.* New York: Fordham University Press.

Butler, J. (2006) *Precarious Life: The Powers of Mourning and Violence.* London and New York: Verso.

Butler, J. (2009) *Frames of War: When is Life Grievable?* New York: Verso.

Butler, J. (2012) *Parting Ways: Jewishness and the Critique of Zionism.* New York: Columbia University Press.

Butler, J. (2015) *Notes Toward a Performative Theory of Assembly.* Boston, MA: Harvard University Press.

Butler, J. and Spivak, G. C. (2007) *Who Sings the Nation-State?* Calcutta, New York and Oxford: Seagull Books.

Carver, T. and Chambers, S. A. (eds.) (2008) *Judith Butler's Precarious Politics: Critical Encounters.* New York: Routledge.

Castro Varela, M. (2014a) 'Lazy Politics. Antisemitismus, Rassismus und die Notwendigkeit politischer Arbeit' in Hentges, G. and Nottbohm, K. (eds.). *Sprache – Macht – Rassismus.* Berlin: Metropol, pp. 17–34.

Castro Varela, M. (2014b) 'Uncanny Entanglements: Holocaust, Colonialism and Enlightenment' in Dhawan, N. (ed.), *Decolonizing Enlightenment: Transnational Justice, Human Rights and Democracy in a Postcolonial World.* Berlin and Toronto: Opladen, pp. 115–38.

Castro Varela, M. and Dhawan, N. (2006) 'Das Dilemma der Gerechtigkeit: Migration, Religion und Gender', *Das Argument*, 266, pp. 427–40.

Castro Varela, M. and Dhawan, N. (2015a) *Postkoloniale Theorie: Eine kritische Einführung*. Bielefeld: transcript.

Castro Varela, M. and Dhawan, N. (2015b) 'Postkoloniale Studien und Internationale Beziehungen: Die IB dekolonisieren' in Masala, C. and Sauer, F. (eds.), *Handbuch Internationale Beziehungen*. Wiesbaden: VS.

Caygill, H. (2002) *Levinas and the Political*. London and New York: Routledge.

Demirović, A., Adolphs, S. and Karakayali, S. (eds.) (2010) *Das Staatsverständnis von Nicos Poulantzas: Der Staat als gesellschaftliches Verhältnis*. Baden-Baden: Nomos.

Dhawan, N. (2015) 'Homonationalism and State-Phobia: The Postcolonial Predicament of Queering Modernities' in Lavinas Picq, M. and Viteri, M.A. (eds.), *Queering Narratives of Modernity*. New York: Peter Lang, pp. 51–68.

Fanon, F. (2004 [1961]) *The Wretched of the Earth*. New York: Grove Press.

Foucault, M. (1994) *Dits et écrits IV*. Paris: Gallimard.

Foucault, M. (2011) *The Government of Self and Others: Lectures at the College de France, 1982–83*. Basingstoke: Palgrave Macmillan.

Gramsci, A. (1971) *Selections from the Prison Notebooks*. New York: International Publishers.

Ludwig, G., Sauer, B. and Wöhl, S. (eds.) (2010) *Staat und Geschlecht: Grundlagen und aktuelle Herausforderungen feministischer Staatstheorie*. Baden-Baden: Nomos.

Ludwig, G. and Sauer, B. (2010) 'Engendering Poulantzas oder: Sinn und Zweck feministischer Anrufung materialistischer Staatstheorie' in Demirovic, A., Adolphs, S. and Karakayali, S. (eds.), *Das Staatsverständnis von Nicos Poulantzas: Der Staat als gesellschaftliches Verhältnis*. Baden-Baden: Nomos, pp. 173–88.

Neiman, S. (2015) *Evil in Modern Thought an Alternative History of Philosophy*. Princeton: Princeton University Press.

Osterhammel, J. (1995) *Kolonialismus. Geschichte – Formen – Folgen*. Munich: Beck.

Pateman, C. (1988) *The Sexual Contract*. Stanford, CA: Stanford University Press.

Poulantzas, N. (2002 [1978]) *Staatstheorie: Politischer Überbau, Ideologie, Autoritärer Etatismus*. Hamburg: VSA.

Quijano, A. (2008) 'Coloniality of Power, Eurocentrism, and Social Classification' in Moraña, M., Dussel, E. and Jáuregui, C. A. (eds.), *Coloniality at Large: Latin America and the Postcolonial Debate*. Durham, NC: Duke University Press, pp. 181–224.

Said, E. (1983) *The World, the Text and the Critic*. Cambridge, MA: Harvard University Press.

Said, E. (1997) 'Zionism from the Standpoints of Its Victims' in McClintock, A., Mufti, A. and Shohat, E. (eds.), *Dangerous Liaisons: Gender, Nation, and Postcolonial Perspectives*. Minneapolis, MN: University of Minnesota Press, pp. 15–38.

Said, E. (2000) *Reflections on Exile and Other Essays*. Cambridge, MA: Harvard University Press.

Said, E. (2001) *The End of the Peace Process: Oslo and After*. New York: Pantheon Books.

Sauer, B. (2001) *Die Asche des Souveräns: Staat und Demokratie in der Geschlechterdebatte*. Frankfurt am Main: Suhrkamp.

Seemann, B. (1996) *Feministische Staatstheorie: Der Staat in der deutschen Frauen- und Patriarchatsforschung*. Opladen: Leske und Budrich.

Shohat, E. (1988) 'Sephardim in Israel: Zionism from the Standpoint of Its Jewish Victims', *Social Text*, 19/20, pp. 1–35.

Spivak, G. C. (2004) *Death of a Discipline*. Calcutta: Seagull Books.

Spivak, G. C. (2012) *The Aesthetic Education in the Era of Globalization*. Cambridge, MA: Harvard University Press.

6

CHRISTIAN ISRAEL

Didi Herman

This chapter offers a counter-narrative on the Israeli state. It is intended to be a contribution to two rarely connected fields – the critical study of Christianity – and critical scholarship of 'the left' on Israel.[1] In terms of the former, I discuss Israel as an example of the formative power of Christianity and Christendom – how Christianity, as a social and political force, has been instrumental in the making and sustaining of Israel. In terms of the latter, left scholarship on Israel, I hope to show why the concept of Christianity is highly relevant to our understandings of Israeli state formation, even if, indeed perhaps *because of*, how progressive scholarship largely ignores it. My aim is not to replace concepts such as 'settler colony', 'race' or 'apartheid' – those consistently reiterated in left scholarship[2] – but to argue that Christianity is also foundational. That Israel is a Jewish state goes without saying. It privileges Jews in state law, and privileges Jewish law in the state. But Israel is not just or only a Jewish state. It is a state established on land with a polytheistic, Jewish, Orthodox and Latin Christian, and Islamic history that goes back thousands of years. We can conceive of Israel as no more (nor less) than a Western settler colony engaged in a project of dispossession and genocide against an indigenous population. But, if we can *also* understand Israel in its historical, regional and spiritual contexts, I would argue that our imaginings of Israel's past, present and futures

---

1 I use the phrase 'left scholarship' to denote the work of a range of diverse academics who are writing on Israel/Palestine (see note below). The phrase obviously lacks subtlety, but it is a shorthand that I find useful. In terms of this chapter, it is accurate to say that whatever their differences, 'left' scholarship, on the whole, ignores Christianity's role in the making and sustaining of Israel.

2 See e.g. Abu-Laban and Bakan, 2008; Abu El-Haj, 2010; Bakan and Abu-Laban, 2009; De Jong, 2017; Ghanim, 2008; Goldberg, 2008; Khoury, 2012; Lentin, 2008; Lloyd, 2012; Massad, 2006; McMahon, 2014; Morgensen, 2012; Nadeau and Sears, 2010; Razack, 2010; Rodinson, 1973; Rose and Rose, 2008; Said, 1980; Salaita, 2011; Shalhoub-Kevorkian, 2014; Veracini, 2010, 2014; Wolfe, 2006, 2012.

are enhanced. The story of Christianity in the making of Israel is a neglected one that this chapter is intended to elucidate.

My deployment of the terms 'Christianity' and 'Christendom' is not intended to homogenise Christianity nor to marginalise the fact that Christianity is riven by historical and contemporary dissent and fissures. Nonetheless, Christianity, despite the different forms it takes in different contexts, can be analysed as a constellation of elements.[3] These would include not only clearly faith-based principles – for example, that the messiah arrived in the form of Jesus, and that he will eventually return to usher in a new world – but also ways of knowing and being that can be articulated as non-religious or secular, but are associated with reason, civility and supercession.[4] Christianity, unlike the short-hands of 'race' and 'colonialism', has received minimal attention in left scholarship on Israel/Palestine. This is not surprising; as Gil Anidjar has said more generally, 'Christianity has yet to be recognised as a concept' (2009b: 386) and, I would add, as a practice.

I make four arguments that Israel owes much (not all) of its creative impulse and contemporary formation to Christianity, and that, as a result, Israel can, with some validity, be called, in part, 'Christian', and not just or only Jewish. First, centuries of Christian Judeophobia[5] directly led to the emergence of Jewish national aspirations in the 'nation state era'. Second, the British conquering of Palestine in 1917, an event that arguably was required before the concept of a Jewish state could be viable, can be placed within a context of approximately 1,500 years of European Christian empire building and that it is important to see these continuities of Christendom's enterprise as manifested in a modern state like Israel. Third, during the nineteenth century, Protestant theology and individual Protestant evangelicals had a significant influence on the development of Jewish national thought, on the orientation of Jewish nationalist leaders and early Ashkenazi settlers, and on British support for the notion of a Jewish 'return to Palestine'. Protestantism continues to play an important role in Israel, and in terms of support for Israel elsewhere. Fourth, Israel itself and its defenders have created a Christ-like messiah out of the state, an entity on earth to deliver prophetic destiny and as redemption for Holocaust sacrifice.[6] At the same time, Israel's critics may participate in a reverse form of this discourse by insisting that Israel is outside international law's comity of nations, namely, though never named, Christendom.

3 I cannot do justice to the literature here, but see, for example, Jakobsen and Pellegrini (2008) and further references later in the chapter.

4 See my discussion of the English judiciary in *Jews and Other Uncertainties* (2011) for further development of this point.

5 I prefer the term 'Judeophobia' to antisemitism for reasons I have explained elsewhere: see Herman, 2011: 25.

6 For a recent example of Christian Zionist thinking in this regard, see https://www.washingtonpost.com/amphtml/news/made-by-history/wp/2018/02/01/the-apocalyptic-vision-behind-mike-pences-holocaust-comments/ (accessed 11 April 2019).

Christian Judeophobia

Although rarely considered in progressive writing on Israel today, it is not controversial to say that European Judeophobia first arose in parallel with the gradual consolidation and state institutionalisation of Christianity as something separate to both 'Jews and pagans' (Lieu, 2004; Buell, 2005). Buell has shown how very early Christians sought to distinguish themselves from Jews through a framework of universalism against particularism: 'By distinguishing Christianity as universal and racially unmarked, Judaism is constructed as its constitutive other – the racially marked in particular' (2005: 28). However, in practice, Christian universalism simply meant that non-Christians could and should become transcendent, supercessionary Christians (Buell, 2005: 3ff). It was in the second Christian century that early Christian thinkers developed their 'origins story' with 'Jesus as the founder of a new descent group' (Buell, 2010: 178). For centuries thereafter, Christian martyrs, theologians and rulers were the foremost promulgators of Judeophobia's many dimensions of which the allegation of 'particularism' was just one. In addition to this work on early Christianity theology and practice (see also Boyarin, 2004; Ruether, 1996), an immense body of work exists on the recurrent violence towards, demonisations and expulsions of Jews throughout Europe from the Middle Ages to the Nazis' Final Solution. As Heschel has argued, there is an 'underlying affinity between racism and Christian theology' (2010: 212; see also Byron, 2002).

In the nineteenth century, Jewish nationalism arose in response to centuries of Christian Judeophobia as a political movement dedicated to finding a place where Jews could live free of persecution.

> I say that we cannot hope for a change in the current of feeling . . . The nations in whose midst Jews live are all either covertly or openly Anti-Semitic (Herzl, 1988 [1896]: 2010).

Where this place might be – whether it would be a 'Jewish state' or a safe space for Jews within some other state – these were all matters of intense debate within a movement that was not monolithic in composition or intent. Jewish 'national homes' were pursued in Angola, Australia, Canada, Madagascar, Surinam, Uganda and the US, as well, of course, in Palestine (Alroey, 2016; Rovner, 2014). What united most nationalists was their view that Jews would never be safe within Christian Europe. The pogroms in the East, the histories of expulsion and then the Dreyfus affair in the West – these and other events convinced many Ashkenazi Jewish thinkers that the only alternative was to find somewhere else to go. Eventually, for a confluence of reasons (see, for example, Alroey, 2016), Palestine became the only choice for the dominant voices within the nationalist movement.

As Campos discusses (2011), indigenous Jews living in Ottoman Palestine were generally not sympathetic to the Ashkenazi nationalist agenda. While a Hebraic revival movement was popular in Palestine, it was normally not proposed as a step towards Jewish political autonomy, but rather as a 'real contribution to the rest of the Ottoman *umah*' (2011, p. 208):

The rebirth of the Jewish people, in its cultural, social, and economic dimensions, would work to the benefit of the empire at large. Hence, the Palestinian Sephardi commitment to Zionism should be characterised as an Erez-Israel commitment within the Ottoman body politic (Campos, 2011: 208).

Practices towards Jews (and Christians) in the Muslim world, while not free of distinctive supercessionary elements present in the Koran, were very different from those in Christendom. It is hardly surprising that Jewish political nationalism emerged in the latter world.

For these reasons, Israel owes its existence, foundationally, to Christian Judeophobia. It was the fact that Jews were never permitted to be 'at home' in Europe that led to their seeking a way out. This foundational inspiration for Jewish nationalist thought and practice – European Christian Judeophobia – has been left behind in so many discussions of Israel. Instead, left and right argument about antisemitism begins, and ends, with the Holocaust, as if the Holocaust was all there was to say about Judeophobia in Europe. The right claims the Holocaust as justification for Israel and everything Israeli governments choose to do. In 2011, Benjamin Netanyahu declared to the US Congress, 'We are a nation that rose from the ashes of the Holocaust' – as if Jewish nationalism began in the 1940s.[7] The left tends to claim the Holocaust as either an opportunity to compare 'Zionists' to 'Nazis', an artefact of an antisemitism now defunct, or as a terrible event for which Palestinians should not bear the consequences.[8] In both frameworks of understanding, Christianity and the legacies of Christian Judeophobia are rarely to be seen.

European Christian empire building

The history of European colonialism, including in Palestine, cannot be fully understood without giving proper consideration to the role Christianity has played in colonialism within Europe. During the early centuries of Latin Christian expansion into Eastern and Northern Europe, indigenous peoples were dispossessed of their lands, Christian settlement took place in the taken lands, and local peoples were either enslaved, converted, expelled or killed (Bartlett, 1994). Contrary to Atlantic-centred narratives, European colonialism did not begin in Africa and the

---

7 http://www.pmo.gov.il/English/MediaCenter/Speeches/Pages/speechcongress240511.aspx (accessed 11 April 2019) or, from 2014,

'Unlike the Holocaust, when the Jewish people were like a wind-tossed leaf and utterly defenseless, we now have great power to defend ourselves, and it is ready for any mission. This power rests on the courage and ingenuity of the soldiers of the IDF and the men and women of our security forces. It is this power that enabled us, against all odds, to build the State of Israel': http://www.pmo.gov.il/English/MediaCenter/Speeches/Pages/speechholo270414.aspx (accessed 11 April 2019).

See also Mike Pence's tweet about Holocaust Remembrance Day 2017: 'A few days ago, Karen & I paid our respects at Yad Vashem to honor the 6 million Jewish martyrs of the Holocaust who 3 years after walking beneath the shadow of death, rose up from the ashes to resurrect themselves to reclaim a Jewish future. #HolocaustRemembranceDay #NeverAgain'.

8 The last argument made most eloquently by Edward Said, 1980.

Americas, but on continental European lands, and in the waters of the Irish, North and Black Seas. Original European imperial expansion and colonialism were, in the first instance, about the Christian conquest of 'pagan' Europe. The laboratories of European terror, violence, conversion and enslavement were Ireland, Poland, Finland and other places on the periphery of the early Latin and Greek Christian empires (Bartlett, 1994; see also Constable, 1996; Phillips, 1985).

In terms of Palestine in particular, Latin and Greek Christendoms and Islamic empires struggled for dominance in Palestine (as in the region more widely) from the first Islamic conquests in the seventh century (the Greek church eventually becoming the second largest landholder in Jerusalem and remaining so now).[9] European Christian theological and intellectual engagement with Palestine had developed from around the fourth century (Swanson, 2000), with Palestine representing, for many Latin and Orthodox Christians, 'our native land' (Hopwood, 1969: 9; see also Housley, 2000: 38; Price, 2000). One could say that Christians considered themselves to have a form of indigeneity in Palestine and certainly the Christian churches saw themselves as the only natural and legitimate guardians of Palestine's holy sites. This indigeneity, and I recognise it is controversial to use that word, would not have been an uninterrupted connection with land over a long period of time (as is the case in most definitions of the term today). Rather, this is the indigeneity of an origins story, a story of *Christian* origin that is in keeping with the idea of Christian supercessionary 'peoplehood' I noted earlier and also in keeping with stories of Jewish origin in Palestine and Muslim origin in what is now Saudi Arabia (I return to the idea of Christian indigeneity later).

As is well known, a series of Crusades in the eleventh and twelfth centuries sought to provide Latin Christianity with literal ownership of what they perceived as 'their' Holy Land – a superiority they asserted even over the eastern orthodox. Unfortunately for the Christian crusaders, the Ottomans eventually emerged victorious from such encounters and ruled Palestine and large parts of Eastern Europe for the next 500 years or so, promoting a steady stream of Muslim settlement in the taken lands and converting many others already living there. However, by the nineteenth and early twentieth century, following several centuries of Russian Christian conquest, and Greek, Bulgarian and other independences during the waning years of the Ottoman Empire, much of what had been Muslim Balkan and Eastern Europe had been Christianised and cleared of Muslims (Brubaker, 1998). From the 1820s to the 1920s, approximately 5 million Muslims were killed, and millions more dispersed from Eastern Europe and the Caucuses to various parts of the remaining Ottoman Empire, including Turkey, Syria and also Palestine (Chatty, 2010; McCarthy, 1995).[10] The First World War ended the Ottoman Empire's many centuries of rule in Palestine with the conquest of Jerusalem by Britain in December 1917. Given the imperial histories briefly reviewed above, it is unsurprising that

---

9 C. McGreal, 'Greek Orthodox Church Mired in Jerusalem Land Row' (22 March 2005), available at https://www.theguardian.com/world/2005/mar/22/israel (accessed 11 April 2019).

10 Many Jews were also targeted in these Christian campaigns; see sources noted in text.

this conquest was seen at the time as a victory for a twentieth-century Christian Crusade – as the *London Times* wrote:

> In its essence it is a vindication of Christianity. At a moment when Christendom is torn by strife, let loose by the apostate ambitions of those who have returned in practice to the sanguinary worship of their 'Old German God' it stands forth as a sign that the righteousness and justice that are the soul of Christian ethics guide Christian victors even in the flush of triumph.[11]

Without Christianity's victory over Islam in Palestine, it is unlikely there would have been a Jewish state a mere 30 or so years later.[12]

The British colonial regime established the first modern nation-state in Palestine, as the land up until that point had been part of a much larger Ottoman region. There is obviously a significant literature on the details and impact of the Mandatory regime on Palestine, but here I am only concerned with one dimension almost entirely lacking in this scholarship – Christianity. When British power acquired Palestine, a particularly Christian understanding of 'religion' was imposed by the mandatory state. Christianity's invention of 'religion' is a story I cannot do justice to here, but one that has been explored by a range of scholars (e.g. Anidjar, 2008; Anidjar, 2015; De Vries, 2009; Fitzgerald, 2014; Jakobsen and Pellegrini, 2008; Masuzawa, 2005; see also Batnitzky, 2011). Christian (specifically Anglican) power in Palestine accomplished at least two things in relation to the making of Israel: it turned Muslims, Jews and Christians into competing religious supplicants; it propagated the myth of 'the Arab' versus 'the Jew'.

Laura Robson, one of the only scholars writing in this area, argues that British rule, which lasted from 1917 until 1948, brought religious sectarianism to Palestine, as it did to India: British colonial policy turned spiritual affiliations into political identities (2011b). The British took over an Ottoman legal system that for hundreds of years had recognised Jews and Orthodox Christians (and later some Catholics, but never Protestants) as indigenous 'millets' – separate but not equal communities within the Muslim world (Robson, 2011b: 5, 57–8; Tsimhoni, 1984). The British did not dispense with the millet system – they expanded it by creating a Muslim millet, something that would have been an absurdity under Ottoman rule, but made sense from a colonial Christian 'religion' perspective (one enshrined in the Balfour Declaration – see later).

> The British created the Palestinian Muslim millet to appease what they assumed was a strong religious feeling among Palestinian Muslims, who through their international connections could pose a threat to Britain's colonial holdings in such far-flung places as Egypt, Malaysia, and, above all, India (Robson, 2011b: 58).

11 *The Times* (London), 13 December 1917, Issue 41660, p. 9.
12 For a thorough discussion of the broader effects of the Mandate, see Kattan (2009), although he ignores the role of Christianity.

Thus, Palestinian courts that were previously 'state' courts became Islamic courts enforcing Sharia law for Muslims alone. The British created the position of 'Grand Mufti' to represent all Muslims, and the main political representative body for non-Jewish Palestinians, including Christians, became the Supreme Muslim Council – an organisation that had no history of engaging with a millet system (Robson, 2011b: 59–60; Tsimhoni, 1984: 169–70).[13] Orthodox Judaism was authorised as the spokesperson for 'the law of the Jews', in contrast to other possibilities active at the time, such as the non-statist Hebrew Courts of Peace discussed by Shamir (2000).

Thus, under the Mandate, designated Jewish leaders, despite representing the smallest faith community in Palestine, received a half-share of political representation and Muslim leaders the other half, with Palestinian Christians largely ignored. This new cleavage led to intensified faith identities (including the increased power of Judaism and Islam in Jewish and Arab nationalisms) where colonial subjects vied for British attention and resources. For the colonial power, 'divide and rule' was hardly a new experience. British imperialism had thrived elsewhere through the promotion of politicised identities, including in Ireland, Malaysia, India, Ceylon, Kenya and Cyprus. In Cyprus, for example, 80 years of British rule succeeded in solidifying the separation of Orthodox Christians and Muslims as 'Greeks' and 'Turks' (Pollis, 1973; but see also Gates, 2013). According to Pollis, the British in Cyprus fostered an 'apartheid mentality' (1973: 590) that resulted in a mythology of primordial enmity. In a passage that could just as easily have been written about Palestine, Pollis writes of Cyprus:

> The British thus strengthened identification within each community, sharpened the cleavages between them, and drew the communities into political relationships perhaps relevant for a modern nation-state, but irrelevant to the previously existing communal social order and to the premises which sustained it. Thus, a social order composed of a Muslim and Orthodox governing elite was gradually redefined into two vertically divided religious groups; and this was further redefined into two antagonistic nationality groups-Greeks and Turks. There were no policies instituted to create even the structural requisites of a unified community (1973: 591).[14]

'The Jew' and 'the Arab', like the 'Greek' and the 'Turk', or 'the Hindu' and 'the Muslim' in India (Kapila, 2007), are, in part, products of Christian racial thinking:

---

13 Palestinian Christians were, ironically, almost completely ignored by British rule for a number of complicated reasons discussed by Robson (2011b, 66ff) and also Tsimhoni (1984), including British rivalries with other Christian powers, British Protestant millenarianism (see below), and that it had never been British imperial policy (unlike French) to privilege Christianity in its Middle Eastern and Asian colonial territories (see also Pollis, 1973). Furthermore, as some Catholics and all Protestants were never recognised as millets under the Ottomans, and the Eastern Orthodox communities were diverse, it would not have been straightforward to incorporate all 'Christians' into something new.

14 In response to Pollis, Gates (2013) argues that the British were not so deliberately calculating, but more muddling through.

'For to uphold the division between Jew and Arab, between Jew and Muslim, is to reproduce the origins of racism and of antisemitism at once: the history of Christian prejudice' (Anidjar, 2009a: 267). Until the twentieth century, there was little to differentiate Jews from Muslims in the mind of Christendom – they were both viewed as backward peoples lacking Christian virtue: the Semites (Arab Christians rendered invisible then as now) (Anidjar, 2008: 31; Renton, 2013, 2017; Buell, 2005). The rise of pan-Arab and pan-Jewish nationalisms, each accompanying the other during the 'age of nationalism', coalesced into 'the Jew' versus 'the Arab', a differentiation born out of imperial war, racial thinking and the Christian conquest of Ottoman territory. This is not to say that distinctions were not present before Christian conquest, nor that many 'Jews' and 'Arabs' did not do their best to capitalise on them under British rule and after (for one example, see Halabi, 2014). Rather, my argument is that British colonial rule in Palestine interacted with these distinctions in Christian ways to 'undo' the Semite (Renton, 2017: 124–5) and to bring 'the Jew' and 'the Arab' into the operation of the colonial state. Thus, what then became the hegemonic nationalism of the new Israeli state was produced in interaction with Christian colonial power.

I narrate the imperial history above in an attempt to place Palestine within the context of gradual Christian expansionism within Europe *and the eastern Mediterranean in particular*. Regional, historical and – for lack of a better word – religious context has been lost in most progressive scholarship that equates Jewish colonialism in Palestine with European conquests across the Atlantic – whereas Palestine had long been either an Islamic or a Christian colony before it became a Jewish one. Palestine, and therefore Israel, is embedded within the historic (and continuing) struggle between Christianity and Islam, a struggle which cannot simply be conflated with the encounters and dispossessions that took place in South and North America (see also Busbridge, 2018).

Protestant pre-millennialism

Latin and Greek Christianity's approach to Judaism had been fairly straightforward: conversion or expulsion (with a few exceptions) – the same policy applied to Muslims once Islam emerged. Jews and Judaism were not major players in pre-Reformation Christian salvation stories (Melchionni [Ferrari trans.], 1993). However, following the Protestant Reformation, The Book of Revelations became more significant for Northern European Christians and, for many, a blueprint for how the end-times would unfold. In Revelations, 'the Jews' were seen to play a crucial role in Christ's Second Coming. Protestant readings of this story have been well covered elsewhere (Almond, 2007; Haija, 2006; Herman, 1997; Matar, 1985; Smith, 2013), but to summarise: Jews will go to live in Palestine and rebuild Jerusalem; Jews will convert to Christianity; Jews who do not convert will die before or when Christ returns (along with all other non-believers) to usher in the new millennium – 'heaven on earth'. Although pre-millennialism was and is by no means subscribed to by all Protestants, this eschatology has nonetheless had a significant impact on Palestine, historically, and in the present. The necessity of Jews 'returning' to Palestine was an important (though not dominant) aspect of Protestant theology from the sixteenth century onwards. Post-Reformation, the Jewish role in the end-times became added to pre-existing Christian Judeophobia; Jews did not belong in Europe, but they did belong in Palestine.

In their studies of English and American Protestantism, Matar (1985) and Smith (2013) show how, from the seventeenth century, Protestant eschatology was inextricably tied to ongoing battles with two concepts: 'Rome' and 'the Turk' (see also Almond, 2007). For many (not all) Protestants, the role of 'the Jews', therefore, was as prophetic allies in these monumental struggles with what was perceived as Satanic force. However, there was no commitment to a 'Jewish state' in Palestine; Jews were eventually to convert and the Holy Land was to be Christian (Matar, 1985: 132). The necessity of Jewish migration to Palestine was both to rid Europe of Jews and establish a front-line Christian crusader force in the Holy Land (made up of Jews) to fulfil prophecy (see also Robson, 2011a).

Many scholars have argued that a literal Jewish migration to the actual land of Palestine has little or no basis in Judaic theology or philosophy and ultra-orthodox Jews have never supported it (e.g. Boyarin and Boyarin, 1993; Rabkin, 2012; Raz-Krakotzkin, 2013). Jewish nation-statism emerged in the nineteenth century 'age of nationalisms' as an obvious, perfectly rational strategy to deal with European Judeophobia. When, after much debate (see e.g. Alroey, 2016), it eventually became centred on Palestine as the land for settlement, it did so with Protestant pre-millennial theology as its background and precursor, not Judaism. The idea that Jews *must*, literally, 'return' to Palestine is a Christian, not a Jewish, idea (see also Raz-Krakotzkin, 2013; Goldman, 2009), as is the wrongly quoted but often repeated phrase, 'a land without people for a people without land' – a phrase that, slightly differently composed, had its origins in British Protestant evangelical thinking about Jews (Garfinkle, 1991; Goldman, 2009: 22–3). As Goldman has shown (2009), several Jewish nationalist thinkers were directly inspired by their engagements with Protestant evangelicals, including Herzl. As Piterberg has argued (2008), Palestine-centred Jewish nationalists developed a reading of the 'Old Testament' that was Protestant in approach. In other words, they relegated Jewish interpretive texts to the margins (e.g. the Mishna and Talmud) in favour of a literal reading of 'the return' (2008: 27ff). Given the nineteenth-century Protestanisation of Judaism (discussed further below), such a move is not surprising.

From an elite Anglican British perspective (such as the evangelicals Lloyd George and Arthur Balfour), the twin goals of fulfilling Protestant prophecy and removing eastern Jews from Europe were nicely facilitated by the Balfour Declaration, the latter equally motivated by other expedient political considerations of the day (Van Oord, 2008; Kimmerling, 2005; Renton, 2007). Bar-Yosef argues that English Protestant millennialists were marginal to mainstream British culture (2005), and Renton also dismisses their input into the Balfour Declaration (2007). Yet, while it is prudent not to overplay the impact of millennialism on wider English society, its role in the formation of British elite political support for a 'Jewish home' and for providing Jewish nationalists with the idea of 'restoration' was important. Minimising millennialism's impact in these respects risks further obfuscation of Christianity's role in Israel's formation (see also Scholch, 1992).

As has been well documented (Haija, 2006; Herman, 1997; Smith, 2013), the basis for conservative Protestant support for Israel now is little different from what it once was: actual Jews need to be settled on that land to fulfil Christian prophecy. Also continuing, if in a different form, is 'the Jews' prophetic role in holding back forces of evil (e.g. Islam) out to destroy Christianity. As Shindler has explored (2000), successive Israeli governments have made good use of conservative Protestant support (while continuing to ignore the conversion aspect of their scenario). Further, as Durbin (2013) and Williams (2015) have more recently documented, American Christian zionism has undergone shifts in recent years that have resulted in not simply increasing support for Israel, but Christians' personal spiritual identification with historical and contemporary Israel. Durbin notes a Christian zionist shift in emphasis from Revelations to Genesis; contemporary Israel is God's plan made manifest and it must be protected from attack (2013). Williams has explored how American evangelicals have taken on Jewish rituals (such as blowing the shofar, Friday night services, wearing Jewish prayer shawls[15]) and made them integral to their Christian practice, exporting these practices to their global ministries (2015).

This taking on of Jewish ritual evokes a Christian relationship to Palestinian indigeneity that, as I noted earlier, has been present since Christianity's inception and throughout its colonial enterprises. Early 'Christian peoplehood' was developed through differentiating Christians from Jews, with Christianity, by the time of the Crusades, becoming the legitimate inheritor of Palestinian land itself. For many contemporary American evangelicals, their selfhood and sense of mission are increasingly achieved through identifying not against Jews, but with the Jewish state. In this sense, many contemporary Christian evangelicals see the 'Jews of Israel' as safeguarding their Christian heritage from Islamic onslaught in a shared biblical homeland (see Feldman, 2007).[16]

My argument in this section is intended to facilitate analysis necessary to making sense of America's fascination with and support for Israel, as well as, in part, the origins of the Balfour Declaration. The latter was the product of a number of forces coming together (Jewish nationalism and imperial rivalries being the most studied), but one important factor, usually ignored or marginalised, was the influence of pre-millennial theology on the British Protestant architects of the Declaration. The Balfour Declaration was not simply or only an imperial moment in the lead-up to the creation of a Jewish settler state – it was the product of a complex set of

---

15 In 2017, I saw Jewish prayer shawls for sale when I visited The Holy Land Experience, a Christian biblical theme park in Orlando, Florida: https://holylandexperience.com/ (accessed 11 April 2019). Christian zionist pilgrimage to Israel/Palestine is a significant industry related to the arguments in this chapter, but I cannot do justice to it here.

16 See also the new Museum of the Bible in Washington, a Christian enterprise partly intended to deepen ties with Israel, https://www.museumofthebible.org/ (accessed 11 April 2019).

circumstances and beliefs that included Protestant theological principles. In terms of America's obsession with Israel, it, too, cannot be properly understood without taking account of Protestant pre-millennialism in the US, its evolution over time and the political power of the conservative Protestant movement in the US.[17]

Orienting towards Christendom

Israel was not simply incubated by Christian conquest and theology as I argued above, but its own early leaders and settlers also turned to Christian Europe and America for inspiration and allegiance. It is not surprising that Jewish settlers in Palestine looked to the Protestant, modernising West as that to which they aspired; within Western Europe, Judaism itself had already been Protestantised in various ways as Khazzoom and others have explored (see Khazzoom, 2003), including being turned into a 'religion' by Christians and Jews alike, as Batnitzky has discussed (2011). Jewish nationalist leaders not only hoped to make a Jewish state in Northern Europe's image, but also its Jewish settlers were to be de-orientalised and turned towards the West, rejecting any Eastern/Semitic affinity they could have had for those already living in Palestine (including the Sephardi and Mizrachi Jews already living there) (Renton, 2012; Shamir, 2000). For Central and Western European leaders of the nation-state movement, the 'return' to and takeover of 'backward Palestine' would enable the *ostjuden* to become civilised Westerners (Penslar, 2001). As Shohat has noted: 'In Palestine, freed of its progenitor the Ostjuden, the New Jew could paradoxically live in the "East" without being of it' (2003: 49).[18] The *ostjuden* would undergo their transformation in a Jewish state, rather than exacerbating the already precarious position of Jews in Western Europe through further migration.

While the 'Western' aspect of this orientation is reasonably well known, its *Christian* character is seldom reflected upon. However, 'the West' was not simply 'the West' – it was also 'enlightened', Protestant Christendom:

> Thus, paradoxically, the exodus from Europe and the hope of creating a separate Jewish entity in the east was a way of joining the Christian West through a complete identification with the Western self-image. It was perceived as the basis for joining – for being assimilated into – the history of the Christian West, the narrative of European redemption (Raz-Krakotzkin, 2013: 47).

Jewish settlers even modelled their settlements on Christian ones in Palestine – the German Templar colonies established in the late nineteenth century provided

---

17 For one such organisation particularly active in anti-BDS activity, see https://unitedwithisrael.org/about-us/ (accessed 11 April 2019). There is some evidence that younger American evangelicals are less sympathetic to Israel: see https://www.washingtonpost.com/world/the-long-uneasy-love-affair-of-israel-and-us-evangelicals-may-have-peaked/2018/01/27/6d751bd0–0051–11e8–86b9–8908743c79dd_story.html?hpid=hp_hp-more-top-stories_israelevangelicals-710pm%3Ahomepage%2Fstory&utm_term=.dd9ddf28d59b (accessed 12 April 2019).
18 Echoes of these sentiments were also found in early zionist utopian writing (see Eliav-Feldon, 1983).

inspiration, among others (Goldman, 2009: 11). Given such influences, it is therefore perhaps not surprising that Israel, over time, has taken on more and more of a Christian form.

As a number of scholars have argued, Israel gradually claimed for itself a prophetic embodiment. Rose (2005), Raz-Krakotzkin (2013), Kimmerling (2005) and others have all explored Israel's political messianism, how the Jewish state became the saviour of the Jews, itself the long-awaited messiah (see also Barell and Ohana, 2014). As Zertal (2005) and others have discussed, the sanctification of the Holocaust in Israel became an important piece of this messianism – much like the sanctification of Christ's suffering does for many Christians. Leaders present Israel as on earth to deliver prophetic destiny, as embodying the risen ashes of the Holocaust, they sanctify life and glorify sacrifice, the life and sacrifice of the Jewish state at all costs. If we attempt to think through Israel as, in part not in whole, Christian *in theological form*, we have a very different picture of its past, present and futures than if we simply take its own self-description as 'the Jewish state' as all there is to say. That the messiah has already come – in this case in the form of Israel – is, or was, a Christian, not a Jewish idea.

At the same time, some of Israel's critics participate in a similar but reverse discourse by insisting that Israel consistently violates the norms of 'proper' international behaviour; for these critics, Israel exists outside the comity of nations (Kattan, 2009), namely (though significantly never named) the Christian comity of nations. While Israel itself takes an increasingly Christian form, its critics indirectly argue it is not Christian enough. Palestinians' appeal to international law is an understandable strategic tool; when it becomes a resource to justify Israel's relegation to pariah state status, its Christian character should not be ignored. Especially when evoked by the Christian West, perhaps particularly against non-Christian states, the deployment of international law rhetoric risks further entrenching Christian imperial history and contemporary practice.

This is an implicit not explicit argument – but it is readable through Israel critics' appeal to, idealisation of and disappointment in international law (see e.g. Kattan, 2009). But international law as we know it today is deeply embedded in the history of Christian (Iberian Catholic) colonialism and, for the most part, its norms have been imposed on – not cooperatively developed by – the non-Christian world (Anghie, 2007; Beard, 2007; see also Moyn, 2015; Paz, 2016).

> Whether examined as an abstract vocabulary about political life on the globe or empirical practices among sovereigns, international law is deeply embedded in Christian dogmas, worldviews, rites and hierarchies. It would not be hard to defend the proposition that 'international law is a Christian discipline' (Koskenniemi, 2017: 16).

International law, and in particular international human rights, was a means of confining international society 'to the Christian community, bound by Christian law' (Beard, 2007: 133). As Franklin Roosevelt proclaimed in 1942: 'We shall win this war, and in victory we shall seek not vengeance but the establishment of an international order in which the Spirit of Christ shall rule the hearts of men and of nations'.[19] Thus, Israel's failure to abide by United Nations and other international law edicts can be read as a failure to enter Christendom – perhaps even the ongoing, stubborn Jewish refusal to accept Christ himself. As Stephen Salaita has written: 'Israel is the least likely of nations to have a soul' (2011: 10). The world of international law is presented as secular space where 'Jewish tribalism' (i.e. zionism) does not belong. For some, Israel's illegal acts are 'depraved' and 'evil' (Salaita, 2011: 38, 142); for others they are 'stubborn' (Wintemute, 2017: 94); either way, Christian tropes, and the Christian mission (Paz, 2016), play their historical role.

Conclusion

I have argued that all the processes above – Christian Judeophobia and Christian colonialism within Europe, the early-twentieth-century Christian conquering of Palestine, the Protestant theological influence on the development of Israel-zionism, Protestants' continued involvement in propping up successive Israeli governments, the orientation of Israel-zionist leaders and settlers towards Northern European Christianity, the political-theological form that Israel has come to take, and the Christian production of the 'Jews' and 'Arabs' forever at war – have had an enormous impact on the character and politics of Israel. It is insufficient to say the least to consider only 'race' and 'apartheid' or 'Western settler colonialism' minus its Christianity as social processes worth attention. Conceiving of Israel as *only* a Jewish/Zionist state committing genocide against an indigenous population facilitates a caricature that obscures as much as it illuminates.

The Christian world's rendering of Jews, and the left's rendering of 'Zionists', as committing 'evil deeds' (Salaita, 2011: 142) is nothing new. The demonisation of Israel and 'Zionists' by the left is the reverse side of the coin of the demonisation of 'Islamic terrorists' by the right. Both caricatures are understandings that are Christian in origin, and derive much of their power from Christianity's supercessionary ideology and its accompanying relegation of Judaism (and then Islam) to the part of Christianity's inferior antagonist (even Christian zionism is waiting for Jesus's return so that all non-Christians will die or convert). The pro-Israel right is wrong to compare its left opponents to Nazis – that is pure hyperbole. However, the left draws on a tradition much older and more entrenched than twentieth-century Nazism. Christianity was and is implicated in the making of Israel, and Israel's critics need to reflect on how we draw on Christianity's archive to imagine the Jewish state.

Finally, this chapter perhaps begs the question: What would a less Christian, more Jewish state look like? While it is impossible to think through a response outside conditions of Christian hegemony, one answer, or set of answers, can be found

19 Catholic Action, January 1942.

by going back to early Jewish nationalist thinkers and movements, those that stood opposed to or were otherwise outside the zionism that focused on Jewish settlement in Palestine. Whether within the debates over what sort of Jewish state should be established that roiled the early nationalist movements (Alroey, 2016; Conforti, 2010; Rovner, 2014), or a circle of Central European Jewish thinkers in the early twentieth century, some of whom advocated for the abolition of all states in preparation for the messiah's coming (Löwy and Larrier, 1980), or among anti-Western Eastern European Jewish movements concerned with Jewish culture (Goldstein, 2010) – all of these alternatives perhaps offered more Jewish solutions than what became Christianised Israel.

But we can also approach the idea of the Jewish state differently – as a state of being in the world, rather than as a territorial refuge. 'Diaspora' as a concept has been taken up by a range of left Jewish scholars to develop ideas of justice, community and ethics in order to ground an explicitly non-nationalist Jewish politics. Daniel and Jonathan Boyarin, for example, in a piece that influenced many others, proposed the concept of diaspora as an alternative to one of 'national self-determination' (1993: 711). The Boyarins employ 'diaspora' as a way of understanding that "'peoples and lands are not naturally and organically connected"; that historical and cultural identities can be maintained at the same time as a "renunciation of sovereignty"' (723). In fact, they argue that this insight of diaspora may be 'the most important contribution that Judaism has to make to the world' (723). However, in their insistence that political Israel-zionism has no place in traditional Judaism, they also argue that: '[If] Jews are to give up hegemony over the Land, this does not mean that the profundity of our attachment to the Land can be denied' (715). The attachment to an origins story rooted in 'actual land' remains despite opposition to the taking of contemporary Palestine as a Jewish homeland.

Judith Butler, in her book *Parting Ways*, reiterates both the Boyarins' critique of sovereignty and their recovery of 'diaspora', or exile, as a Jewish value, but she is perhaps more emphatic that diaspora is not an exclusively Jewish value (2012; see also Castro Varela's contribution in this volume). In a piece critical of the 'identity' or 'Jewishness' focus of both the Boyarins and Butler,[20] Julie Cooper argues that the history of anti-semitism and the appeal of political nationalism requires the articulation of a Jewish polity, but not necessarily a Jewish nation-state. For Cooper, the point is not to imagine a better or more Jewish 'Jewish state', whether a nation-state or a state of being, but, in a return to Arendt (2009), to offer a political alternative to Israel – to elucidate a non-nationalist form of Jewish political representation that responds to anti-semitism. Perhaps it is impossible to say what a Jewish state or non-state might look like outside conditions of Christian hegemony – but arguably it would not look like Israel.

20 '. . . the relevant debate to pursue, in this expanded conversational arena, is whether, at this juncture, Jews need a nation-state – not what "Jewishness" means . . . The pressing question for diasporic thinkers, I submit, is how to envision political agency in polities other than the nation-state' (Cooper, 2015: 83–4).

Acknowledgements

For helpful comments on earlier drafts, I would like to thank: Gil Anidjar and the book and book series editors. I would also like to thank my Kent colleagues, Luis Eslava, Sara Kendall and Rose Parfitt, for pointing me towards some helpful readings in international law.

References

Abu El-Haj, N. (2010) 'Racial Palestinianization and the Janus-Faced Nature of the Israeli State', *Patterns of Prejudice*, 44(1), pp. 27–41.

Abu-Laban, Y. and Bakan, A. B. (2008) 'The Racial Contract: Israel/Palestine and Canada', *Social Identities*, 14(5), pp. 637–60.

Almond, P. (2007) 'Thomas Brightman and the Origins of Philo-Semitism: An Elizabethan Theologian and the Restoration of the Jews to Israel', *Reformation & Renaissance Review*, 9(1), pp. 3–25.

Alroey, G. (2016) *Zionism without Zion: The Jewish Territorial Organization and Its Conflict with the Zionist Organization*. Detroit, MI: Wayne State University Press.

Anghie, A. (2007) *Imperialism, Sovereignty and the Making of International Law*. Cambridge: Cambridge University Press.

Anidjar, G. (2008) *Semites: Race, Religion, Literature*. Stanford, CA: Stanford University Press.

Anidjar, G. (2009a) 'Can the Walls Hear?', *Patterns of Prejudice*, 43(3–4), pp. 251–68.

Anidjar, G. (2009b) 'The Idea of an Anthropology of Christianity', *Interventions*, 11(3), pp. 367–93.

Anidjar, G. (2015) 'The Forgetting of Christianity', *Reorient*, 1(1), pp. 27–36.

Arendt, H. (2009) *The Jewish Writings*. New York: Schocken.

Bakan, A. B. and Abu-Laban, Y. (2009) 'Palestinian Resistance and International Solidarity: The BDS Campaign', *Race & Class*, 51(1), pp. 29–54.

Barell, A., and Ohana, D. (2014) '"The Million Plan": Zionism, Political Theology and Scientific Utopianism', *Politics, Religion & Ideology*, 15(1), pp. 1–22.

Bartlett, R. (1994) *The Making of Europe: Conquest, Colonization and Cultural Change 950–1350*. London: Penguin.

Bar-Yosef, E. (2005) *The Holy Land in English Culture 1799–1917: Palestine and the Question of Orientalism*. Oxford: Clarendon Press.

Batnitzky, L. (2011) *How Judaism Became a Religion: An Introduction to Modern Jewish Thought*. Princeton, NJ: Princeton University Press.

Beard, J. (2007) *The Political Economy of Desire: International Law, Development and the Nation State*. Abingdon: Routledge.

Boyarin, D. (2004) *Border Lines: The Partition of Judaeo-Christianity*. Philadelphia, PA: University of Pennsylvania Press.

Boyarin, D. and Boyarin, J. (1993) 'Diaspora: Generation and the Ground of Jewish Identity', *Critical Inquiry*, pp. 693–725.

Brubaker, R. (1998) 'Migrations of Ethnic Unmixing in the "New Europe"', *International Migration Review*, pp. 1047–65.

Buell, D. K. (2005) *Why This New Race: Ethnic Reasoning in Early Christianity*. New York: Columbia University Press.

Buell, D. K. (2010) 'God's Own People: Specters of Race, Ethnicity, and Gender in Early Christian Studies' in Nasrallah, L. and Schussler Fiorenza, E. (eds.), *Prejudice and Christian Beginnings: Investigating Race, Gender, and Ethnicity in Early Christian Studies*. Minneapolis, MN: Fortress Press, pp. 211–34.

Busbridge, R. (2018) 'Israel-Palestine and the Settler Colonial "Turn": From Interpretation to Decolonization', *Theory, Culture & Society*, 35(1), pp. 91–115.

Butler, J. (2012) *Parting Ways: Jewishness and the Critique of Zionism*. New York: Columbia University Press.

Byron, G. L. (2002) *Symbolic Blackness and Ethnic Difference in Early Christian Literature*. London: Routledge.

Campos, M. (2011). *Ottoman Brothers: Muslims, Christians, and Jews in Early Twentieth-Century Palestine*. Stanford, CA: Stanford University Press.

Chatty, D. (2010) *Displacement and Dispossession in the Modern Middle East*. Cambridge: Cambridge University Press.

Conforti, Y. (2010) 'East and West in Jewish Nationalism: Conflicting Types in the Zionist Vision?', *Nations and Nationalism*, 16(2), pp. 201–19.

Constable, O. R. (1996) 'Muslim Spain and Mediterranean Slavery: The Medieval Slave Trade as an Aspect of Muslim-Christian Relations' in Waugh, S. L. and Diehl, P. D. (eds.), *Christendom and Its Discontents*. Cambridge: Cambridge University Press, pp. 264–84.

Cooper, J. E. (2015) 'A Diasporic Critique of Diasporism: The Question of Jewish Political Agency', *Political Theory*, 43(1), pp. 80–110.

De Jong, A. D. (2017) 'Zionist Hegemony, the Settler Colonial Conquest of Palestine and the Problem with Conflict: A Critical Genealogy of the Notion of Binary Conflict', *Settler Colonial Studies*, pp. 1–20.

De Vries, H. (2009) *Religion: Beyond a Concept*. New York: Fordham University Press.

Durbin, S. (2013) '"I am an Israeli": Christian Zionism as American Redemption', *Culture and Religion*, 14(3), pp. 324–47.

Eliav-Feldon, M. (1983) 'If You Will It, It Is No Fairy Tale: The First Jewish Utopias', *Jewish Journal of Sociology London*, 25(2), pp. 85–103.

Feldman, J. (2007) 'Constructing a Shared Bible Land: Jewish Israeli Guiding Performances for Protestant Pilgrims', *American Ethnologist*, 34(2), pp. 351–74.

Ferrari, S. (trans.) (1993) 'The Vatican, the Palestine Question and the Internationalization of Jerusalem (1918–1948)', *Rivista Di Studi Politici Internazionali*, 60(4)(240), pp. 550–68.

Fitzgerald, T. (ed.) (2014) *Religion and the Secular: Historical and Colonial Formations*. London: Routledge.

Garfinkle, A. M. (1991) 'On the Origin, Meaning, Use and Abuse of a Phrase', *Middle Eastern Studies*, 27(4), pp. 539–50.

Gates, C. (2013) 'The 'Turkish' Minority in Cyprus: An Artificial Identity?', *Journal of Imperial and Commonwealth History*, 41(5), pp. 870–86.

Ghanim, H. (2008) 'Thanatopolitics: The Case of the Colonial Occupation in Palestine', in Lentin, R. (ed.), *Thinking Palestine*. London: Zed Books, pp. 65–81.

Goldberg, D. T. (2008) 'Racial Palestinianization' in Lentin, R. (ed.), *Thinking Palestine*. London: Zed Books, pp. 25–45.

Goldman, S. (2009) *Zeal for Zion: Christians, Jews, and the Idea of the Promised Land*. Chapel Hill, NC: University of North Carolina Press.

Goldstein, Y. (2010) 'Eastern Jews vs. Western Jews: The Ahad Ha'am–Herzl Dispute and Its Cultural and Social Implications', *Jewish History*, 24(3), pp. 355–77.

Haija, R. M. (2006) 'The Armageddon Lobby: Dispensationalist Christian Zionism and the Shaping of US Policy towards Israel-Palestine', *Holy Land Studies: A Multidisciplinary Journal*, 5(1), pp. 75–95.

Halabi, R. (2014) 'Invention of a Nation: The Druze in Israel', *Journal of Asian and African Studies*, 49(3), pp. 267–81.

Herman, D. (1997) *The Antigay Agenda: Orthodox Vision and the Christian Right*. Chicago, IL: University of Chicago Press.

Herman, D. (2011) *An Unfortunate Coincidence: Jews, Jewishness, and English Law*. Oxford: Oxford University Press.

Herzl, T. (1988) [1896] *The Jewish State* [trans. Jacob M. Alcow]. New York: Dover Publications.

Heschel, S. (2010) 'Race as Incarnational Theology: Affinities between German Protestantism and Racial Theory' in Nasrallah, L. and Schussler Fiorenza, E. (eds.), *Prejudice and Christian Beginnings: Investigating Race, Gender, and Ethnicity in Early Christian Studies*. Minneapolis, MN: Fortress Press, pp. 211–34.

Hopwood, D. (1969) *The Russian Presence in Syria and Palestine, 1843–1914: Church and Politics in the Near East*. Oxford: Clarendon Press.

Housley, N. (2000) 'Holy Land or Holy Lands? Palestine and the Catholic West in the Late Middle Ages and Renaissance' In Swanson, R. N. (ed.), *Holy Land, Holy Lands*. Cambridge: Boydell & Brewer, pp. 228–49.

Jakobsen, J. R. and Pellegrini, A. (eds.) (2008) *Secularisms*. Durham, NC: Duke University Press.

Kapila, S. (2007) 'Race Matters: Orientalism and Religion, India and beyond c. 1770–1880', *Modern Asian Studies*, 41(3), pp. 471–513.

Kattan, V. (2009) *From Coexistence to Conquest: International Law and the Origins of the Arab-Israeli Conflict, 1891–1949*. London and New York: Pluto Press.

Khazzoom, A. (2003) 'The Great Chain of Orientalism: Jewish Identity, Stigma Management, and Ethnic Exclusion in Israel', *American Sociological Review*, 68(4), pp. 481–510.

Khoury, E. (2012) 'Rethinking the Nakba', *Critical Inquiry*, 38(2), pp. 250–266.

Kimmerling, B. (2005) *The Invention and Decline of Israeliness: State, Society, and the Military*. Berkeley, CA: University of California Press.

Koskenniemi, M. (2017) 'International law and religion: no stable ground' in

Koskenniemi, M., Garcia-Salmones Rovira, M. and Amorosa, P. (eds.), *International Law and Religion: Historical and Contemporary Perspectives*. Oxford: Oxford University Press, pp. 3–21.

Lentin, R. (ed.) (2008) *Thinking Palestine*. London: Zed Books.

Lieu, J. (2004) *Christian Identity in the Jewish and Graeco-Roman World*. Oxford: Oxford University Press.

Lloyd, D. (2012) 'Settler Colonialism and the State of Exception: The Example of Palestine/Israel', *Settler Colonial Studies*, 2(1), pp. 59–80.

Löwy, M. and Larrier, R. B. (1980) 'Jewish Messianism and Libertarian Utopia in Central Europe (1900–1933)', *New German Critique*, 20, pp. 105–15.

Massad, J. (2006) *The Persistence of the Palestinian Question: Essays on Zionism and the Palestinians*. London: Routledge.

Masuzawa, T. (2005) *The Invention of World Religions: Or, How European Universalism Was Preserved in the Language of Pluralism*. Chicago, IL: University of Chicago Press.

Matar, N. I. (1985) 'The Idea of the Restoration of the Jews in English Protestant Thought 1661–1701', *Harvard Theological Review*, 78(1–2), pp. 115–48.

McCarthy, J. (1995) *Death and Exile: The Ethnic Cleansing of Ottoman Muslims, 1821–1922*. Princeton, NJ: Darwin Press.

McMahon, S. F. (2014) 'The Boycott, Divestment, Sanctions Campaign: Contradictions and Challenges', *Race & Class*, 55(4), pp. 65–81.

Morgensen, S. L. (2012) 'Queer Settler Colonialism in Canada and Israel: Articulating Two-Spirit and Palestinian Queer Critiques', *Settler Colonial Studies*, 2(2), pp. 167–90.

Moyn, S. (2015) *Christian Human Rights*. Philadelphia, PA: University of Pennsylvania Press.

Nadeau, M. and Sears, A. (2010) 'The Palestine Test: Countering the Silencing Campaign', *Studies in Political Economy*, 85(1), pp. 7–33.

Paz, R. (2016) 'Religion, Secularism and International Law' in Orford, A. and Hoffman, F. (eds.), *Oxford Handbook on International Law*. Oxford: Oxford University Press.

Penslar, D. J. (2001) 'Zionism, Colonialism and Postcolonialism', *Journal of Israeli History*, 20(2–3), 84–98.

Phillips, W. D. (1985) *Slavery from Roman Times to the Early Transatlantic Trade*. Manchester: Manchester University Press.

Piterberg, G. (2008) *The Returns of Zionism: Myths, Politics and Scholarship in Israel*. London: Verso.

Pollis, A. (1973) 'Intergroup Conflict and British Colonial Policy: The Case of Cyprus', *Comparative Politics*, 5(4), pp. 575–99.

Price, R. M. (2000) 'The Holy Land in Old Russian Culture' in Swanson, R. N. (ed.), *Holy Land and Holy Lands*. Cambridge: Boydell & Brewer, pp. 250–62.

Rabkin, Y. (2012) 'Religious Roots of a Political Ideology: Judaism and Christianity at the Cradle of Zionism', *Mediterranean Review*, 5(1), pp. 75–100.

Razack, S. (2010) 'A Hole in the Wall; a Rose at a Checkpoint: The Spatiality of Colonial Encounters in Occupied Palestine', *Journal of Critical Race Inquiry*, 1(1), pp. 90–108.

Raz-Krakotzkin, A. (2013) 'Exile, History, and the Nationalization of Jewish Memory: Some Reflections on the Zionist Notion of History and Return', *Journal of Levantine Studies*, 3, pp. 37–70.

Renton, J. (2007) *The Zionist Masquerade: The Birth of the Anglo-Zionist Alliance, 1914–1918*. Houndsmills: Palgrave Macmillan.

Renton, J. (2012) 'Yad Chaim Weizmann and the Westernness of Israel', *Jewish Historical Studies*, 44, pp. 27–50.

Renton, J. (2013) 'The Age of Nationality and the Origins of the Zionist-Palestinian Conflict', *The International History Review*, 35(3), pp. 576–99.

Renton, J. (2017) 'The End of the Semites' in Renton, J. and Gidley, B. (eds.), *Antisemitism and Islamophobia in Europe: A Shared Story?* London: Palgrave Macmillan, pp. 99–140.

Robson, L. (2011a) 'Church, State, and the Holy Land: British Protestant Approaches to Imperial Policy in Palestine, 1917–1948', *Journal of Imperial and Commonwealth History*, 39(3), pp. 457–77.

Robson, L. (2011b) *Colonialism and Christianity in Mandate Palestine*. Austin, TX: University of Texas Press.

Rodinson, M. (1973) *Israel: A Colonial-Settler State?* [trans. D. Thorstad]. New York: Pathfinder Press.

Rose, H. and Rose, S. (2008) 'Israel, Europe and the Academic Boycott', *Race & Class*, 50(1), pp. 1–20.

Rose, J. (2005) *The Question of Zion*. Princeton: Princeton University Press.

Rovner, A. L. (2014) *In the Shadow of Zion: Promised Lands before Israel*. New York: New York University Press.

Ruether, R. (1996) *Faith and Fratricide: The Theological Roots of Antisemitism*. Eugene, OR: Wipf & Stock.

Said, E. W. (1980) *The Question of Palestine*. New York: Vintage Books.

Salaita, S. (2011) *Israel's Dead Soul*. Philadelphia, PA: Temple University Press.

Scholch, A. (1992) 'Britain in Palestine, 1838–1882: The Roots of the Balfour Policy', *Journal of Palestine Studies*, 22(1), pp. 39–56.

Shalhoub-Kevorkian, N. (2014) 'Human Suffering in Colonial Contexts: Reflections from Palestine', *Settler Colonial Studies*, 4(3), pp. 277–90.

Shamir, R. (2000) *The Colonies of Law: Colonialism, Zionism and Law in Early Mandate Palestine*. Cambridge: Cambridge University Press.

Shindler, C. (2000) 'Likud and the Christian Dispensationalists: A Symbiotic Relationship', *Israel Studies*, 5(1), pp. 153–82.

Shohat, E. (2003) 'Rupture and Return: Zionist Discourse and the Study of Arab Jews', *Social Text*, 21(2), pp. 49–74.

Smith, R. O. (2013) *More Desired than Our Owne Salvation: The Roots of Christian Zionism*. Oxford: Oxford University Press.

Swanson, R. N. (ed.) (2000) *Holy Land and Holy Lands*. Cambridge: Boydell & Brewer.

Tsimhoni, D. (1984) 'The Status of the Arab Christians under the British Mandate in Palestine', *Middle Eastern Studies*, 20(4), pp. 166–92.

Van Oord, L. (2008) 'The Making of Primitive Palestine: Intellectual Origins of the Palestine–Israel Conflict', *History and Anthropology*, 19(3), pp. 209–28.

Veracini, L. (2010) *Settler Colonialism: A Theoretical Overview*. Houndmills, Basingstoke: Palgrave Macmillan.

Veracini, L. (2014) 'What's Unsettling about *On Settling*: Discussing the Settler Colonial Present', *Critical Review of International Social and Political Philosophy*, 17(2), pp. 235–51.

Williams, J. (2015) 'The Pentecostalization of Christian Zionism', *Church History*, 84(1), pp. 159–94.

Wintemute, R. (2017) 'Israel-Palestine through the Lens of Racial Discrimination Law: Is the South African Apartheid Analogy Accurate, and What if the European Convention Applied?', *King's Law Journal*, 28(1), pp. 89–129.

Wolfe, P. (2006) 'Settler Colonialism and the Elimination of the Native', *Journal of Genocide Research*, 8(4), pp. 387–409.

Wolfe, P. (2012) 'Purchase by Other Means: The Palestine Nakba and Zionism's Conquest of Economics', *Settler Colonial Studies*, 2(1), pp. 133–71.

Zertal, I. (2005) *Israel's Holocaust and the Politics of Nationhood*. Cambridge: Cambridge University Press.

7

USING THE MASTER'S TOOLS

Rights and radical politics

Ruth Kinna

The story of origins and the possibility of reimagining the state

What do we reimagine when we reimagine the state? Perhaps one of the reasons that political theorists tend to shy away from this question is that they lack a normative language to address it. As Chandran Kukathas notes, the concepts used to analyse our political orders have been moulded by the historical experience of the European state and they are 'as contentious as the notion of the state' itself (2014: 357). Kukathas chooses the concept of 'legitimacy' to illustrate the point. But there are plenty more. Amnon Lev's discussion of sovereignty is another example: the meaning it now assumes is derived from the 'historical analytics of power that relate to the semantic and aesthetic resources that made it possible to present sovereignty as a *political* force and hence, by implication, a force for good' (2014: 3, emphasis in the original). It is no coincidence that sovereignty moved centre stage in the political theology that prevailed during of the period of the European state's formation.

Working from the premise that the tools available to political theorists have been shaped by the prevailing order, Jens Bartleson argues that a substantial body of political theory has been unable to reimagine the state. Scrutinising the history of anti-state theory, he diagnoses the theoretical problem of the state in the construction of 'anarchy'. However this condition is described, anarchy is cast as the foil for the state. It is both integral to stories of the state's genesis and to the conception of the state as a political order. In Bartleson's view, 'anarchy' haunts political theory, inventing a domestic 'inside' and international 'outside' that fixes the parameters of intellectual enquiry; not even anti-state theorists have managed to break free. Indeed, rather than reimagining the state, Bartleson finds that they have only been able to replicate it. At one and the same time, 'modern political discourse ceaselessly questions the form and content of authority, its legitimacy and proper boundaries' and 'makes questions about the ultimate foundations of authority difficult to ask, let alone answer' (Bartleson, 2001: 3). While 'its actual manifestations in political theory and practice are criticized from a variety of actual viewpoints', the state's presence is taken for granted (Bartleson, 2001: 3). Similar problems pervade cognate disciplines. Tuori's analysis of legal anthropology reveals how assumptions about the genius of the European state helped sustain unenlightening distinctions between 'primitive' or 'savage' and law-governed 'cultured' peoples in historic (and some contemporary) scholarly investigations into the origins of law (2015).

Frustrated by this theoretical *cul-de-sac*, anarchists have turned to sociology, geography and anthropology to contest claims about the state's necessity and normative arguments about its historic achievements (Kropotkin, n.d. [1902]; Morris, 2005; Scott, 2009). Yet, bringing these insights to bear on mainstream political theory has largely failed to advance our understanding of the state or anarchy. The concepts which anarchists deploy to present their alternative conceptions of order are too easily misconstrued in the context of state theory and by the binaries it supports: law/lawlessness, government/chaos, freedom/licence. The political theory that casts anarchy as 'other' to the state, ontologising both (Dhawan in this volume), survives intact. As a result, the anarchist reimagining of the state remains unintelligible.

The historical response to the question of the state's reimagining was to return to the story of its origins. These stories revolve around the idea of the contract and they are told to explain how and why individuals agreed to establish government. Contracts are thus imagined as foundational agreements, which establish the basis for the state's just constitution. They also define the limits of legitimate protest, empowering citizens to act when the terms of the agreement they are purported to have made are breached. The approach fell out of vogue as the process of European state-building advanced during the seventeenth and eighteenth centuries. Indeed, Bartleson notes that Kant cautioned his fellow philosophers to stop delving into accounts of the state's 'origins'. The project was both speculative and dangerous: '[t]he origin of supreme power . . . is not *discoverable* by the people who are subject to it'. So, the 'subject *ought not* to indulge in *speculations* about its origin with a view to acting upon them' (emphases in the original). It is 'futile' to ask whether 'an actual contract originally preceded their submission to the state's authority, whether the power came first and the law only appeared after it, or whether they ought to have followed this order'. The people were 'already subject to civil law' and to question why or how constituted 'a menace to the state' (Kant in Bartleson, 2001: 3).

Alarmed by the systemic injustices perpetuated by liberal democratic states, some contemporary political theorists have recognised the constructive aspects of this destructive work. Yet in crossing Kant's line, they have not so much asked questions about the state's origins as query the contractual devices that post-war political theorists have resurrected to ground justice within the state. John Rawls's *Theory of Justice* is the seminal work for this review.

For Charles Mills and Carole Pateman, both leading contemporary critics of contract, there is no 'before' or 'after' the state, which theory can realise or access. The role of political theory is to dissect our political orders and explore and expose persistent, entrenched injustices and inequalities. By lifting the lid on the relationship between our prevailing institutional arrangements and the theory that undergirds them, both ask how far contract is a master's tool or, as Audre Lorde argued in another context, a device that allows 'only the most narrow perimeters of change' (Lorde, 2007 [1979]: 111). For Charles Mills, one of the most celebrated liberal critics of liberalism, this is an exercise in thinking about what can be salvaged from liberal contract theory. For Carole Pateman, it is about developing an alternative to it. Both take a lead from Jean-Jacques Rousseau: Mills does this in order to develop a subversive contract that de-racialises mainstream contract theory, while Pateman seeks to recover the idea of free agreement that the social contract suppresses.

To what extent do these critiques help us reimagine the state? In what follows, I tackle this question by considering how far each advances prefigurative change. This term is borrowed from contemporary anarchist political thought and it is suggested by Mills's robust defence of his deployment of the master's tools to drive social transformation. As will become clear, Pateman's rejection of contract reveals the limits of Mills's project. My argument has four parts: first, it outlines Mills's reclamation of 'the master's tools'; second, it discusses prefiguration. This provides, third, the platform to discuss Pateman's critique of contract and domination. The final section briefly discusses two recent examples of activism and the reclamation of the master's tools to support prefigurative change.

Charles Mills: Rawls, Rousseau and the subversion of contract

In an important essay entitled 'Rousseau, The Master's Tools, and Anti-Contractarian Contractarianism', Charles Mills presents a qualified critique of contemporary contract theory, defending himself against critics who accuse him of adopting tools of domination to address racial injustice (Mills, 2015: 171ff). He rejects the claim, put forcefully by Audre Lorde, that 'the master's tools can never be used to dismantle the master's house' (ibid.: 172). Contesting the generality of this claim, he argues that the theoretical devices used to sanction systematic white racist violence and oppression can be emptied of their 'moral viciousness' (ibid.: 173). His special interest is in contract theory and he takes Rousseau's eighteenth-century critique of John Locke's seventeenth-century account of contract for his model. Styling himself a sympathetic critic of contract or an 'anti-contractarian contractarian', Mills contends that it is possible to use contract both to counter white supremacism in mainstream political philosophy and to redress the historic injustices that the contract has helped sustain. As will be seen, Mills diverges from Rousseau in significant ways, but follows Rousseau's lead in redeveloping an existing account of contract to reveal its flaws. The *Theory of Justice*, John Rawls's twentieth-century restatement of liberal contract theory, is Mills's target.

After its publication in 1971, the *Theory of Justice* defined mainstream Anglo-American political theory and played an important role in the resurrection of twentieth-century political philosophy (Klosko, 2011: 458). It was elaborated in a period of intense unrest in America when civil rights, anti-Vietnam War protest, women's and Black liberation movements drew attention to the failure of liberal political institutions to uphold liberal principles and values (Daniels, 1989 [1975]: XXXV). As a modified version of social contract theory, the *Theory of Justice* introduced the device of the 'original position' to imagine what principles of justice parties to a hypothetical contract would choose in order to ground their political institutions. The 'original position' facilitated a thought-experiment about ideal political arrangements and fulfilled a role that was roughly equivalent to the hypothetical 'state of nature' in historical contract theory. However, Rawls departed from traditional theory in two ways. First, he invoked the metaphor of contract to devise what he called the 'basic structure' of society, not as Locke and Rousseau had done, to recommend ideal constitutions. The basic structure balanced liberty against equality and advanced a set of distributive rules that were open to a range of governmental arrangements. Second, whereas contract theorists drew their ideal constitutions from more or less chaotic descriptions of a 'natural' pre-government condition, Rawls modelled the basic structure on the choices individuals made behind the 'veil of ignorance'. This meant that the contract was imagined as an agreement between individuals who knew everything about the world, but who were ignorant about their personal circumstance or status within it. Using the uncertainty created by the veil to model the behaviours of his contractors (notably, their unwillingness to take significant risks or gamble on their life-chances), Rawls defended the fairness of the principles of justice with reference to the fairness of the process used to generate them. As the veil was removed, choosers were able to reflect on the justness of the chosen principles by examining 'hard cases' and fine-tuning them accordingly.

Mills's critique of the *Theory of Justice* turns on the distinction Rawls makes between 'ideal' and 'non-ideal' theory. Rawls explains that the ideal 'presents a conception of a just society that we are to achieve if we can. Existing institutions are to be judged in the light of this conception' (Rawls in Simmons, 2010: 7). Non-ideal theory instead 'asks how this long term goal might be achieved or worked toward' (ibid.). As Feinberg notes, ideal theory regulates 'well-ordered' societies where 'everyone always acts justly' (Feinberg, 1989 [1975]: 117). Non-ideal theory focuses on real-world non-compliance and the permissible, feasible and effective measures that might be taken to address injustice.

By presenting a conception of a just society that is strictly compliant with the principles of justice, ideal theory is supposed to help 'with real-life problems of the non-ideal world' by 'mediating our "natural duty" to promote just institutions' (ibid.). In this logic, ideal theory may bear little relation to the real world, but it is a mistake to think that it is therefore 'simply irrelevant'. In fact, Simmons argues, ideal justice guides '*activists* in the cause of justice'. Ideal justice is 'strongly *transitional* . . . in character' (Simmons, 2010: 22, emphases in the original) and Rawls outlines 'an ideal of justice toward which [nonphilosopher activists] take their campaigns to be ultimately directed' (ibid.: 35–6).[1]

---

1 In this context, 'transitional justice' describes the use of theoretical benchmarks as drivers for political change, not post-conflict transformation and the transition from war to peace building.

Mills's objections to the *Theory of Justice* are multiple: it adopts a classic liberal social ontology which casts individuals as equal and undifferentiated, so removing relations of 'structural domination, exploitation, coercion, and oppression' (Mills, 2005: 168); it attributes idealised capacities to them, removes cognitive distortions from their reasoning and idealises their social institutions. How the family, the economic structure or the legal system actually operate to 'disadvantage women, the poor and racial minorities' is of no consequence (ibid.: 169). Above all, ideal theory is silent on historic oppression. As Simmons also notes, the rational choosers who select principles of justice from behind the veil of ignorance are asked to think only about the future. They are not required to take past injustices into account. Simmons writes: Rawls paid 'no attention to the long histories of injustice to people of color, to women, to various groups that constitute minorities in their religious convictions or sexual orientations'. Similarly, his ideal conception 'pays no attention to the modern destruction of community and social and family networks, to the neglected pursuit of genuinely common ends, to the threat posed by liberal society to the values of culture and ethnicity' (ibid.: 32–3).

Unlike Simmons, Mills considers this neglect highly material to the ideal's transformative potential. Normatively, Rawls's exclusion of racial injustice 'from the start' (Mills, 2015: 177) results in the construction of a 'perfectly just society' in which 'no race would have been discriminated against' and where 'no rectificatory measures would be needed'. To compound the problem, Rawls's *'factual* assumptions about the shaping of the modern world' are defective. His discussion of international justice, elaborated after the publication of the *Theory of Justice*, simply glosses over 'European imperialism, the genocide of native peoples, and the Atlantic slave trade' (Mills, 2015: 177, emphasis in the original).

If Rawls were motivated to address the failures of liberalism identified by civil rights activists in the 1960s, then Mills's finding is that the *Theory of Justice* clearly fails to provide an adequate response. Mills's conclusion is that Rawls's contract is not only conservative, it is ideological. Mills's controversial claim is that his work contributed to the perpetuation of 'illicit group privilege' by embedding and concealing white racial domination (Mills, 2005: 166; Stemplowska and Swift, 2012: 378–9). Rawls's view that actual injustice can only be grasped through the lens of the ideal erased actual injustice from view and provided a cover for everyday oppression. In short, as it is currently configured, the *Theory of Justice* is of 'little help to us in trying to adjudicate appropriate public policies to deal with the actual history of racial subordination in societies like the United States, where . . . racial discrimination has been the norm' (Mills, 2015: 177).

Rather than re-run the contract using a different choice problem and retain the priority of ideal over nonideal theory, Mills argues that non-ideal theory should be reframed and its priority reversed. His aim is to develop robust 'principles of *transitional* justice' (ibid.: 177, emphasis in the original). To do this, he turns to historical contract theory and argues that Rawls repeats the mistake that Rousseau had identified in Locke: he adopts a consensual model of contract to defend liberal principles and values and treats consent as an indicator of fair process. Rousseau, Mills observes, showed that the Lockean contract was mistaken because it took the existence of inequality and privilege for granted. In doing so, he exposed the structural domination that liberal constitutions actually entailed and explained how voluntary agreements concluded in these imagined conditions cemented injustice by legitimising real-world injustice.

Mills's project differs from Rousseau's in two important respects. In the first place, he notes that the story of the origins of inequality that Rousseau told focused on class domination. Mills widens the analysis arguing that the 'restrictive' contract Rousseau described is adaptable to the analysis of other types of oppression. Indeed, even while Rousseau was 'sexist and arguably . . . racist', Mills contends that his 'innovative concept of an exclusionary contract' can be 'applied more broadly than he himself intended' – to encompass sex and race (ibid.: 174). Second, unlike Rousseau who devised a new social contract as an alternative to the Lockean model, Mills limits his ambition to 'purge' liberalism of 'its historic injustice' (ibid.: 176). He deploys contract as a 'minimalist', drawing 'normatively' on the recognition of the equal moral status of human beings central to liberal-democratic ideals and 'factually on the simple insight that humans create the sociopolitical' (Mills in Pateman, 2008: 14). The normative claim sets a benchmark for the marginalised and disadvantaged to assess existing institutions and guide justice struggles. His factual insight grounds the priority Mills attaches to non-ideal theory. Invoking the liberal commitment to moral equality to assess actual and historical injustices, Mills strips ideal theory of the status Rawls gives it and reconfigures the hypothetical contract to focus on nonideal realities:

> The 'anti-contractarian contractarianism' I am advocating, then, corrects this grossly misleading factual picture of modernity by (following Rousseau) representing the actual 'contract' as a domination contract, a racial contract imposed by whites on people of colour. Correspondingly, the normative mission becomes the rectification of the resulting 'non-ideal' 'basic structure': what public policies, what institutional measures, would we choose behind the 'veil of ignorance', worried that we might turn out to be black in what will be a white-supremacist sociopolitical order? (Mills, 2015: 177).

Mills's critique of the *Theory of Justice* is that it constrains the possibilities for social transformation by measuring non-ideal justice against an ideal in which injustice is already embedded. Instead, as a political demand, the commitment to moral equality empowers the dominated to challenge prevailing systems of domination in accordance with liberal values and principles. The reclamation of contract from the master is a critical tool, but it also gives real weight to the constitutional instruments that the principle of moral equality enshrines in liberal democratic states. There 'is nothing in the definition of *rights* or *freedoms* that limits them to white males' (ibid.: 183, emphases in the original), Mills argues. The feebleness of these tools is explained by the imperfect imagining of perfect justice. Rawls's ideal theory wrongly suggests that these rights and freedoms have been perfected. Shattering this illusion enables citizens to articulate their just demands and use the rights and freedoms available to them to advance transformative, egalitarian and emancipatory change. Unlike Rousseau, who invited us to reimagine the state built anew, Mills deploys the masters' tools imaginatively to encourage us to challenge the relationships of domination that structure our existing institutions. We reimagine the state through our actions by bringing our experiences of injustice in alignment with our egalitarian principles.

Prefiguration and the rejection of the master's tools

The activist objection to Mills's argument is that the deployment of the master's tools corrupts the campaigns they are designed to advance. This was Lorde's warning: the master's tools only give access to the master's house. Using them 'may allow us temporarily to beat him at his own game, but they will never enable us to bring about genuine change' (Lorde, 2007 [1979]: 112). The same argument, though often articulated as a fear of co-optation, is expressed in contemporary radical politics as a commitment to prefigurative change.

Prefiguration is the idea that the ends and means of political action must be aligned. Particularly associated with horizontal social movement activism and anarchistic anti-hierarchical organising, prefigurative politics establishes a framework for political action that limits the possibilities for engagement in the mainstream and militates against the use of existing representative institutions to advance political change. The adoption of consensus decision-making in many social movement actions is an example of a prefigurative approach: the embrace of the practice is integral to the participants' commitment to struggle for a future participatory, transparent and direct democratic politics.

How far prefiguration entails a refusal to use the master's tool, as Mills envisages, is a moot point. Uncertainty emerges from the complex relationship between the theory and practice of prefiguration and disagreements about the role and nature of utopian goals and visions as part of collective action for social change. Hostility to using master's tools has its roots in a historical argument rehearsed in the European socialist movement about the instrumental use of the state to realise revolutionary goals. Subsequently theorised, prefiguration amounts to a meta-ethic of revolutionary activity. Absorbed into movement politics, the idea is also linked strongly to a principled commitment to direct action, that is, action which advances change by disregarding institutional mechanisms, rules and norms. This also has a historic root and extends naturally from the rejection of participation in conventional politics. The strap line, 'be the change you want to see', is sometimes invoked to describe prefiguration in this sense. These three aspects of prefiguration prompt questions about the ways in which marginalised or historically dominated groups should articulate their demands and about the latitude they have to use rights without compromising principles of direct action.

The first view, that the use of the master's tools is inevitably corrupting, has its origins in a nineteenth-century debate about the possibility of capturing state power to deliver anti-state, anti-capitalist change. On the assumption that anarchist and non-anarchist revolutionary socialists shared the same socialist, egalitarian ends, anarchists argued that their anarchist methods alone were appropriate for the state's destruction or abolition.[2] Although the term was not then used, prefiguration underpinned three separate anarchist positions: (1) *the rejection of political action*, that is, the refusal either to enter into parliamentary institutions where circumstances allowed, or to be bound by constitutional rules; (2) *the disavowal of proletarian dictatorship*, i.e. the Marxist idea that the proletariat must temporarily seize control of the machinery of government to secure its position against the bourgeoisie; and (3) *the condemnation of vanguardism*, the view expressed most forcefully by Lenin, that the oppressed cannot fully emancipate itself without the support of enlightened party workers.

The second view, more familiar in contemporary anarchist political theory, treats prefiguration as a distinctive meta-ethics. There are two versions of the thesis. For Benjamin Franks, a leading analyst of prefigurative ethics, prefigurative politics is a rejection of consequentialism and deontology. Consequentialism evaluates the rightness of actions by their outcomes rather than the actor's intentions or motives and deontological approaches refer to the application of binding moral rules (accepted as such by autonomous, rational individuals). In distinction to both, prefiguration leaves the evaluation of the rightness of actions to the actors themselves. It closes the gap between means and ends by defining ethical behaviour as behaviour designed to realise short- or long-term increases in autonomy, irrespective of the action's 'success'. The 'moral framework' requires 'agents of change' to 'act autonomously to end their own oppression' (Franks, 2006: 114). The methods are 'pragmatic and local, as no ultimate or universal ground for "the good" exists' (ibid.).

Saul Newman advances another version of the thesis. His account resonates with Franks's rejection of 'instrumentalist strategies that appeal to the ultimate end of millennial events such as "the revolution"' (ibid.). However, Newman follows the nineteenth-century egoist Max Stirner to flesh out his model, and so ties prefiguration to the self-liberation of sovereign beings. Prefiguration is coupled with a type of 'hyper-liberalism' that Franks rejects. For Newman, it involves the abandonment of all predetermined 'utopian' ends or political causes. It describes continuous disobedience or insurrection (Newman, 2016: 64ff). In Newman's words, it is 'an expression of ownness', a 'reclamation of the self' and a 'constant work on oneself to invent subjectivities and relationships which are self-governing and no longer enthralled to power' (ibid.: 65).

In the third view, prefiguration describes a form of activism that is elaborated through movement practices. Examples include the development of alternative cooperative and democratic practices and 'anti-utopian utopian' imaginaries; anti-representational politics, horizontal organisation, 'nowtopian' experimentation and

2 The socialist anarchist view is that the state and capitalism are co-constituted and it diverges from minimal state, right libertarianism and so-called anarcho-capitalism, which typically call for the removal of state controls on markets and the enforcement of contracts by states to uphold the inequalities markets create.

community building, the ethics of mutual aid and the practice of anti-oppression politics. The common principle is direct action. Marianne Maeckelbergh explains: 'prefiguration is not a theory of social change that first analyses . . . and then sets out a . . . plan for changing the existing landscape' (2011: 3). It is 'a different kind of theory, a "direct theory" that theorizes through action, through *doing*' (ibid., emphasis in the original). Uri Gordon describes it as a form of action intended to 'challenge the basic legitimacy' of the state through a particular commitment to build movement principles into everyday life (Gordon, 2008: 18). It involves a principled rejection of the state's legitimacy, disallows actions that are designed as appeals to governments and demands for the introduction of reforms, whether or not the methods are legal. The line between prefigurative and non-prefigurative action is not entirely solid. While actions designed to reveal the dynamics of oppression usually fall into the prefigurative category, Gordon suggests that civil disobedience typically falls outside. This describes:

> a selective refusal to obey some of the regime's laws or politics, as a means of pressuring it into changing them. Tax strikes, refusal of conscription, and sitting in the 'wrong' section of a segregated bus all fall into this category. There is no intention to overthrow the regime, only to force it to negotiate (ibid.: 52).

The important point is that direct action is not merely illegalism. For example, at the turn of the twentieth century, anarchist women often classified illegal women's suffrage campaigns as pragmatic appeals to the state, which reinforced its legitimacy. Even though they adopted direct action (and 'terrorist' tactics), the suffragettes' actions were not prefigurative because they struggled calculatedly for the extension of the vote and sought the most effective means available to secure them.

To summarise: prefigurative politics variously denies the possibility of realising revolutionary change through the seizure of state power. It commits activists to locally determined direct actions that are intended to increase autonomy and it is substantively defined by sets of activities and projects that activists undertake. These different conceptions intersect in multiple ways, but proponents of prefigurative politics typically focus their attention on resistance to the state in an effort to realise alternatives in the 'here and now'. In advancing a particular politics of transformative change, they address issues of systematic, legally sanctioned injustice and the tools that may be used to combat it.

Advocates of prefigurative politics have little to say about contract. Nevertheless, the concept of prefigurative change sheds interesting light on Mills's project. Prefigurative approaches beg two questions about the transformative potential of Mills's subversive contract. The first is about the extent to which the retention of an ideal standard of justice necessarily restricts the local determination of action and constrains activism by keeping it within boundaries that are defined and enforced by the state. The second is about the extent to which the constitutional instruments – rights, for example – guaranteed by states can be used prefiguratively in direct actions to combat injustice. Does prefiguration rule out both the acceptance of a principle of justice and the appropriation of the tools that Mills's contract defends? Carole Pateman's critique of Mills indicates that prefiguration is incompatible with the logic of contract, but that the tools states use to regulate justice may be used prefiguratively. To the extent that activists engage in direct actions and resist tying justice to any fixed agreement, they are also free to appropriate the master's tools to struggle against domination and oppression.

Contract and free agreement

Carole Pateman's critique of Mills develops two interrelated lines of argument: first, she rejects contract as a potential tool for recuperation from the master and, second, she recommends a concept of 'free agreement' as an alternative to contract (Pateman and Mills, 2008: 15). The thrust of her critique is that Mills's 'anti-contractarian contractarianism' fails fully to combat relations of domination and, insofar as it recommends an ideal conception of justice, it re-inscribes the state. In contrast, 'free agreement' provides a route to its reimagination. To explain the difference, I set Pateman's critique of Mills alongside Michael Bakunin's anarchist critique of Rousseau's social contract and then turn to Martin Buber's anti-contractarian, anti-state critique of Rousseau to recover the concept of free agreement as the practice that contract suppresses.

Like Mills, Pateman depicts contract theory as part of the state's ideological machinery. She argues that contract was advanced during a tumultuous period of European state formation and was deployed to justify 'specific forms of political order' (Pateman and Mills, 2008: 20). Ultimately smoothing the passage from absolutism to liberalism and republicanism, contract cemented constitutional protections for private property ownership, political liberties, rights and, for Pateman, the systems of structural inequality that these regimes regulate and protect. Contract is 'about the creation of the modern state and structures of power, including sexual and racial power' (ibid.). The generic order it defends, which extends beyond the particular constitutional settlements that contract theorists variously recommended, is one of domination.

Pateman's fundamental objection to contract is that it requires individuals 'to give up their right of self-government' (ibid.: 15). Rousseau 'was well aware' of this. Taking up the story of contact with Rousseau's *Social Contract* (at the point Mills leaves it), she argues that contract theory introduces a counterfactual condition, which denies the material reality that 'humans create their own social and political structures and institutions' (ibid.: 14). For Pateman, this counterfactual plays a primary role in legitimising patterns of actual domination in modern states by sustaining an idea of consent that is highly restrictive.

Pateman's critique has a strong anarchist flavour. Exposing the ideological role that contract played in legitimising inequalities in the state was a central concern of nineteenth-century anarchists and Rousseau was a particular target of their critiques. For Bakunin, Rousseau's error was to mis-describe the processes that explained the imposition of the contract of domination. He concluded that Rousseau had advanced a brilliant critique of tyranny and slavery through his analysis of

Locke, but that his alternative construction of the social contract proceeded from the faulty and inconceivable assumption of 'primitive men enjoying absolute liberty only in isolation' (Bakunin, 1972 [1895]: 175–6). In the *Origin on the Discourse of Inequality*, Rousseau narrated a novel story that described insecurity in physical and psychological terms. Yet, in telling it, Bakunin argued, Rousseau recycled the contractarian fallacy that human beings are 'antisocial by nature' and 'destroy each other's freedom' when 'forced to associate' (ibid.). Having misconstrued politics as a field demanding a solution to the problem of mutual destruction, Rousseau had mistakenly argued that natural beings were obliged to 'conclude a contract, formal or tacit, whereby they surrender some of their freedom to assure the rest' (ibid.).

Bakunin acknowledged that contract was only one of several theoretical devices available to advocates of state organisation and he classified it as particular expression of the principle of domination. Domination has its roots in what Bakunin called 'political theology'. In common with other theories of government, the contract rested on a pervasive belief that humans were imperfect, corrupt beings who required discipline and external guidance to straighten out their crookedness and bring them to perfection. Contract theorists were typically political liberals, individualists and Kantians. Yet, their idea of government dovetailed with the conceptions of conservatives who considered the state 'the work of God' and the metaphysicians – notably Hegelians – who founded the state on a 'more or less mystical realisation of objective morality' (ibid.: 174). Having placed human fallibility and frailty at the heart of politics, Bakunin complained that all these political theologians passed off their preferred systems of government as ideal, perfect and beyond contention.

Bakunin's understanding of political theology helps explain Pateman's opposition to Mills's anti-contractarian contract. The divergence between Pateman and Mills is not about the fairness of the power relationships contract cements, but about the intelligibility of re-theorising justice within the state with reference to a contractual arrangement. Pateman takes issue with Mills's view that the moral equality of persons central to the minimal contract enables us to remain alert to domination and injustice. Her concern is that his invocation of contract is inherently conservative because it relies on an ideal that is inevitably skewed by prevailing power relations.

Pressed by Mills, Pateman acknowledges that contract can be construed in different ways. A contract may take the form of either 'contractarianism' or of 'contractualism'. In Pateman's reading, contractarianism refers to the bargains struck by individuals deemed to possess property in themselves, who contract to sell their labour and/or acquire services, goods and chattels. Contractualism, by contrast, promotes the moral philosophy of personhood and the duty not to treat others as mere means.[3] Locke advanced a form of contractarianism. Mills, on the contrary, places himself in the tradition of Kant and Rawls and proposes contractualism. Yet,

3 The more familiar distinction between contractarianism and contractualism turns on the derivation of the content of morality. Contractarianism is linked to Hobbesian traditions and the maximisation of self-interest in bargains with others. Contractualism is associated with Kantianism and requires

Pateman considers both as forms of domination. Contractarianism is particularly pernicious because it embeds economic inequalities in the state: rich and poor are said to agree to rules that maintain the principles of equality that underpin class differences. Contractualism operates differently in theory, but Pateman maintains that it is tainted by the power relations that states regulate, and, which contract theory has already helped normalise. Unable to see the relationships of domination that structured eighteenth-century societies, Kant had advocated moral equality and endorsed a social contract that subordinated workers to owners, women to men and non-white peoples to whites. Kantianism cannot now 'be washed clean' (Pateman and Mills, 2008: 21) precisely because the 'actual "contract" that has established the present social order' is not 'so radically different from the sanitized version presupposed' by the theory, as Mills contends (ibid.: 23). Pateman agrees with Mills that Rawls's contractors are anything but abstract trans-historical individuals who can help us model ideal justice. They are persons with interests who perpetuate forms of domination managed by states. Yet, her conclusion is that re-theorising the injustices arising from those relations will not upset the power advantages that are embedded within contract. Pateman argues:

> [c]ontract, in particular contracts about property in the person, is the major mechanism through which these unfree institutions are kept alive and presented as free institutions. Contemporary contract theory provides no help in either of its guises if we wish to create a more democratic and a more free society (ibid.: 20).

Turning to the alternative, Pateman refers to free agreement as 'a voluntary mutual undertaking' which genuinely recognises that human beings create the socio-political realm (ibid.: 15). In anarchist political thought, free agreement is distinguished from contract in three ways. First, it is a process of continual adjustment, driven by social forces that are unequal and fluid. Second, like contract, free agreement relies on individual judgment and consent, but this is secured by means of cooperation and through the social practices and institutions that individuals collectively construct (Kropotkin in Baldwin, 1970 [1910]: 284–5). Third, free agreement gives expression to justice through the constant negotiation of social and individual rights. According to this view, transformative change is driven by the perception of the gaps between actual injustice and its ideal, but the ideal is elaborated through social interaction not determined in advance. As injustices are addressed, the conception of the ideal thus also changes. Kropotkin took his lead from Proudhon, who, he argued:

> ascribed great importance to idealization, to the ideals that in certain periods acquire ascendancy over the petty daily cares, when the discrepancy between the law, understood as the highest expression of justice, and actual life as the

---

individuals to pursue their interests in a way that can be justified to others (Ashford and Mulgan, 2007/18).

power of legislation, acquires the proportions of a glaring, unbearable contra-diction (Kropotkin, 1968 [1924]: 272).

The state's enforcement of contractual obligations compromises free agreement in each of these spheres. And the repercussions are felt both in the construction of state-civil society relations and within in civil realm. Contracts regulating property, labour and marriage are all unfree (Kropotkin, 1985 [1906]: ch. 11).

To show how the state deliberately represses free agreement, anarchists returned to the story of contract. Bakunin's pithy analysis honed in on the relationship of the state to society. The contract 'becomes the foundation of society, or rather of the State, for we must point out that in this theory there is no place for society; only the State exists, or rather society is completely absorbed by the State' (Bakunin, 1972 [1895]: 176). Writing in the twentieth century, Martin Buber, a sympathetic critic of nineteenth-century anarchism, developed Bakunin's insight. Buber explained the pervasiveness of statism in political theory with reference to the 'defective differenti-ation between the social and the political principles' (1957: 161). Tracing the roots of the confusion to classical thought, he explored the implications in a genealogy that tracked the absorption of the social principle in a narrow concept of 'the political'.

For Buber, the incorporation of the social in the political was a process charac-terised by the excision of the rights vested in independent associations through the state's constitution. This process was eased, Buber felt, by the wrongful claim that the state represented society. Contract theory was a powerful part of this pretence. Turning to Hobbes, Buber observed that the civil society associations that embody the social principle are painted out of existence in the anarchy that Hobbes had imagined. Individuals possess rights, but there are no social rights because individu-als in the state of nature are said to lack the capacity to cooperate. Moreover, the natural rights they possess are nearly all surrendered to the state as a condition of its order. Buber concluded that:

> [i]n Hobbes' view 'civil society is entirely identical with the State'. Hobbes was aware of the 'social principle' and the 'free contracts between individu-als for the recognition and preservation of the rights of ownership'. Yet the thrust of Hobbes's argument is that the state's perfection entails the annihila-tion of the 'last vestige of society' (ibid.: 168).

Taking the analysis forward to the eighteenth century, Buber argued that Rous-seau had reworked Hobbes's thesis, replacing Leviathan with the general will: the invention of the general will thoroughly confused 'the social and political princi-ples'. Although Rousseau had been perfectly able to 'distinguish between the social contract and the establishment of the State in a legal manner', he had called for free associations to be expunged from the body of the state. In the *Social Contract*, Buber contended, Rousseau had prohibited the existence of:

> any society which is constituted of various large and small associations; that is to say, a society with a truly social structure, in which the diversified spontaneous

contacts of individuals for common purposes of co-operation and co-exist-
ence, i.e. the vital essence of society are [sic] represented (ibid.: 169).

Buber's idea was that contract theory sat within a statist logic. It formalised
the state's actual subordination and regulation of all other associations according
to the terms of the one-off choices that rational, morally equal individuals had
purportedly made. It was still possible to conclude free agreements in the body of
the state, but not through the legal mechanisms that contact established within it.
Civil society associations are, then, able to contest the arrangements or decisions
that issue from the state, but not the principles on which the decisions are based.
The substitution of free agreement for contract means leaving the terms on which
agreements are made and remade to groups and individuals organised in infinitely
plural bodies.

In recovering the 'social' from political theory, Buber also recovered an understanding of rights that contract theory smothers and distorts. He defined rights
as powers that regulate relations within and between self-governing associations.
Contract theorists imagined that states introduced or guaranteed rights and entitlements through the establishment of law (Dhawan, in this volume). Buber argued
that rights are located in the social sphere and are simply part of a matrix of regulatory tools that social groups use to structure their relations. Where free agreement
prevails, the legal enforcement of contracts is relinquished to the 'societies, groups,
circles, unions, co-operative bodies, and communities varying very widely in type,
form, scope, and dynamics' that comprise civil society (Buber, 1957: 173). Rights
function in the same way within and between local communities. In 'the social-
federative sphere', Buber argued, 'Society (with a capital S)' realises its object. He
continues:

> Just as Society keeps individuals together in their way of life by force of habit
> and custom and holds them close to one another and, by public opinion, in
> the sense of continuity, keeps them together in their way of thinking, so it
> influences the contact and the mutual relations between the societies (ibid.).

The power imbalances, dysfunctions and transgressions that states and societies
confront are similar. Buber commented: 'Society cannot . . . quell the conflicts
between different groups; it is powerless to unite divergent and clashing groups'
(ibid.). Yet, the grounds on which contract and free agreement are secured and
evaluated are divergent. Contract refers back to the original terms of the agreement,
assuming those terms to be fair, and enforces compliance, treating it as consent. Free
agreement has no such authority and it assumes social conflict as well as the possibility of injustice as a result of interest, custom and tradition. Like contract, free
agreement thus recognises the limits of consent and the possibility of domination
in perpetuity.

In what sense can free agreement help reimagine the state? Pateman's argument
that free agreement replaces contract has two implications. The first is that groups

and individuals must articulate ideal principles themselves and not just accept ideals as part and parcel of a contractual arrangement. The moral equality of persons is only one possible standard of judgment that the disadvantaged may use to combat actual injustice. Free agreement gives individuals and social groups latitude to articulate principles to address problems of domination. Decoupling justice from any fixed contractual principle ensures that existing arrangements are always open to renegotiation. Even if habit and custom in fact militate against this, no contractual obligation exists to pre-empt or hinder the possibility of free agreement. Second, the relocation of rights from the political to the social sphere reinforces Mills's view that the master's tools can be used to destroy the master's house, while significantly altering the grounds of the argument. Buber's analysis of contract suggests that asserting a right is not, as Mills suggests, to appropriate a master's tool. It is to argue that the right was never the master's in the first place.

Prefiguration, free agreement and rights

Free agreement is incompatible with Mills's subversive contractualism for two reasons. First, it perpetuates the principle of domination vested in contract and, second, it introduces a fixed principle of justice. Mills argues that the minimal contract treats humans as creators of the socio-political realm and that the liberal commitment to moral equality provides a yardstick to assess the injustices of actual societies in ways that facilitate redress. Advocates of free agreement worry that the commitment to moral equality does not empower the dominated to challenge prevailing systems of domination because contract wrongly obliges social groups to adopt the standards that 'masters' use to settle disputes, rather than allow the dominated to explore problems of justice and injustice as they perceive or experience them. This concern suggests that the minimal contract is incompatible with prefiguration, too, because it restricts the autonomy of local agents. As Benjamin Franks argues, prefigurative politics is compatible with the 'use of a moral framework to assess anarchist methods' (2006: 97), but not with the identification of a ready-made principle of justice.

At the same time, the relocation of rights from the narrowly political to the social realm opens up a space for the reclamation of the master's tools or, in other words, prefigurative direct actions that challenge systemic injustices without reinforcing the state's claims to legitimacy.

Because the line between prefigurative and non-prefigurative action is sometimes blurred, it is difficult to determine the limits of this reclamation. Analysing shifts in the politics of Occupy Wall Street, Gordon argues that the participants blunted the critique of corporate capitalism even as they adopted 'quintessentially anarchistic modes of organizing', which were 'non-hierarchical, decentralized, consensus-based, and mindful of the need to overcome enactments of domination among the participants' (n.d.: 49). The protestors' error, he suggests, was to appeal to the will of the sovereign people to call for social justice and policy change at elite level. By issuing this call, they mistakenly legitimised the proxy power government claims.

The potency of Gordon's view depends on the ways in which transformative claims are made and the content they are given. Demanding the right to free speech can be prefigurative, although is it often now expressed as a demand by one social group that the state silence another. The direct actions by the feminist performance group Speaking of IMELDA, which called on political elites to repeal the 8th Amendment of the Irish Constitution (which prohibited abortion in Ireland), are similarly prefigurative. Their performances explicitly challenged the legitimacy of government to determine birthrights on behalf of women and were designed to uncover the dynamics of patriarchal power in church and state. The Aboriginal Embassy protest in Canberra is another example of a direct action that reclaims a tool from 'masters' to advance transformative change. Established in 1972 to assert the land rights of Indigenous people against the claims of the settler government, the Embassy consists of a set of tents and signs outside the Old Parliament Building in Canberra. The establishment and persistence of the Tent Embassy is designed to highlight the illegitimacy of the settler government. As Paul Muldoon and Andrew Schaap explain, '[b]y speaking from a position outside the constitution, the Aboriginal Embassy makes present the anomaly of Indigenous people within the Australian polity':

> The demonstrators act, on the one hand, as Australian citizens who are made alien in their own land by the continuing process of colonial dispossession with which the constitutional order is complicit. On the other hand, they act as members of a pan-Aboriginal sovereign nation, whose recognition the constitutional order requires to become legitimate. In doing so, the Aboriginal Embassy provokes the decolonization of the Australian state and society (2014: 219–20).

Aligned with free agreement, prefiguration is compatible with the use of the master's tools because it denies the rights of masters to grant them as permissions or to pronounce authoritatively on the legitimacy of actions. Rights are powerful tools available to activists involved in prefigurative struggles. Many anarchists, including Franks and Newman, argue that individuals also have rights as members of groups in both the social and the political realm, society and the state. To this extent, free agreement gives individuals latitude to reclaim in prefigurative actions what masters have misappropriated from the social realm. It allows them to assert rights individually and in groups, whether or not those rights actually exist in law, as long as the right is asserted in ways that avoid reinforcing the master's permissive power.

Conclusion: Reimagining the state

I have argued that Mills rightly demonstrates the potential for using the master's tools prefiguratively to advance transformative change. Drawing on anarchist thought to develop Pateman's critique of contract, I have also argued that vestiges of the state's power to determine the justice of transformative actions are retained in Mills's anti-contractarian contractarianism. In drawing attention to Rousseau's critique of Locke, Mills shows that contractual agreements, made on the basis of a presumed consent, entrench social, cultural and economic inequalities to perpetuate patterns of domination. Pateman's conception of free agreement acknowledges the dynamic relationship between non-ideal and ideal theory that Mills advances, but jettisons the liberal principles and values which Mills recommends to support justice campaigns. Free agreement recommends open negotiation to realise justice and thus articulates a principle of non-domination that does not compromise prefigurative commitments to the determination of justice by local actors.

Seen through the lens of contract and domination, the state is constructed as a sociological reality, which cannot be reimagined, but which can be anarchised through prefigurative action. This involves attacking established notions of justice without dispensing with moral rules and redeveloping the principles of political association collaboratively and cooperatively, rather than abandoning them, as the convention construction of 'anarchy' disingenuously suggests. It requires that disputes and conflicts are resolved through negotiation, not *diktat*, and that justice is not determined in advance of the negotiations. Indeed, it might be argued that because anarchists reject the state, they are especially obliged to pay attention to showing how 'societal processes in which one can be held responsible for his or her acts' can be made 'known . . . before hand [sic] and be developed fairly' (Holterman, 1993: 350). Challenging the state is a conceptual and creative process, which involves both rethinking political theory and reinventing practice. According to the anthropologist James Scott, the uplands in Southeast Asia, home to approximately 100 million marginal people, have not yet been colonised by the state (2009: ix). In this huge geographical area, which he refers to as Zomia, the inhabitants practice a range of sophisticated arts to avoid being governed. For most of the rest of us, the state is already our reality and there is little prospect of escape. What arts can we learn to reimagine it? One is to refashion the tools that masters call theirs as our own and use them to fight domination as if our agreements were free.

Acknowledgements

I'm grateful to Davina Cooper and Nikita Dhawan for their encouragement and helpful comments and to Robert Knight, Phil Parvin, Simon Stevens and Judith Suissa for their feedback on earlier drafts.

References

Ashford, E. and Mulgan, T. (2007/18) 'Contractualism', *Standford Encyclopedia of Philosophy* [online]. Available at https://plato.stanford.edu (accessed 19 September 2018).

Bakunin, M. (1972) *Oeuvres*, vol. 1: *Fédéralisme, Socialisme et Antithéologisme* [1895]. Paris: PV Stock.

Bartleson, J. (2001) *The Critique of the State*. Cambridge: Cambridge University Press.

Buber, M. (1957) 'Society and the State [1951]' in Friedman, M S. (ed. and trans.), *Pointing the Way: Collected Essays by Martin Buber*. New York: Harpertorch Books, pp. 161–76.

Daniels, N. (1989) [1975] 'Introduction' in Daniels, N. (ed.), *Reading Rawls: Critical Studies on Rawls' 'A Theory of Justice'*. Stanford, CA: University of Stanford Press, pp. xxxi–lvi.

Feinberg, J. (1989) [1975] 'Rawls and Intuitionism' in Daniels, N. (ed.), *Reading Rawls: Critical Studies on Rawls' 'A Theory of Justice'*. Stanford, CA: University of Stanford Press, pp. 108–23.

Franks, B. (2006) *Rebel Alliances: The Means and Ends of Contemporary British Anarchisms*. Edinburgh and Oakland: AK Press/Dark Star.

Gordon, U. (n.d.) 'Insurrectionary Patriotism and the Defusion of Dissent', *Anarchy A Journal of Desire Armed*, 75, pp. 48–53, 71.

Gordon, U. (2008) *Anarchy Alive! Anti-Authoritarian Politics from Practice to Theory*. London: Pluto.

Holterman, T. (1993) 'Anarchism and Legal Science', *Archiv für Rechts un Sozialphilosophie/ Archives for Philosophy of Law and Social Philosophy*, 79(3), pp. 349–59.

Klosko, G. (2011) 'Contemporary Anglo-American Political Philosophy' in Klosko, G. (ed.), *The Oxford Handbook of the History of Political Philosophy*. Oxford: Oxford University Press, pp. 456–79.

Kropotkin, P. (n.d.) [1902] *Mutual Aid: A Factor of Evolution*. Boston: Extending Horizon Books.

Kropotkin, P. (1968) [1924] *Ethics: Origin and Development*. Friedland, L. S. and Piroshnikoff, J. R. (trans.). New York: Benjamin Blom.

Kropotkin, P. (1970) '"Anarchism" from the Encyclopaedia Britannica [1910]' in Baldwin, R. (ed.). *Kropotkin's Revolutionary Pamphlets*. New York: Dover Publications, pp. 284–300.

Kropotkin, P. (1985) [1906] *The Conquest of Bread*. London: Elephant Editions.

Kukathas, C. (2014) 'A Definition of the State', *University of Queensland Law Journal*, 33(2), pp. 357–66.

Lev, A. (2014) *Sovereignty and Liberty: A Study of the Foundations of Power*. London: Routledge.

Lorde, A. (2007) 'The Master's Tools Will Never Dismantle the Master's House [1979]' in *Sister Outsider: Essays and Speeches by Audre Lorde*. Berkeley, CA: Crossing Press, pp. 110–13.

Maeckelbergh, M. (2011) 'Doing is Believing: Prefiguration as Strategic Practice in the Alterglobalization Movement', *Social Movement Studies*, 10(1), pp. 1–20.

Mills, C. W. (2005) '"Ideal theory" as Ideology', *Hypatia*, 20(3), pp. 165–84.

Mills, C. W. (2015) 'Rousseau, The Master's Tools, and Anti-Contractarian Contractarianism' in Gordon, J. A. and Roberts, N. (eds.), *Creolizing Rousseau*. London: Rowman & Littlefield, pp. 171–93.

Morris, B. (2005) *Anthropology and Anarchism Their Elective Affinity*. London: Goldsmiths University of London.

Muldoon, P. and Schaap, A. (2014) 'The Constitutional Politics of the Aboriginal Embassy' in Foley, G., Schaap, A. and Howell, E. (eds.), *The Aboriginal Tent Embasssy: Sovereignty, Black Power, and Rights and the State*. London: Routledge, pp. 219–34.

Newman, S. (2016) *Postanarchism*. Cambridge: Polity Press.

Pateman, C. and Mills, C. (2008) 'Contract and Social Change: A Dialogue between Carole Pateman and Charles W. Mills' in ibid., *Contract and Domination*. Cambridge: Polity Press, pp. 10–34.

Scott, J. C. (2009) *The Art of Not Being Governed: An Anarchist History of Upland Southeast Asia*. New Haven, CT: Yale University Press.

Simmons, A. J. (2010) 'Ideal and Nonideal Theory', *Philosophy and Public Affairs*, 38(1), pp. 5–36.

Stemplowska, Z. and Swift, A. (2012) 'Ideal and Nonideal Theory' in Estlund, D. (ed.), *The Oxford Handbook of Political Philosophy*. Oxford: Oxford Handbooks [online]. Available at www.oxfordhandbooks.com (accessed 30 August 2017).

Tuori, K. (2015) *Lawyers and Savages: Ancient History and Legal Realism in the Making of Legal Anthropology*. London: Routledge.

PART III
Prefigurative practices

8

ANTICIPATORY REPRESENTATION

Thinking art and museums as platforms
of resourceful statecraft

Chiara De Cesari

This chapter illuminates the ways in which artists and cultural producers can participate in forging, quite literally, the nation-state by performing its institutions, and by mocking its operations.[1] Can nation-state building and avant-garde, activist art be brought together? Most scholars of nationalism would agree that the nation is a socio-cultural construct. It is the product of multifarious practices of social imagination that allow a group of people to think of themselves as belonging to the same 'imagined community' (Anderson, 1983), despite not really knowing one another. Representations of the nation, from flags to national anthems, are activated through particular rituals (ceremonies, commemorations and so on), and then reproduced and circulated through a variety of media and everyday practices. Less widespread but growing in influence, particularly among anthropologists, is the idea that also the state must be discursively constructed as a bounded singularity in order to produce a 'state effect' (Mitchell, 1991).

This chapter explores how a particular nation-state – one that does not yet (fully) exist – is prefigured through a set of artistic and cultural practices, and reflects on their institutional effects. I examine three different projects that blur the boundaries between reality and fiction: two stage a Palestinian national museum, and the third a Palestinian biennial. These projects also represent the first national cultural institutions of this kind in Palestine, and, particularly in the third case, promote the establishment of a comprehensive national cultural management infrastructure. I examine these projects not only as sites for the (re)production of the imagined community of the nation, but also as platforms to imagine – and to instantiate in embryonic form – a set of institutions that contribute to the making of the future

---

1 Portions of this chapter are drawn, with permission, from Chiara De Cesari, 'Anticipatory Representation: Building the Palestinian Nation(-State) through Artistic Performance' (2012) *Studies in Ethnicity and Nationalism*, 12(1), pp. 82–100.

Palestinian state, as a form of Blochian concrete utopia. I focus on the museum as an important 'ideological state apparatus' (Althusser, 1971), investigating how Palestinian artists and cultural producers have played with the format of the national museum in order to realise it despite the absence of a sovereign Palestinian state and Palestine's diasporic condition. The paradox is that with the continuing occupation of the Palestinian territories and many Palestinians living in the diaspora, a national museum can only exist within a transnational setting.

Is the state and its institutions also the product of imaginative practices? This question has become the object of much anthropological enquiry, at a time when nation-states worldwide have entered a phase of wide-ranging transformations. While it is questionable whether the Weberian model of the state as a centralised, coherent and rational entity detached from society ever represented a historical reality, globalised late capitalism has brought with it the gradual erosion of some of the key features and powers of the modern nation-state, in particular traditional forms of sovereignty. In anthropology, the project of rethinking the state has been deeply influenced by Michel Foucault (1991) and his notion of governmentality (see also Rose et al., 2006), which has highlighted the role of knowledge and the imagination in government, as well as the plurality of agencies involved therein.

Inspired by Foucault, recent anthropological theorising has questioned the unity of the state, and emphasised the great deal of cultural, imaginative work that goes into making the state into a unitary entity, that is, into making an autonomous and coherent institution out of a congeries of sites and agencies, often located across national borders, which carry out (what we have historically come to understand as) 'state' functions (see e.g. Gupta and Sharma, 2006; Thelen et al., 2014; Krupa and Nugent, 2015). Also in political theory, in the context of a shift towards participatory modes of governance, there have been several calls to 'decentre' the nation-state by examining how plural governance formations participate in it, and by uncovering progressive potential and forms of 'activist statehood' in the cracks and gaps between these formations, particularly those embedded in grass-roots organising (Cooper, this volume; see also Painter, 2006; McConnell et al., 2012; Iveson, 2016).

Yet, what does contemporary art have to do with the socio-cultural production of the state, and with tactics of 'activist statehood'? While museums have long been seen, at least by critical scholars, as key ideological apparatuses of the state, crucial for the production of proper citizens and the forging of consent through representations of the nation as a longstanding and civilised community (see e.g. Bennett, 1995), avant-garde art has rarely been viewed as a site for the reproduction of the power of the nation-state. But recently, the relationship between aesthetics and politics has resurfaced as a prominent area of interdisciplinary study. While a number of philosophers have claimed that a process of growing aestheticisation of knowledge, reality and politics has taken place from the latter part of the twentieth century onwards (e.g. Debord, 1983 [1967]; Welsch, 1997), one can observe a parallel politicisation of artistic practices and the proliferation of so-called 'political art' and 'artivism' (e.g. Groys, 2014; Thompson, 2015; Weibel, 2015) and practices that cross the boundaries between representation, invention and intervention. Intersubjectivity and the blurring of boundaries between representation and intervention is indeed a mark of much contemporary art. Curator and art theorist Nicolas Bourriaud (2002) has defined a set of prominent art practices since the 1990s as 'relational art': that is, art as an endeavour fundamentally concerned with producing social relationships, with 'modelling possible universes' and microtopian communities.

Along with this social turn, a number of shifts have taken place in how contemporary avant-garde art functions, including a movement away from the traditional relationship between the artwork and the audience, previously grounded in the latter's contemplation of the former, and towards interactivity and participation. Also, the artwork no longer functions as a 'discrete, portable, autonomous work of art that transcends its context' (Bishop, 2004: 54) and communicates a set of universal meanings, but rather as a constructed situation à la Debord, as a stage for possible future scenarios, and as a space for 'imagining things otherwise' (Esche, 2004). To sum up, moving from *mimesis* to *poiesis*, from representing to remaking and changing the world – in other words, abolishing art's autonomy – seems to be a core objective of contemporary avant-garde art. Responding to these shifts, critical theorists like Jacques Rancière have argued that 'the materiality of art has been able to make of itself the anticipated materiality of a different configuration of the community' (2006: 32). Such *anticipated materiality* is also what contemporary Palestinian art tries to accomplish.

I explore two experiments in setting up a Palestinian national museum, which are also art projects in themselves. Moreover, I pay heed to the first Palestinian art biennials, organised by a Palestinian non-governmental organisation (NGO) in 2007 and 2009 in various locations across the Mediterranean. The biennials, too, were simultaneously an artwork and a real event, as well as an institutional beginning. Indeed, the blurring of the boundary between artistic representation and reality was a defining feature of each of these projects. All three stage a particular institution of power, the museum, which has been fundamentally concerned with national representation since its full development as part of the infrastructure of the nation-state in the nineteenth century. Yet, they are all cosmopolitan, travelling projects. While their representations of the nation(-state) are staged largely in exile, these projects are animated by the promise of return, acquiring their full meaning as a prefiguration of institutions soon to come to Palestine. Moreover, there is a further friction. Art biennials constitute the latest transmutation of the museum form, and as such have inherited much of the latter's logic and organisational infrastructure. Although they occur in a transnational context, and are currently proliferating across the world, biennials are fundamentally concerned with national representation, as well as nation and city branding (see Filipovich et al., 2010). More importantly, they are usually organised by state cultural institutions: organising a biennial reflects a city's or state's desire to be included on the global map of cultural and tourism flows (as well as its desire to attract capital investments for local development). Yet, the organisers of the Palestinian biennials, as well as the main actors behind both national museum projects, all belong to the transnational Palestinian civil society. These are all 'state-like' initiatives instituted by non-state actors who playfully engage with these ambiguities.

It is my argument that the biennials and the experiments in establishing a Palestinian national museum constitute a kind of artistic practice that does not just imitate or represent the social world, however critically; rather, they are artistic practices that purport to *produce* new social arrangements, in particular a set of new 'state' (art and cultural) institutions. They participate in the making of the Palestinian state-to-come through a tactic of *anticipatory representation*. By exploring these very peculiar cases of a national museum and an art biennial, my broader aim is to examine contemporary artistic practices as sites for the performance and creative reforging of state institutions.

The political context of the current Palestinian cultural mobilisation

Palestine is neither a nation-state nor a postcolonial entity; today, it is a fragmented, diasporic and occupied nation. Most Palestinians live as refugees outside of their original homeland, the descendants of those forced to leave what became the state of Israel in 1948. Many others live in the West Bank and Gaza, or else in Israel. In 1994, the Oslo Accords set up the Palestinian Authority (PA) as the Palestinian 'proto-state', that is, as an interim body to oversee the transition to statehood in the occupied territories. Yet, the failure of the so-called peace process left that transition suspended. Today, the PA is a non-sovereign entity that administers a series of disconnected areas of the West Bank and Gaza from which the Israeli military has withdrawn; around these areas, colonisation and settlement building proceed uninterrupted, and Israel retains control of external borders, airspace and all movement in and out of the Palestinian enclaves. Effectively, the occupation continues in a mutated form (Halper, 2000; Ophir and Azoulay, 2012). Politically, then, the Palestinian territories are characterised by what I would call 'asymmetric dispersion': Israeli colonial rule continues, while key state functions are performed by international donors and aid agencies, and a local infrastructure of Palestinian organisations working to provide essential services. Divided since 2007 into two major sections, one controlled by Islamist Hamas (Gaza) and the other by the secular-nationalist Fatah party (the West Bank), the PA is only one actor in this complex field, and clearly not the most powerful. These circumstances and particularly the tremendous growth of Israeli colonies since Oslo have made several pundits doubt the viability of a two-state solution to the Israeli-Palestinian conflict (Hilal, 2007).

In recent years, this fractured and conflict-ridden terrain has been the platform for a great flourishing of cultural activities and museum projects, including the initiatives described below. Its agents understand themselves as participating in a culture of resistance, yet, according to some critics, they are actually contributing, albeit unintentionally, to a kind of normalisation of the occupation and the current status quo.

The impossible institution: Designing a Palestinian national museum

Since the Oslo Accords granted Palestinians a degree of autonomy, a number of small museums and exhibition spaces have been set up, in addition to older folklore-focused institutions. In most cases, these institutions are not PA but charitable societies, private foundations, NGOs and other 'civil society' institutions. A symptom of the PA's failure thus far in completing its project of state building, a national museum in Palestine has long been, in the words of Jack Persekian (whose work we will return to shortly), a 'practical impossibility' (Pelgrom, 2007: 3).[2] The establishment of the PA as an interim body was for many a promise of Palestinian statehood; yet, the latter has not come to pass. With no sovereign state, functioning national institutions have made room for improvised arrangements. National museums have been made possible only thanks to the creative nomadic practices of a number of Palestinian artists and cultural operators.

The Palestinian Museum is the institution that probably most closely resembles a national museum in the territories. This project, however, is a civil society one, initiated in the 1990s and still run by one of the major Palestinian NGOs, the Welfare Association (WA), financed with expatriate Palestinian capital. Tasked with producing a new concept, noted historian Beshara Doumani took over the Palestinian Museum in the late 2000s after the failure of earlier projects. He describes the story of the museum in the following way:

> The early iterations of this project conceived of it as a traditional national museum. That is, a major commemorative structure built around a single chronological narrative from ancient times to the present. I conceptualize it, instead, as a *mobilizing and interactive cultural project* that can stitch together the fragmented Palestinian body politic by presenting a wide variety of narratives about the relationships of Palestinians to the land, to each other and to the wider world (2010, emphasis added).

The WA museum initiative highlights the difficulties of building a nineteenth-century-style national museum outside of the infrastructure of a sovereign state, and the challenges that arise when an NGO steps in to substitute for the latter. As Doumani emphasises, there is both a problem of the scale and 'magnitude' involved (an NGO undertaking a project with costs ranging into the hundreds of million of dollars) and a problem of representation (who has the right to represent the diversity of Palestinian voices?) (2011). Rarely self-sustainable, museums are very expensive to maintain and require guarantees of long-term institutional support.

2 Major obstacles to a Palestinian national museum project include a lack of funding and expertise, and crucially, the problem of its location: while this museum can only be located in Jerusalem, which Palestinians consider their historic capital, Israel opposes any kind of Palestinian institutional presence in the city it views as its capital and effectively controls (if against international law and UN resolutions, see B'Tselem, 2006).

Museums' operational time frames are not those of the typical NGO, which works with a limited budget and short-term, project-like timetables. Doumani's proposed means for overcoming these obstacles was a transnational museum: in his words, 'not a museum-state as much as a museum-nation' (2010), made up of a network of transnational centres or 'rings' as nodes of knowledge production and social mobilisation.[3] This museum concept is in contrast to the traditional monumental building in a fixed location, marked by a large, costly collection and a single over-arching narrative; as such, it was expected to mirror the diversity of Palestine and the plural meaning of Palestinianness, and to allow for different voices to be heard. Doumani wanted such a museum to act as an inclusive platform on which to pro-duce interconnectivity, and as a true 'embodiment of the Palestinian body-politic' in its multiplicity, and as itself an 'arena for the performance and reproduction of . . . peoplehood by Palestinians' (2010) in the face of dispersion and fragmentation.

But the Palestinian museum that was eventually built in Birzeit is much closer in its architectural form to the earlier 1990s monumental conception rather than to the knots of memory idea espoused by Doumani and the long-time head of the museum's task force, Omar Al-Qattan. A large museum building of stone and glass was completed in 2016 at a cost of $25 million and towers now over a landscaped, terraced garden of 40,000 m² next to Ramallah; a further expansion is already planned. The architectural firm designing the museum is also building the new Grand Egyptian Museum by the pyramids (apparently, the largest ever archaeologi-cal museum), as well as a number of national cultural institutions across the world in what appears like a grand style of the nation-state in globalised times. While the original curatorial team wanted to make an exhibition without objects to represent the loss and dispossession at the heart of the Palestinian condition and to prob-lematise national narratives, there were a series of disagreements, and so this team resigned and the museum was inaugurated empty. A less provocative and more consensual approach was then chosen for the first exhibition of the museum, which opened in late 2017.

The impossible national museum thus appeared possible only 'in a transnational not territorially-fixed setting', or as an art performance. In this context of inter-rupted statehood, with its failed or (at the very least) troubled institutions, a few more 'national museums' have been realised in the form of mobile, cosmopolitan art projects. Blurring repetition and mockery of its standard form, these projects radically dislocate the museum by making it 'portable': a 'nomadic' project in exile. At the same time, these projects take their roles very seriously; in fact, they represent the very first instances of a Palestinian national museum and, more broadly, of a national art infrastructure. By mocking the museum format, they plant and nurture the seeds for future institutions.

---

3 If not otherwise noted, all following quotes in this section as well as the information and data on the WA Palestinian Museum come from my interview with Beshara Dumani (2011). He is, however, no longer the director of the project.

Khalil Rabah's Palestinian Museum of Natural History and Humankind

First shown internationally at the 2005 Istanbul Biennial, artist Khalil Rabah's museum prompted visitors to ask themselves: 'But is it real?' (Paynter, 2006). The same must have happened the year after, when the museum was installed in the shadow of the New Acropolis Museum in Athens. Although it changes according to the context of each exhibition, this installation usually consists of a museum-like display of artefacts organised thematically in a set of cabinets. The visitors' movement across the installation space is also organised as if in a museum, framed by an entrance marked by a ticket desk and with a café at the end of the exhibition. This museum clearly mocks the traditional form of the so-called universal museum, those vast collections ranging from natural history to archaeology and art that constituted the core of the first national museums in the metropolitan centres (often born of colonial plunder, see Bennett, 1995; Bal, 1996). On display are fossils, bones and meteorites; upon closer inspection, however, one discovers that these are not 'natural' specimens, but artefacts, carefully crafted by Rabah out of wood from the olive tree, which is a key symbol of Palestine and Palestinian nationalism. Playing with the nature/culture dichotomy and its confusion, this critical device reveals a key convention of colonial displays, and indeed their enduring legacy within postcolonial national institutions.

But Rabah's objective is not simply to critique the museum form and its entanglement with the colonial project and the oppression of native peoples. He turns a chief colonial institution such as the museum against itself. His project is not only one of critical representation – of *mimesis* – but also of *poiesis*, in the Ancient Greek sense of creation and making. At the Istanbul Biennial, the artist presented a show from the (allegedly) permanent collection of the 'Museum of Natural History and Humankind' with these comments:

> Here this Museum presents an exhibition, 'Palestine before Palestine' from the permanent collection of the museum, which tells people that there is a museum with an established, permanent collection, and yet it only exists as an institution within an institution, in the transient event of the biennale.[4]

This museum manifests itself in a number of museum-like operations, (mock) rituals of the art and cultural world. For example, in 2004, it organised one of the first 'art' auctions on Palestinian ground, the 'Third Annual Wall Zone Sale' at Ramallah's Khalil Sakakini Cultural Center. Here, Rabah auctioned off objects collected around the Separation Wall in an ironic act of political protest at the devastations wrought by the eight-metre-high barrier that imprisons West Bank Palestinians in a number of enclaves. Another initiative, hosted by the London Brunei

---

4 This quote appears in 'Displacement and Re-placement', available online from http://www.culture base.net/culturebase.net/artistfa7c.html?164 (accessed 6 March 2018).

Gallery, involved the reading of over 50,000 names of the owners of the old buildings inscribed on the first Palestinian national inventory of historic properties – a
counterpoint to the nearby display of ancient Oriental archaeology from Gaza of
the colonial Petrie Collection (see O'Reilly, n.d.). Instantiations of the museums
continue to this day in various locations across the globe, the last one, as I write,
being the compilation of the museum catalogue by a group of scholars and artists.

Noteworthy is the name of the Museum of Natural History and Humankind's
exhibition 'Palestine before Palestine' (an exhibition within an exhibition within an
exhibition, and here the boxes multiply), whose content is claimed to have come
from the permanent collection of the museum. The preposition 'before' points to
a crucial temporal dimension that is common to all of the initiatives discussed in
this chapter. What I would call a 'temporality of the promise' is typical of national
museums, particularly historical ones, but becomes overamplified in these initiatives.
Donald Preziosi (2010) has argued that museums work by manufacturing belief in
the prior existence and independent agency of what their objects are taken to represent, which is often the very spirit of a nation. Moreover, and this is crucial, they are
marked by a peculiar sense of time that governs the relationship between museum
representations and that which is represented. What Preziosi calls the mythological,
'uncanny space-time of museology' refers to

'A certain sense of time as *aspect*: time as a syntactical relation between events
connected in a causal relation of *incompletion* and *fulfillment*. In this regard, the "past"
of the artefact/relic is not uncommonly staged as an incomplete manifestation or a
prologue to what has now come to pass in the present place of observation. Every
artefact is thus the relic of an absence: of an absent past which at the same time
prefigures our present, which in turn fulfils, completes or "proves" what we imagine
the past imagines to be its future' (2010: 58).

Similarly, Rabah's museum is a device that produces a sense of incompleteness
and anticipation (Palestine before Palestine) and that calls for a future fulfilment.
It is a promise of permanence, both of the museum itself (it is, after all, a museum
with a permanent collection!) and of the entity evoked by its artefacts. This is not
just a museum, however; rather, it is an artwork representing a particular museum,
the Palestinian National Museum, which does not yet exist. Not simply a critical
representation of such an institution, it becomes an anticipatory one.

Contemporary Art Museum Palestine (CAMP)

This temporality of promise and anticipation is further apparent in another Palestinian national museum initiative, namely, the Contemporary Art Museum Palestine (CAMP). In a way, CAMP is a more 'real' museum than Khalil Rabah's art
installation, particularly when viewed in light of the institution that the initiative
prefigures and invokes. In this case, the collection itself does not yet really exist; at
present, it is largely a promise, or a series of artists' agreements on paper.

CAMP is an ongoing project that has changed over the years, the result of curator Jack Persekian's long-term involvement in cultural organising in East Jerusalem.

Written agreements to donate artworks to CAMP, signed by over 35 artists, are stored in a folder in the Al-Ma'mal Foundation for Contemporary Art in Jerusalem, while a small selection of these works found a 'surrogate home' (as Persekian used to call CAMP's host museums in the diaspora) in the Van Abbemuseum in Eindhoven, the Netherlands. This small mobile collection is 'in exile' because of the lack of a proper home in Jerusalem.[5] The long-term goal of the project is to create a national Palestinian museum of the arts in Jerusalem, on Palestinian ground. Under the current political circumstances, however, the return of the collection to the city is 'deferred', suspended in a way that mirrors the stalemate concerning the right of Palestinian refugees to return to their original homeland (see Pelgrom, 2007).[6] The status of this collection in exile also mirrors the enduring de-territorialised, diasporic condition of the Palestinian nation and the current suspension of Palestinian statehood.

In the Van Abbe interview, Persekian, who today is a key cultural operator and art promoter in the Middle East, narrates the history and the purpose of the museum, which he describes as a 'practical solution to several questions'.[7] The project is structured around a 'practical impossibility', referring to the feasibility of a national Palestinian museum being established in Jerusalem. It stems from the simultaneous need for such a museum to house a growing art collection, and for it to serve as an identitarian laboratory, a connective space of knowledge and cultural production, just as Doumani suggests. It also stems from a set of concrete questions and dilemmas; for example, how is a Palestinian institution to preserve, exhibit and circulate the fruits of the growing artistic productivity and the current cultural mobilisation in the territories?

CAMP has, however, a home in the Old City of Jerusalem too. In the late 1990s, Persekian, together with a number of artists and other key Palestinian cultural operators, created the Al-Ma'mal Foundation for Contemporary Art, which has since become the focal point of a steadily growing Palestinian experimental art scene, setting up residencies, exhibitions, film screenings and all kinds of educational initiatives and workshops. Today, the Al-Ma'mal is a small but clearly structured art workshop, running three main programmes: the Artist-in-Residence; the Workshops initiative, to encourage local communities and youths to engage with art and creative self-expression; and an exhibition programme. Each year since 2007, the Ma'mal has also organised the Jerusalem Show, a show of contemporary artworks in the alleys of the Old City. At the foundation, both local and non-local artists live and work in Jerusalem for a few weeks, take part in workshops in the West Bank and Gaza, and participate in young people's programmes with Palestinian schools, organisations and universities.

5 If not otherwise noted, all following quotes by Jack Persekian come from his video interview, which is part of the first installation of CAMP at the Van Abbemuseum (Eindhoven, the Netherlands), shown within 'The Politics of Collecting – the Collecting of Politics' exhibition (25 September 2010–6 February 2011). I thank Jack Persekian for providing me with a copy of the taped interview.

6 See also Persekian's Van Abbemuseum interview (n. 5).

7 See n. 5.

The foundation continues to provide a thriving meeting ground for international and Palestinian artists, thus sustaining the nascent local art scene. Such productivity also means that the foundation is responsible for a growing number of art works, with over 35 pieces (either actual installations or, much more commonly, deeds signed by their creators) donated over the years by both Palestinian and international artists. This has occurred in a situation where professional knowhow, as well as funding and, of course, institutional support, was absent. This collection and its troubled history provided the inspiration for the founding of CAMP. Indeed, a surrogate home had to be found for the collection to be conserved, but the project's diasporic nature was transformed from a deficiency into a 'lever for new opportunities and dynamic multicultural productivity'.[8] Its function is not only to 'tell the history of a place through the artists' work', but also to connect Palestine with other cultural realities, providing a 'nomadic site where dialogue, growth, and resourceful experimentation are encouraged' (see also Balaram, 2005; Rayyan, 2005). In the course of its development, CAMP's philosophy has shifted from the idea of a nomadic collection, travelling from host museum to host museum, to the project of a museum in exile.[9] A museum in exile responds to the problem of the 'absence of representation' for the Palestinian diaspora (Persekian, 2011), and indeed to the crucial dilemma of representation for the PA itself, a truncated institution that is hardly representative even of West Bankers and also fundamentally vulnerable to Israeli diktats. Ultimately, CAMP is a critique of the fragility of Palestinian national representation in both its symbolic and its political connotations.

In the Van Abbe, CAMP was exhibited as a collection of artworks and as an art project in itself: the concept of a national museum in exile, which is at the same time the promise of a national institution to come. CAMP, then, is not a representation of a museum in a mimetic sense, but rather a projection, a *prefiguration* of a future museum: it is the anticipation of an impending institution rather than the representation of a pre-existing one. This is a performance of a national museum in the sense of a performative statement, calling into being the very entity it describes; it is an action that invokes the spells of art to conjure into being an impossible institution.

The Palestinian biennials

Like the two museum initiatives discussed above, the Palestinian art biennial has been organised not by the PA Ministry of Culture, but by Palestinian NGOs. The first organisation to set up an art&architecture biennial was Riwaq (Centre for Architectural Conservation). The official name for this event was the 'Riwaq Biennale'; however, both the organisers and the public in general saw it as the Palestinian national biennial. Indeed, Riwaq is not only Palestine's primary heritage NGO and a key cultural operator in the West Bank; it also functions as the Palestinian

8 See n. 5.
9 If not otherwise noted, information and quotes in this paragraph are taken from my interview with Jack Persekian (2011).

shadow ministry of culture. Founded in 1991, three years before the PA, Riwaq's main focus of activity is the conservation of historic buildings, but the organisation has done much more than restoring many Ottoman and Mamluk structures all over the West Bank. For example, it has compiled a national register of historic buildings, contributed to the drafting of new cultural heritage legislation, and led pioneering projects of conservation planning in towns and villages. With Riwaq drafting legislation, compiling national surveys and building policy frameworks, this organisation's territorial presence and national role are both wider-ranging and more influential than that of the PA's own agencies within the Ministry of Culture and the Ministry of Tourism and Antiquities. The organisation has also forged strong connections between preserving the heritage of the past and producing culture in the present; the biennial itself is a good example of this philosophy, as well as of Riwaq's propensity to 'think national' and operate like a (counter-)state agency.

James Ferguson and Akhil Gupta (2002) have re-theorised the role of NGOs as part of new apparatuses of 'transnational governmentality' to describe current practices of government that undermine the older system of nation-states without replacing it. They identify a redeployment of state functions as a key feature of governance in globalisation, referring to a partial transfer of state power from national sites to infra-, supra- and particularly transnational ones (see also Trouillot, 2001). Increasingly, non-state transnational entities and NGOs are invested with governmental functions. Calling into question what he terms the 'vertical topography of power' characteristic of hegemonic views of Third World politics, Ferguson suggests that NGOs 'may be better conceptualized not as "below" the state, but as integral parts of a new, transnational apparatus of governmentality' (Ferguson, 2004: 392). The cases to which Ferguson and Gupta refer all involve situations where states have been in place long before the arrival of NGOs, and in this respect the Palestinian condition is, of course, exceptional. Nonetheless, their reflections are still largely applicable to Palestinian NGOs. Riwaq is a case in point.

The first biennial took place in 2005, but here I wish to focus on the 2007 and 2009 events. Artist Khalil Rabah, curator of the Museum of Natural History and Humankind and a member of Riwaq, was the director of these biennials, which had a similar philosophy to his museum project. Distinctive features of these events were their nomadic existence and the absence of any large-scale central exhibition. During the 2007 biennial, movement occurred only within Palestine. The event took place over several weeks and consisted of a series of 'gatherings' and 'journeys' that structured what the organisers called 'curated conversations and interactions' between Palestinian and international artists, architects, planners, conservationists, archaeologists, curators and theorists (Rabah, 2007). Specifically, the calendar included several trips around the West Bank, with forays into Israel for those with a permit, as well as a large symposium (also partly comprised of countryside walks), several workshops, screenings, and small installations and exhibitions in different locations across the territories.

Palestinians living in the West Bank experience daily life incarcerated in a guarded enclave; the biennial aimed to transform this area into one node of a global network of cosmopolitan cultural production, and to explore the synergies released by that transformation. In other words, the main aim of the biennial was to connect the occupied territories with transnational cultural flows, even if only for a few people over a few days. But there was also a second crucial objective: during the event, Riwaq launched its '50 Villages' project, together with a major fundraising campaign to finance this ambitious scheme of long-term national heritage preservation. The goal of the project is to preserve and rehabilitate the 50 most significant historic centres of the West Bank and Gaza, selected from the properties listed in the national historic heritage register, also produced by Riwaq. The 50 Villages project highlights how, in Palestine, a major national plan of heritage conservation is being devised, coordinated and carried out by an NGO, and promoted under the rubric of an art biennial.

The 50 Villages became the focal point (both spatially and thematically) for the 2009 biennial, significantly entitled 'A Geography: 50 Villages', which took place over several months at different sites within and beyond Palestine. The organisers emphasised the connectivity dimension discussed above; but in contrast to the 2007 biennial, the 2009 edition was run in collaboration with local communities and was entirely Palestinian-funded.[10] Moreover, the 2009 biennial was spread across the whole Mediterranean region. It began in Italy, with the inclusion of a Palestinian 'pavilion' in Venice as a collateral event at the 53rd International Art Exhibition La Biennale di Venezia. This was the first time Palestine had had such a pavilion, which was presented under the title 'Palestine c/o Venice' (Mikdadi, 2009); it consisted of a one-day symposium and an exhibition of Palestinian art, including the installation '50 Local Pavilions' by Rabah. The latter consisted of a performance of Riwaq's cultural management activities, including a seminar-like event, and even featured the Venetian presence of the mayor of a town with which Riwaq was working. As Rabah put it, this was 'a biennale within a biennale, an art work representing an institution'.[11]

As in the case of the two museums discussed above, the question of national representation loomed large at 'Palestine c/o Venice'. National pavilions at art biennials, especially those as celebrated as Venice, are statements of nationhood and national status, presented by the cultural institutions of the nation-state in question. Inevitably, the Palestinian pavilion turned this state of affairs on its head: it was put together by civil-society organisations and intellectuals, and it both critiqued and mocked the standard practices of national representation from a position, in a sense, of impossibility. From a procedural perspective, this is precisely what a 'Palestinian Pavilion' is at present, and indeed, at the official level, 'Palestine c/o Venice' was not a national pavilion, but simply a collateral event. This is because pavilions at the Venetian biennale are meant to represent only those nation-states formally

---

10 Funding for the 2007 biennale came from the Palestinian private sector, the UNDP and some European donors; for the 2009 edition, support came largely from the Palestinian private sector.
11 Introduction to the Palestine pavilion symposium, Venice, 5 June 2009. All quotes in this section come from audio recordings I made at the symposium.

recognised by Italy; the fact that 2009 was the first time that Palestine had been officially represented at the Venice Biennale is also a consequence of this rule.

In spite of its uncertain status, Riwaq and the curators insisted on calling the Palestinian Venetian event the 'Palestinian Pavilion'. For Riwaq, appropriating the idiom of the pavilion was a performative statement of (the right to) nation-statehood; behaving 'as if' the Palestinian exhibition were a proper national pavilion was a way to evoke the future existence of the Palestinian state through what I call *anticipatory representation*, the performance or prefiguration of an institution that does not yet fully exist.[12] Other artists and critics, in contrast, questioned the very concept of national pavilions and demanded their deconstruction and/or destruction. Regardless of such disagreements, a common if implicit understanding united all participants in the Palestinian biennial debate, which was a sense of a close association (and a particular temporal experience of anticipation and fulfilment) between representation and its object, in this case, the pavilion and the Palestinian state-to-come. In this debate, arguments about the pavilion and its labelling as such intersected with appeals for a Palestinian state, and the fact that the pavilion was taken to signify a commitment to the state was clearly apparent in, for example, Persekian's provocative suggestion that a Palestinian pavilion should find its 'place in the Giardini [the central and most prestigious Biennale venue] . . . next to the Israeli pavilion, especially considering that numerous people support a two-state solution, side by side in peace and harmony' (2009: 20). Others pointed out how all positions in relation to the debate assumed the existence (sooner or later) of Palestine as a state, and that this assumption was an 'absurdity' given the current circumstances of the Israeli-Palestinian conflict.[13] Rather than being an absurdity, however, I contend that Palestine's non-pavilion of a non-state organised by 'civil society' was a performance of statehood and a contribution to the construction of its nascent institutions. Indeed, the biennials have been instrumental in the realisation of the '50 Villages' project and the emergence of a national historic heritage management infrastructure in the West Bank; and since then, many projects in the 50 Villages have been carried out using funds raised during the biennials. (By 2018, Riwaq has managed to work in 20 of the 50 Villages.) Moreover, the early Riwaq biennials, together with the Jerusalem Show, have set the stage for a partnership between the key Palestinian cultural organisations, which, together, have organised a larger Palestinian biennial ever since 2012 – with the express aim

12 This tactic of anticipatory representation reminds me of the notion of *figura*, which the literary critic Eric Auerbach (1984 [1959]) has magisterially described as a key Christian concept shaping the early representation of reality in Western literature, particularly in medieval times. Figural interpretation identifies historical or literary figures and events as 'real prophecies', that is, as pre-figurative or shadowy versions of other events, which are read as the former's fulfilment. In Auerbach's conceptualisation, the first event signifies – in the sense of both representing and announcing – the second one, which fullfils the former. Both events, but particularly the first one, the *figura*, are marked by an unfinished, incomplete and temporary quality, and both refer to a future event, which constitutes the fullest realisation of the process.

13 See n. 11.

of creating a supporting infrastructure for cultural and art practice in Palestine and beyond.

A controversial issue that figured prominently in discussions surrounding the Palestinian biennials concerned the representativeness or otherwise of Palestinian NGOs (for a discussion of this phenomenon, see De Cesari, 2010; Hammami, 2006). Do NGOs and intellectuals have the right to represent Palestine and Palestinians on such a prominent stage? Are projects like the museums and the biennials not elite enterprises that are out of touch with ordinary Palestinians' experiences, needs and desires? This controversy goes beyond the cultural sector. The West Bank, in particular, can count on a vibrant civil society that has gone through vast changes in recent years with the huge inflow of financial aid in the wake of the Oslo Accords. West Bank intellectuals and NGO professionals have faced repeated accusations of elitism and detachment from their former grassroots constituencies and the realities of life in present-day Palestine. Such arguments were evoked at the Venice exhibition in the sound installation *Ramallah Syndrome*, a group dialogue among young Palestinian artists and theorists, which challenged the symbolic politics enacted through the show. These artists/activists highlighted not only the problems of representation at the core of contemporary Palestinian politics, but also the persistence of the colonial regime and the waning of resistance thereto through a kind of 'hallucination of normality', the fantasy that 'it is as if the establishment of a sovereign Palestinian state – in effect, indefinitely postponed – will be achieved through pure illusion'.[14]

Conclusions

This chapter has discussed how the Palestinian museums and the biennials contribute to the creation of new state-like cultural institutions. 'Prefiguration' is a notion of radical politics that social movement studies has recently expanded to address what Davina Cooper first called 'everyday utopias' (2014), then conceptualised as 'counter-states' (2016) and 'activist statehood' (this volume). These notions are to grasp diverse experimental institutional simulations that produce democratic, politically transformative formations that straddle and engage, even as they also oppose, formal institutions of the state. By performing nation-statehood, also the Palestinian projects instantiate similar modes of experimental stateness, or rather *statecraft* (cf. Peck and Theodore, 2015). While Rabah's and Persekian's museums can be said to be the very first Palestinian national museums, the CAMP project in particular *prefigures* a future national art museum by gathering the seeds (the artists' agreements) of this museum's collection, and by testing and 'incubating' it in the Netherlands. Both projects anticipate what is now an impossible national museum by playing with the ambiguities between reality and (critical) representation, and

---

14 See http://ramallahsyndrome.blogspot.com, extracts from conversation N. 1 October 2008 (accessed 6 March 2018).

by producing a representation of this future institution in the here and now. The organisation of a Palestinian biennial on Palestinian ground and the very presence of a Palestinian (quasi-)pavilion on the Venetian stage were symbolically important steps in placing Palestine on the map of cultural and knowledge flows, and in giving it the semblance of a nation-state. It can be argued that in the absence of real sovereignty, these are merely trappings, empty rituals and paraphernalia of the nation-state. But it is the conclusion of this chapter that the Palestinian museums and the biennials as artistic performances do have a real impact by reimagining national cultural institutions *before* they actually exist and thus instantiating them even if in embryonic, experimental form.

Mimicry, play, resourcefulness, precarity and experimentation are key elements of this form of creative statecraft – as are failures. This chapter was originally written in 2011 and first published in 2012; since its writing, in the context of a veritable 'museum fever' that has gripped the West Bank (De Cesari, 2019; Khaldi, 2015), some of the projects I have described above have failed or at least suffered a set-back, a change or multiple changes in direction. While (some) NGO projects are increasingly 'stately' (like the Palestinian Museum), PA ones are NGOising. Two of the most important museums that have inaugurated since, the Yasser Arafat Museum&Memorial and the Mahmoud Darwish Museum&Memorial, are run by foundations formally independent from but in fact deeply tied to (and sponsored by) the Palestinian Authority. Interestingly, this solution has allowed the PA to accomplish what it had not been able to do in the previous years, when it was ministry units in charge of creating museums. Beyond the PA, the Ramallah-centred cultural scene, of which museums are part, has expanded and become more institutionalised. Grassroots organisations and NGOs are not only more established, but have begun coordinating with each other and building a network of institutions that is solidifying into a broader infrastructure with a set programme of actions. The (new) Palestinian art biennial is a good example of this trend. Since 2012, Riwaq has teamed up with several other organisations like the Palestinian Museum and the Al-Ma'mal Foundation to produce a truly national biennial: initially, it was mostly established institutions from the Ramallah/Jerusalem area, the de facto capital and cultural centre of Palestine, but over recent years the organisers have made a conscious effort to involve also Palestinian cultural institutions active in Gaza and Israel. While the Riwaq biennial and other previously separated events have evolved into this broader infrastructure, CAMP, on the other hand, was dealt a serious blow when a joint funding application with the Vanabbemuseum was turned down by the Dutch government – a development that highlights the precarity of Palestinian cultural organising and its extreme dependency on international aid. The latter has created no few problems for Palestinian institutions, such as when a major cultural funder, the Ford Foundation, decided to move its activities to Egypt and so to cut off the lifeblood of many Palestinian cultural organisations. But in many cases, Palestinian institutions have reacted by reorganising and networking among themselves, coming up with creative partnerships and shared, inventive solutions, so as to become more independent of external agendas.

Amid the ebbs and flows of projects, experiments and mistakes, failures and ad hoc, imaginative solutions to deal with them, Palestinian artists and cultural producers call into being, through critical representations, institutions that do not yet fully exist. By mocking cultural institutions that exist elsewhere but not yet in Palestine, Palestinian counter-institutional projects give shape to the first such institutions on Palestinian ground. Like the state in exile of the Sahrawi refugees analysed by Jacob Mundy, these Palestinian projects are 'pre-figurative lived model[s]' of what the future could look like (2007: 275): critiques of present, global institutions, that is, anti-institutions that function both as prototypes of a future-to-be and as handy if tentative and imperfect devices of an evolving present. In this process, anticipatory representations produce new forms of imaginative statecraft in the here and now that open up both possibilities and predicaments. Cultural producers and artists turned 'cultural managers' see the risks of becoming 'a stultified bureaucracy', as Omar Al-Qattan (2015) put it, and lose experimental and democratic steam. Strikingly, some NGO museums appear much more state-like now as opposed to 2011. But the lesson for me is that it is also by 'failing', by making and unmaking the state, that institutions like the Palestinian Museum remain sites of institutional productivity and experimentation. By making and unmaking the state, Palestinian organisations help us reconceive what progressive statehood might mean.

References

Al-Qattan, O. (2015) 'Full Interview between Omar Al-Qattan & Yasmine Eid-Sabbagh' [online]. Available at http://qattanfoundation.org/en/qattan/media/news/full-interview-between-omar-al-qattan-yasmine-eid-sabbagh (accessed 3 March 2019).

Althusser, L. (1971) 'Ideology and Ideological State Apparatuses' in *Lenin and Philosophy and Other Essays*. Brewster, B. (trans.). London: New Left Books.

Anderson, B. (1983) *Imagined Communities: Reflections on the Origin and Spread of Nationalism*. London: Verso.

Auerbach, E. (1984 [1959]) 'Figura' in *Scenes from the Drama of European Literature*. Manheim, R. (trans.). Minneapolis, MN: University of Minnesota Press.

Bal, M. (1996) 'Telling, Showing, Showing Off' in *Double Exposure: The Subject of Cultural Analysis*. New York: Routledge.

Balaram, G. (2005) 'All for Art's Sake' [online]. Available at http://www.hindu.com/mag/2005/07/24/stories/2005072400200500.htm (accessed 3 March 2019).

Bennett, T. (1995) *The Birth of the Museum: History, Theory, Politics*. London: Routledge.

Bishop, C. (2004) 'Antagonism and Relational Aesthetics', *October*, 110, pp. 51–79.

Bourriaud, N. (2002). *Relational Aesthetics*. Paris: Presses du réel.

B'Tselem. 2006. 'A Wall in Jerusalem: Obstacles to Human Rights in the Holy City'. Jerusalem: B'Tselem [online]. Available at http://www.btselem.org/download/200607_A_Wall_in_Jerusalem.pdf (accessed 3 March 2019).

Cooper, D. (2014) *Everyday Utopias: The Conceptual Life of Promising Spaces*. Durham, NC: Duke University Press.

Cooper, D. (2016) 'Enacting Counter-States through Play', *Contemporary Political Theory*, summer, pp. 1–9.

De Cesari, C. (2010) 'Creative Heritage: Palestinian Heritage NGOs and Defiant Arts of Government', *American Anthropologist*, 112(4), pp. 625–37.

De Cesari, C. (2019) *Heritage and the Cultural Struggle for Palestine*. Stanford, CA: Stanford University Press.

Debord, G. (1983 [1967]) *The Society of the Spectacle*. London: Rebel Press.

Doumani, B. (2010) 'A Post-Territorial Museum: Interview with Beshara Doumani. Interview by Ursula Biemann', *ArteEast Quarterly*, spring [online]. Available at http://www.arteeast.org/pages/artenews/extra-territoriality/268/ (accessed 3 March 2019).

Doumani, B. (2011) 'Interview by the Author', 18 October, conducted on Skype.

Esche, C. (2004) 'What's the Point of Art Centres Anyway? Possibility, Art and Democratic Deviance', *Republic Art*, April [online]. Available at http://republicart.net/disc/institu tion/esche01_en.htm (accessed 3 March 2019).

Ferguson, J. (2004) 'Power Topographies' in Nugent, D. and Vincent, J. (eds.), *A Companion to the Anthropology of Politics*. Oxford: Blackwell.

Ferguson, J. and Gupta, A. (2002) 'Spatializing States: Toward an Ethnography of Neoliberal Governmentality', *American Ethnologist*, 29(4), pp. 981–1002.

Filipovich, E., van Hal, M. and Øvstebø, S. (eds.) (2010) *The Biennial Reader*. Bergen/Ost fildern: Bergen Kunsthall and Hatje Cantz.

Foucault, M. (1991) 'Governmentality' in Burchell, G., Gordon, C. and Miller, P. (eds.), *The Foucault Effect: Studies in Governmentality*. Chicago, IL: University of Chicago Press.

Groys, B. (2014) 'On Art Activism', *e-flux* #56, June [online]. Available at http://www.e-flux.com/journal/on-art-activism/ (accessed 3 March 2019).

Gupta, A. and Sharma, A. (2006) 'Globalization and Postcolonial States', *Current Anthropology*, 47(2), pp. 277–307.

Halper, J. (2000) 'The 94 Percent Solution: A Matrix of Control', *Middle East Report*, 216, pp. 14–19.

Hammami, R. (2006) 'Palestinian NGOs since Oslo: From Politics to Social Movements?' in Beinin, J. and Stein, R. L. (eds.), *The Struggle for Sovereignty: Palestine and Israel, 1993–2005*. Stanford, CA: Stanford University Press.

Hilal, J. (ed.) (2007) *Where Now for Palestine? The Demise of the Two-State Solution*. London: Zed Books.

Iveson, K. (2016) '"Making space public" through Occupation: The *Aboriginal Tent* Embassy, Canberra', *Environment and Planning A*, 49(3), pp. 537–54.

Khaldi, L. (2015) 'The Fugitive Object and the Hollow Museum', MA thesis, European Graduate School.

Krupa, C. and Nugent, D. (2015) 'Off-Centered States: Rethinking State Theory through an Andean Lens' in Krupa, C. and Nugent, D. (eds.), *State Theory and Andean Politics: New Approaches to the Study of Rule*. Philadelphia, PA: University of Pennsylvania Press.

McConnell, F., Moreau, T. and Dittmer, J. (2012) 'Mimicking State Diplomacy: The Legitimizing Strategies of Unofficial Diplomacies', *Geoforum*, 43(4), pp. 804–14.

Mikdadi, S. (2009) 'Palestine c/o Venice' in *Palestine c/o Venice*. Beirut: Mind the Gap.

Mitchell, T. (1991) 'The Limits of the State: Beyond Statist Approaches and Their Critics', *American Political Science Review*, 85(1), pp. 77–96.

Mundy, J. (2007) 'Performing the Nation, Pre-figuring the State: The Western Saharan Refugees, Thirty Years Later', *Journal of Modern African Studies*, 45(2), pp. 275–97.

Ophir, A. and Azoulay, A. (2012) *The One-State Condition: Occupation and Democracy in Israel*. Stanford, CA: Stanford University Press.

O'Reilly, K. (n.d.) 'The Palestinian Museum of Natural History and Humankind' [online]. Available at https://www.soas.ac.uk/gallery/50320names/file24018.pdf (accessed 3 March 2019).

Painter, J. (2006) 'Prosaic Geographies of Stateness', *Political Geography*, 25, pp. 752–74.

Paynter, N. (2006) 'A Lack of Solemnity Is Not Necessarily a Lack of Seriousness', *Art Lies* 49 [online]. Available at http://www.artlies.org/article.php?id=1305&issue=49&s=0%20-%2013k (accessed 3 March 2019).

Peck, J. and Theodore, N. (2015) *Fast Policy: Experimental Statecraft at the Thresholds of Neoliberalism*. Minneapolis, MN: University of Minnesota Press.

Pelgrom, E. (2007) 'Dare 2 Connect. Report of the Meeting: Café Mediterranée – An Encounter with the Middle Eastern Cultural World, 14 September 2007, Felix Meritis' [online]. Available at www.sica.nl/sites/default/files/pdf/071127_verslag_cm_14sept.pdf (accessed 3 March 2019).

Persekian, J. (2009) 'Act of Reconciliation' in Mikdadi, S. (ed.), *Palestine c/o Venice*. Beirut: Mind the Gap.

Persekian, J. (2011) 'Interview by the Author', 9 September, Jerusalem.

Preziosi, D. (2010) 'Myths of Nationality' in Knell, S. J., Aronsson, P., Amundsen, A. B. and Barnes, A. (eds.), *National Museums: New Studies from around the World*. London: Routledge.

Rabah, K. (2007) 'Riwaq Biennale: To Set in Motion' in *The Second Riwaq Biennale Guide*. Ramallah: Riwaq.

Rancière, J. (2006) *The Politics of Aesthetics*. Rockhill, G. (trans.). London: Continuum.

Rayyan, A. (2005) 'Al Ma'mal Foundation for Contemporary Art', *Nafas Art Magazine*, March [online]. Available at http://universes-in-universe.org/eng/nafas/articles/2005/al_ma_mal_foundation (accessed 3 March 2019).

Rose, N., O'Malley, P. and Valverde, M. (2006) 'Governmentality', *Annual Review of Law and Social Sciences*, 2, pp. 83–104.

Thelen, T., Vetters, L. and von Benda-Beckmann, K. (2014) 'Introduction to Stategraphy: Towards a Relational Anthropology of the State', *Social Analysis*, 58(3), pp. 1–19.

Thompson, N. (2015) *Seeing Power: Art and Activism in the 21st Century*. Brooklyn, NY: Melville House Publishing.

Trouillot, M. R. (2001) 'The Anthropology of the State in the Age of Globalization: Close Encounters of the Deceptive Kind', *Current Anthropology*, 42(1), pp. 125–39.

Weibel, P. (ed.) (2015) *Global Activism: Art and Conflict in the 21st Century*. Karlsruhe, Germany: ZKM, Center for Art and Media.

Welsch, W. (1997) *Undoing Aesthetics*. Inkpin, A. (trans.). London: Sage Publications.

9

CONCEPTUAL PREFIGURATION AND MUNICIPAL RADICALISM

Reimagining what it could mean to be a state

Davina Cooper

This chapter takes up the challenge of reimagining the state as a prefigurative conceptual task.[1] Rather than focusing on the state's reform or, conversely, on its elimination, prefigurative conceptualising asks two questions.[2] First, what state meanings arise when we imagine better kinds of states; second, how might these meanings be enacted in the present? In other words, how might we actualise these meanings – operating *as if* they were already viable? This does not mean other meanings and institutionalised practices, especially established ones, are absent or gone. Like other forms of prefigurative practice, prefigurative conceptualising *knowingly* takes place on terrain already structured by prior dominant understandings. It involves acting as if the terms of the present were otherwise, while knowing that they are (probably) not. A key question therefore becomes: what can enacting prefigurative meanings *do*? If activists, policy-makers, academics, and others take up understandings that trouble, or fail to cohere with, conventional ones, what political traction, if any, might this have?

In some cases, new meanings can be advanced through their practice. Living gender, for instance, in non-binary, queer, feminist or a-gendered ways seems likely to impact on what gender means and is. But can states be transformed by grassroots actors prefiguring more desirable state meanings; or is a level of capacity missing, especially when it comes to the nation-state? In the case of the state, prefigurative conceptualising suggests a far more partial and tentative form of actualisation,

---

1 As Ruth Kinna (this volume) discusses, prefigurative politics is typically positioned against state politics rather than as a register for state recuperation. But if we are to explore what doing the state *as if it were otherwise* requires, reimagining what it means to be a state is crucial.

2 It thus forms one thread of broader prefigurative practice. On the latter, see Boggs (1977); Maeckelbergh (2011); Yates (2015). Margaret Davies (2017) also develops a helpful account of prefigurative theorising in *Law Unlimited*.

one likely to be overwhelmed by the very present, hard-to-shield-off, status quo. I return to the question of performativity, and what the enactment of new meanings can (and cannot) do, in the final part of this chapter. However, before getting there, I want to explore a counter-hegemonic conception of the state, drawing inspiration from two quite different sources: legal pluralism, which has provided a flexible and dynamic response to the analogous question of how to conceptualise law in ways that give an account of community-level normativity; and, second, British municipal radicalism (BMR) as an instance of more radical state-craft. But first, I want to respond to the question that reimagining the state begs: why should we reclaim, even in transformed form, the concept of the state?

Retrieving the state: But on what terms?

For many on the left – anarchist-inspired writers and activists, most prominently – the state holds little prefigurative appeal (see Ince, 2012; Springer, 2012). According to Holloway (2010: 58): 'The state is a way of doing things: the wrong way of doing them.'[3] An extensive literature names and critiques the coercive, exploitative and disciplinary activities of states from policing, war and imprisonment to social security, colonialism and capital accumulation. Other chapters in this volume detail some of the many harms states cause. Some critics identify the problem as lying with particular kinds of state – capitalist, neoliberal, colonial; others identify the state itself as inherently and always problematic. Saul Newman (2001) describes the state as 'an abstract principle of power and authority that has always existed in different forms, yet is more than these actualisations'. In other words, while states have a material presence, performing power and authority in everyday life, they also signal and stand in for a more abstract kind of force. For critical state scholars, radical change cannot emerge from within state apparatuses, but only from the 'outside'; and it is the presence or *potential* for an outside which is key. Discussing the alterglobalisation movement, Maeckelbergh (2011: 13–14) writes, '[t]he aim of developing . . . new structures is to slowly make the state and multilateral organizations obsolete'.

But, of course, not all critical writers and activists reject the state (see, for instance, Dhawan, 2016; Newman, 2012; Newman and Clarke, 2014). Arguments in favour of some kind of state or analogous institutional form are various as chapters in this book explore. They include the value of differently scaled not-for-profit bodies developing public goods, redistributing resources, undertaking planning and coordination, managing externalities and other harms, and facilitating learning, public discourse and cultures. Yet, even if we temporarily bracket the critiques that each of these state activities or purposes engenders, this does not tell us much about the kind of state required or, indeed, what it means to be a state. Work on the Global

---

3 However, see Ordóñez et al. (2018) for discussion of anarchists' engagement in electoral politics in the Spanish context.

South recognises a wide range of types of states – varying in their form, scale and register of respectability and legitimacy (e.g. Aretxaga, 2003). By contrast, writing on post-industrial neo/ liberal states in the Global North is often narrower in its gaze. Implicitly (or otherwise), it focuses on capitalist nation-states, assuming state-hood comes with defined territory, formal institutional structures, representative versions of democracy and impersonal, juridical norms. Writers and activists may argue over the capacity of these neo/liberal states to support interests and agendas contrary to those of dominant forces, as they may also argue over the composi-tion and placing of state boundaries, and the ontological plane on which the state operates (virtual, material, as-if real). But, in these debates and disagreements, what states are deemed able to do is defined and limited by a backward-facing concep-tual form; in other words, by addressing what states already appear to have been and done. A prefigurative conceptualisation, in contrast, approaches the question of what it means to be a state by considering *what could become possible and imaginable*. In other words, it develops its account of what statehood could mean by considering what it could become. At the same time, this chapter complicates the assumption that prefiguration, in facing towards imagined futures, is driven by desires and hopes for changes located exclusively in some time ahead. Instead, it turns to a historic instance of progressive statehood in order to reflect on what statehood could come to mean. However, first I want to turn to legal pluralism to help unsettle the notion that states necessarily mean nation-states.

State pluralism

Can we imagine the state in more pluralist ways, where the nation-state – with its histories of exclusions, dominations, exploitative extractions and claims to prestige and grandeur – appears as just one kind of state among others, in a list that could also include guerrilla, micro, city, regional and global states (e.g. Aretxaga, 2003)? Adopting this kind of approach does not reject the language of states in the way anarchist-inflected work does, but instead takes up the terms of statehood *as if* they were unexceptional. This parallels legal pluralism's approach to law. While other literatures, including in political science and international relations, have addressed state pluralism,[4] legal pluralism is particularly helpful for thinking about states beyond the nation-state because it directs attention to questions of definition (what counts as law or the state), the ways in which different legal (or state) entities inter-act; and to questions of form (in conditions where plurality may or may not be mutually intelligible or recognised).

Developed to illuminate normative and regulatory diversity, and to challenge the idea that the only real law was state law,[5] legal pluralism starts from the pre-sumption that more than one system of law (or normative ordering) can exist in

---

4 See, for instance, Morefield (2005); also Laski (1919); Hirst (1997).
5 International law, of course, has always been far more pluralistic and provisional in relation to the question of what constitutes 'law'.

any social field (e.g. Griffiths, 1986; Macdonald et al., 2006: 611; Merry, 1988). While legal (and normative) orders are treated as being unequal in their power, at the same time, no order is treated as fully sovereign, with absolute and exclusive dominion. Yet, the question of dominion through, or in terms of, a governing structure or text opens an important distinction between 'strong' and 'weak' legal pluralism (e.g. Griffiths, 1986).[6] Weak legal pluralism identifies a situation where subjects and spaces are regulated by different legal norms emerging from different sources. However, subordinate sources of law acquire (and depend upon) superordinate permission − whether from a central legislature, judicial system or governing constitutional text. In weak legal pluralism, different sources of authority fit to form a single coherent whole, and authority clashes are treated as resolvable. Strong legal pluralism is different; and it is this version of legal pluralism which is most useful here. In strong legal pluralism, law and its legitimacy do not derive from one superordinate body or principle, but from multiple, potentially incommensurable sources, as plural forms of authority are *claimed* rather than given. This means activities a nation-state considers illegitimate or illegal may be authorised by the rules or norms of a less powerful or dissident body − a radical political party, free school, militant trade union or teenage gang, for example, or by countervailing authorities, such as religious legal orders. But strong pluralism can also mean a community's rules, norms and rule-makers are not always apparent to other normative communities. Even cases of conflict may be unevenly recognised as communities discount, ignore or trivialise the law-making activities of others (see Cooper, 2019).

Legal pluralism helps us, by analogy, to think about states beyond the conventional nation-state. In its strong variant, it opens up possibilities for nested or overlapping states to exist, based on different sources of authority and even different criteria of statehood. In the latter case, where state formations, and their sources of authority, are incommensurable, they may not meet on the same political plane. They may not even notice each other or at least not in ways that would render tensions and disagreement intelligible as one involving competing *state* formations. But, as with law in legal pluralism, once the state is no longer equated with the nation-state, we need to ask: how should we understand what it means to be a state? Adopting a prefigurative conceptual approach may suggest we can understand and imagine statehood (or stateness) in any way we choose, thus bringing − at least potentially − fantastic imaginaries into our current practice. But while this may be theoretically practicable, questions of intelligibility arise, particularly if others' *recognition* of alternative conceptualisations of stateness is important. So, we might ask: Should prefigurative conceptualisations of statehood still involve territory, membership, institutions, procedures, systems, subjects, powers, economic, political and social functions? In other words, do they require elements associated with the nation-state even if the national scale is then subtracted? This is the 'Gulliver fallacy'

---

6 This distinction can be understood as normative, descriptive or interpretive (and, not uncommonly, slides between the three).

described by Anderson (1996: 151); states can be big or small, but are broadly assumed to be the same kind of thing. Or, can we hold on to the concept of statehood while not only decentring the nation-state, but also troubling the notion that states must be significantly alike?

Brian Tamanaha (2000) suggests one way forward in the parallel discussion regarding law. Rather than requiring *non*-state legal orders to resemble state ones, he suggests law is whatever people, through their social practices, recognise and treat as law. Analogising from Tamanaha's (2000) approach would seem to support a far more pluralistic, multi-perspectival conception of statehood (see also Anderson, 1996; Ruggie, 1993). Foregrounding internal recognition means, fundamentally, accepting as states those entities recognised (or treated) by members as states regardless of how they are perceived by others working with other criteria. This seems to support prefigurative thinking. If the state is whatever some people say it is, this validates projects for fashioning new state conceptions in ways that allow prefigurative imaginings to develop and flourish. But there are also difficulties with this kind of formulation in relation to issues of translation, recognition and power. Along with the question of what it means for others to *recognise* a body as a state in these conditions, how do we know when people are treating their own 'internal' practices as law or statehood, rather than something else, particularly when terminology diverges? What does it mean for members to 'treat' something *as a state*? Did the members of Frestonia, the micro-nation established to oppose demolition of a west London street squat by the GLC, in 1977,[7] treat Frestonia as a *state*? Certainly, they sought recognition from official state bodies (including the British government and the United Nations), drew on the symbols of statehood – passports, borders, named ministers, postage stamps and so on – and, as a squat, organised many of their affairs at a self-authorised distance from the formalities of British law and state governance. But, in other respects, the playful quality of their endeavour meant they did not act *as if* Frestonia governed them.[8] And while state figures played with the idea of Frestonia as a state, and the royal mail briefly recognised their postage stamps, such acknowledgment did more to trivialise Frestonia than to affirm its statehood.

Pluralism can be an important conceptual departure from a normative framework of statehood organised around the sovereign, territorially exclusive, nation-state. However, when it comes to defining the political substance of states, something more than openness and polyvalence is required to produce a progressive prefigurative account, something that gives positive content to what it means to be a state. In the discussion that follows, I consider what this might be by exploring one sustained episode of prefigurative state practice. Typically understood in terms of what it trialled and accomplished, this episode can also be read (in both historic and current terms) as prefiguring a different conception of what it could mean to be a state. This prefiguring, in both its meaning and form, does not exist in isolation.

7 http://www.frestonia.org/ (accessed 5 September 2018).
8 See also Cooper (2016, 2017); for a different example of protest-based state-claiming, see Routledge (1997).

Just as new prefigurative imaginaries gain critical traction from recognising the meanings they express do not currently prevail, so state practices, such as the one discussed below, get formed in counter-relation to a very different form and understanding of statehood.

My aim, in the discussion that follows, is to trace the contours of British municipal radicalism as it took shape in the 1980s. In doing so, I do not want to argue for the renaissance of an urban socialist politics, cast in the particular form it took three decades ago.[9] BMR is not presented here as a blueprint, a past political project that ought to be re-installed. Aside from its own limitations and failings (apparent to outsiders and to those of us who were participants – I was an active councillor in Haringey from 1986 to 1990), the very different contemporary political context makes any notion of return, even in urban Britain, naively nostalgic. However, I take up this episode to help stimulate imaginaries of what statehood could viably mean and entail. Pickering and Keightley (2006: 921) write, there is 'a distinction between the desire to return to an earlier state or idealized past, and the desire not to return but to recognize aspects of the past as the basis for renewal and satisfaction in the future' – a renewal, of course, which may take a very different form from the past that is politically ploughed.

State conceptualising from the municipal left

Municipal radicalism may seem, for some, a dated ground from which to reimagine the state. However, despite sustained attention paid to transnational movements and global governance networks, and despite also urban governance's ties to contemporary neoliberalism (e.g. see Miller, 2007; Purcell, 2008), *municipal* statehood remains a site where radical innovation and democratic resurgence in different countries takes place (e.g. see Russell 2019). While many on the left treat local government as a relatively uninteresting and insignificant assemblage, responsible for social consumption and the competitive development of investment-friendly urban infrastructures, the following discussion approaches municipal government as an open, embodied, networked formation that is far more than a small, local part of a nation-state apparatus (see Cumbers, 2015; Russell, 2019). Without denying what else local government does, I want to consider how its *state-enacting* work might contribute to a pluralist imagining of transformative progressive statehood, recognising that some municipal time-space contexts may inspire and support such imaginaries more than others.

1980s British municipal radicalism (BMR) is one such context. Rooted in democratic, left Labour politics, community activism, radical unionism and socialist thinking (Lansley et al., 1989), BMR sought to present, in Sheffield city leader

---

9 Taking up a historical (rather than present-day) episode underscores the capacity of prefigurative conceptualising to create new conceptual lines across time and space. So, historic practices are interpreted in relation to new imaginaries, which they may inspire and support, but also challenge and complicate.

David Blunkett's words, 'what we could do as a Socialist government at national level'.[10] As Peter Saunders (1984: 43) remarked:

> Cheap bus fares in South Yorkshire, a responsive system of council house management in Walsall and support for worker cooperatives in the West Midlands . . . are visible manifestations of an alternative philosophy . . . undermin[ing] the assertions of political leaders who claim that there is no option but to follow the logic of the market.

British councils have pursued radical initiatives and rebellion at other times (Branson, 1980; Gyford, 1985; MacIntyre, 1979). My account and take-up of 1980s BMR does not depend on its exceptionalism. Nevertheless, BMR, at this time, proved a distinctive formation. Driven by anger at the Thatcher government, and its mix of authoritarian, neo-conservative and market-expansionist politics, BMR emerged out of a confluence of people, informed by community activism, the women's movement, alternative economics, environmentalism, anti-racism and socialism, who entered (or engaged with) local government as officers, advisers, councillors, activists and Labour Party members. I discuss the details of BMR further below. As a political project, it was characterised by three key features that asserted an independence of spirit – if not always of practice: willingness to resist and defy the Thatcher government, including by breaking the law; experimentation and innovation in policy (including in ways described by opponents as 'loony'); and a readiness to subject the local state to the richly diverse and tumultuous shape of community politics.

Yet, while 1980s BMR was distinguished from other British moments of municipal radicalism by its comprehensive character, and by the breadth of councils involved, it was neither a cohesive political project nor one that involved every urban Labour-controlled council. Taking shape in metropolitan authorities (before they were abolished by the Thatcher government in 1986) – most notably the GLC, Merseyside and South Yorkshire – alongside urban councils in London, Liverpool, Edinburgh, Manchester and Sheffield (among others), left-run councils demonstrated patchy and uneven engagement with socialist and new urban left politics. Aside from the ways in which these two politics often found themselves in tension with each other, some local authorities were more deeply immersed in BMR than others. The involvement of particular councils as well as particular parts of councils changed as the 1980s wore on. Nevertheless, for close to a decade, British municipal radicalism constituted a distinct project of statecraft as BMR authorities promoted progressive institutional alternatives to neoconservative and neoliberal rule, around the themes of participatory democracy, progressive economics, solidarity, environmental stewardship and equality. Can we then draw from the BMR experience to reimagine what it could mean to be a good or 'better' state, attending along the way to some of the challenges for progressive statehood this example raises?

---

10 David Blunkett quoted in Gyford et al. (1989: 329).

British municipal radicalism

In many respects, BMR offers a familiar account of multi-purpose state entities, spatially arrayed, with hierarchical, bureaucratic systems, and formal, regularised procedures, policy-making on behalf of communities. Like other formations identified as state formations, BMR councils condensed the social relations of their locality, managed cleavages and conflict, and presented themselves as acting on behalf of particular constituencies, as well as the area as a whole. Yet, in other respects, BMR offered something more than a 'business as normal' local state temporarily directed towards progressive ends. To start with, BMR demonstrated how statehood could be *claimed*, in ways that were unauthorised and unaccepted from 'above', as bodies 'gave themselves the law'. This included rejecting national legislative authority, refusing to comply with politically controversial new legislation, and creatively interpreting municipal powers to advance controversial priorities and agendas (Cooper, 1996; Loughlin, 1996).

BMR's claims to legal autonomy should not be overstated. Most government legislation was followed, and different municipal departments continued to be subject to the policies and instructions coming from central government ministries. BMR councils may, at times, have acted like a state or claimed to be one,[11] but they also paid plenty of attention to their formally subordinate institutional status. Yet, despite these various provisos, I want to draw on those aspects of municipal practice that exemplify strong state pluralism, with its competing sources of authority, legitimacy and power (Lansley et al., 1989; Seyd, 1987). For it is these aspects which can enrich our understanding of what conceptually prefiguring the state could mean.

Refusing their 'lowly' place, BMR councils challenged the constrained scale and focus of municipal action (see also Hobbs, 1994). They supported international struggles against oppression, colonialism and apartheid. They also challenged the notion that peace and collective safety were beyond their domain of concern by introducing, among other measures, 'nuclear-free zones' (Gyford, 1985: 16). At the same time, attention was paid to local experiences and needs, particularly among those facing exclusion, marginality and impoverishment. Thus, councils subsidised public transport and childcare services; supported alternative arts-based projects; sought to monitor and control local police forces; and instituted a progressive economic agenda, oriented to public urban regeneration, community planning, democratic control, liveable wages, social useful production and cooperative economics (Boddy, 1984; Lansley et al., 1989; Parkinson, 1989: 430). In short, BMR developed a rhizomatic form of local governance – stretching out, activating and incorporating community projects within a constantly evolving governmental form that intensively and reflexively engaged with the question of what local government could do.

---

11 On the relationship between acting like a state and claiming to be a state, see also McConnell (2016); Navaro-Yashin (2012).

Certainly, the extroverted *governmentalisation* of left politics raised concerns in some quarters that municipal government was taking over activist agendas, quashing in the process space for 'autonomous' political action. And while this concern presupposes a particular imaginary of a vertical and powerful state, the concern powerful bodies will dominate, and so shape (and contain), political agenda is a real and important one. But BMR also took a distinctively more introverted direction, opening up its spaces and processes to local people.

> Town halls were opened up as meeting rooms and advice centres, and for crèches and exhibitions. London's County Hall, in particular, became a giant meeting room for women's groups, black groups, community organisations and Labour party activists (Lansley et al., 1989: 75).

Consultative fora, community-facing equality units, organisational representatives on council committees and decentralisation initiatives (devolving service delivery and, sometimes, decision-making to local neighbourhoods) were just some of the participatory formats councils developed (see Fudge, 1984; Gyford, 1985: 58; Hambleton, 1988). BMR asserted itself as a different kind of state project. As such, it did more than simply take the machinery of conventional municipal governance into new policy areas. It also reimagined and re-enacted what it could mean to be a state. But how can its historic instantiation help inspire progressive imaginaries of the plural state today? In the discussion that follows, I explore three aspects in more detail: democratic embeddedness, activism and care.

Embedded in everyday life

Left-wing state criticism routinely depicts the state as vertical and dominating, luxuriating in a remoteness and grandeur (Rai, 2010) that elevates it above society (Lefebvre, 2009: 86). But if this is a necessary part of what it means and is to be a state, how can states be part of democratic everyday life? One answer is that we need to bracket the nation-state paradigm that too often dominates state thinking. Local government, in general, and BMR, in particular, may offer a different trope – one that treats states as embedded, mundane, prosaic and accessible. As a controversial local government project, an immediate quality of BMR was its limited power, lacking the capacity to *impose* order and solutions. Without the dominating authority and coercive tools associated with nation-states in the Global North, and struggling to retain hegemony in the face of competing forces, BMR might indeed be described as a 'failed state' (see also Krämer, this volume); one whose lifespan was too short to even count as a state (see also Lansley et al., 1989). But this suggests a *normative* vision of states as long-living, machinic, powerful structures. Thus, a different reading might foreground the provisional and contested character of BMR, and its short life, as reflecting what embedded states are and could be like when the vertical distance (that progressive scholars disavow) is missing. Far from sitting atop society and threading through elite global and domestic networks, embedded progressive states are enmeshed in everyday non-elite relations.

In the case of BMR, one striking example of this enmeshing involved role sentanglement (Gyford, 1985; Seyd, 1987), challenging the conventional notion that politicians, bureaucrats and service users have distinct, discrete interests. Some degree of entanglement is inevitably present in local government, given politicians are required to live locally, and many staff inevitably do so, and therefore, as residents, also use council services. Role entanglement is also far from being the preserve of the left and the tangled ties between local elites and municipal power structures has long been noted. However, in BMR, role-overlaps between residents, workers, councillors, community activists and party members within, but also across, different left-wing councils was particularly pronounced. What made these overlapping roles especially significant was their politicisation as people took up different statuses and positions (particularly through municipal trade unions, Labour Party and community organisations), and the opportunities, access and visibility these positions made available, to argue for militant municipal policies and stances. The militancy associated with role overlaps did not go uncriticised (Gyford et al., 1989). Conservative central government also acted to legally restrict certain overt forms (set out in the Local Government and Housing Act 1989), in which officials in one authority were politicians in another. However, read through the prism of an embedded state, overlapping roles may appear both inevitable and beneficial. More commonly seen in micro-forms of governance, such as a communal village or commune, what BMR accomplished was to create a progressive version of role-overlap at a larger scale.

If subjecting states to grass-roots agendas and control is one aspect of a more quotidian state imaginary, another is a re-evaluation of the everyday. In his striking account of 'prosaic' state practices, Joe Painter (2006: 753) signals the 'intense involvement of the state in so many of the most ordinary aspects of social life'. This is particularly evident at municipal level. In local government, the micro-materiality of life: from food, housing and streets, to refuse, drains and sewage, comes constantly to the fore. Routinely dismissed as boring and insignificant against the flashier concerns of nation-states, the politicisation of these issues through BMR elucidates their social importance and interest, as disputes about pavement curbs, traffic, housing and pollution became explicitly sutured to inequalities of gender, race, class and disability (e.g. see Goss, 1984; Ouseley, 1984).

BMR affirmed the everyday character of stateness, permeated by social justice issues even in relation to infrastructural issues, such as pavement curbs, perceived by many as mundane. But it also went further to reveal how the everyday, including of the state, could be a site of new kinds of experimental and playful politics.[12] Through funds, staff, spaces and publicity, BMR supported an explosion of cultural activities, much of which took place in municipal venues. By enrolling community

---

12 I explore this further in Cooper (2019).

activists within policy decision-making, especially in relation to new controversial agenda, such as lesbian and gay equal opportunities, councils found themselves (not always happily) subject to activist enthusiasms and ideas. In Haringey, for instance, in 1986, the new lesbian and gay unit (LAGU), a mini-department composed of staff with backgrounds in gay, feminist, anti-racist and disability politics, wrote to all schools telling them of a fund to support 'positive images'. Writing directly, they circumvented the 'proper procedure' of going through the education service, who would undoubtedly have defused or blocked this initiative (Cooper, 1994). Locally and then nationally, the right took up this 'error' to exemplify the excesses and state wildness of 'loony' councils (leading eventually to section 28 of the Local Government Act 1988 prohibiting the promotion of homosexuality). Meanwhile, the council were forced through community and party pressure to stand behind LAGU and support positive images.[13]

State activism

The quotidian state emphasises embeddedness, the politics of everyday governance, the pleasures of policy innovation and the possibilities for a non-sovereign, less forceful state. State activism highlights other characteristics. Discussing BMR, Gyford (1985: 53) describes how:

> The concept of the town hall as a machine for service delivery was to be supplemented, though not supplanted, by the notion of using it as a political base from which to campaign within the community.

BMR was obviously not unique in using state resources to advance a political agenda. However, what made it distinctive was its readiness to campaign, and not simply govern, on behalf of marginal and subjugated interests. Gyford (1985: 54) describes the typically activist paraphernalia produced by councils: 'petitions, periodicals, pamphlets, leaflets . . . posters, badges . . . marches . . . exhibitions . . . concerts'. Here, I want to focus on two other aspects. The first concerns the expressive assertion of harms and wrongs.

Acting politically on behalf of disadvantaged groupings is rarely associated with states. More commonly, states appear as the targets of grassroots campaigning, as activists mobilise against institutional apparatuses that are identified as securing and safeguarding elite interests. But if states are to be conceptualised in ways that make progressive forms thinkable and possible, their readiness to combat dominating interests is important. BMR adopted a campaigning position, oriented to social justice, around a number of extra-territorial moral and political issues. These ranged

---

13 See also John Gyford (1985), who describes the initiatives, learning and mistakes that occurred as left-wing politicians experimented with new roles and formats, often in the face of intransigence (or its threat) from the more traditional staff that many BMR councils had inherited (also Boddy and Fudge, 1984).

from South African apartheid to Britain's military presence in Northern Ireland, the miners' strike and nuclear armaments. We can read this municipal action as a form of 'glocalisation' in which locally materialising practices help to build global connections and attention (Swyngedouw and Kaïka, 2003; see also DeFilippis, 2001). But BMR also 'drilled down', rejecting the compartmentalisations which treated corporate decision-making, gay sex and domestic violence as too private or morally settled for local state interest.

Tied to this politics of municipal advocacy and solidarity was a second aspect: the deployment of powers, *including unexpected powers*, to advance social justice, and to oppose and resist reactionary forms of harm. Discussing BMR, Stewart Lansley and his co-authors (1989: 67) remark: 'Lawyers were sent off to find new powers, and to reinterpret existing ones.' Instead of perpetuating an arrangement in which particular tools and resources aligned with particular policies, municipal activism mixed and switched resources to strengthen the ability of state bodies and their allies to advance political objectives. One striking feature of this process was the deployment by BMR councils of quasi-private powers. For instance, councils sought to use contracting, procurement and land ownership powers to boycott companies involved in apartheid South Africa or with 'bad' employment practices. In other cases, complex financial powers were used, such as through creative accounting, to generate the resources required to advance progressive social justice agendas. Many of these measures were not explicitly illegal because their use had not been contemplated. Thus, until the courts ruled on their legality, councils were able to engage in interest rate swaps and creative leasing arrangements, leveraging monies in ways that risked future indebtedness, as they gambled unsuccessfully on a 1987 Labour election victory and future government 'bail-out'. But while creative accounting illustrates those subterranean forms of municipal power which only surface when exercised, what this example also reveals is the intricately connected character of state bodies – both in their present and imagined future form.

I have suggested BMR asserted its self-driving authority as a political governing project. At the same time, BMR was not a movement for secession, but embedded in a hoped-for future of progressive national government. Prefigurative conceptions of statehood may emphasise plurality, but this does not mean state bodies identify themselves, or should be read, as discrete atomistic entities. This is important. It is easy to read plurality as the multiplication of separate, here sovereign, things. But reimagining the state prefiguratively invokes other conceptions of statehood – indeed, stateness may be a better word for the interconnected forms of governance that develop. What state activism brings to this imaginary is a way of thinking about the relationship between different interlinked governmental forms and between political agendas across different temporalities. Present state connections, particularly top-down controlling ones, may be rejected by less powerful state bodies in their pursuit of contentious political aims. But other forms of connection, in hoped-for better times, may be expressed – whether as something desired, sought after or practically built.

State care

Using state resources to express spatially extended relationships of responsibility, anchored in attention and concern rather than culpability, highlights a third feature associated with progressive statecraft: namely, of care (see also Newman, this volume). Approaching care as an expansive responsibility challenges the conventional territorial notion[14] that what 'belongs' to a state, namely, its people, land and infrastructure, can be legitimately extracted, deployed and exploited according to state justifications.[15] It also challenges a narrow reading of states as responsible only for their settled and legal inhabitants. Like the later sanctuary city movement (Darling, 2009; McDonald, 2012), BMR unsettled the assumption that care should be distributed in favour of established British residents over more recent incomers (particularly those with precarious status). Many BMR councils, for instance, controversially refused to give 'local people' or a 'local connection' priority when allocating municipal housing; resources were also expended in extending community language translations and supporting minority community organisations.

We can interpret the support for new residents, and the refusal to privilege long-established ones, as revealing a different relationship between states and national borders, explored in more detail by Nick Gill (this volume). It also coheres with a less boundary-conscious basis for action. Local government, typically, adopts an 'open border' approach when it comes to goods, money and people (although in many cases, service availability and subsidies may depend on residence).[16] What BMR and similar municipal acts of care demonstrate is how 'open borders' do not have to mean welfare's withdrawal (as neoliberal, 'no borders' politics sometimes suggests). Instead, it invokes an approach to responsibility that extends outwards from residing migrants to migration-producing conditions (such as war, economic colonialism and persecution) to transnational forms of geopolitical support (see also Massey, 2007).

The pursuit of more expansive forms of state-based care, however, is not seen unequivocally as progressive. Anarchists and other critical left scholars have long expressed anxiety about the paternalistic character and implications of states taking responsibility for people's well-being, using their resources and systems to cultivate subjects according to publicly prescribed norms. Bauman's (1991) influential discussion of the 'gardening state' identifies some of the problems deemed to arise when states determine what should grow, flourish, wither or die; where pursuing

14 Contemporary work on territory is extensive; for some interesting accounts, see Blomley (2016); Brenner and Elden (2009); Elden (2010); and Painter (2010).
15 The refusal to capitalise territory, to focus on well-being rather than commercial (or other) value, contrasts with local government practice in other contexts where councils are expected to compete to optimise investment opportunities, and to attract business. While misleading to suggest no competition existed among BMR councils for investment, their explicit orientation was to managing and meeting needs rather than supporting commercial growth.
16 Municipal borders can also function as part of the governmental machinery of resource redistribution as monies move from rich local states to poorer ones (thereby also dampening the incentive for inter-municipal competition).

happiness, security and peace is seen as displacing the advancement of freedom. Bauman's account has been widely drawn upon (e.g. Binkley, 2009; Mottier, 2008; Schiel, 2005). However, what often gets lost in the critique of the gardening state is the *particular* gardening imagery at stake; namely, of healthy species, rational resource husbandry and the elimination of 'alien nature' (also Comaroff and Comaroff, 2001; Mottier, 2008). When it comes to thinking about progressive forms of state care, we might want to turn to other kinds of gardening: 'guerrilla gardening', 'non-native' plant cultivation, growing or protecting heterogeneous, wild spaces and community gardening as a form of public action (McKay, 2011). BMR demonstrates how states can mix these different forms. While it sought to strengthen marginalised communities, BMR's advancement of different, and sometimes competing, progressive agendas suggests a form of political gardening that was often improvised, unpredictable, and sometimes chaotic, conflictual and disruptive.

I have explored some ways in which BMR, as an episode of innovative statecraft, might stimulate and nourish progressive state imaginaries, focusing on the everyday, activist and care-based dimensions of statehood. It is important, though, to recognise that these dimensions are neither fully distinct nor always in harmony. I have not explored BMR in order to generate a neat, fixed imaginary of governance, but rather to highlight some of the dynamics that new state imaginaries might entail. In this case, tensions take different forms. For instance, while state activism appears oriented to visibility – to expressing its politics in ways that are noted, the everyday state casts its actions in shadow. Relations of care suggest a division between governing and governed that democratically embedded states may disavow. The everyday state reflects and condenses relations of power, which the activist state seeks to transform. The activist state expresses commitment; the everyday state expresses contradiction and ambivalence. The activist state places itself in opposition to the status quo; the caring state represents itself as that which governs. Finally, while state activist and gardening-as-care projects rely upon and mobilise desires and fantasies about the future, the everyday state extends the present across the future.

The value of reimagining the state

Tensions between activist, caring and everyday forms of statehood may be important to sustain in developing new conceptual imaginaries. But I want, finally, to turn to a question posed at the start: What political value does reimagining the state have? This chapter has drawn on legal pluralism and a historical episode of state radicalism in order to think about what statehood could mean. But do modes of reimagining that jettison aspiration – 'I wish one day the state would become . . .' in order to act *as if the meaning of the state was already otherwise* replicate problems endemic to more idealist forms of normative conceptualising in refusing or failing to *adequately and critically represent* what is? Arguably, imagining the concept of the state *as if* it were already otherwise risks masking, and so by default enabling, the state's relationship to dominant social relations – a risk Lefebvre (2009: 55) lays bare when he declares:

> Someone who does not begin with … critique of the existing State apparatus is simply someone who operates within the framework of existing reality, who does not propose to change it and who absolutely does not deserve the title of socialist.

Of course, 'socialist' is not the only form of left politics at stake here, but the relationship of prefiguration to critique is an important one.

Prefigurative state conceptualising, like other kinds of prefigurative practice, does not centre critique – at least not overtly. Nevertheless, it does take place acutely aware of the limits, flaws and problems endemic to formations conventionally understood as state formations. Thus, in reimagining what it means to be a state, conceptual prefiguration operates *in relation to* other state imaginaries, including dominant ones. At the same time, reimagining recalibrates which practices, systems and forms are to count as those of the state. In other words, conceptual prefiguration does not retain, and work with, an already framed or cut-out state. Instead, it combines present-day concerns and values with readings of other times and spaces to rethink and re-engage with the here and how. But, the question remains, what does this *do*? Beyond unsettling common-sense notions of what states are invariably like, to what extent can conceptual prefiguration, with its reimagined ideas of what it means to be a state, *affect* social and political practice?

This is a crucial and complex question, which I cannot fully do justice to here, not least because it requires far more research. Certainly, writers have explored the contested character and consequences of what gets treated as a state part (e.g. Mitchell, 1991); and a growing body of work has addressed the question of why activist, official and public conceptions of the state matter; how they affect the actions and decisions that people and organisations make (e.g. Brissette, 2015; Fuglerud, 2004; Gill, 2010; Navaro-Yashin, 2002; Yang, 2005). For the most part, however, these accounts focus on *non*-prefigurative state imaginaries. To the extent they address progressive politics, their focus, as in Nick Gill's (2010) work, is on how different *critical* perceptions of the state inform activist organisations' strategies. In Britain, *prefigurative* state thinking has largely occurred on the neoliberal right (e.g. Ridley, 1988). The last three decades have witnessed extensive reimagining and re-actualisation of the 'proper' or 'right-course' state as right-wing politicians, officials and academics publicly rethought and refashioned what it could mean (and be) to be a state, foregrounding commercial involvement, inter-state investment competition, market practices and financial rule (Cerny, 1997). *Imagining* states in the Global North in intensively market-supporting ways was not enough alone. Accomplishment needed regulatory, economic and social reforms as well. However, in neoliberalism's political expansion, developing a new imaginary proved central to this process – inspiring, legitimating and rationalising socio-material and policy shifts, alongside expectations of what states should and could do. If the state is a concept that can be imagined in multiple ways, neoliberal political projects not only redefined the state, but reassembled, imaginatively as well as practically, those elements deemed part of it.

My argument in this chapter has stressed the importance for progressive politics of reimagining what it could mean to be a state; and enacting this imagining – whether through radical state projects, the development of counter-institutions or through forms of ambitious going-beyond-what-is-currently-realisable play (see Cooper, 2019). I have focused on the first possibility here, in part to emphasise that prefiguring the state is not only about meaning in its ideational form. Acting as if meanings were otherwise stresses the importance of materiality and doings. BMR demonstrates how, through such doings, new meanings and accounts of what a state could be then emerge. But conceptual prefiguration, even of the state, does not have to centre institutional practices. It also can occur in the many other ways differently situated actors express and assume particular meanings. Deliberately using the concept of the state to counter prevailing understandings may not bring those preferred meanings into practical usage or realisation (see De Cesari, this volume). Still, it contributes to a project that refuses to relinquish institutional formations (and what they might offer to progressive politics) to elite actors for them to possess – and in possessing to determine their meaning, and the cuts and joins that inevitably make them up.

Conclusion

In recent years, debate about political government in post-industrial states has questioned many certainties, including commitment to liberal norms of democratic state-based rule. In some academic quarters, analytical and normative paradigms have shifted from state to governance to recognise and affirm plurality and inclusive horizontal relations. But 'general purpose' or functionally split governance structures, such as those described by Hooghe and Marks (2003), are not necessarily progressive alternatives to the nation-state. In some cases, they may co-exist in seeming comfort with it; in other cases, they offer a corporatist, less democratic means of providing public goods, where fragmentation undermines more holistic and expansive forms of public responsibility. Swyngedouw (2005) explores some of the deficits governance-beyond-the-state produces in terms of representation, accountability and legitimacy. Complementing his critique, this discussion has suggested that progressive politics could benefit from a different turn, one that holds onto the concept of the state while prefiguratively reimagining what gathers in its name. This makes it possible to recognise micro, shadow, guerrilla, embryonic, dying, local, national, regional and supranational states as political governing formations, reflecting back their constitutive social relations, while also acting on these relations in transformative or maintenance-based ways.

What can imagining ourselves dwelling in a world of diversely formed, over-lapping, multi-scaled states contribute to progressive politics? Recognising micro, guerrilla and regional states as states may undercut the grandeur and assumed (or defended) sovereignty of the nation-state; but simply extending the category of statehood to differently scaled, bounded forms of institutionalised diversity does not seem enough to significantly advance a progressive understanding of what statehood could entail. I therefore turned to one imaginary of a progressive 'better state' inspired by 1980s British municipal radicalism. With all its tensions and failings, BMR provides a productive ground from which to think about statehood (and other political governance formations): how we might imagine states, at least at certain scales, as seeking to advance and model themselves around relations of public responsibility, social justice, participation, care, activism and creativity.[17] Allowing this imaginary to surface, and to be actualised by activists, writers, policy-makers and others *as if* it identifies what it could mean to be a state, is not enough to *realise* the states being prefigured. Still, it rubs hard against the nation-centric qualities conventionally associated with states, of coercion, patriotism, territory, protection of dominant interests and the abandonment of those deemed to 'drain' resources. It is also a state imaginary that resonates with political initiatives far beyond 1980s British municipal government, including the 'right to the city' movements with their anti-neoliberal urban imaginaries (Portaliou, 2007); the sanctuary city projects intended to protect undocumented migrants (Darling, 2009); and new initiatives to municipalise energy infrastructures (Cumbers, 2015).

Conceptual prefiguration has its limitations. Like other forms of prefigurative practice, it may over-read the political agency available to think and act effectively in ways that are at odds with the status quo, underestimating, also, the preconditions and temporal specificity of political change (including the conditions that enable thinking to acquire particular shapes). But because the scope of political agency is both uncertain and emergent, prefiguration tacitly treats the risk of over-reading as less problematic than the reverse, which is to assume such agency's absence. Whether nationally scaled states (let alone global ones) could ever adequately resemble radical municipal governments seems unlikely (although the relentless municipalisation of nation-states may be making it more credible). However, as new kinds of political governance formations emerge, including at global and regional scale, radical politics needs to engage with the fantasy of what stateness could and should entail. If neoliberal politics reimagines 'good' states as corporations within a marketplace, reimagining 'better' states through a radical municipal lens – reversing the expectation that if Frestonia became a state it should look like a nation-state – seems no less valuable.

Acknowledgements

I am grateful for comments and feedback from Didi Herman, Nikita Dhawan, Janet Newman and the series editors, Sarah Keenan and Sarah Lamble; an earlier version of this chapter was published as 'Prefiguring the State' (2017) *Antipode*, 49(2), pp. 335–56.

References

Anderson, J. (1996) 'The Shifting Stage of Politics: New Medieval and Postmodern Territorialities?', *Environment and Planning D: Society and Space*, 14(2), pp. 133–54.

17 See also Fung and Wright (2003) on 'empowered participatory governance'.

Aretxaga, B. (2003) 'Maddening States', *Annual Review of Anthropology*, 32(1), pp. 393–410.

Bauman, Z. (1991) *Modernity and Ambivalence*. Cambridge: Polity Press.

Binkley, S. (2009) 'Inventado: Between Transnational Consumption and the Gardening State in Havana's Urban Spectacle', *Cultural Studies↔Critical Methodologies*, 9(2), pp. 321–44.

Blomley, N. (2016) 'The Territory of Property', *Progress in Human Geography*, 40(5), 593–609.

Boddy, M. (1984) 'Local Economic and Employment Strategies' in Boddy, M. and Fudge, C. (eds.), *Local Socialism?* Houndmills, Basingstoke: Macmillan, pp. 160–91.

Boddy, M. and Fudge, C. (1984) *Local Socialism?* Houndmills, Basingstoke: Macmillan.

Boggs, C. (1977) 'Marxism, Prefigurative Communism, and the Problem of Workers' Control', *Radical America*, 11(6), pp. 99–122.

Branson, N. (1980) *Poplarism, 1919–25: George Lansbury and the Councillors' Revolt*. London: Lawrence & Wishart.

Brenner, N. and Elden, S. (2009) 'Henri Lefebvre on State, Space, Territory', *International Political Sociology*, 3(4), pp. 353–77.

Brissette, E. (2015) 'From Complicit Citizens to Potential Prey: State Imaginaries and Subjectivities in US War Resistance', *Critical Sociology*, doi: 10.1177/0896920515582091.

Cerny, P. G. (1997) 'Paradoxes of the Competition State: The Dynamics of Political Globalization', *Government and Opposition*, 32(2), pp. 251–74.

Comaroff, J. and Comaroff, J. (2001) 'Naturing the Nation: Aliens, Apocalypse, and the Postcolonial State', *Social Identities*, 7(2), pp. 233–65.

Cooper, D. (1994) *Sexing the City: Lesbian and Gay Politics within the Activist State*. London: Rivers Oram.

Cooper, D. (1996) 'Institutional Illegality and Disobedience: Local Government Narratives', *Oxford Journal of Legal Studies*, 16(2), pp. 255–74.

Cooper, D. (2016) 'Enacting Counter-States through Play', *Contemporary Political Theory*, 15(4), pp. 453–61.

Cooper, D. (2017) 'Transforming Markets and States through Everyday Utopias of Play', *Politica and Società*, 2, pp. 187–214.

Cooper, D. (2019) *Feeling like a State: Desire, Denial, and the Recasting of Authority*. Durham, NC: Duke University Press.

Cumbers, A. (2015) 'Constructing a Global Commons in, against and beyond the State', *Space and Polity*, 19(1), pp. 62–75.

Darling, J. (2009) 'A City of Sanctuary: The Relational Re-imagining of Sheffield's Asylum Politics', *Transactions of the Institute of British Geographers*, 35(1), pp. 125–40.

Davies, M. (2017) *Law Unlimited*. London: Routledge.

DeFilippis, J. (2001) 'Our Resistance Must Be as Local as Capitalism: Place, Scale and the Anti-Globalization Protest Movement', *City*, 5(3), pp. 363–73.

Dhawan, N. (2016) 'Homonationalism and State-Phobia: The Postcolonial Predicament of Queering Modernities' in Viteri, M. and Picq, M. L. (eds.), *Queering Paradigms V: Queering Narratives of Modernity*. Oxford: Peter Lang, pp. 51–68.

Elden, S. (2010) 'Land, Terrain, Territory', *Progress in Human Geography*, 34(6), pp. 799–817.

Fudge, C. (1984) 'Decentralisation: Socialism Goes Local' in Boddy, M. and Fudge, C. (eds.), *Local Socialism?* Houndmills, Basingstoke: Macmillan, pp. 192–214.

Fuglerud, O. (2004) 'Constructing Exclusion: The Micro-Sociology of an Immigration Department', *Social Anthropology*, 12(1), pp. 25–40.

Fung, A. and Wright, E. (2003) *Deepening Democracy: Institutional Innovations in Empowered Participatory Governance*. London: Verso.

Gill, N. (2010) 'Tracing Imaginations of the State: The Spatial Consequences of Different State Concepts among Asylum Activist Organisations', *Antipode*, 42(5), pp. 1048–70.

Goss, S. (1984) 'Women's Initiatives in Local Government' in Boddy, M. and Fudge, C. (eds.), *Local Socialism?* Houndmills, Basingstoke: Macmillan, pp. 109–32.

Griffiths, J. (1986) 'What Is Legal Pluralism?', *Journal of Legal Pluralism and Unofficial Law*, 24, pp. 1–55.

Gyford, J. (1985) *The Politics of Local Socialism.* London: Allen & Unwin.

Gyford, J., Leach, S. and Game, C. (1989) *The Changing Politics of Local Government.* London: Unwin Hyman.

Hambleton, R. (1988) 'Consumerism, Decentralization and Local Democracy', *Public Administration*, 66(2), pp. 125–47.

Hirst, P. (1997) *From Statism to Pluralism.* London: UCL Press.

Hobbs, H. H. (1994) *City Hall Goes Abroad: The Foreign Policy of Local Politics.* Thousand Oaks, CA: Sage Publications.

Holloway, J. (2010) *Crack Capitalism.* London: Pluto Press.

Hooghe, L. and Marks, G. (2003) 'Unraveling the Central State, But How? Types of Multi-Level Governance', *American Political Science Review*, 97(2), pp. 233–43.

Ince, A. (2012) 'In the Shell of the Old: Anarchist Geographies of Territorialisation', *Antipode*, 44(5), pp. 1645–66.

Lansley, S., Goss, S. and Wolmar, C. (1989) *Councils in Conflict: The Rise and Fall of the Municipal Left.* Houndmills, Basingstoke: Macmillan.

Laski, H. (1919) 'The Pluralistic State', *The Philosophical Review*, 28(6), pp. 562–75.

Lefebvre, H. (2009) *State, Space, World: Selected Essays* (Brenner, N. and Elden, S. eds.). Minneapolis, MN: University of Minnesota Press.

Loughlin, M. (1996) *Legality and Locality: The Role of Law in Central-Local Government Relations.* Oxford: Oxford University Press.

Macdonald, R., Scott, F. R. and Sandomierski, D. (2006) 'Against Monopolies', *Northern Ireland Legal Quarterly*, 57(4), pp. 610–33.

MacIntyre, S. (1979) 'Red Strongholds between the Wars', *Marxism Today*, 23, pp. 85–90.

Maeckelbergh, M. (2011) 'Doing Is Believing: Prefiguration as Strategic Practice in the Alterglobalization Movement', *Social Movement Studies*, 10(1), pp. 1–20.

Massey, D. (2007) *World City.* Cambridge: Polity.

McConnell, F. (2016) *Rehearsing the State – the Political Practices of the Tibetan Government-in-Exile.* New York: John Wiley & Sons.

McDonald, J. (2012) 'Building a Sanctuary City' in Nyers, P. and Rygiel, K. (eds.), *Citizenship, Migrant Activism and the Politics of Movement.* London: Routledge, pp. 129–45.

McKay, G. (2011) *Radical Gardening: Politics, Idealism & Rebellion in the Garden.* London: Frances Lincoln.

Merry, S. E. (1988) 'Legal Pluralism', *Law and Society Review*, 22(5), pp. 869–96.

Miller, B. (2007) 'Modes of Governance, Modes of Resistance: Contesting Neoliberalism in Calgary' in Leitner, H., Peck, J. and Sheppard, E. (eds.), *Contesting Neoliberalism.* New York: Guilford Press, pp. 223–49.

Mitchell, T. (1991) 'The Limits of the State: Beyond Statist Approaches and Their Critics', *American Political Science Review*, 85(1), pp. 77–96.

Morefield, J. (2005) 'States Are Not People: Harold Laski on Unsettling Sovereignty, Rediscovering Democracy', *Political Research Quarterly*, 58(4), pp. 659–69.

Mottier, V. (2008) 'Eugenics, Politics and the State: Social Democracy and the Swiss "Gardening State"', *Studies in History and Philosophy of Science Part C: Studies in History and Philosophy of Biological and Biomedical Sciences*, 39(2), pp. 263–9.

Navaro-Yashin, Y. (2002) *Faces of the State: Secularism and Public Life in Turkey.* Princeton, NJ: Princeton University Press.

Navaro-Yashin, Y. (2012) *The Make-Believe Space: Affective Geography in a Postwar Polity*. Durham, NC: Duke University Press.

Newman, J. (2012) *Working the Spaces of Power: Activism, Neoliberalism and Gendered Labour*. London: Bloomsbury.

Newman, J. and Clarke, J. (2014) 'States of Imagination', *Soundings: A Journal of Politics and Culture*, 57(1), pp. 153–69.

Newman, S. (2001) 'War on the State: Stirner's and Deleuze's Anarchism', *Anarchist Studies*, 9(2), pp. 147–64.

Ordóñez, V., Feenstra, R. A. and Franks, B. (2018) 'Spanish Anarchist Engagements in Electoralism: From Street to Party Politics', *Social Movement Studies*, 17(1), pp. 85–98.

Ouseley, H. (1984) 'Local Authority Race Initiatives', in Boddy, M. and Fudge, C. (eds.), *Local Socialism?* Houndmills, Basingstoke: Macmillan, pp. 133–59.

Painter, J. (2006) 'Prosaic Geographies of Stateness', *Political Geography*, 25(7), pp. 752–74.

Painter, J. (2010) 'Rethinking Territory', *Antipode*, 42(5), pp. 1090–118.

Parkinson, M. (1989) 'The Thatcher Government's Urban Policy: A Review', *Town Planning Review*, 60(4), pp. 421–40.

Pickering, M. and Keightley, E. (2006) 'The Modalities of Nostalgia', *Current Sociology*, 54(6), pp. 919–41.

Portaliou, E. (2007) 'Anti-Global Movements Reclaim the City', *City*, 11(2), pp. 165–75.

Purcell, M. (2008) *Recapturing Democracy: Neoliberalization and the Struggle for Alternative Urban Futures*. New York: Routledge.

Rai, S. M. (2010) 'Analysing Ceremony and Ritual in Parliament', *Journal of Legislative Studies*, 16(3), pp. 284–97.

Ridley, N. (1988) *The Local Right: Enabling Not Providing*. London: Centre for Policy Studies.

Routledge, P. (1997) 'The Imagineering of Resistance: Pollok Free State and the Practice of Postmodern Politics', *Transactions of the Institute of British Geographers*, 22(3), pp. 359–76.

Ruggie, J. G. (1993) 'Territoriality and Beyond: Problematizing Modernity in International Relations', *International Organization*, 47(1), pp. 139–74.

Russell, B. (2019) 'Beyond the Local Trap: New Municipalism and the Rise of the Fearless Cities', *Antipode*. 51(3), pp. 989–1010.

Saunders, P. (1984) 'Rethinking Local Politics', in Boddy, M. and Fudge, C. (eds.), *Local Socialism?* Houndmills, Basingstoke: Macmillan, pp. 22–48.

Schiel, T. (2005) 'Modernity, Ambivalence and the Gardening State', *Thesis Eleven*, 83(1), pp. 78–89.

Seyd, P. (1987) *The Rise and Fall of the Labour Left*. Houndmills, Basingstoke: Macmillan.

Springer, S. (2012) 'Anarchism! What Geography Still Ought to Be', *Antipode*, 44(5), pp. 1605–24.

Swyngedouw, E. (2005) 'Governance Innovation and the Citizen: The Janus Face of Governance-beyond-the-State', *Urban Studies*, 42(11), pp. 1991–2006.

Swyngedouw, E. and Kaïka, M. (2003) 'The Making of "Glocal" Urban Modernities', *City*, 7(1), pp. 5–21.

Tamanaha, B. Z. (2000) 'A Non-Essentialist Version of Legal Pluralism', *Journal of Law and Society*, 27(2), pp. 296–321.

Yang, S.-Y. (2005) 'Imagining the State: An Ethnographic Study', *Ethnography*, 6(4), pp. 487–516.

Yates, L. (2015) 'Rethinking Prefiguration: Alternatives, Micropolitics and Goals in Social Movements', *Social Movement Studies*, 14(1), pp. 1–21.

10

REGULATING WITH SOCIAL JUSTICE IN MIND

An experiment in reimagining the state

Morag McDermont and the Productive Margins Collective

What might it mean to engage in reimagining the state? What different interests and experiences would be at stake? And what role might research play? In this chapter, I use understandings developed in the course of a programme of research that drew on the experiences and expertises of communities at the margins in order to reimagine regulatory systems and practices.

Regulation is a central role of states as they seek to protect citizens from the consequences of global markets and unfettered competition in activities such as securing food safety, ensuring institutional probity or improving air quality. However, regulation has now become a key target of the anti-statist, anti-expert political mobilisations that have been witnessed in, for example, the discourse around the UK exiting the European Union.

While regulatory systems are encountered on a daily basis – in education, social work, immigration, food safety, consumer protection or housing construction standards – regulatory systems are seen as remote, technocratic, run by 'experts'. Indeed, it is the technocratic nature of regulatory practices that is attractive to governmental bodies: the technocratic 'fixes' of regulatory practice appear non-ideological, and transportable across boundaries, whether they be system boundaries or national borders. Through deploying regulatory practices, acts of governing are portrayed as outside politics; yet they tend to be experienced as remote and exclusionary. It was this 'problem' that was the basis of a five-year programme of research: 'Productive Margins: Regulating *for* Engagement',[1] a collaboration between two universities (Bristol and Cardiff) and community organisations in Bristol and South Wales.[2]

---

1 ESRC Grant No: ES/K002716/1.
2 The community organisations in the partnership were: 3G's Development Trust, a social enterprise, established in 1995 at the head of a Welsh valley in the Gurnos and Galon Uchaf, previously coal-mining and steel-making communities; Building the Bridge, which emerged out of the New Labour

These included social enterprises, partnership bodies, creative media organisations, community development associations and a range of grassroots organisations. Our aim was to examine whether it was possible to reimagine regulatory practices through strategies of 'co-production', bringing in the experience and expertise of communities at the margins to address the central question of how individuals and communities might engage with regulation in ways that promoted community-based understandings of social justice.

In setting out alternative imaginaries, we begin by exploring the current state of regulation scholarship and practice, discussing the move from hierarchical, command-and-control to decentred regulation, with its emphasis on risk-based regulation and self-regulation. We argue that the premise on which much regulation is brought into being, and the tools adopted, tend to the creation of relatively closed circuits of regulators, companies and other technocratic intermediaries, their shared understandings and shared languages thereby excluding most citizens.

The following section interrogates four themes that emerged in attempting to generate 'progressive'/alternative strategies through forms of coproduction: expertise, experience, deliberation and creativity. We outline the strategies used to foster a collaborative approach, and offer examples of how the creative practices deployed took different forms in relation to specific sites of regulation.

However, notions of co-production have been criticised for not paying sufficient attention to disparities of knowledge and power. The final section, then, argues for the need to reimagine politics as an integral element of any attempt to 'reimagine the state'. We argue for a concern for the *infrastructure* that can support the emergence of expertise by experience, enable community-level understandings of social justice to come to the fore and maintain space for difference.

Understandings of regulation

Theories and practices of regulation have developed over recent decades, with a shift from regulation as centralised and operating through mechanisms of 'command-and-control' to ideas of 'decentred' regulation (Black, 2001), 'regulatory space' (Hancher and Moran, 1989) and 'regulation in many rooms' (Nader and Nader, 1985).

---

government's Prevent agenda as a participatory mechanism that institutionalised a new relationship between Bristol City Council, the Police, various statutory agencies and Bristol's diverse Muslim community; Coexist, a Community Interest Company and umbrella organisation for grass-roots organisations and community groups, which occupies a formerly derelict office building in Stokes Croft, Bristol; Knowle West Media Centre, a creative-media organisation and registered charity based in one of the most economically deprived areas of Bristol; Single Parents Action Network (SPAN), a Bristol-based organisation established to empower one-parent families throughout the UK; Southville Community Development Association (SCDA), a social enterprise and charity running a community building, a café, a nursery, a pre-school and pre-/after-school club and older people's services; and South Riverside Community Development Centre (SRCDC), a charity and a company registered by guarantee, which had been funded through the Welsh government's Communities First programme to support the most disadvantaged communities in the Butetown, Riverside and Grangetown areas of Cardiff.

In all of these ways of thinking and talking about regulation, space plays an important role: the boundaries between regulator and regulated become elusive, shifting and highly context dependent.

A focus on the decentred nature of regulation, and the 'regulatory space' metaphor in particular, has focused regulation thinking away from hierarchical, top-down concepts of 'command and control' (CAC), onto the fragmentary and dispersed nature of regulatory power. In regulatory space, the resources of, and relations between, the various occupants of the space are critical in holding it together (Scott, 2001). We can think of these as 'powers of association' (Latour, 1986) which create interdependencies between the actors as human and non-human items are exchanged and bargained as part of the functioning of power (see McDermont, 2007).

However, if we move away from ideas of regulation as being 'government commanding, others obeying', then what is regulation? Perhaps the narrative that suggests a shift from 'command-and control' to decentred regulation is a myth; after all, governing has always taken place 'beyond the state' (Rose and Miller, 1992). However, in these narratives 'decentred regulation' is used both as a description of how regulation *is* operationalised in actuality, and as a normative set of prescriptions of how regulation *should* be operationalised. To decentre regulation is to recognise 'issues of complexity, the fragmentation and construction of knowledge, the fragmentation of the exercise of power and control, autonomy, and interactions and interdependencies' (Black, 2001: 123), but this tends to make the idea of regulation either elusive, or too all encompassing. To provide focus for the multi-disciplinary co-investigators in the research programme (on which more below), we suggested that regulation had five qualities: (1) it is process oriented (not defining outcomes, but governing how outcomes are to be achieved); (2) it is codified (there are rules to the game, most are explicit, but they can be tacit); (3) it seeks behaviour modification; (4) it engages regulator and regulatee (i.e. both have agency) so regulation has a negotiated character; and (5) it can be facilitative, enabling experimentation and allowing for innovation in how things get done.

However, the ways in which regulation has been operationalised, through practices of risk-based regulation and 'self-regulation', have contained very narrow understandings of who, or what, forms part of the regulatory system. The occupants of regulatory space are generally restricted to relatively powerful organisations; the regulatory bodies, the companies/organisations that are to be regulated and a myriad of advisers, consultants, financiers and others. In regulatory space, there is little, if any, room for engagement from individuals and communities who also experience being regulated by, for example, the decisions of supermarkets as to where to locate and what to sell, or of housing associations as to what to build and whom to house. Engagement seldom moves beyond establishing a consumer advisory panel, or having a tenant on a housing association board (e.g. McDermont et al., 2009). So, although the tendency towards decentred regulation would appear to offer the possibility of opening up regulatory spaces, we would rather point to the closing down that occurs — regulatory space may include a broader conception of 'others', but by drawing boundaries it also excludes.

These exclusionary tendencies arise from a number of directions. First, the technocratic nature of regulation, which deploys specialised expertise, makes it attractive for governments (and others). Regulation appears as non-ideological, as politically neutral. This allows regulations to travel globally as 'seemingly fluid and flexible instruments of rule' (Turem and Ballestero, 2014: 3). So, while regulation scholars recognise the fragmentary and constructed nature of regulatory knowledge with no single actor holding all the information necessary to solve regulatory problems (Black, 2001: 107), the more inclusionary concept of regulation this generates only recognises the knowledge of *organisations* that are the subject of regulation (and their consultants and financiers) as relevant. The result is to make systems *more* internally referential. Second, the invention of regulatory systems and practices frequently arises not from a desire to prevent a social harm, but rather as a response to demands from 'cohesively co-ordinated groups, typically industry or special interest groups' (Veljanovski, 2010: 25) to protect a field from intrusion by 'outsiders'. The design of the regulatory system thus reflects the need of the actors inside the system to create authority and control. For example, UK housing associations in the 1970s worked with the government to set up a system of regulation with a centralised state regulator (McDermont, 2007); or the various measures, standards and certification procedures which are crucial to both the creation and partial stabilisation of free trade space (Lewis et al., 2017). Third, the practices that have become vital in decentred regulation – 'risk-based' and 'self'-regulation – also work towards the narrowing down of the focus and attention of those operating in regulatory space. 'Risk-based' regulation has become a leading influence on the design of regulation, being seen as a way of reducing the 'burden' of regulation by targeting resources (e.g. in the UK, the Hampton Report (2005)). What risk-based mechanisms do is focus resources on inspection of those organisations that are judged to pose the greatest risk, so ignoring wider societal risks. They 'tend to focus on known and familiar risks [and in doing so they] fail to pick up new or developing risks and will tend to be backward looking and can get "locked in" to an established analytical framework' (Baldwin and Black, 2008: 66).

Self-regulation, also in vogue because it seemingly saves state resources, leads to practices and procedures based on internal (organisational or sectoral) knowledge. The many meanings of self-regulation all revolve around mechanisms of regulation that put the organisation – or the sector – at the centre of regulatory practice (Black, 2001). So self-regulation might mean passing the regulatory function down to the level of the firm, where organisations are required to establish their own departments that monitor and inspect, a sort of 'enforced self regulation' (Ayres and Braithwaite, 1992); or it might refer to a sector or industry carrying out its own regulatory functions with some oversight by government, sometimes termed 'coregulation' (Grabosky and Braithwaite, 1986: 83).

So, decentred regulation, and the tools and techniques that this gives rise to, results in spaces open only to regulatory institutions (with a variety of attachments to, or detachments from, the state) working alongside relatively powerful actors: companies, consultants and other intermediaries. This 'decentring' of regulation may have produced more efficient and effective regulation from the perspective of regulators and regulated organisation. However, these multiple, discrete systems that have evolved technocratic fixes to regulatory problems allow little, if any, reference to the lived experience of those who themselves are regulated: the person seeking asylum, living in poor housing or wanting to buy healthy, affordable food. Regulatory systems as discrete, technocratic solutions seem to have little relation to values of 'social justice' as they might be expressed by people and communities who come to feel they are 'at the margins'. As some regulation theorists have noted:

> . . . the globalization of law has decentred law-making from nation-states to various sectors of society: contracting parties, technical committees, epistemic communities . . . not the 'warm communal bonds' of rural or traditional communities, but in the 'cold technical processes' of specialist networks (Black, 2001: 144; referencing Teubner, 1997).

Teubner, Black and others have argued for some time that regulatory systems need to become more reflexive through 'proceduralisation', a 'democratisation of administration' (Black, 2000: 614). For Teubner, each regulatory system is autonomous, with its own set of normative values and associated practices. He argues for a 'reflexive law' that can 'foster mechanisms that systematically further the development of reflexion structures within other social systems' (1983: 275).

Recently, however, Black (2013) has suggested that calls for the democratisation of administration have achieved little. If regulators are to regulate in a 'really responsive' way, they need to 'develop socially enriched mechanisms for seeing and knowing' that move away from regulatory knowledge dominated by economics-thinking, to encompass socio-political and anthropological perspectives.

Contesting regulation: Expertise, experience, deliberation and creativity

These were the problems of regulation that inspired the creation of a programme of research which attempted to rethink the theory and practice regulation. 'Productive Margins: Regulating *for* Engagement' was a collaboration between community organisations and higher education researchers to examine whether it is possible to reimagine regulatory practices through strategies of *co-production*.[3] The *co-*(llaborative) *production* of a programme of research, we hoped, would foreground the experience and expertise of communities at the margins. This would enable us to address the central question of how to promote understandings of social justice developed by communities.[4] The programme sought to explore both the tensions around systems of regulation *and* the tensions that arose when trying to rethink

---

3 There is a growing literature on theories and practices of co-production. For overview of co-production in research, see e.g. Facer and Enright, 2016; in public services, see e.g. Boyle et al., 2010.

4 'Community' is a problematic term, and over-used. There are many levels of 'community' involved in this research project – we have tried, in our practices and writing, to remain open to this multiplicity, but this is difficult and we recognise that we frequently do not succeed.

regulatory systems through the mechanisms and perspectives of co-production. As a programme, we therefore wanted to challenge assumptions of 'expertise', both within the regulatory systems we were exploring and within the research process. We came to see that these two aspects were inextricably linked. If regulatory systems were to become more responsive to the needs and demands of regulated *citizens* (as opposed to companies and organisations), they need to both develop different ways of seeing and knowing the practices and impact of their regulation, and ways in which communities at the margins could become engaged in designing those regulatory systems. We hoped that the processes and practices of co-production, as put into practice in our programme, including working with artists and creative practices, could open up such new ways of seeing, knowing and redesigning. Therefore, our insights from experimenting with co-production (in research) were directly relevant to the co-production of regulatory systems. In the remainder of this section, we interrogate some of the questions of expertise, experience, deliberation and creativity that arose in attempting to generate 'progressive'/ alternative strategies through forms of co-production.

Our methodology of co-production began with two principles: academics and community organisations are equal partners in the design and delivery of the research programme; and new understandings arise when we reflect what we think we know against others who bring to the field different perspectives. In this model of collaborative working, expertise is viewed as 'embodied ensembles of political, institutional and relational knowledge' (Newman, 2017: 94). The programme partnership between researchers in two universities and practitioners in seven community organisations embodied a multiplicity of expertises.

The community organisations were all sites of expertise: they were multiply placed organisations often representing and advocating for several constituencies. They were well able to reinvent and reposition themselves. They provided services – nurseries for local children, drop-in advice sessions, clubs for older residents – as well as galvanising local campaigns: for example, challenging poverty and disadvantage at local and national levels.

Some of the community-based co-investigators had come to their work through the professional route of community development and, in discussions, often pointed to the similarities in the principles behind co-production and of community development. However, their expertise was also heavily grounded in the 'institutional knowledge' of their organisations: in the knowledge, expertise and experience of staff, of those who took part in their organisation's activities and services, and of trustees or others involved in governance. A key role played by these community organisations was intermediating, brokering and advocating for the communities they were embedded within. The community organisation workers brought these many forms of knowledge and expertise to the collaboration, along with their organisation's skills in summoning disenfranchised populations into new participatory projects.

The community organisations were attracted to the research process for several reasons. It could aid their constant search for new funding for their work; being associated with a university could provide legitimacy to their claims; and through an interest (personal and organisational) in research in its own right (several of the community-based co-investigators had previous attachments to higher education, as Masters or PhD students, or researchers).

The academic research team similarly embodied multiple expertises and disciplines, acknowledging, for example, that methods from drama, literature and the other creative arts are as relevant and important as those from social science. The academics involved in the programme were also multiply facing actors. They were not 'simply' academics; they were also activists, artists and trustees of civil society organisations. Much of the work they did as academics involved working with, and/or for, non-academic organisations.

The structure of the programme was also a recognition that academics and community organisation practitioners, while having equal claims to expertise, embody different *forms* of expertise. This difference mattered: in our programme, it was not the intention that academics should take on the role or work of community workers. However, the Productive Margins collaboration was very deliberately constructed as a partnership between organisations, as well as a partnership of co-investigators located in organisations. The principal innovation in the approach to research, as we saw it, was the co-production of the research programme itself. Rather than the academics starting with a list of the fields for enquiry and pre-scribed research projects, the approach of Productive Margins was for this to be a *collaborative* enterprise.

Problems of deliberation

Our principal site of co-production was the Productive Communities Research Forum, which was intended to be:

> An innovative mechanism where academics and communities together will identify research projects that develop regulatory regimes for engaging communities, projects that arise out of everyday lives rather than the bureaucratic needs of mainstream institutions (McDermont, 2012).

The Research Forum, which would co-produce the content of the research programme, was an attempt to create alternative spaces in which to think, theorise, gather data and analyse, a site in which the academic and community organisation workers were all 'co-investigators'. This was an attempt to use co-production as a way of moving on from flawed governmental models of consultation that left no space for issues to emerge and local concerns to be addressed. However, it was not without its tensions as we discuss below.

Research Forum meetings, which were day-long events held every two to three months, were our principal site of co-production in the first phase of the programme. Recognising that knowledge and expertise is situational, Forum meetings moved around between the partner organisations in the programme. The first time we met in a partner's 'home', our day began with a site visit around the organi-sation's facilities and local spaces and places that were important in making up the local community. We experimented with format and design, with the host organisation for each Forum having a role in designing the shape of the day and methods used. At the first Forum, everyone brought an object which represented their understanding of 'regulation'; at the second we worked with maps; at the third some of us did bread-making; at the fourth we brought in an external facilitator.

Having spent four meetings coming to understand the issues and concerns of each of the partners, we then moved on to identifying themes and devising research questions using flipcharts and post-it notes. Three subject areas emerged from dis-cussions over the previous year, each of which brought together concerns of two or more of the partner organisations: (1) isolation and loneliness in older people; (2) poverty; and (3) the regulation of food. At this point, the Research Forum for-mat evolved: working groups were set up around each of these themes, comprising academics and community organisations which, at different paces, developed ideas.

Despite intentions that all should be 'equal partners' in the research process, ine-qualities of power were ever present. The fact that the funding came from a *research council* and hence was all channelled through the lead university dictated both financial procedures and management structures. So, although the Research Forum was placed as the principal site of co-production, the concern (of our university systems and the funder's review panel) that the grant needed 'robust' management meant we established several layers of management, which were then perceived as excluding most of the non-academic partners. This was a constant tension in the programme, leading some to say we were not doing 'true co-production'.

Co-production requires time (see e.g. Theodore, 2015). If we were to gain new understandings by putting unfamiliar perspectives together, there had to be time for trust to develop. Here, we benefited from a five-year research funding, but the *slowing down* of working practices was something that many of the co-investigators, from the universities and community organisations alike, found difficult. Many participated in the Forum meetings simultaneously worrying about the deadlines waiting for them outside this space that we had carved out for collaboration.

Our principal mechanism for involving community members was as 'peer researchers', supported by a training programme. This approach to co-producing research raised important questions of critique, which are discussed more fully else-where (Thomas-Hughes, 2018). Here, we discuss two issues related to expertise and experience. First, the reasons to become engaged in the programme as peer-researchers were various: for some, this was a way of using skills developed through-out a working life, enabling (for example) continued commitment and engagement in retirement. One group, who were the peer researchers for the 'Isolation and Loneliness' project (see below), tended to challenge the notion of 'training', being relatively sure of the value of their own expertise and experience.

For others, involvement in the research programme was viewed as a route through to the university: education as a means of escaping existing restrictions, of improving life/life chances. Here, the role of research participant was more as a participant in learning, one which was at times in contradiction with the aims of creating *community* researchers. So, for example, one group of (mainly Somali) women went through a ten-week programme of learning about research interview techniques and co-designing an interview schedule. However, when it came to the final workshop where peer researchers were to interview each other using this schedule, no one wanted to be interviewed. What followed was an impromptu conversation where peer researchers discussed personal and 'community' experiences of being interviewed by the Home Office, Social Services or the Police and reflected that there were negative associations which came forth at the prospect of 'actual' interviewing which had not been experienced during role-play activities (for more detail, see Thomas-Hughes, 2018).

One result of the two-stage approach to co-producing knowledge – the first in the Research Forum, around what issues should be the subject of investigation, the second in working groups at project design and data collection stage – was a challenge from the peer researchers that the community organisation workers 'knew' about the concerns of the community. Three of the community organisations grouped together around issues of the regulation of food under a project title 'Who Decides What's in My Fridge' (see below). However, when women from the Somali community in Bristol were brought together as the community researchers on this project, some questioned why they were talking about food at all: access to food was not the problem. As the community and university researchers unpicked the issues around perceptions of an over-supply of fast-food takeaways serving poor quality food, it became clear that concerns centred not only around the health impact of fast food, but also around issues of space and its use. In this inner-city area, there was a perceived lack of alternative spaces in the community for children, young people and women. With few other options in the area, the fast-food takeaway queue had become the congregating point for the Somali youth, providing an arena for anti-social behaviour and gangs. So, while the project raised issues of the licensing of fast-food takeaways which have since been taken on by local councillors, limited time and resources for the research project meant this element could not be further developed. This raises important questions about the *infrastructure* required for community engagement in decision-making to be sustained, discussed in the concluding section.

Questions of creativity

The research programme asked: How can the regulatory architecture of spaces of participation support community engagement? One important dimension to the programme was our commitment to working with arts and humanities mixed-mode practices to produce different modes of regulating spaces of engagement (McDermont, 2012: 2). The programme was intended to elicit experiments that might show how regulatory practices could be reconfigured to accommodate and encourage perspectives that dissent from the mainstream. Each of the project working groups took up the idea of using arts practices enthusiastically – in part encouraged by the separate pot of money available for each project to commission artists – but in different ways. Here, we briefly highlight work in three of the seven projects.

'Life chances': Co-producing sociological fiction[5]

The process of collaborative production took us not to specific issues of regulation, but rather to broad areas of common concern. 'Poverty', recognised by all in the Research Forum as a key concern for regulatory practices, specifically resonated with two of the community organisations that had been set up to challenge poverty and disadvantage in multicultural areas of Bristol and Cardiff respectively. The working group's initial research question was around 'what would regulatory systems look like if children were put at the centre?' In narrowing this down, the working group focused on 'low-income families in modern urban settings: poverty, austerity and participatory research'. This arose in part from a desire to subvert the UK Coalition Government's 'Big Society' discourse, with its attack on the welfare state as a driver for social and moral decline (McKee, 2015), and its institutionalisation of participatory engagement to control resistance (Cohen et al., 2017).

A turning point for the poverty working group was commissioning artists Close and Remote. The artists wanted to move away from the needs-based model of 'poverty' to a focus on community assets. Having stumbled upon the UK Coalition Government's twitter account for its 'Life Chances' programme (#LifeChances), they sought to disrupt its images of hetero-normative, mono-racial and largely fictionalised family types and to re-appropriate the term.

The artists developed a set of practices, which was to result in a co-produced novel, a work of 'sociological fiction' (Poulter et al., 2016). In workshops with volunteers, community workers, researchers and artists, fictional characters were created, loosely based on individuals' lives. The novel uses factual material to create fictional storylines that explore the different 'life chances' of families with children as their lives are affected by regulatory systems. The storylines interweave encounters with the welfare benefits system, housing officers, child protection and the immigration and asylum system, with the regulatory relationships created by employment, schooling and encounters with social workers, illustrating how regulatory systems often fail to match the reality of the lives of the people who use them. However, the approach was not just to document oppression by looking at situations now; it also sought to explore different futures, highlighting different utopias from those envisaged by government policy. As a mechanism for involving through doing, the artists got participants to make jewellery. In the novel, a Life Chances Jewellery Community Interest Company (CIC) is set up. The CIC offers space for mutual support and learning, especially for women. As well as being creative, people use existing skills and develop new ones, and establish a network and

5 More can be found on other projects on the programme website, https://productivemargins.blogs.bristol.ac.uk/ (accessed 1 May 2019), including links to papers, books and performances discussed here.

knowledge of regulatory systems that affect them. People can work in the CIC while also receiving Unconditional Credit (a form of Basic Income); they hear about exciting new developments in Children's Services, such as parent advocates (to help avoid children being taken into care) and citizen involvement on local council committees. Recent entrants to the UK can access language and skills support so they can contribute quickly to the local economy.[6]

Following the formal completion of 'Life Chances' as a research project, some of the community members set up a Community Interest Company of their own. The research also produced the 'Game of Life Chances', played with facilitators on a carpet. The game has the potential for use in communities and workplaces, opening up discussion between 'players' about the various regulatory 'blockages' experienced by the actors because of their differing 'life chances', particularly about immigration status and education background.

What both the novel and the game allow for are modes of seeing and knowing regulation through different senses, a 'feeling' of regulatory systems, or perhaps an 'aesthetics' of regulation (Evans and Piccini, 2017). The novel demonstrates very vividly the ways in which the myriad of practices and relationships that regulatory systems generate come to feel impenetrable, that the successive layering of regulation on people's lives becomes *laminated* into one strong, oppressive 'system'. Insights like this, which can emerge in more 'playful' means of engagement (cf. Cooper, 2016), are not visible if the focus of study is simply on a specific regulatory system.

Who decides what's in my fridge?

Food is a site of regulation on multiple levels, whether this be standards of product safety and food hygiene, the licensing of food outlets, or the ways in which supermarkets regulate what we buy through their decisions about what they purchase, from whom, under what conditions, and the siting and accessibility of stores. The food working group, a collaboration between three community organisations and academics working on food-related research, came together around a desire to explore 'how people experience the regulation of their food habits in their community' (Webster et al., 2016: 3). Each organisation had separately worked on issues around food: one working with residents of Knowle West, the other with residents of Easton, the third through a community kitchen. But there was little feeling of similarity between the concerns of the three groups; each was a strong organisation with its own history and strong personalities. The intention was to enable dialogue between the communities of Knowle West and Easton as:

> together the groups were all interested in further exploring the spatial regulation of food habits; how local environments and neighbourhoods work to influence the decisions that we make about food, and how to create change (ibid.).

6 Watson et al., 'Life Chances: Re-imagining Regulatory Systems for Low-Income Families in Modern Urban Settings' (2016). Available at https://www.bristol.ac.uk/policybristol/policy-briefings/life-chances/ (accessed 1 May 2019).

Food, we hoped, would perform the function of a 'boundary object', able to create communication because it is both adaptable to different viewpoints, while being robust enough to maintain identity across them (Star and Griesemer, 1989). Sharing different foods together became a useful way to initiate conversations about food habits, and enabled deeper discussions about cultural identity and experiences of migration. However, background tensions arising from the different socio-economic circumstances in the two communities were felt throughout the life of the project.

For this working group, the commissioning of an artist was also a critical turning point in being able to take the project 'into the world'. The artist repurposed an old milk float as a Somali Kitchen, which was set up outside the local library, sharing Somali food cooked by members of the Women's Group. They shared their vision for the local community through a leaflet, 'They put magic in it' (the 'magic' came from a quote from one of the research participants 'Why do our children love takeaways so much? What do they put in it? They put magic in it'):

> We want to work together with others in the community to improve the health of our community and provide a cleaner, healthier environment for our families. We want to promote fresh, nutritious food and a thriving, affordable local food culture in Easton.[7]

Some of the peer researchers, formalised as a Somali Women's Group, became interested in actively campaigning on the issue of fast food in the area, and eventually presented their case to local City Councillors at a local neighbourhood forum. At the end of the project, some members registered the Somali Kitchen as a CIC. As in the Life Chances project, one response to regulation was to turn to social enterprise as a route for creating new possibilities, initially, at least, framed within the possibility that 'enterprise' could encompass political action.

However, one of the difficulties with the research project as a mechanism for challenging regulatory systems is the short, project-focused timescale. For the outer-city residents, the problem was not too easy access to food, but too little: closed down shops, no local supermarket or shops that sold fresh food at affordable prices, issues that they had campaigned on for many years. There was a feeling that the problems of the two areas, only separated by a few miles, were worlds apart: 'Their [problem] was junk food, mainly, shops; with us, we don't have shops' (Webster et al., 2016: 22). The food research project achieved a high profile for local initiatives in growing food and foraging (including on BBC radio), but was unable to get near the regulatory problem of markets' inability to provide affordable food in local shops. The project surfaced at the gap between conventional approaches to food regulation (through health and safety, etc.) and the regulatory effects of markets, which fail to make healthy, affordable food available in particular localities.

7 See https://www.facebook.com/SomaliKitchen/ (accessed 6 March 2019).

Such highly local concerns are invisible through general systems of state regulation, demonstrating that 'really responsive' systems of food regulation need community knowledge and expertise.

Isolation and loneliness in older people

The issue of isolation and loneliness experienced by older people was identified as a matter of concern at one of the early Research Forum meetings. The aim of this project was to explore how regulation not only produces loneliness, but can also be a means of tackling it. Two of the organisations had significant elderly populations in their neighbourhoods; however, in other respects they were very different areas. Gurnos is situated at the head of a South Wales valley with high levels of unemployment; the Southville area of Bristol had been the site of gentrification over the last few decades and so had a very mixed population. The community association in Southville was involved in the Bristol Aging Better partnership (led by Age Concern) to develop services for older people in the city. These spatial and demographic differences led to the two groups developing in very different ways.

In Southville, the local residents who became the group of community researchers had all been professionals before retiring and very much took the lead. They worked with a range of methods to try to contact 'isolated' older people, including a tea trolley that was taken around shopping centres and other places used by older people and a worker sitting on the community transport bus engaging passengers in conversation. They conducted interviews with older people and then worked with a dramaturge to make them into a series of monologues. At this point, they became actors (with the support of a professional director). The resulting performance, 'Alonely', contained a series of frequently emotional scenes depicting feelings of isolation experienced following retirement, when a partner dies and other life-changing events.

With this project, political action has given it a life beyond the research programme. The peer researchers formed themselves into the Local Isolation and Loneliness Action Committee (LILAC). The community organisation successfully bid for funding for a worker to work alongside them to develop issues that arose from the research. One of the monologues begins with a male actor exclaiming 'Skype! What a wonderful thing', followed by his story of how Skype has enabled him to keep in touch with his children and grandchildren. This led LILAC to set up 'Tech&Talk' sessions in a local cafe (with the help of a Big Lottery grant) to provide informal learning opportunities for older people to use their digital devices with support being provided by younger people, providing for intergenerational/ multigenerational interactions, as well as a way for people of all ages to get to know one another in an informal, non-threatening and common-purpose way. The interviews also identified the point of retirement as a pivotal time that shifted their possibilities for social contact, particularly for men. LILAC is now seeking funding for 'Hyper-local retirement courses', locally based workshops in which participants could both explore what retirement would mean for them and make contact with others from the area who were in a similar situation to them, enabling the development of contacts and local social networks. Currently, LILAC is applying for Arts Council funding to take the 'Alonely' monologues on tour.

Political reimaginings were critical to enabling this much wider engagement. The local residents who became the peer researchers were clear that what was needed was an *action* committee; in putting into action their voluntary effort they did not want to become burdened with administration and legal technicalities. This was made possible because the community organisation could provide the administrative support, and enabled their existence (and being able to benefit from grants) without having to become a legally incorporated entity. The community organisation in effect provided important *infrastructure* that enabled the action committee to focus on political action. However, it also demonstrates the inequalities perpetuated by demographics: the possibilities for similar action happening in the area covered by the 3Gs association is less optimistic as the organisation, and many other community associations throughout Wales, struggle to continue, following the Welsh government's decision to withdraw the funding for the Communities First programme.[8]

These research projects demonstrate the value of co-productive and creative practices in opening up spaces for seeing and knowing regulation differently, providing space for a regulatory aesthetics. But co-production also regulates, creating new exclusions at the same time as new ways of working (see Innes et al., 2018; McDermont, 2018). The creative reimaginings showed that thinking regulation differently means opening spaces for *political* reimaginings, for ways that can provide an infrastructure for engaging expertise and experience in new ways.

Political reimaginings of regulation

We have argued in this chapter for the need to find different ways of seeing and knowing regulatory systems; ways that engage the expertise and experience of communities at the margins of regulatory decision-making. We have traced how the mechanisms of co-production, and the practices of creative artists, provide possibilities for doing so. We have outlined experimental forms that aimed to enable such expertise and experience to become part of the reshaping of regulatory processes, practices, values and principles. However, in calling upon regulatory systems to recognise that people are 'experts-by-experience' (Noorani, 2013), are we in danger of setting up a false opposition between 'ordinary people' and 'experts' (Clarke, 2010; Newman and Clarke, 2009)? Of suggesting that 'ordinary people' are above the 'sordid, dirty business' of party politics, with 'everyday preoccupations [that] are local and particular, operating "beneath the radar" of political organization, mobilization, and institutional structures' (Clarke, 2013: 212)? In this final section, we

8 This is the subject of another research project under the Productive Margins programme, 'Weathering the Storm'. See https://productivemargins.blogs.bristol.ac.uk/.

discuss the ways in which a reimagining of regulation must be coupled with a reimagination of politics: a reimagining that views 'ordinary people' not as individualised citizen-consumers, but (also) as members of collectivities. In this political reimagining, we need to consider that new forms of *intermediation* or *brokering* might open up regulatory spaces to those living and or working in communities at the margins. This suggests a focus on the importance of the *infrastructure* that is required to maintain projects and initiatives. Such infrastructure can support the *emergence* of forms of expertise by experience and community-level understandings of social justice, while allowing space for difference.

Regulatory governance has long recognised the role of 'intermediaries'. However, these are generally understood as intermediating between governments/regulators and regulated *organisations*, as in the Regulator-Intermediary-Target (RIT) model of regulation:

> Regulation is frequently viewed as a two-party relationship between a regulator (R) and the targets of its regulation (T). This volume conceives of regulation as a three-party system, in which intermediaries (I) provide assistance to regulators and/or targets, drawing on their own capabilities, authority, and legitimacy (Abbott et al., 2017: 6).

This somewhat linear model of regulatory systems is one which frequently appears in the regulation and governance literature. It is one that largely ignores citizens; it sometimes acknowledges 'ordinary people' as the beneficiaries of regulation. What this linear model misses is that the companies who are the 'targets' of regulation are themselves frequently also its beneficiaries (see also Koenig-Archibugi and Macdonald, 2017). The Productive Margins programme has shown a more complex and mesh-like view of regulatory systems, with the many layers of regulation (from social-workers and the asylum and immigration system to employers, supermarkets and digital platforms) experienced as being *laminated* and impenetrable. In this world of regulatory systems, there is an evident need for intermediation, translation and brokering for communities at the margins.

In the RIT literature, regulatory intermediaries 'often enter the system through contract, delegated authority or other formal arrangement' (Abbott et al., 2017: 7). The partners in this research programme spoke of themselves as brokers and intermediaries, as 'in between' (or 'umbrella') organisations that could support the work of smaller, focused groups or enterprises, 'curating' others. In one Forum meeting, some spoke of themselves as 'experts in nothing very much'; but it looks more like experts in everything, running community centres and calling on other experts as needed. They translated between local communities and citizens and regulators (knowing, for example, who to ask, or to be able to pick up the phone and talk to the right person in the local authority).[9] Elsewhere, we have highlighted the

9 From notes of a Research Forum meeting in April 2017.

brokering role played by advice organisations in supporting people in employment disputes (McDermont and Kirk, 2017) and other instances involving engagement in legalised spaces (e.g. Kirwan, 2016).

Larner and Craig discuss community organisations as 'strategic brokers' who:

> spend a great deal of time building and maintaining relationships . . . the domain of their expertise [is] explicitly geared to process issues, they can facilitate, mediate and negotiate, nurture networks, and deploy cultural knowledge and local knowledge in ways that enable traditionally 'silent' voices to be heard along with the articulate, persistent and powerful (2005: 417–18).

The focus on the role as *strategic* is important. Community organisations as intermediaries need to be understood as part of an infrastructure that supports engaged regulatory systems, in much the same way as cooperative development agencies and secondary housing cooperatives provided an important infrastructure that supported the development and sustainability of the UK cooperative sector in the 1970s and 1980s. These organisations provided legal, financial and management support that enabled embryonic cooperatives to both get off the ground and have a sustained existence. In a similar way, a number of the partners in Productive Margins provided support, for example, to local actions groups, providing administrative support so that their members could get on with the 'doing', and enabling them to operate under their umbrella so as to avoid the legal complications of becoming incorporated bodies. Others provided flexible workspaces and acted as intermediaries with the local authority on issues such as the payment of business rates.

We need, however, to avoid romanticising 'community'. Newman describes the complex and difficult terrain negotiated by intermediaries. This work is political (Newman, 2012: 134), taking place both inside and outside of organised, institutional structures of local and central government. The position of 'bridging the borders between policymakers and "ordinary people" – the communities and citizens on whom policy was likely to have an impact' (ibid.: 133) was precarious, involving multiple identities. In our programme, one organisation spoke of having to be '*not too radical*' (in its relations with the local authority and the landlord of the building they occupied), despite its counter-culture, radical roots.

Often, it is the regulatory impact of funding regimes that shape an organisation's capacity to make political interventions. Brokers and intermediaries, such as Citizens Advice,[10] can shape social policy from the margins, and can also be watchdogs, highlighting breaches of regulations (or lack of regulation). But this work can be compromised because of their reliance on funding from government and from the industries they challenge (for example, the financial services industry through Money Advice contracts). So political reimagining is not just a focus on process, on using co-production and creative methods to open up ways of seeing. It is about

10 See https://www.citizensadvice.org.uk.

tackling the precarity of organisations that can be effective intermediaries – difficult in a climate of austerity governing and cuts in public funding.

Earlier in this chapter, we highlighted Black's argument that regulatory systems needed to be able to see and know differently if they were to be 'really responsive'. However, our frustration with the regulation and governance literature is that it never seems to deliver ways of seeing and knowing differently. This chapter has shown how empirical research through mechanisms of co-production is one way of recognising other forms of expertise and experience that do not currently exist in regulatory space. But co-production can only ever be part of the answer: political infrastructure matters. Without an infrastructure that can support communities at the margins, co-production is likely to be ineffective. And co-production itself is not unproblematic. We have shown in this chapter how questions of what counts as representation, and expertise and experience, remain unresolved. Inequalities of power and expertise cannot be altered through co-production; politics matter too.

Acknowledgements

The Productive Margins Collective includes academics at Bristol and Cardiff universities and the organisations listed in n. 2.

References

Abbott, K. W., Levi-Faur, D. and Snidal, D. (2017) 'Introducing Regulatory Intermediaries', *ANNALS of the American Academy of Political and Social Science*, 670(1), pp. 6–13.

Ayres, I. and Braithwaite, J. (1992) *Responsive Regulation: Transcending the Deregulation Debate*, New York: Oxford University Press.

Baldwin, J. and Black, J. (2008) 'Really Responsive Regulation', *Modern Law Review*, 71(1), pp. 59–94.

Black, J. (2000) 'Proceduralising Regulaion Part 1', *Oxford Journal of legal Studies*, 20(4), pp. 597–614.

Black, J. (2001) 'Decentring Regulation: Understanding the Role of Regulation and Self-Regulation in a "Post-Regulatory" World', *Current Legal Problems*, 54(1), pp. 103–46.

Black, J. (2013) 'Seeing, Knowing, and Regulating Financial Markets: Moving the Cognitive Framework from the Economic to the Social', *LSE Law, Society and Economy Working Papers*, 24/2013.

Boyle, D., Slay, J. and Stevens, L. (2010) 'Public Services Inside Out: Putting Co-production into Practice' [online]. Available at https://www.nesta.org.uk/report/public-services-inside-out/ (accessed 1 May 2019).

Brigstocke, J. (2013) 'Democracy and the Reinvention of Authority' in Noorani, T., Blencowe, C. and Brigstocke, J. (eds.), *Problems of Participation: Reflections on Democracy Authority and the Struggle for Common Life*, pp. 7–12. Authority Research Network [online]. Available at www.authorityresearch.net/essay-collection-problems-of-participation.html (accessed 3 March 2019).

Clarke, J. (2010) 'Enrolling Ordinary People: Governmental Strategies and the Avoidance of Politics?', *Citizenship Studies*, 14(6), pp. 637–50.

Clarke, J. (2013) 'In Search of Ordinary People: The Problematic Politics of Popular Participation', *Communication, Culture & Critique*, 6, pp. 208–26.

Cohen, S., Herbert, A., Evans, N. and Samzelius, T. (2017) 'From Poverty to Life Chances: Framing Co-produced Research in the Productive Margins Programme' in Ersoy, A. (ed.), *The Impact of Co-Production: From Community Engagement to Social Justice*. Bristol: Policy Press, pp. 61–84.

Cooper, D. (2016) 'Enacting Counter-States through Play', *Contemporary Political Theory*, 15(4), pp. 453–61.

Evans, P. and Piccini, A. (2017) 'The Regulatory Aesthetics of Co-Production' in Ersoy, A. (ed.), *The Impact of Co-Production: From Community Engagement to Social Justice*. Bristol: Policy Press, pp. 99–118.

Facer, K. and Enright, B. (2016) 'Creating Living Knowledge: The Connected Communities Programme, Community-University Relationships and the Participatory Turn in the Production of Knowledge', Connected Communities Programme [online]. Available at https://connected-communities.org/wp-content/uploads/2016/04/Creating-Living-Knowledge.Final_.pdf (accessed 3 March 2019).

Grabosky, P. and Braithwaite, J. (1986) *Of Manners Gentle: Enforcement Strategies of the Australian Business Regulatory Agencies*. Melbourne: Oxford University Press.

Hancher, L. and Moran, M. (1989) 'Organizing Regulatory Space' in Hancher, L. and Moran, M. (eds), *Capitalism, Culture and Economic Regulation*, Oxford: Clarendon Press, pp. 271–99.

Innes, M., Davies, B. and McDermont, M. (2018) 'How Co-roduction Regulates', *Social & Legal Studies*, 28(3), 370–91.

Kirwan, S. (ed.) (2016) *Advising in Austerity: Reflections on Challenging Times for Advice Agencies*, Bristol: Policy Press.

Koenig-Archibugi, M. and Macdonald, K. (2017) 'The Role of Beneficiaries in Transnational Regulatory Processes', *ANNALS of the American Academy of Political and Social Science*, 670(1), pp. 36–57.

Larner, W. and Craig, D. (2005) 'After Neoliberalism? Community Activism and Local Partnerships in Aotearoa New Zealand', *Antipode*, 37(3), pp. 402–24.

Latour, B. (1986) 'The Powers of Association' in Law, J. (ed.), *Power, Action and Belief: A New Sociology of Knowledge?*, London: Routledge, Kegan & Paul, pp. 264–80.

Lewis, N., Le Heron, R. and Campbell, H. (2017) 'The Mouse that Died: Stabilizing Economic Practices in Free Trade Space' in Higgins, V. and Larner, W. (eds.), *Assembling Neoliberalism: Expertise, Practices, Subjects*. New York: Palgrave Macmillan, pp. 151–70.

McDermont, M. (2007) 'Territorializing Regulation: A Case Study of "Social Housing" in England', *Law & Social Inquiry*, 32(2), pp. 273–398.

McDermont, M. (2012) *Case for Support* [online]. Available at https://productivemargins.blogs.bristol.ac.uk/ (accessed 1 May 2019).

McDermont M. (2018) 'Alternative Imaginings of Regulation: An Experiment in Co-production', *Journal of Law & Society*, 45(1), pp. 156–75.

McDermont, M., Cowan, D. and Prendergrast, J. (2009) 'Structuring Governance: A Case Study of the New Organizational Provision of Public Service Delivery', *Critical Social Policy*, 29(4), pp. 677–702.

McDermont, M. and Kirk, E. (2017) 'Working in Law's Borderlands: Translation and the Work of an Advice Office', *Onati Socio-Legal Series*, 7(7), 1445–64.

McKee, K. (2015) 'An Introduction to the Special Issue – The Big Society, Localism and Housing Policy: Recasting State-Citizen Relations in an Age of Austerity', *Housing Theory and Society*, 32(1), pp. 1–8.

Nader, L. and Nader, C. (1985) 'A Wide Angle on Regulation: An Anthropological Perspective' in Noll, R. (ed.), *Regulatory Policy and the Social Sciences*. Berkeley and Los Angeles, CA: University of California Press, pp. 141–59.

Newman, J. (2012) *Working the Spaces of Power.* London: Bloomsbury.

Newman, J. (2017) 'The Politics of Expertise: Neoliberalism, Governance and the Practice of Politics' in Higgins, V. and Larner, W. *Assembling Neoliberalism: Expertise, Practices, Subjects.* New York: Palgrave Macmillan, pp. 87–106.

Newman, J. and Clarke, J. (2009) *Public, Politics and Power: Remaking the Public in Public Services.* London: Sage.

Noorani, T. (2013) 'Service User Involvement, Authority and the "Expert-by-Experience" in Mental Health', *Journal of Political Power,* 6(1), pp. 49–68.

Poulter, S., Mellor, S., Evans, N. et al. (2016) *Life Chances: A Work of Sociological Fiction.* Available at https://www.closeandremote.net/life-chances/novel/ (accessed 1 May 2019).

Rose, N. and Miller, P. (1992) 'Political Power beyond the State: Problematics of Government', *British Journal of Sociology,* 43(2), pp. 173–205.

Scott, C. (2001) 'Analysing Regulatory Space: Fragmented Resources and Institutional Design', *Public Law,* summer, pp. 329–53.

Star, S. L. and Griesemer, J. (1989) 'Institutional Ecology, "Translations" and Boundary Objects: Amateurs and Professionals in Berkeley's Museum of Vertebrate Zoology, 1907–39', *Social Studies of Science,* 19(3), pp. 387–420.

Teubner, G. (1983) 'Substantive and Reflexive Elements in Modern Law', *Law & Society Review,* 17(2), pp. 239–85.

Teubner, G. (1997) '"Global Bukowina": Legal Pluralism in a World Society' in *Global Law without a State.* Aldershot: Dartmouth Gower, pp. 3–28.

Theodore, N. (2015) 'Subject Spaces: Towards an Ethics of Co-production' [online]. Available at http://www.ijurr.org/lecture/2015-aag-ijurr-lecture/ (accessed 3 March 2019).

Thomas-Hughes, H. (2018) 'Critical Conversations with Community Researchers – Making Co-production Happen?' [online]. Available at https://ahrc.ac.uk (accessed 3 March 2019).

Thomas-Hughes, H. and Barke, J. (2018) 'Community Researchers and Community Researcher Training: Reflections from the UK's Productive Margins: Regulating for Engagement Programme', University of Bristol Law Research Series #010 2018. Available at http://www.bristol.ac.uk/media-library/sites/law/documents/Thomas-Hughes%20and%20Barke%20BLRP%20No.%2010%20-%20July%202018%20merged.pdf (accessed 1 May 2019).

Turem, Z. U. and Ballestero, A. (2014) 'Regulatory Translations: Expertise and Affect in Global Legal Fields', *Indiana Journal of Global Legal Studies,* 21(1), 1–25.

Veljanovski, C. (2010) 'Economic Approaches to Regulation' in Baldwin, R., Cave, M. and Lodge, M. (eds.), *The Oxford Handbook of Regulation.* Oxford: Oxford University Press, pp. 17–38.

Webster, K., Millner, N. and Productive Margins Collective (2016) *Who Decides What's in My Fridge?* Productive Margins. Available online at https://productivemargins.blogs.bristol.ac.uk/ (accessed 1 May 2019).

PART IV

Reimagining otherwise

11

HARMFUL THOUGHTS

Reimagining the coercive state?

John Clarke

Why do we keep returning to the state? It remains an object of both constant fascination and constant anxiety. I suspect that one of the seductions that draws us back to the state centres on issues of power: what other formation offers the prospect of enabling and enforcing progressive politics and policies on a large scale (at least national, but also international)? Yet, it is precisely this sense of reach and power that brings with it a sense of anxiety, or even dread, about the state. Most of the time, I have little difficulty in imagining the state as a means of delivering social value – creating supports for welfare, well-being and social improvement, or providing the machinery to redress past and present harms and inequalities. This conception of a progressive state draws on well-established (if seriously flawed) social democratic imaginaries of reform and progress. Taking it forward would certainly demand challenging and moving beyond some of the severe constraints of social-democratic conceptions of 'universal' welfare, not least their nationalism, productivism and familialism (Clarke, 2010). Nevertheless, such constraints are open to political challenge, while thinking of the state as what Gramsci called the democratic-bureaucratic system brings me up against what might be the *limits of politics*: more precisely, against questions of how political desires become translated into policies and then become translated into practices.

This issue was central to Gramsci's view of the state as a double structure – the idea that the bureaucratic parts of the complex formation offered a place where power and dominant interests could be both *installed* and *insulated* from democratic incursions. Here, even small progressive steps (in terms of politics and policies) have to engage in that passage through the institutions where they may be translated, adapted and assimilated to the prevailing dispositions of the bureaucracies (see the complex sagas of equality policies, e.g. Cockburn, 1991; Cooper, 2004). These insti-tutional dispositions may take a variety of forms – legal, professional, managerial, organisational and so on – which may (or may not) align or fuse into blocks of power. But these conditions of power within state bureaucracies create the possibility of refusal, resistance, dilution and diversion, as in the capacities of professional/occupational cultures to reproduce patriarchal, racialised and other forms of discriminatory practice and embodiment (from the university to the hospital). Of course, sometimes they may provide the resources to create and enact progressive directions, but my concern here is with their *recalcitrant* capacities: their ability to soak up or defuse radical innovations: as Tony Platt has recently argued in the context of criminal justice in the US, 'we need to grapple with the legacy of stubborn resistance to meaningful structural change' (2019: 23). We know that there have been diverse approaches to regulating and reforming these bureaucratic capacities and dispositions that have gone beyond the writing of laws or policies and expecting them to be implemented. Among them have been the reform of professional cultures; the deployment of target-setting (or management by objectives) in pursuit of progressive outcomes; the installation of political supervisors within the bureaucracies; and the creation of localised political control (ranging from workers' committees to community representation).

Before exploring such issues, however, there is a prior question that organises this chapter: *How can we reimagine the state's coercive powers?* This is, I realise, a rather old-fashioned phrasing after Foucault's strictures on power. However, I think that even coercive forms of power might usefully be thought of as productive rather than omitted from discussion or consigned to the conceptual dustbin. In pursuing this question, I need to turn away from all those positive images of the state as enabling, developmental, welfarist, etc. (even while acknowledging that such images conceal highly contradictory politics, policies and practices, including forms of discipline, control and coercion). Instead, I begin from images of the security state, the military state, the penal or carceral state, and the police state; such images speak of forms of power that have to be addressed in any project of reimagining the state. Each of these forms of power has become more significant in the context of the re-composition of states of the Global North during the period of neo-liberalisation (see e.g. Hall et al., 1978; Wacquant, 2009). Can we imagine states without coercive powers? At the moment of writing, I do not think I can – although exactly what and who are the objects of coercion may be open to question. In what follows, I explore these issues by addressing three questions: (1) Can existing coercive powers and agencies be reimagined? (2) What do we imagine are the purposes of coercion? (3) Can popular control be exercised over state apparatuses? I confess that my aim in this chapter is to sketch these issues, rather than offer coherent and consistent answers to the questions.

Turbulent states: Old problems and new possibilities

As indicated above, the state remains a source of profound ambivalence – we are variously seduced and repulsed by its promise of power.[1] One way of starting to

---

1 This sentence originally read 'The state continues to drive us crazy – in theory as well as in practice'. However, a critical comment on an earlier draft suggested that, from a critical mental health/disability perspective, it would be better to avoid the word 'crazy'. I think this view misunderstands the cultural

disentangle these contradictory reactions is to clarify some of the terminology: what is this thing called The State? Let me begin by refusing the definite article ('The') and the singular form ('State'): we are necessarily dealing with states, plural, that vary in form, shape and tendency in different spatio-temporal contexts. They are acted upon and shaped by very diverse social relations and political forces with the result that 'The state, in every country, is to some extent the trace in social reality of social conquests' (Bourdieu, 1998: 33). Nor can such states be grasped as singular entities with a coherent institutional form and structure. Rather, they might be best understood as a more or less loose assemblage that combines *places* (from windowless offices to symbolic constitutional sites), *people* (heterogeneous agents variously empowered to act as if they embody The State, from tourism officers to torturers), *policies* (that range from defining membership of the 'political community' to the criminalisation of selected acts and actors) and *practices* (in which people come to encounter The State, such as disability assessments or dietary advice). Such states have complicated – and changeable – scalar architectures in which local, regional, national and supra-national elements are combined and condensed. Finally, the boundaries of such states are variably porous and mobile, not least in their relationships with what is often termed civil society. As Gramsci argued, these are complexly connected formations, rather than divided and opposed entities. In the present, that elusive boundary has been refigured through various state-like capacities and powers being devolved to non-state agents and agencies, which range from paramilitary death squads to service-providing NGOs (see e.g. Sharma, 2006, on the complex articulation of NGOs and state-ness). For the purposes of this chapter, I will be concentrating on some of the clusters of places, people, policies and practices through which states often come to seem most State-like: the apparatuses of coercion and control, such as policing, prisons and the law. But even these need to be thought of as assemblages rather than singular and coherent entities: they are always both internally complex (e.g. the struggles between inmates, staff and managers over the internal control of prisons) and externally coupled through strained relations with other assemblages, not least the different incarnations of finance ministries or budgetary control and accounting systems.

The arguments in this chapter try to work with these shifting and unsettled understandings of states (and their efforts to appear stately) in relation to a set of issues and an inherited set of ideas, concepts and concerns about the coercive capacities of states. My interest in the coercive powers of states – and their relationship to popular and progressive politics – has been re-animated by two relatively recent movements. The first emerges from the efforts of families and friends to

---

politics of language in assuming that 'crazy' (or any other word) has a singular meaning. I would rather follow Raymond Williams and consider the shifting and contested 'historical semantics' of such words. So, the dominant articulation – accusing someone of being crazy – is indeed a way of diminishing, dehumanising and disempowering them, their views and their actions, but this does not exhaust the word's meanings. I think that ideas of feeling crazy, or even more, being *driven* crazy, are commonplace expressions of conflicted or profoundly unsettled emotional states. Patsy Cline singing Willy Nelson's *Crazy* is a testament to such expressions and their popular potency.

discover the truth of how 96 people came to die in a crowd at a football game on 15 April 1989 at the Hillsborough stadium in Sheffield, England (Scraton, 2016 [1999]). So far, it has taken two inquests (1991 and 2016) and two inquiries (1990 and 2012) for the criminal responsibility of the policing of the event to be publicly confirmed. Before then, most of the official accounts had deflected blame onto the supporters themselves (not least through collusion between police, local politicians and media in the immediate aftermath of the event). There have been several organisations involved in the campaign to get justice for the Hillsborough families and survivors, including the Hillsborough Families Support Group (https://en-gb. facebook.com/HFSGOfficial/) and the Hillsborough Justice Campaign (writing in 1998):

> The Hillsborough disaster still remains in the memories of football supporters, although for a whole new generation, it is an event from almost another era. We need to reach out and teach this new generation what happened almost 10 years ago when 96 men, women and children went to a football game and came home in coffins. Even people old enough to remember may have been deliberately misled by the tabloid gutter press into believing that it was 'Scousers' who killed the 96.
>
> We have had to contend with these despicable lies by printing and distributing the personal testimonies of those of us that were there. We will be silent no more and we hope that this website reflects our ability to conduct a campaign for Justice in a manner which best serves the interests of the families and survivors. We are an open, democratic organisation and if we have missed out on some point which you would like to see raised then we welcome any suggestions or questions. We appeal to anyone, be they a football supporter or otherwise to show solidarity with our campaign by helping in whatever way they can (http://www.contrast.org/hillsborough/ whoweare.shtm).

The event matters politically because it raises questions about the persistent impunity of state agents to popular accountability (this is the same regional police force, South Yorkshire, that was also at the heart of violently policing the miners' strike of 1984–85). It matters to me personally because I grew up in Sheffield and attended that football ground on hundreds of occasions without dying. It is important to pay tribute to the persistence not only of the families and friends of those who died, but also the committed intellectual work of Phil Scraton in recording, reporting and pursuing the Hillsborough families' claims to justice.

The second movement emerged in response to the killings of young black and Hispanic men in the United States (Trayvon Martin, Mike Brown and many more: see *Killedbypolice.net*, for example). Such killings underlined a structural vulnerability in the relationship between black people and the coercive apparatuses of the US state, long known and remarkably persistent (e.g. in the history of racialised incarceration in the US: Christie, 1996; Morley and Petras, 1998; Wacquant, 2009).

The issue of police killings was made into a focus of political attention by the mobilisation organised under the banner of *Black Lives Matter*, beginning in 2013:

> The Black Lives Matter Global Network is a chapter-based, member-led organization whose mission is to build local power and to intervene in violence inflicted on Black communities by the state and vigilantes.
>
> We are expansive. We are a collective of liberators who believe in an inclusive and spacious movement. We also believe that in order to win and bring as many people with us along the way, we must move beyond the narrow nationalism that is all too prevalent in Black communities. We must ensure we are building a movement that brings all of us to the front.
>
> We affirm the lives of Black queer and trans folks, disabled folks, undocumented folks, folks with records, women, and all Black lives along the gender spectrum. Our network centers those who have been marginalized within Black liberation movements.
>
> We are working for a world where Black lives are no longer systematically targeted for demise.
>
> We affirm our humanity, our contributions to this society, and our resilience in the face of deadly oppression.
>
> The call for Black lives to matter is a rallying cry for ALL Black lives striving for liberation (https://blacklivesmatter.com/about/).

Black Lives Matter's mobilisation around the racialised violence of the US state (and elsewhere) has made visible once again the long history and present reality of the ways in which the US functions as a racial formation (Omi and Winant, 1986). In a moment where US populism has taken the form of celebrating white supremacist conceptions of the nation, such contestations of the racialised formation of the state and its coercive capacities raise vital questions about how popular control of such agencies might be achieved (and demonstrate the risks of failing to achieve such control).

Although the focus of my work in recent decades has been on matters of citizenship, welfare states and public service reform, these two examples have drawn my attention back to the coercive elements of state power and, in particular, reminded me of the ways in which they could be insulated from popular politics and struggles for popular control. This sense of the recalcitrance of such institutions poses questions of how to reimagine some of the most *intractable* parts of state power for progressive purposes. Although both examples come from the Global North, the issues that they bring into view – the prospects and problems of controlling state power – have echoed around popular, liberatory and revolutionary politics in very different settings. Popular movements have often sought to protect various subjects (the vulnerable, the subordinate) from violence, including violence by states. Meanwhile, other movements have sought to use state powers to protect subjects (such as the people, the nation, the revolution) from the dangers of reaction and regression. The issues raised by the Hillsborough disaster and Black Lives Matter have taken me back to older concerns – notably with race and policing (Hall et al., 1978) – and some of the conceptions and resources that were important to me then, from debates in what was then called 'state theory' to the developments of critical/radical criminology in the UK, Europe and the US (see e.g. the journal *Social Justice*, formerly *Crime and Social Justice* – and that *Crime and* in the original title was significant!).

This inheritance gives a rather strange dynamic to the work of *imagining* that goes on in this chapter. In particular, it gives it a very odd temporality, juxtaposing older resources, current issues and projected possibilities in strained and uncomfortable ways. The results feel like rather idiosyncratic encounters that make imagining a work of reaching for connections – reaching for in both the sense of bringing them (back) into view, but also the sense of spinning them out of fragile tissue, and as a consequence, running the risk of over-reaching and failing to grasp the object of my desires. Finally, the temporal sensibility of this discussion is also unsettled by my feeling that thinking about coercive state powers emerges somewhere at the intersection of *prefigurative practices* (such as Black Lives Matter trying to build blocs that might achieve 'local power') and *exhausted experiments* – from moments of 'popular justice' to the diverse ways in which attempts have been made to secure 'progressive' policies within state agencies. The result feels uncomfortably like a conversation between different parts of myself – 'reimagining' as a sort of dialogic thinking out loud. This odd conversation wanders across a variety of topics around which there are many debates in political philosophy, politics and even economics (e.g. about regulating the commons) about the relationship between social order, the state and coercion. But I am going to begin from an older set of concerns: what the Hungarian Marxist István Mészáros called the 'necessity of social control' when considering how the transition to a socialist society would necessitate processes and systems of social control. In his Isaac Deutscher Memorial Lecture, he argued that:

> The manifest failure of established institutions and their guardians to cope with our problems does not put, of course, these problems out of existence; only intensifies their complexity as well as the explosive dangers of a deadlock. And this takes us back to our point of departure: the imperative of an adequate social control which 'humanity needs for its sheer survival'.
>
> Its establishment will, no doubt, take time and will require the most active involvement of the whole community of producers, activating the repressed creative energies of the various social groups over matters immeasurably exceeding in importance issues like deciding the colour of local lamp-posts to which their 'power' of decision-making is confined today.
>
> The establishment of this social control will, equally, require the conscious cultivation – not in isolated individuals but in the whole community of producers, to whatever walk of life they may belong, of an uncompromising critical awareness coupled with an intense commitment to the values of a socialist humanity which guided the work of Isaac Deutscher to a rich fulfilment (Mészáros, 1971; see also Mészáros, 1972).

In the Marxist tradition, the state was understood as necessary to manage the transition from capitalism (before 'withering away', of course). Actually existing socialist societies indicated some of the problems of trying to 'capture' the state for progressive purposes, not least the risks of being captured by the state and its power (and its fantasy of power). So, any reimagining of the state, and of its coercive powers in particular, has to wrestle with these contradictions. Nevertheless, Mészáros points to a central problem about progressive social transformations: they do not happen all at once. There is not a single revolutionary moment in which a whole new society is born fully formed and complete. The question of transition necessarily raises questions and problems of 'social control' as people attempt to secure or deepen social changes. In what follows, I try to explore some of these dilemmas that emerge at the unsettling intersection of 'state desire' (including what Stef Jansen, 2015, nicely calls 'yearnings' for a state) and 'state phobia' (see also the discussion by Nikita Dhawan in this volume).

Can existing powers and agencies be reimagined?

It may be useful to distinguish between the claimed purpose of existing state agencies and their actual practices, not least because the claimed characteristics of the liberal states (the rule of law; the control of crime; the defence of the nation, membership of the international community, etc.) conceal practices that are both more particular and more contradictory than the general statements imply. For example, who and what are criminalised always involves specifying a particular set of identities and behaviours (paralleled in those identities and behaviours that are selectively not criminalised). We can see the traces of these specifications in the racialised and racialising dynamics of criminalisation, exemplified in the 'racial profiling' in the use of stop and search powers in the UK, or in the grossly disproportionate incarceration of black men and the use of deadly force against young black and Hispanic males by police in the US.

Similarly, the idea of the Rule of Law occludes the rule of very specific laws, including those that are socially, economically and politically oppressive. This is a dilemma that E. P. Thompson famously addressed at the end of his study of the Black Act of 1723, which ruthlessly enforced processes of enclosure in forests and woodlands. Having demonstrated the full class power of the rule of this law, Thompson nonetheless concluded that:

> And if the actuality of the Law's operation in class-divided societies has, again and again, fallen short of its own rhetoric of equity, yet the notion of the rule of law is itself an unqualified good (1975: 267).

Thompson argued that the rule of law offered the possibility of a defence against authoritarian and despotic uses of state power. This position was much debated at the time and remains a subject of argument (see e.g. Cole, 2001; Fine, 1994; Peluso, 2017). These controversies find echoes in a variety of past and continuing struggles to use the existing legal agencies and powers to redress inequalities, for example, in equalities legislation (e.g. Hepple et al., 2000) or the criminalisation of 'hate crimes' (Lamble, 2013). Such issues also evoke a wider debate about the possibility of extending the state's reach to a range of 'harms' that are currently exempt from or only thinly addressed by existing laws and agencies of regulation (see Hillyard et al., 2004).

Sites of continuing conflicts include issues of corporate responsibility for animal and human welfare, environmental abuses and deaths at work/from work. One example of the possibilities and limitations of the criminalisation strategy can be found in the issue of 'corporate manslaughter' (Tombs and Whyte, 2013). Indeed, Pearce and Tombs have argued that 'a *punitive policing* strategy is necessary, desirable and practicable' to address corporate harms (1990: 440, my emphasis). This points to a tension between criminalisation and decriminalisation as elements of progressive strategies. Decriminalisation strategies (e.g. around drugs and sex work) have aimed to take particular behaviours (and potentially vulnerable social actors) out of the purview of state power; while criminalisation approaches have sought to redirect state power to redress injuries and harms previously immune to social control. Sarah Lamble (2013) has explored the contradictions of 'hate crime' as a setting for the deployment of state power, noting how it enrols those it 'defends' (such as gay, lesbian and trans people) into the contradictory space of 'neoliberal citizenship'. In particular, she points to the punitive penality of such criminalising processes, directed against other subordinated groups. This testifies to the dilemmas of using the criminal law as a means of enforcing desired social changes. There are alternatives to criminalisation and penality as strategies of social control through state power, for example in the politics of abolitionism, long established in the domain of penal politics (see Mathiesen, 1974), which argues that withdrawal from the use of prisons is a necessary precondition of any humane or progressive social order. In a different register, arguments for 'restorative justice' and 'transformative justice' have suggested that it is possible to intervene into social disorders in non-punitive ways – although this remains a contested view, not least for questions about the relationships between justice and social justice (Acorn, 2004; Braithwaite, 1989; Evans, 2018; UNODC, 2006).

The apparatuses of law and policing have long been seen as the core of states' coercive and repressive capacities. They raise three particularly difficult questions for progressive imaginations. First, in what ways can harms in the present be controlled or even redressed without the capacity of state power? There are – and always have been – forms of 'informal social control' that regulate social behaviour without recourse to the state. Indeed, some authors (e.g. Ranasinghe, 2017) argue for the privileging of such 'private ordering' over the material and symbolic violence of state law. Of course, such informal social controls can reproduce oppressive and unequal relationships – rather than regulating or contesting them. Inequalities and power are multi-sited and not only located in the state. Second, in the face of persistent harms or disorders, can we imagine a progressive politics of punishment? If so, what principles would govern such progressive approaches (redress, restitution, restorative justice)? Equally importantly, through what mechanisms or agencies would such policies be enacted? These are, I think, not just tactical questions that follow from larger decisions about progressive political programmes, but are at the core of any modelling of a better social order and its nurturing. They are questions that carry critical choices about 'social control' and how it might be organised given our persistent ambivalence about state power. The points of potential intersection are many: for example, I was fortunate enough to attend the Institute for Political Ecology's 'Green Summer Academy' (on the island of Vis, Croatia, 2016: http:// ipe.hr/en/category/green-academy/), during which there was a fascinating debate about how the Commons might be governed if it took the form of a 'social commons', as well as an economic one. In the process, we discussed the eight principles that Elinor Ostrom identified for governing the Commons – and these pose interesting questions about social control:

8 Principles for Managing a Commons

1   Define clear group boundaries.
2   Match rules governing use of common goods to local needs and conditions.
3   Ensure that those affected by the rules can participate in modifying the rules.
4   Make sure the rule-making rights of community members are respected by outside authorities.
5   Develop a system, carried out by community members, for monitoring members' behavior.
6   Use graduated sanctions for rule violators.
7   Provide accessible, low-cost means for dispute resolution.
8   Build responsibility for governing the common resource in nested tiers from the lowest level up to the entire interconnected system (Walljasper, 2011; see also Chatre and Agrawal, 2008).

For my purposes here, there is an admirable clarity about these principles (locally appropriate regulations, nested layers of participatory rule-making and responsibility, accessible dispute resolution, etc.). But there are also some conceptual and political ambiguities: what would the 'system' for monitoring behaviour look like, and what form would a set of 'graduated sanctions' take? Ostrom's terms are disconcertingly neutral descriptors of a system and agents that might, in other terms, be thought of as practices of policing the commons and punishing rule violators. There were a couple of other points, which triggered some political doubts. I understand why 'defining a clear group boundary' might be invoked in the context of a local commons, but in terms of other social orders, such exclusivist reasoning is disconcerting (especially in a political moment of increasing nationalism and nativism). The questions of such membership and the associated forms of entitlements and obligations are rightly vexed and troubling ones. This is not intended to be a discussion of the commons, but a demonstration that questions of collectivity and social order get us quickly – perhaps more quickly than we would like – to matters of rules and their enforcement: the problem of 'social control'.

This question of membership connects to a critical cluster of issues that emerge if we take apart the hyphenated form in which states usually appear to us – the nation-state (on the hyphen, see Gupta, 1998: 316–27; on the national form of the state, see also Newman, this volume). Some of these concern the military forms of the coercive capacities of the state – the Janus-faced apparatuses of 'national defence' that can be deployed against both external and internal 'enemies'. The shifting cast of characters who come to be 'enemies of the people' should warn us against taking the defence of the nation as a simple matter of identification and loyalty: in the UK, terrorists, judges and Members of Parliament have all been recently declared enemies and traitors. One of the critical questions about imagining 'pacifist states' (Crook, 2016) is whether (and how) they might exempt themselves from an international political (dis)order that presumes forms of military capacity and generates national investment in them (in both material and affective ways). There have been different answers to this question, ranging from neutrality to building alliances with the more powerful (or at least militarily more powerful) nations. Similarly, the unfolding of progressive or revolutionary politics has often had complicated relationships with military power, including the participatory model of people's militias and the expectation (or hope) that professional standing armies will take the side of 'the people' rather than the people's enemies. This hope has been sometimes fulfilled – from St. Petersburg in 1917 to Tunisia in 2011 where the army announced it would serve as a 'guarantor of the revolution' (see 'No One Is Really in Charge', *The Economist*, 27 January 2011, http://www.economist.com/node/18014117). However, these issues take me way beyond my limited capacities (of space and imagination), so I am not going to pursue these questions of the military and security apparatuses here, despite the problems they pose as the agencies perhaps most deeply insulated from popular politics. But the question of who or what is to be 'defended' – and by what means – remains a persistent *political* challenge.

Finally, in the Global North, the national character of existing states means that there are necessary corollaries concerning the politics, policies and practices – and the forms of power in which they are entangled – that have taken us from colonialism to neo-colonialism. Can we imagine a national state that would take internationalism and its international obligations (to other places, other people and the global environment) seriously? These questions take shape at the intersection of networks of relations and institutional forms – ranging from historical questions of redress and reparations to the current movements of people (see Nick Gill's chapter in this volume). The national scale currently dominates over others, not least because the dominant international organisations are typically the embodiment of an *inter-state* system, but it is clear that the dilemmas of progressive politics cannot be confined within one national territory – and its accompanying state. Necessarily, then, the questions of coercion – of protection, redress and regulation of disorders – also outrun the existing national borders.

What do we imagine coercion might be used for?

Mészáros's concern with 'social control' in the transition to a more fully human society provides a starting point for this question. How is such a transition to be regulated, safe-guarded and enforced? At the moment, I cannot imagine a progressive politics that is not committed to the protection of people from various forms of violence – ranging from physical assaults and emotional abuse through to the varieties of structural violence associated with inequalities, exclusions and subordinations. While other progressive policies might be dealing with questions of redress, recognition and redistribution, the protection of people from harassment, attacks and harms demands collective capacities of control, constraint and coercion. So, there will remain a need for powers to control violence, to separate, constrain or exclude people who come to be defined as 'dangerous' in the emerging order, and to enforce compliance with progressive social norms. No doubt coercion comes at one end of a spectrum of strategies – reconciliation or reintegration (Braithwaite, 2002), re-socialisation, reparative measures (Meertens and Zambaro, 2010) and the enforcement of compliance. Power can take many forms before it arrives at the point of direct coercion (Allen, 2003; Morris, 2012). Equally, the justice processes of such a progressive state might be explicitly integrated with its social justice programmes rather than being institutionally separated. But how might such coercive powers or capacities be organised, directed and enacted? Clearly, we might imagine such powers could be organised and governed in the form of Committees, Tribunals, Forces, Services and so on – but do they not tend to look like, sound like and, indeed, feel like what we currently call a state? This is, of course, one of the dilemmas at stake in reimagining states: to what extent do the things that we imagine resemble actually existing states? If they do resemble such things, has our act of reimagining gone far enough? But if these reimagined entities do not seem stately, have we imagined something else? What stately qualities should our reimagined states possess, and which should they lose in the process?

Turning back to the question of coercive powers, we might also need to see coercion as a necessary part of any progressive programme of social and economic reform. Suppose that policies for progressive taxation were enacted, then establishing an apparatus for identifying and collecting taxes due would be a corollary, and the enforcement of such policies on individuals and collective entities such as corporations would be essential to make both taxation policies and the reforms they might fund become a reality. Similar questions surround the control of environmental harms. In both of these instances, there are larger questions about the nominal national limits of the state and the existence of harms, injustices and inequities that flow across contingent national boundaries. There is a parallel problem about the policing of agents and agencies that are transnational, not least around the potential expropriation of ownership and resources, which points to the limitations of the conventional national, and nationalising, imaginary of the state (and the scale of its powers).

I have tried to suggest that there are a range of issues – from interpersonal violence to transnational harms – that require us to think about the need for coercive powers. As indicated above, I do not think social control is only about coercion: there is a large repertoire of both informal and formal processes through which social life can be governed – through which conduct can be conducted. So, coercion is neither the only, nor even the first, recourse of a progressive collectivity trying to engage in the challenges of social development, social ordering and social protection, but neither can I see that such a collectivity could easily forego coercive powers.

Can popular control be exercised over state apparatuses and agents?

The final question brings me back to the challenge of what Gramsci called the democratic-bureaucratic system, in which we can see the complex, if not con-tradictory, terrain for the potential articulation of politics (the democratisation of power) and policies (the apparatuses and capacities for delivering progressive out-comes). While I do not underestimate the problems of formulating and agreeing to progressive policies or directions on a whole variety of fronts, the really difficult challenge concerns how to ensure their realisation through networks of agencies and agents that may not be 'fit for purpose' in the new order. As I noted at the beginning, the coercive apparatuses of states have proven particularly resistant to popular politics and progressive policies. This is, of course, not coincidental. Here, I propose to take up two issues. The first concerns problems of popular control of coercive capacities; the second involves questions about the techniques and tech-nologies through which state agencies and agents might be brought into alignment with progressive policies. First, then, there have been many examples of forms, sites and practices of popular control over state apparatuses, including ones that emerge from the politics of popular justice (de Sousa Santos, 2014 [1982]; Abel, 2014). Sally Engle Merry notes that:

> Popular justice has appeared in a wide variety of forms in and in highly diverse locations throughout the world: in revolutionary socialist states, in fascist states, in capitalist welfare states, and in postcolonial socialist states . . . Popular justice has a basic temporality, a historically formed and changing quality. In this respect, it differs from the formal legal system, which typically has far greater continuity and stability. Although a particular manifestation of popular justice may be short-lived, new forms continually emerge. Some are initiated by the state, some by more or less distinct social groups endeavour-ing to assert some autonomy from the state, and some by dissident groups protesting the power of the state (Merry, 1995: 31–2).

Merry points to political ambiguities around the idea of the popular – an issue to which I will return shortly. But first I want to pursue the ways in which popular justice differentiates itself from the 'formal legal system' because the formality of the legal system is one of the crucial mechanisms that produce the 'state effect' (Mitch-ell, 1990). The Law distances itself from the people – and achieves its ideological dominance – partly through a variety of organisational and discursive devices: for-malisation, professionalisation, an architecture of power and a cool or even frozen style of discourse (see, inter alia, Edelman, 2007; Ewick and Silbey, 1998; on the frozen style, see Joos, 1961). Popular justice innovations attempt to disrupt or displace these characteristic distancing effects of Law and to create new settings, styles and practices to enact the popular. For example, Boaventura de Sousa Santos has argued that, in the context of the Portuguese revolutionary crisis of 1974–75, popular justice signified the following:

> It is class justice; that is, it appears as justice exercised by the popular classes parallel to or in confrontation with the state administration of justice. It embodies alternative criteria of substantive legality or at least alternative criteria for the interpretation and enforcement of pre-existing legality. It is based on a concrete notion of popular sovereignty (as opposed to the bourgeois theory of sovereignty) and thus on the idea of direct government by the people. Consequently it requires that judges be democratically selected by the relevant communities and act as representative members of the masses, who are autonomously exercising social power. It operates at a minimum level of institutionalization of bureaucratization (a nonprofessional justice with very little division of legal labour and immune to systematic rationality). Rhetoric tends to dominate the structure of discourse mobilized ... (2014 [1982]: 253).

Here, we can see one route to constructing a different sort of apparatus – one that in its processes and styles aims to engage the people in the process of creat-ing – rather than merely administering – justice. Merry's observations about the distinctive temporality of popular justice point to one of the dilemmas here – how to institutionalise such informal, dynamic and emergent organisational forms. This troubled and unstable relationship between popular politics and institutionalisations of popular justice is also evoked by the Committee of Public Safety, established in Paris 1793 to embody Danton's claim that 'This Committee is precisely what we want, a hand to grasp the weapon of the Revolutionary Tribunal'. The Commit-tee might stand for the dilemmas and contradictions of an imagined progressive reform of state apparatuses – facing, as it did, the challenge of counter-revolution, the external military threat of Austrian invasion, and the domestic instability occa-sioned by external agitators and spies (from Britain, in particular). That combina-tion imposed a distinctive political/administrative temporality on the Committee and its works: a state of permanent emergency. But, of course, the Committee is also recurrently mobilised as a symbol in a very different imaginary, this time as a warning of the dangers of progressive or revolutionary political transformation – in which 'the Terror' functions as a salutary tale of the evils of non-gradual political change (see Wahnich, 2012).

These two examples point to characteristic revolutionary fusions of the people and power – but such fusions are also a source of discomfort for more modern (post-modern?) political sensibilities. They raise the question of who can speak for The People or even a 'community' in the face of heterogeneous identities and interests. This is a particularly pressing issue in situations where challenges to forms of state power involve redressing past harms or inequalities. It returns us to the problem of 'membership': who counts as (or gets to be counted as) members of the community-at-issue is constantly contested. It contains – and often conceals – nested problems of voice and representation. For instance, Southall Black Sisters have raised important questions about how minority communities – of ethnicity and faith – have come to be represented by 'community leaders' or representatives who exclude, subordinate and silence other bodies and voices within those communities (see e.g. Dhaliwal and Yuval-Davis, 2014; Southall Black Sisters, 2011). These problems of membership and voice are particularly pertinent for arguments that state agencies and their personnel should be more representative of the communities they serve or govern. The argument about state representativeness makes apparently straightforward claims – that we should be served, policed or judged by 'people like us'.

The persistence of social inequalities – of gender, race, class, sexuality and more – highlights problems in the ways that public services are *embodied*. As a result, the demand for representativeness is multifaceted. First, it applies to the 'front line' embodiment of public services – demanding that they should resemble the communities that they serve. Here, the question of statistical representativeness quickly bumps into the more difficult dynamics of organisational cultures, where existing norms, orientations and practices may prove intractable, and often work to either acculturate the 'outsiders' or to only include them in subordinate positions. As a result, the second front of the representation struggle necessarily opens around questions of advancement, promotion and the management of the organisation, as the problems of overcoming forms of subordinated inclusion become apparent. The third front of the struggle for representation concerns the sites of control and governance: how is popular control, direction and accountability to be established?

The difficult political dynamic at stake, however, is that 'people like us' is a constantly contestable concept, just as the 'people' is an always emergent collectivity. So, part of the challenge of progressive reimagining of the state is the struggle to find new forms of representation and voice that address past exclusions without reifying or over-solidifying new identities. We might see the claim for better representation as pointing to a horizon, rather than being a readily achievable one-off target. The issues of representation, voice and effective power over services are general ones for progressive politics, but take on a sharper form in relation to the coercive capacities of states precisely because these apparatuses have historically been so insulated against the prospect of popular control. As I indicated earlier with the examples of the Hillsborough disaster and Black Lives Matter, the coercive agencies tend to ignore or deny popular demands for redress and reform. Consequently, there is a recurring challenge to find the means by which, for example, policing might be made responsive to, accountable to, or even subject to its local, national and international 'communities'. The dilemmas are familiar and so are the defensive claims that seek to renew the insulation of policing: policing needs to be independent, be subject to the Law not politics, and be a matter of professional judgement in terms of both operational management and the actions of the individual officer. Such refusals treat the current state of affairs as 'normal': policing as non-political? Independent of whom? Subject to the rule of which laws? Bureau-professionalism as the embodiment of social neutrality? Such questions make clear both the obfuscations of the present and the difficulties of overcoming them.

The difficulties of transforming the personnel and cultures of public services, especially those with coercive capacities, has led to an interest in the possibilities of 'managerial' techniques and technologies to bring about compliance with progressive policies and objectives. For example, efforts to control 'racial profiling' in the use of stop-and-search police powers attempted to enforce accountability through recording requirements (providing grounds for each particular 'stop') and other rules of engagement. Not surprisingly, police forces have been slow to adapt (Dodd, 2017). Such rules have been the subject of recurrent conflicts between attempts to control by regulation and professional resistance elaborated on the basis that reform 'was overly bureaucratic and officers were being tied up with red tape' (Barrett, 2014). More recently, body cameras have emerged as a favoured technology for monitoring police–public encounters – with mixed and uncertain results (see, inter alia, Ariel et al., 2017; Urban Institute, 2015). The uncertainty is hardly surprising given that it remains unclear whether the technology is intended to control aggressive police behaviour or aggressive members of the public, and the continuing problem of the interpretation of visual 'evidence' (Vertesi, 2015). Such issues have acquired renewed salience in the struggles around police violence towards black men in the US (signified in the arguments of, and around, *Black Lives Matter*), but are recurrent issues that arise at the intersection of the complex politics of representation and the deployment of the coercive capacities of states.

And finally?

I have tried to explore the 'dark side' of the state through these questions about coercive power because I find it the most difficult set of issues to confront in the process of reimagining the state for progressive purposes. As will be obvious, I don't have any satisfactory answers to the questions that surround these issues. But I do think they are central to dealing with the seductions of the state and the relationship of ambivalence that entangles us. In short, I think a progressive politics has to think about the question of coercive power – its purposes, its forms and its control. It may be possible to think about such questions aside from the state, but, as will be clear, I find it hard to disentangle them. If an alternative social order is emerging, it will need the means to install itself, and to ensure compliance, as well as enthusiasm. Those needs lead inexorably to the question of 'social control' and, in my view, to the challenge of reimagining the coercive powers of states in the service of progressive politics. They also suggest why doing so may be difficult.

Acknowledgements

I am deeply grateful to Davina Cooper for the original invitation to think about this question and for her comments on an earlier draft. Thanks also to the participants in the original workshop and a subsequent meeting for the thought-provoking discussions and to Nick Gill for his comments on a previous draft. Subsequent comments from the editors and others have suggested possibilities for improvement. If I have failed to live up to them, their efforts to help me think better are still much appreciated.

References

Abel, R. (ed.) (2014) *The Politics of Informal Justice*, vol. 2: *Comparative Studies*. Amsterdam: Elsevier.

Acorn, A. (2004) *Compulsory Compassion: A Critique of Restorative Justice*. Vancouver: University of British Columbia Press.

Allen, J. (2003) *Lost Geographies of Power*. Oxford: Wiley-Blackwell.

Ariel, B., Sutherland, A., Henstock, D. et al. (2017) 'The Deterrence Spectrum: Explaining Why Police Body-Worn Cameras "Work" or "Backfire" in Aggressive Police–Public Encounters', *Policing: A Journal of Policy and Practice* [online]. Available at https://doi.org/10.1093/police/paw051 (accessed 3 March 2019).

Barrett, D. (2014) 'Theresa May Introduces New Restrictions on Stop and Search Powers', *The Telegraph*, 26 August [online]. Available at http://www.telegraph.co.uk/news/uknews/crime/11054788/Theresa-May-introduces-new-restrictions-on-stop-and-search-powers.html (accessed 3 March 2019).

Bourdieu, P. (1998) *Acts of Resistance*. Cambridge: Polity Press.

Braithwaite, J. (1989) *Crime, Shame and Reintegration*. Cambridge: Cambridge University Press.

Braithwaite, J. (2002) *Restorative Justice and Responsive Regulation*. New York and Oxford: Oxford University Press.

Chatre, A. and Agrawal, A. (2008) 'Forest Commons and Local Enforcement', *Proceedings of the National Academy of Science*, 105(36), pp. 13286–91.

Christie, N. (1996) 'Crime and Civilisation', *New Internationalist*, 282, pp. 10–12.

Clarke, J. (2010) 'New New Deals: Reforming Welfare Again?', *Occasion: Interdisciplinary Studies in the Humanities*, 2 (December) [online]. Available at https://arcade.stanford.edu/occasion/new-new-deals-reforming-welfare-again (accessed 30 April 2019).

Cockburn, C. (1991) *In the Way of Women: Men's Resistance to Sex Equality in Organizations*. Basingstoke: Macmillan.

Cole, D. H. (2001) '"An Unqualified Human Good": E. P. Thompson and the Rule of Law', *Journal of Law and Society*, 28(2), pp. 177–203.

Cooper, D. (2004) *Challenging Diversity: Rethinking Equality and the Value of Difference*. Cambridge: Cambridge University Press.

Crook, J. (2016) 'The Non-Coercive State: The Creation of Pacifist Societies', *New Intrigue*, 22 March [online]. Available at https://newintrigue.com/2016/03/22/the-non-coercive-state-the-creation-of-pacifist-societies/ (accessed 3 March 2019).

Dhaliwal, S. and Yuval-Davis, N. (2014) *Women against Fundamentalism: Stories of Dissent and Solidarity*. London: Lawrence & Wishart.

Dodd, V. (2017) 'Stop and Search: Police 'Unacceptably Slow' to Comply with New Rules', *The Guardian*, 2 February [online]. Available at https://www.theguardian.com/law/2017/

feb/02/stop-and-search-police-unacceptably-slow-to-comply-with-new-rules (accessed 3 March 2019).

Edelman, B. (2007) *Quand les Juristes Inventent le Réel*. Paris: Hermann.

Evans, M. (2018) *Transformative Justice: Remedying Human Rights Violations beyond Transition*. London: Routledge.

Ewick, P. and Silbey, S. (1998) *The Common Place of Law: Stories from Everyday Life*. Chicago, IL: University of Chicago Press.

Fine, R. (1994) 'The Rule of Law and Muggletonian Marxism: The Perplexities of Edward Thompson', *Journal of Law and Society*, 21(2), pp. 193–213.

Gupta, A. (1998) *Postcolonial Developments*. Durham, NC: Duke University Press.

Hall, S., Critcher, C., Jefferson, T., Clarke, J. and Roberts, B. (1978) *Policing the Crisis: Mugging, the State and Law and Order*. London: Macmillan (revised edn, 2013).

Hepple, B., Coussey, M. and Choudhury, T. (2000) *Equality: A New Framework: Report of the Independent Review of the Enforcement of UK Anti-Discrimination Legislation*. London: Hart Publishing.

Hillyard, P., Pantazis, C., Tombs, S. and Gordon, D. (eds.) (2004) *Beyond Criminology: Taking Harm Seriously*. London: Pluto Press.

Jansen, S. (2015) *Yearnings in the Meantime: 'Normal Lives' and the State in a Sarajevo Apartment Complex*. New York and Oxford: Berghahn.

Joos, M. (1961) *The Five Clocks*. New York: Harcourt, Brace & World.

Lamble, S. (2013) 'Queer Necropolitics and the Expanding Carceral State: Interrogating Sexual Investments in Punishment', *Law Critique*, 24(3), pp. 229–53.

Mathiesen, T. (1974) *The Politics of Abolition*. London: Martin Robertson.

Meertens, D. and Zambrano, M. (2010) 'Citizenship Deferred: The Politics of Victimhood, Land Restitution and Gender Justice in the Colombian (Post?) Conflict', *International Journal of Transitional Justice*, 4(2), pp. 189–206.

Merry, S. E. (1995) 'Sorting Out Popular Justice' in Merry, S. E. and Milner, N. (eds.), *The Possibility of Popular Justice: A Case Study of Community Mediation in the United States*. Ann Arbor, MI: University of Michigan Press, pp. 31–66.

Mészáros, I. (1971) 'Alienation and Social Control' in *Socialist Register 1971*. London: Merlin Press, pp. 1–20.

Mészáros, I. (1972) *The Necessity of Social Control*. London: Merlin Press (2014 edn: New York: New York University Press).

Mitchell, T. (1990) 'Society, Economy and the State Effect' in Steinmetz, G. (ed.), *State/Culture: State-Formation after the Cultural Turn*. Ithaca, NY and London: Cornell University Press, pp. 76–97.

Morley, M. and Petras, J. (1998) 'Wealth and Poverty in the National Economy: The Domestic Foundations of Clinton's Global Policy' in Lo, C. and Schwartz, M. (eds.), *Social Policy and the Conservative Agenda*. Oxford: Blackwell.

Morris, C. W. (2012) 'State Coercion and Force', *Social Philosophy and Policy*, 29(1), pp. 28–49.

Omi, M. and Winant, H. (1986) *Racial Formation in the United States: From the 1960s to the 1980s*. New York: Routledge.

Ostrom, E. (1999) 'Coping with the Tragedies of the Commons', *Annual Review of Political Science*, 2, pp. 493–535 [online]. Available at https://doi.org/10.1146/annurev.polisci.2.1.493 (accessed 3 March 2019).

Pearce, F. and Tombs, S. (1990) 'Ideology, Hegemony and Empiricism: Compliance Theories of Regulation', *British Journal of Criminology*, 30(4), pp. 423–43.

Peluso, N. L. (2017) 'Whigs and Hunters: The Origins of the Black Act by E. P. Thompson', *Journal of Peasant Studies*, 44(1), pp. 309–21.

Platt, T. (2019) *Beyond These Walls: Rethinking Crime and Punishment in the United States*. New York: St. Martin's Press.

Ranasinghe, P. (2017) 'The (Non)Violence of Private Ordering', *Oñati Socio-legal Series*, 7(7), pp. 1532–56 [online]. Available at http://opo.iisj.net/index.php/osls/article/view File/846/1062 (accessed 3 March 2019).

Santos, B. de Sousa (2014 [1982]) 'Law and Revolution in Portugal: The Experiences of Popular Justice after the 25th of April 1974', reprinted in Abel, R. (ed.), *The Politics of Informal Justice*, vol. 2: *Comparative Studies*. Saint Louis: Elsevier, pp. 251–80.

Scraton, P. (2016) [1999] *Hillsborough: The Truth*. London: Random House.

Sharma, A. (2006) 'Crossbreeding Institutions, Breeding Struggle: Women's Empowerment, Neoliberal Governmentality, and State (Re)Formation in India', *Cultural Anthropology*, 21(1), pp. 60–95.

Southall Black Sisters (2011) *Cohesion, Faith and Gender Report*. London: Southall Black Sisters [online]. Available at http://www.southallblacksisters.org.uk/news/cohesion-faith-and-gender-report-2 (accessed 3 March 2019).

Thompson, E. P. (1975) *Whigs and Hunters: The Origins of the Black Act*. London: Allen Lane.

Tombs, S. and Whyte, D. (2013) 'The Myths and Realities of Deterrence in Workplace Safety Regulation', *British Journal of Criminology*, 53(5), pp. 746–62.

UNODC [United Nations Office on Drugs and Crime] (2006) *A Handbook on Restorative Justice*. New York: UNODC.

Urban Institute (2015) 'Evaluating the Impact of Police Body Cameras', Washington, DC: *Urban Institute Debates* [online]. Available at https://www.urban.org/debates/evaluating-impact-police-body-cameras (accessed 3 March 2019).

Vertesi, J. (2015) 'The Problem with Police Body Cameras', *Time*, 14 May [online]. Available at http://time.com/3843157/the-problem-with-police-body-cameras/ (accessed 3 March 2019).

Wacquant, L. (2009) *Punishing the Poor: The Neo-Liberal Government of Social Insecurity*. Durham, NC: Duke University Press.

Wahnich, S. (2012) *In Defence of the Terror: Liberty or Death in the French Revolution*. Fernbach, D. (trans.). London: Verso.

Walljasper, J. (2011) 'Elinor Ostrom's 8 Principles for Managing a Commons', *On the Commons* [online]. Available at http://www.onthecommons.org/magazine/elinor-ostroms-8-principles-managing-commmons#sthash.SLvjuybQ.dpbs (accessed 3 March 2019).

12

BORDER ABOLITION AND HOW TO ACHIEVE IT

Nick Gill

'[I]t is vital to express the unfinished.'

Thomas Mathiesen, 1974: 16

It is difficult to conceive of 'progressive' states that continue to employ exclusionary, militarised and subjugating border controls. Contemporary international border control practices are not only coercive, but also help to perpetuate the conditions for economic exploitation and the large-scale wastage of human lives in camps and precarious forms of status around the world. While not everyone is inhibited by border controls, the differential mobility of the world's population, striated along lines of racial, gender, national and economic difference, is a hallmark of modern society. Conversely, border liberalisation has been associated with a recognition of the equal moral worth of persons (Carens, 1987), an increased ability to exercise the fundamental human right of movement (Jones, 2019a), increased global prosperity (The Economist, 2017), greater human freedom (Bauder, 2017), enhanced peace (Gill, 2009) and a greater capacity to adapt to global environmental change (Geddes and Jordan, 2012).

Scholarship that discusses large-scale border liberalisation has given much attention to whether or not such a project would be a good idea. As advocates for a world without restrictions on immigration, for example, Pécoud and de Guchteneire (2007) set out the case for large-scale border liberalisation from the perspectives of ethics and human rights, economics and global society, and with respect to the practical aspects of a world without border controls. In a similar vein, Jones (2019b) systematically critiques the major arguments against border liberalisation, concluding that 'there is not a moral, legal, philosophical, or economic case for limiting the movement of human beings at borders' (ibid.: 5). Far less attention has been given to how a large-scale project of border liberalisation could be brought about, however. This has been described by Bauder (2017: 57–58) as a tendency to simply:

> . . . call for an end to migration restrictions without developing alterna-
> tive models of migration or governance. In other words [critical scholars]
> *negate* the contemporary condition of closed and controlled borders . . . As
> pure negation, however [they] say nothing about the conditions under which
> unconstrained human migration ought to occur . . . As pure negation, the
> 'dream' of freedom of migration remains intangible (ibid.: 57–58, emphasis
> in the original).

This chapter focuses precisely on the question of 'how' to achieve border abolition. In doing so, it flirts with James Ferguson's call to develop a more sophisticated Left art of government. Rather than occupying a position of pure critique in
response to the international proliferation of border controls, which can get caught
in a cycle of 'gestures of refusal' (Ferguson, 2011: 62) that is 'always 'anti', never 'pro'
(ibid.: 62), Ferguson entreats us to forgo:

> . . . the pleasures of the easy, dismissive critique and instead turn a keen and
> sympathetic eye toward the rich world of actual social and political practice,
> the world of tap-turning and experimentation (ibid.: 67–8).

Going someway down this road, the chapter undertakes something of a thought
experiment by exploring the role that states themselves might play in the process
of border abolition. While critical scholars have tended to view states and border
controls as inextricable, the chapter explores the possibility that states could feature
in a world without international border controls, and could even be employed in
bringing such a world about. Key to this argument is a set of distinctions: between
borders and boundaries, between border abolition and both open borders and no
borders, and between sudden and gradual forms of border liberalisation.

The primary purpose of this chapter is to expose the extent of, and embark
upon, the intellectual and practical experimentation that becomes necessary if we
are to be able to talk about borderless states. The argument is divided into four parts.
In the first, a specific understanding of the notion of abolition is set out that admits
a role for states in abolitionist politics. In the second, the implications of this understanding are explored in the context of border control by distinguishing border abolition from both 'open borders' and 'No Borders' as they are currently understood
in literature that deals with large scale border liberalisation. In the third, one possible
form that border abolition could take, via international treaty, is outlined. And in the
fourth, the chapter reflects on the challenges and risks of such a process.

Abolition

What is abolition? Its simplest definition is 'to put an end to' (Schwarz, 1993), but
a survey of dictionary definitions reveals three further connotations. The first can

be derived from its etymological association with destruction. Coles's *An English Dictionary* (2015) defines abolition as 'destroying, putting out of the memory'. Similarly, the *New Oxford Dictionary of English* (Oxford University Press, 1998) traces the word's origin to 'the Latin abolere, meaning "destroy"'.

A second connotation relates to the 'official' nature of abolition captured in the definitions offered by both the *Oxford Advanced Learner's Dictionary* (2010) and the *Longman Dictionary of Contemporary English* (1995). They define 'abolish' as 'to officially end a law, a system or an institution' and 'to officially end a law, system etc., especially one that has existed for a long time'.

Both, the *Oxford Advanced Learner's Dictionary* (2010) and the *Longman Dictionary of Contemporary English* (1995) also include the third connotation: the notion that abolition can refer to the ending of a *law*. The *Collins English Dictionary* (2015) includes this connotation, too, defining abolition as 'to do away with (laws, regulations, customs etc.)'.

The first two of these connotations hint at the role that states might play in the abolition process. With regard to the first, Max Weber famously defined the state as the monopoly of legitimate violence over a given territory. If we are prepared to make the assumption that violence can be equated with destruction, then both abolition and states are destructive by nature. This implies that states as institutions may be well placed to carry out, support or facilitate abolitionist work. Why? Because they have at their disposal mechanisms of coercion that might be necessary to put an end to deeply culturally and historically engrained practices (see Clarke, this volume, on the agonising ethics of state coercion).

With regard to the second connotation, Bourdieu (2014) identifies being 'official' as central to the symbolic capital of states. The concept of the official refers to 'the idea that there is a group consensus on a certain number of values' (2014: 29). As such, to be official is to represent 'the idea that the group has of itself' (ibid.: 48). Who voices this idea is of utmost importance. Bureaucrats – good ones at least – are adept at what Bourdieu calls 'universalization' (ibid.: 33): that is, the transformation of something particular into something universal that represents a claim about the group as a whole. Officialdom is able to transcend the grounds of disagreement, such that even parties that are disadvantaged by a decision accept it because it has been mandated in what Bourdieu calls a 'trans-personal' way (ibid.: 45). Although states themselves struggle with this process of universalisation, without states it is harder to claim that something is official because they command the technologies best suited to achieving it: including a strong claim to representation (e.g. via democratic accountability) and a whole edifice of cultural and performative resources – from insignia and flags, to uniforms and architectural forms – that Bourdieu labels 'theatrical' technologies (ibid.: 48). So, we might reason that if abolition is indeed to be 'official', then states probably offer the most solid grounds for its fulfilment. States are at the hub of officialdom, and monopolise the discursive and symbolic resources that constitute it.

There are indeed various progressive abolitionist activities that have pitched the coercive and symbolic power of states or the international state system against long-lived violent practices. Many of these represent the search for profit in a capitalist society. These activities include the campaigns for the abolition of slavery, whale, seal and fox hunting, vivisection and child labour. This is not to say that when something is officially, or legally, abolished, it automatically ceases. But state-backed abolition has been seen by activists in these areas as crucial to their success in gaining traction and popular support because it is via states that the idea that society wants 'to have and give of itself' (Bourdieu, 2014: 48), is often established and promulgated.

The third connotation, however, complicates the picture because, unlike the situation in which states either intervene, or are entreated to intervene, in activities that arise owing to the over-enthusiastic pursuit of profit in the market economy, there are other situations in which the focus of abolitionist efforts are aspects of states themselves, such as repressive laws and taxes. Think of the movements to abolish immigration detention and prison, for example. This type of struggle introduces to the notion of abolition a certain tautology. If abolition describes the legal end of a law, then what is necessary to achieve abolition is the contortion of 'the law' against the law itself, or, more broadly, 'the state' against 'the state'. In the specific context of border abolition, this tautology applies even more acutely since it raises the question of how borders can be abolished if borders are prerequisites for the very existence of states themselves.

Such is the challenge of conceiving of the progressivity of states, as set by the editors of this volume, that it is necessary to fashion a response to both the general challenge of tautology with respect to the law, and the specific challenge of tautology with respect to the conditions of possibility of states, before it is possible to continue examining the question of the relation of border abolition to states. In the remainder of this section, I outline two intellectual resources that may help to constitute such responses.

In response to the first challenge, anti-essentialist state theorists emphasise how the state system is constructed through discourse, structural effects and performance, rather than being an ontologically stable 'thing' (Dunn, 2010). The approach is traceable to Philip Abrams, who likened 'the state' to an idea, *the effect of which* is the appearance of something that is coherent and constant. The idea of the state, for Abrams (1988: 79), has the effect of masking and concealing profound inconsistencies in the way in which the state is enacted and practised. According to this view, the state should be examined 'not as an actual structure, but as the powerful, apparently metaphysical effect of practices that make such structures appear to exist' (Mitchell, 2006: 180).

Geographers have adopted this perspective explicitly in dealing with the messiness, inconsistencies and prosaic nature of states (Painter, 2006). Although the history of modernity as it is commonly written features both coherent historical states, as well as a supposed historical correspondence between states and nations, neither of these bears much scrutiny (Massey, 2005; Agnew, 2009). Doreen Massey (2005) is critical of what she regards as the 'isomorphism between space/place on the one hand and society/culture on the other' (ibid.: 64), leading places to be associated with culture, while nation-states have historically been regarded as somehow above or outside cultural influences (see also Mitchell, 2006). In reality, states are culturally and spatially produced and conditional in all sorts of ways, and have been since their inception (Ferguson and Gupta, 2002; Steinmetz, 1999). This insight emphasises the contingency of states, their performance and their improvisation (Jeffrey, 2013). 'One should reject the notion of the state as a natural thing', Dunn suggests, and focus instead upon the 'citational processes that call it into being' (ibid.: 88).

This anti-essentialist view of states allows for plurality within states themselves that underscores their fragility, and therefore their reversibility, malleability and challenge-ability. As Cooper puts it, '[p]lural state thinking makes room for divergent kinds of states', including progressive and inclusive ones (2017: 335).

A key resulting possibility in this literature is that of *contradiction* within 'the state'. Because 'the state' is complex, plural and often rather chaotic, it is not unusual to find that different elements 'within' 'it' are working in opposite directions. This certainly makes the state a difficult phenomenon to study (Abrams, 1988)! It is also worth remembering that states are *peopled* institutions, and that charismatic personalities have often had a determinate effect on the course that states take (Jones, 2011). Indeed, there is a complex sociology of states (Bourdieu, 2014: 6).

If we take seriously the possibilities of contradiction within 'the state', it is possible that abolitionist efforts that target features of the state might find symbolic and financial support from other parts of the state itself, owing precisely to the fictitiousness of the coherence that the label 'the state' purports to convey.

In response to the second challenge, another resource for border abolitionism might be found in a particular distinction between a border and a boundary. 'Borders' are not an unproblematic category, and actually refer to at least two sets of functions: the function of controlling population movement and the function of marking the hinterland of states for the purposes of administration, taxation and the delivery of public services. These two functions can be distinguished relatively easily by referring to the first set as 'border' functions, primarily concerned with the regulation of human movement, and the second as 'boundary' functions, primarily concerned with administrative demarcation.

The conflation of these two sorts of functions might be related to the history of border studies. 'Border studies', writes Paasi (1999: 70), were conceived 'at the turn of the [twentieth] century in order to depict a modern world that was becoming territorialized along rigid boundary lines that characterized a state-centred system'. They concerned themselves with 'removing ambiguity from the process' of 'demarcating political boundaries' (Jones, 2009: 181). Such a history introduces the need to recover, in some way, from the apparent over-signification of borders in historical scholarly work. One way to do this is to recognise that boundaries can be distinguished from borders and should be regarded as 'social ... economic, cultural, administrative and political ... practices and discourses' (Paasi, 1999: 70) rather than lines on maps. Casey (2011) posits that 'borders diverge from boundaries in certain ways' (ibid.: 385), making reference to borders as 'clearly and crisply delineated [and] resistant to the passage of goods or people' (ibid.: 385), while a boundary 'is porous in character (like the human skin), admitting the passage of various substances through it' (ibid.: 385).

This distinction is useful for the current argument because it admits the possibility of a functional edge without an exclusionary border. Indeed, we could turn to certain already-existing boundaries that point towards a possible world without borders but that retains states: such as the boundaries between American states, between England and Wales, and within the European Schengen area (see Kunz and Leinonen, 2007). Boundaries here mark the administrative hinterlands of polities, but are often not policed and securitised by them. In short, it *is* possible, and actually not all that difficult, to conceive of an interface between state territories that exists in administrative terms, but is not concretised through checkpoints, walls and barriers.

Open borders, no borders and border abolition

In the previous section, I reflected on the nature of abolition, noting that abolition may be violent, official and aimed at particular laws. I then suggested that given these characteristics of abolition, states can be in a good position to abolish. If we adopt an anti-essentialist understanding of the state and distinguish borders from boundaries, this applies even when the thing being abolished is part of 'the state' itself (like borders). I now turn to how the pursuit of border abolition with recourse to the symbolic power of states and the international state system sits alongside the concepts of open borders and no borders that dominate existing literature on large-scale border liberalisation. I argue that, in fact, neither model adequately conceptualises the project of border abolition.

Open borders is a position that has been supported by a diverse range of scholars (Bauder, 2017). These diverse perspectives arise from the very different motivations for pursuing free movement – the pursuit of freedom in the case of libertarians, the pursuit of economic growth in the case of market-economic approaches, and the counteraction of the exploitative entrapment of large sections of the global population in low wage and insecure forms of work in the case of Marxism and its variants. Given these differences, it is difficult to generalise about open borders as a coherent school of thought. Nevertheless, the very concept of 'open' borders implies that whatever is open will continue to exist after free population movement has been established, with the implication that, as some future point, it could be closed again. This introduces uncertainty about the longevity and stability of free movement under open borders, which retain the possibility of closure on the basis of national interest. In short, open borders is not *binding* over states because contained within the very possibility of openness is closure itself. Under abolition, by contrast, it would be illegal to close borders again. Borders would not only cease to be closed, they would cease to *officially* exist. The distinction between open borders and border abolition rests, then, on sovereignty. Border abolition would entail wresting sovereignty over borders and their existence away from nation-states.

Might this imply that no borders is more compatible with the abolition of border controls? No borders is part of a wider, usually anarchist, political position that questions a range of relationships of power in the modern era and can be associated 'with demands for a world beyond existing structures of governance' (Bauder, 2017: 64). This world would 'entail the transformation of the ontologies that underlie contemporary political configurations' (Bauder, 2014: 76), giving rise to futures that are 'not yet knowable or even conceivable' (ibid.: 78). Proponents of no borders are critical of open borders thinking, describing what they see as 'The Right's call for open borders which can serve as a continuation, in new form, of the strategy of "accumulation by dispossession"' (Anderson et al., 2009) that characterises exploitative capitalism. Instead of reproducing problematic relations in this way, no borders 'signals a new sort of liberatory project, one with new ideas of "society"' (ibid.: 6). No borders is:

> ... a demand that calls for a fundamental transformation in theoretical, social, psychological and cultural behaviour and norms ... [it] calls into question the conditions of possibility for some of the most basic categories of modern political life: namely, the nation-state, the international system, and citizenship. The demand for No Borders radically challenges modern understandings of the subject and location of the political (ibid.: 40).

As such, no borders does not afford the opportunity to work with the symbolic power of states to abolish border controls, because the dissolution of states is understood to be bound up with a no borders world. As Fernandez et al. (2006: 473) make clear:

> 'No Borders' as a demand on the state, would thus effectively be a demand that the nation-state give up its own condition of possibility, and is thus a demand that can only be effectively utilized if the nation-state is assumed to be suicidal.

While some who are opposed to border controls might well support the dissolution of states as well, it is nevertheless possible to conceive of border abolition separately from wholesale state dissolution if we accept the distinctions already made in this chapter. It may also be desirable. It is worth noting, for instance, that what anarchists mean when they express anti-statism is rejection 'not so much [of] the specific phenomenon of the state but [of] a broader set of asymmetrical social and power relations typified, justified, and institutionalised by the state' (Ince and Barrera de la Torre, 2016: 11). Cooper (2017) lists various ways in which states seek to ameliorate these very relations, albeit with highly variable degrees of success. She includes the fact that states:

> ... provide social welfare, steward resources, establish fora for public debate, make new critical forms of knowledge possible and ... protect populations, including more vulnerable and precarious populations from civil society's violence and discriminations (338).

I am aware that this 'protective' perspective on states is contentious. Indeed, so is Cooper (2017), who also lists a host of historical crimes that states are charged with. The nub of the question that we are wrestling with in this book and in this chapter, however, is not *whether states are* progressive, but rather *how we can make them* progressive. This question insists that states themselves are under construction rather than pre-formed. In other words, it challenges us to prefigure states (Cooper, 2017), which forces a more applied sort of answer than a simple 'yes, states are progressive' or, more typically, 'no, they aren't'. This intellectual move may feel uncomfortable: it is safer, and perhaps easier, to remain in the realms of radical refusal and criticism. In defence of it, though, we might ask: where states do *not* serve the progressive functions Cooper lists, why would we automatically assume that their dissolution is preferable to their improvement? Efforts to rework states towards progressive ends imagines them less like Nietzsche's image of the coldest of all cold monsters and more akin to Derrida's *pharmakon* – both poison and medicine (see Dhawan, this volume). For Martin and Pierce (2013), 'there are latent residual apparatuses of the state which can be activated as part of a systematic progressive politics' (61). 'Resistance cannot and ought not abandon the state', they continue, '[i]f we accept that the state is primarily a shill of neoliberalism, we cede too much' (67).

An internationalist border abolition programme

If states are plural and challengeable, if they can be delineated by boundaries and not borders, and if the symbolic capital of states can be tactically deployed in the pursuit of abolitionist efforts, then perhaps states can be involved in border abolition, as distinct from both open borders and no borders. Having reached this point, I am now able to flesh out the detail of how state-backed border abolition might look.

In what follows, I set out one possibility for mobilising states against borders with recourse to international laws and treaties. Global migration governance has been perceived as weak until recently (Betts, 2011; Hansen, 2011; Koslowski, 2011). As James Hampshire wrote in 2016:

> There is no comprehensive international migration treaty and little by way of an institutional architecture at the global level: no United Nations agency with a mandate for migration – though the United Nations High Commission for Refugees does of course have a mandate for refugees and asylum seekers – and no multilateral forums with the ability to issue binding resolutions (571).

During the course of writing this chapter, progress was made towards two global compacts: the Global Compact for Safe, Orderly and Regular Migration; and the Global Compact on Refugees. Their genesis may signal an increased appetite for international cooperation on migration, although it is too early at the time of writing to say how effective they have been (for an early critical reflection on the refugee compact, however, see Chimni, 2019).

The approach I outline here would enrol the symbolic capital of the international legal and governmental system to unify individual states in collective action, and has the hallmarks of internationalism. I take internationalism to be a political principle, which advocates greater political or economic cooperation among nations and peoples. It has a history in both liberal and socialist movements (Hodder et al., 2015). For example, the Workingmen's International (the first of the four Internationals associated with the development of socialism) was initiated by Karl Marx and contemporaries in 1864 (Featherstone, 2012). It saw a split between the anarchists, who eschewed states, and the Marxists, who advocated the seizure of states in order to establish a workers' government, which would segue to world socialism. This radical form of internationalism was mobilised in different forms during the twentieth century 'by a range of ideologically motivated actors whose objectives are connected . . . by their common desire to overthrow established political structures' (Hodder et al., 2015: 3).

The principle of internationalism has underpinned various developments in international relations and law and, although currently 'beleaguered and unfashionable' (ibid.: 3), it is seen by some as a potent critique of 'the world of states complacent in their sovereignty, inflated with pride and national conceit and prone to war and hatred' (Halliday, 1988: 189).

We might highlight a range of historical internationalist movements and initiatives. Featherstone (2012), for example, recalls the spontaneous international solidarities forged between the working classes in Northern England and the anti-slavery campaigns in America in the 1860s, which had a constraining influence over then-Prime Minister Palmerston's support for the southern pro-slavery American states, despite operating outside the usual elite political machinery. To this bottom-up example we might add more 'top-down' instances of internationalism, including nuclear non-proliferation agreements, the Geneva Convention, the General Agreement on Tariffs and Trade which preceded the World Trade Organization, and the Montreal Protocol. These developments are clearly various, reflecting 'the diverse and often uneven ways in which internationalism has been defined and deployed' (Hodder et al., 2015), and have paved the way for a similar diversity of institutions such as the League of Nations, the International Criminal Court and the United Nations. The rapid development of international human rights laws since the Second World War can also be linked to modern internationalism. While certainly not without problems, contradictions and failings (Žižek, 2006), many of these developments have not been in the immediate, narrowly defined 'national interests' of the states involved.

It is essential to be vigilant against the sort of internationalism that involves an 'acceptance of the asymmetry of international relations and the necessarily dominant, neo-colonial role that rich and powerful countries have to play in enforced and policing [world orders]' (Hodder et al., 2015). With this vigilance in mind, is it possible to conceive of a process within the internationalist tradition that leads towards the abolition of borders?

Consider a process of gradual, cooperative, binding abolition of state controls over migration achieved through international treaty predicated on the central tenet of the right to free international movement. Such a process could include a fund, which we can call the Global Facilitation Fund, which is internationally coordinated and is awarded to countries and areas in proportion to the rate of immigration they experience. The fund's value would increase in proportion to the agreed reduction in border control expenditures among participating countries over time.

The gradualism of this proposal is important. The distinction between gradual and sudden border abolition constitutes the third lynchpin distinction of the chapter alongside the distinctions between borders and boundaries, and abolition, open and no borders that I have already discussed. It is usual to associate border abolition with sudden revolution – the wholesale overthrowing of the old system and the institution of a new form of global inclusivity (Nyers, 2013). But would border abolition necessarily require a revolution? The Merriam-Webster's dictionary (online) offers two relevant definitions of revolution: (1) the usually violent attempt by many people to end the rule of one government and start a new one; and (2) a sudden, extreme or complete change in the way people live and/or work. This understanding of revolution produces a *successionist* disposition. That is, in the context of border abolition, an assumption that global free movement would replace borders relatively abruptly: as one ended, the other would begin (Nyers, 2013).

The expectation of suddenness can sometimes place activist objectives out of practical reach. If activists do not aspire to sudden and complete system change, then they can be figured simply as 'reformers' and important sites and practices of prefigurative, hopeful resistance are seemingly disqualified. The position I am outlining here, in contrast, is that progressive, emancipatory, political struggle need not be sudden or complete, but can be composed of numerous minor acts of intervention and resistance that coalesce into a significant movement over time. This vision of large-scale border liberalisation is compatible with Dummett's view (1992: 23), which advocates for a movement towards border liberalisation that is begun 'in a limited way ... even if the aim [can] not be realized at once'. This view can be derived from the works of abolitionist scholars like Mathiesen (1974), and is related to various concepts in the social sciences such as 'everyday resistance' (Scott, 1987), 'tactical' progressivity (de Certeau, 2011) and 'minor' politics (Squire and Darling, 2013).

In order to make the programme thinkable and operable as a form of intergovernmental cooperation, it is illustrative to specify the scheme more precisely in the following way. Let T_0 be the total financial outlay on border controls globally in time period 0, and let T_x be the total financial outlay on border controls in period x. Let F_x be the total amount of funds available to the Global Facilitation Fund in year x, and let $F_0 = 0$. A preliminary relation between the two values, T_x and F_x, can be expressed by the following two equations:

$$F_x = (x/100) \star T_0$$
$$T_x = (1 - [x/100]) \star T_0$$

Accordingly, in year 0, F_0 would equal zero as per equation one. As x increases from 0 to 100 over the course of 100 periods, the magnitude of the global facilitation fund, F_x, also increases in 1 percent increments, while the magnitude of the total amount spent on border control globally, Tx, reduces at the same rate, as per equation two. In other words, there is a literal diversion of the usage of funds, from border control to the facilitation of safe, global mobility, achieved gradually over 100 periods.

Admittedly, the idea does not address capital flows and only concerns human migration. Yet, capital flows have largely decoupled themselves from the interventions of nation-states in any case. Cities, on the one hand, and global circuits comprised of urban financial centres and electronic global financial markets on the other, have been able to override 'the duality global/national presupposed in much analysis of the relation between the global economy and state authority' (Sassen, 2002: 2).

Innumerable variations on, and developments of, the basic idea can be envisaged. T_0 could be calculated on the basis of average expenditure per period over a predetermined window (e.g. 15 years), for instance, to avoid variability in the process of setting the figure. The process could be expedited or slowed – for example, each increment could be three months, six months, one year or two years. Breaks could be taken if the process hits obstacles, leaps could be taken if the process goes well, and reversals could be considered if the pace proves unmanageable. Regional groupings of countries could embark on the process. Countries not initially included could be incorporated later via a stipulated procedure. Countries that overspent on border controls could be sanctioned by a fine. The behaviour of countries themselves would be subject to monitoring to ensure compliance, which itself could be organised in various ways to maintain independence.

The facilitation fund would eventually be as significant in size as the outlay on border controls is today. It could cover various costs associated with migration, including the following:

- Making impartial and reliable information available about the reception of migrants in destination countries. This would help to reduce migration based on misinformation.
- Securing the safety of those wishing to migrate – for example, via a rapid response rescue organisation and the proper regulation of the current smuggling industry.
- Support for those who had migrated and who were unable to pay for basic education, health care or social security in destination countries.
- Research into adaptive strategies for areas of immigration (and emigration) in the emerging, more connected, global environment.
- Compensation to areas of emigration for their loss of human capital.

A series of operational questions arise, including what to do about serial migrators, whether developed and developing countries would receive the same amount of funding per migrant, how to reckon with internal migration such as the large-scale migrations that both occur and are prevented from occurring in China, what to do about non-contiguous participants in the scheme, what arrangements should be in place in the event of aggression between states and how security interests would be affected. It is not possible here to do justice to all of these questions. My purpose is only to provide a very preliminary sketch of a possible future, rather than to specify it exhaustively, but I do so in the belief that it is better to keep searching for and expressing the potential forms that an alternative global future, even an incomplete one, might take, than to be cowed into silence by the difficulty and risks of achieving it. Politics, here, is not of the sort that waits for the cataclysmic revolution to occur for so long that it 'leaves us in a fearful and fateful deadlock [and] lingers in endless postponement' (Critchley, 2009). Rather, it is composed of practical, if highly demanding, interventions in the present. On this basis, it is worth considering the merits of such a scheme.

An approach such as this would address two major families of objections to multilateral border liberalisation: that of a lack of *concomitance*, meaning that states that act in isolation could be overwhelmed by the resulting in-migration of people, and a lack of attention to *contribution*, referring to the fraught politics of citizenship and entitlement of migrants to welfare, protection and social security in comparison to long-standing residents of an area (Pécoud and de Guchteneire, 2007; Bauder, 2017). On the first point, Pécoud and de Guchteneire (2007) argue that a first principle of large-scale border liberalisation must be multilateralism: 'no state can be expected to progress towards free movement', they write (21), 'if even some other states do not follow the same path'. The process outlined here is not only gradual, but also collective, meaning that the international treaty would act as a coordination device to facilitate the *simultaneous* loosening of border restrictions, thereby dissipating the risk that countries acting in isolation will be 'overwhelmed' by newcomers.

On the second point, an important property of the programme suggested here is that the facilitation fund would deliver support to migrant-receiving destinations in proportion to the immigration they received. In this way, the fund would constitute a response to those states – notably, but not exclusively, in the Global North (Hampshire, 2016) – that are reluctant to entertain the notion of more relaxed border controls due to the supposed financial burden and threats to citizenship that immigration represents. The US and Hungary, for example, have refused to sign the Global Compact for Safe, Orderly and Regular Migration for these sorts of reasons. Of course, we could argue that in reality immigration is often a positive, not a negative, economic influence on a developed receiving country, at least in the medium- to long-term. But bearing in mind the widespread existence of these sorts of reservations, the real value of the fund could be its negotiating potential with states that habitually underestimate immigration's value. It could, therefore, constitute a powerful bargaining tool for initiating a new round of large-scale global migration governance.

One might ask if there would be sufficient funds to compensate the providers of health care, education and social security in destination states upon the arrival of migrants. It might be better to ask *when* there would be sufficient funds. What we have witnessed over the past few decades is a steady escalation in investment in border control, driven by a variety of factors, including fear of terrorism, media sensationalism, rising nationalism and vested corporate interests. Concomitantly, we have seen a decline in the return on this investment, as (1) increasing proficiency in the technological and physical avoidance of controls by migrants has developed and (2) a decline in the costs of migration has occurred as 'technical processes have substantially reduced the costs of travel' (Collier, 2013: 66). Indeed, as populations in Western developed countries have become used to receiving migrants, migrant numbers become large enough to talk not about 'integration' of newly arrived people into a supposedly static and homogenous indigenous population, but about the dynamic 'super-diversity' (Vertovec, 2016) of certain populations in hosting countries. Under these conditions, the costs per migrant of receiving migrant populations also reduces, as schools, hospitals and already-arrived diasporic communities become proficient at meeting the needs of the newly arrived. In other words, border protection is getting more expensive, while migration is getting cheaper. This implies that there is a tipping point – it may well have already been reached (see The Economist, 2017) – at which global cosmopolitanism is cheaper than protectionism.

One way to appreciate the numbers involved is to consider current expenditure on border controls in relation to the number of expected migrants that would result from border abolition. While space constraints preclude a full analysis here, the following reflections are illustrative of the potential of an internationalist border abolition programme. Britain spent £1.8 billion ($3.02 billion; €2.21 billion) on border controls in the financial year 2014/15. Since Britain had a population of 64.61 million people in 2014, this equates to £27.86 ($46.80; €34.24) per person. Assuming, for the moment, that Britain is representative of the developed world, we can extrapolate a rough estimate of the amount that the developed world in general spends on border control by multiplying this £27.86 by the population of the developed world (1.248 billion), yielding an annual expenditure of £34.77 billion ($58.41 billion; €42.73 billion). This exceeds an estimate from the International Organization for Migration in 2003 that, at that time, the 25 richest countries collectively spent $25 to $30 billion per year on the enforcement of immigration laws (Martin, 2003).

Now consider the World Gallup Poll on migration, which conducted interviews with over 400,000 adults in 146 countries between 2008 and 2010. The survey found that '[r]oughly 630 million of the world's adults desire to move to another country permanently . . . if they had the chance' (Esipova et al., 2011: 21). The authors calculate that this figure equates to 14 percent of the world's adult population. For simplicity, let us assume that 14 percent of children would also move if they or their parents had the chance. Taking the world population in 2014 at 7.238 billion, this gives us an estimate of 1.01 billion potential migrants in a world devoid of migration controls.

By dividing the total estimate of border outlays by the developed world by the number of people we would expect to move, we can arrive at a per capita estimate of the size of the facilitation fund upon completion of the programme: it would equate to around £34.43 ($57.84; €42.81) per migrant per year. This is obviously approximate, but might be considered an underestimate, both because the numerator could well be an underestimate and because the denominator is almost certainly an overestimate. With respect to the numerator, the figure Britain spends on border controls may be per capita for the developed world because Britain 'benefitted' from European investment in external border controls in 2014, which we would expect to have reduced the amount that Britain spent directly. What is more, the figure excludes the outlay on border controls of developing countries, which, while less than developed countries below average, would still be significant. With respect to the denominator, not every potential migrant would actually move. It is far easier to say that one would like to migrate than it is to do so and the adjustment of wages and living standards under conditions of free movement is also likely to erode the incentive to move during the period of transition. Nevertheless, we will proceed with this conservative figure.

While £34.43 per migrant per year may not sound like a lot, it is worth bearing in mind that most migrants would migrate to countries close at hand, according to the long-established principle of distance decay identified by geographical models of migration (Samers, 2009). Since most potential migrants are also located in poor countries, then migration would largely be from one developing country to another, meaning that the facilitation fund would function as a de facto redistribution mechanism, allocating funds from richer to poorer countries. This being the case, £34.43 must be considered not in relation to its Western purchasing power, but in relation to its power to improve education and health-care systems in, for example, Sub-Saharan Africa or the poorest areas of Asia and Latin America. If the marketing material of Western charities is to be believed, £30.00 could buy clean water for 30 families, provide over 30 children with effective treatment for malaria, or cover the costs of a child living in poverty to attend pre-school for over half a year. Bearing in mind that most migrants tend to be net contributors to their host as well, the potential of the programme comes into view.

Challenges and risks

It almost goes without saying that such a programme would face a gamut of challenges and risks. Perhaps the primary challenge concerns how to catalyse such a process: how could we possibly hope for such a system to come about or even get started? Border liberalisation on a global scale may appear unrealistic, but as Pécoud and du Guchteneire (2007: 2) argue:

> If one had told a French or a German citizen in, say, 1950, that free movement would be a reality in the European Union a few decades later, he or she may have been difficult to convince. Even in the 1980s it would have been difficult to predict that the free movement of people between Eastern and Western Europe would become normal some three decades later.

Indeed, free movement is by no means 'an absurdity' (ibid.: 25), having been discussed seriously in various regions including West Africa (Adepoju, 2007), the southern African region (Peberdy and Crush, 2007) and South America (Maguid, 2007), while the European Union has achieved high levels of free movement between states. The question remains, though: how can such a process get started?

Progressive pedagogy has historically fulfilled various functions for abolitionism. The perceived economic irrationality of the effort to legally abolish the British slave trade in the late 1700s and early 1800s, from the perspective of British industry, underscores the achievement of the abolitionists (Drescher, 2010). The major challenge they faced was the reduction of cultural and moral distance between the consumers of, and profiteers from, slave produce, and the experiences of slaves, which were largely unknown to the British public. Both female and male abolitionists during the period developed innovative pedagogic techniques to overcome this distancing. A similar challenge faced the American scientists that discovered the negative influence of chlorofluorocarbons (CFCs) on the vital layer of ozone gases that protect the earth from excess ultra-violet radiation linked to skin cancer, as well as damage to plant and animal life. Despite establishing the link between CFCs and depleting levels of ozone in the 1970s, staunch resistance from multinational companies heavily invested in CFCs meant that a consensus was difficult to build. Crucial to breaking the deadlock was the innovative use of time-lapse video technology that gave a compelling visual representation of the development of the 'ozone hole'. The very metaphor of a 'hole' was a key pedagogic intervention that prompted a series of influential actors, including the conservative US President Reagan (who was wholly committed to industry and generally against government intervention), to become sufficiently concerned to intervene.

In order to engender similar support for the abolition of border controls, a comparably well-considered pedagogic arsenal would need to be amassed. Unfortunately, the persistent interest of a global-yet-nationalist, sensationalist, trivialising and exploitative media machine (Herman and Chomsky, 2010), which routinely generates moral panics around migration (Cohen, 2011), introduces specific contemporary challenges that will require the progressive mobilisation of innovative means of counter-visualisation in informational conditions vastly different from, and arguably even harder than, those facing the slave trade abolitionists or the scientists working to abolish CFCs. The perils of constrained migration would need to be not only systematically researched, but also innovatively represented and imparted. The experiences of migration control, including its hidden violence, would need to be relayed in ways that are empathy-building, without pitying or belittling migrant subjects.

In terms of risks, at least four risks of the internationalist programme outlined here present themselves. The first is the naturalisation and normalisation of the state system and the international scale. The way in which the proposal is framed takes as given the primacy of states in the administration of global power, as well as taking a rather quantitative view of power itself (Agnew, 2001). By doing so, it risks becoming active in the very construction of states, while also embodying the assumption that the 'international' is 'the most urgent scale' (Hodder et al., 2015: 2) of intervention. The notion that states are ontologically stable entities that can intervene in a pre-existing and pre-packaged scale of action, both of which remain unaffected by the means of their enactment and operationalisation, is reminiscent of the realist approach to international relations that political geographers have critiqued (Agnew, 2001).

Second, relatedly, without specifying the political and cultural components of the proposal (such as institutions, congresses, summits, societies, etc.), nor giving explicit attention to *who* articulates the international, and from where, the proposal could risk opening the door to the sort of colonial and imperial practices that empires have undertaken in previous epochs. How can the proposal avoid 'the global manifestation of US nationalism' (Hodder et al., 2015: 3), for instance? Featherstone's concern in his study of internationalism is precisely to locate subaltern internationalism outside the corridors of established power, and by extension outside states, and to attend to the ways in which international connections are forged 'from below' (Featherstone, 2012). The risk of proposing an internationalist model such as that put forward above is that it reproduces elite, Eurocentric formations of ideologies and forms of power by not grounding itself and proceeding from local relations and struggles. In order to mitigate this risk, more work would need to be carried out – not only by experts in law, policy, negotiation, economics, diplomacy, international relations, peace studies, migration and political science, but also by migrants and would-be migrants, as well as activists, unions and academics – into the question of 'the relationship between internationalism in the abstract and the geographical specifics of its creation in particular sites' (Hodder et al., 2015: 4). The global sanctuary movement, with its emphasis on locality and welcome, may be in a good position to contribute to this work.

Third, the object of the proposal is the facilitation of markedly freer human movement, the advantages of which are now well known (see Bauder, 2017). The way in which freer human movement might underpin capitalist exploitation of human societies, however, is less frequently discussed (see Gill, 2009). Salter (2013) has explicated the intimate connection between human movement and the liberal world order, including the highly lucrative security and technology sectors that regulate human movement. The system of accumulation that is currently dominant 'simply cannot allow staticity – the entire system is premised on circulation' (ibid.: 11). In this view, what measures would need to be taken to ensure that the liberalisation of borders is not primarily a capitalist endeavour? It is worth remembering that, precisely via their porosity and failure, borders function to admit certain precarious and vulnerable workforces, ripe for exploitation. Certainly, the scale of emigration that large areas of the world could experience (what Collier (2013) calls 'exodus') is capable of consigning these areas to under-development and subordinate positions in the emerging global order. Attention to these risks must accompany any large-scale border abolition initiative.

Fourth, if exclusion is so embedded in society that borders have taken on secondary importance, then the proposal set out here may ultimately miss its target. The risk is that border abolition would be carried out, but that such a development would nevertheless leave intact the primary mechanisms of racist and subjugatory exclusionism that now operate through alternative mechanisms. These include 'internal borders' such as 'administrative, financial, cultural, linguistic and mental barriers' (Pécoud and de Guchteneire, 2007: 24). We might, for example, witness increasing privately financed segregation, higher levels of employment and housing discrimination against newcomers, increasing gentrification and a scaling-up of gated communities (gated cities, for example). All of these risks would need careful thought alongside any practical experiment into the abolition of border controls.

Conclusion

Abolitionism has never been about utopia, though. Abolitionist efforts are not about imagining some woolly, pie-in-the-sky society, but about practical, applied interventions against systems of oppression and marginalisation. A world without borders would also not be utopian (Pécoud and de Guchteneire, 2007; Bauder, 2017). Crime, discrimination, disease, inequality and exploitation would surely outlast such an initiative, but withholding support for partial and imperfect improvements on the basis that such achievements fail to live up to the demands of completeness would require us to adopt a neutered political position. Imagine not supporting the abolition of slavery because capitalism would survive such legislation. Imagine not supporting universal suffrage because of concerns about the first-past-the-post voting method.

Thomas Mathieson (1974) was acutely aware of these difficulties when writing his seminal reflection on the politics of abolition. As he saw it, there arises a dilemma between two strategies. On the one hand, the refusal of short-term reforms might help to maintain an appetite for longer-term, more systemic changes, but this often comes at the price of political paralysis. On the other hand, engaging in short-term reforms may afford abolitionists more political presence, but at the same time can deplete them, dilute their initiative and encourage them to settle for a system that is not fundamentally altered. The solution, for Mathieson, was to identify and support only those short-term reforms that were commensurate with, and clearly made progress towards, the longer-term objective: what he called 'reforms of the abolishing kind' (ibid.: 210). There is a case for viewing a 1 percent increment towards an abolitionist goal, as set out in the proposal above, as an abolishing kind of reform in Mathieson's terms. I will, however, leave it to the readers to decide on the question of whether the abolition of borders via the sort of intergovernmental negotiation outlined here is itself a reform of the abolishing kind on the road towards the elimination of exclusionism, racism and discrimination, or simply likely to re-inscribe these in new forms.

The real challenge facing progressive politics is not the charge of political reformism, but the delicate and practical matter of assessing which battles can and should be fought and won within the current system of domination, and organising campaigns to do so effectively. Whether or not we would sign up to the proposal put forward here, the progressive academic's role in this landscape is fundamentally different from that of a Bartleby-esque dissenter. It is to offer constructive suggestions and critique to progressive factions, with a view to galvanising their activities and opening up new potential fields of winnable struggle. It is to attend to the future systematically, as a technician working to bring about imperfect but improved alternative worlds. Governments, multinationals, security and insurance companies, think-tanks and the military have been undertaking these practices for decades: identifying desirable futures and 'backcasting' the necessary social developments that would be required to bring such futures about (Robinson, 2003). Progressive scholars, too, can develop scenarios as 'a tool to think with and thereafter strategically intervene on the future' (Anderson, 2010: 785).

In this respect, this chapter has sought to reimagine an alternative possible future. It has also, in a minor way, reimagined the role of the progressive academic. To theorise progressively is to move beyond the role of both critic and reformer. This is not a space 'between' revolution and reform, but somewhere else, somewhere full of risk and potential. It is to this project that progressive scholarship invites us.

Acknowledgements

I acknowledge support from the European Research Council, grant number StG-2015_677917

References

Abrams, P. (1988) 'Notes on the Difficulty of Studying the State. Originally published in 1977', *Journal of Historical Sociology,* 1(1), pp. 58–89.

Adepoju, A. (2007) 'Creating a Borderless West Africa: Constraints and Prospects for Intra-Regional Migration' in Pécoud, A. and Guchteneire, P. D. (eds.), *Migration without Borders: Essays on the Free Movement of People.* New York: Berghahn.

Agnew, J. (2001) 'Disputing the Nature of the International in Political Geography: The Hettner-Lecture in Human Geography', *Geographische Zeitschrift,* 89(1), pp. 1–16.

Agnew, J. (2009) *Globalization and Sovereignty.* Plymouth: Rowman & Littlefield.

Anderson, B. (2010) 'Preemption, Precaution, Preparedness: Anticipatory Action and Future Geographies', *Progress in Human Geography,* 34(6), pp. 777–98.

Anderson, B., Sharma, N. and Wright, C. (2009) 'Editorial: Why No Borders?', *Refuge,* 26(2), pp. 5–18.

Bauder, H. (2014) 'The Possibilities of Open and No Borders', *Social Justice,* 39(4), pp. 76–99.

Bauder, H. (2017) *Migration Borders Freedom.* Abingdon: Taylor & Francis.

Betts, A. (ed.) (2011) *Global Migration Governance.* Oxford: Oxford University Press.

Bourdieu, P. (2014) *On the State: Lectures at the Collège de Paris 1989–1992.* Cambridge: Polity Press.

Carens, J. (1987) 'Aliens and Citizens: The Case for Open Borders', *Review of Politics,* 49(2), 251–73.

Casey, E. S. (2011) 'Border versus Boundary at La Frontera', *Environment and Planning D: Society and Space,* 29(3), pp. 384–98.

Chimni, B. S. (2018). 'Global Compact on Refugees: One Step Forward, Two Steps Back', *International Journal of Refugee Law,* 30(4), pp. 630-634.

Cohen, S. (2011). *Folk Devils and Moral Panics.* London: Routledge.

Coles, E. (2015) *An English Dictionary.* London: Andesite Press.

Collier, P. (2013) *Exodus: How Migration Is Changing Our World.* Oxford: Oxford University Press.

Collins Publishing (2015) *Collins English Dictionary*. Glasgow: Collins.

Cooper, D. (2017) 'Prefiguring the State', *Antipode*, 49(2), pp. 335–56.

Critchley, S. (2009) 'Violent Thoughts about Slavoj Žižek', *Naked Punch*, supplement to issue 11.

de Certeau, M. D. (2011) *The Practice of Everyday Life*. Oakland, CA: University of California Press.

Drescher, S. (2010) *Econocide*. Chapel Hill, NC: University of North Carolina Press.

Dummett, A. (1992) 'The Transnational Migration of People Seen from within a Natural Law Tradition' in Barry, B. and Goodin, E. (eds), *Free Movement: Ethical Issues in the Transnational Migration of People and of Money*. New York and London: Harvester Wheatsheaf, pp. 169–80.

Dunn, K. (2010) 'There Is No Such Thing as the State: Discourse, Effect and Performativity', *Forum for Development Studies*, 37(1), pp. 79–92.

Esipova, N., Ray, J. and Pugliese, A. (2011) *Gallup World Poll: The Many Faces of Global Migration*. Geneva: International Organization for Migration.

Featherstone, D. (2012) *Solidarity: Hidden Histories and Geographies of Internationalism*. London: Zed Books.

Ferguson, J. (2011) 'Toward a Left Art of Government: From "Foucauldian Critique" to Foucauldian Politics', *History of the Human Sciences*, 24(4), pp. 61–8.

Ferguson, J. and Gupta, A. (2002) 'Spatializing States: Toward an Ethnography of Neoliberal Governmentality', *American Ethnologist*, 29(4), pp. 981–1002.

Fernandez, C., Gill, M., Szeman, I. and Whyte, J. (2006) 'Erasing the Line, or, the Politics of the Border', *Ephemera: Theory and Politics in Organisations*, 6(4), pp. 466–83.

Geddes, A. and Jordan, A. (2012) 'Migration as Adaptation? Exploring the Scope for Coordinating Environmental and Migration Policies in the European Union', *Environment and Planning C: Government and Policy*, 30(6), pp. 1029–44.

Gill, N. (2009) 'Whose 'No Borders'? Achieving No Borders for the Right Reasons', *Refuge*, 26(2), pp. 107–20.

Halliday, F. (1988) 'Three Concepts of Internationalism', *International Affairs*, 64(2), pp. 187–98.

Hampshire, J. (2016) 'Speaking with One Voice? The European Union's Global Approach to Migration and Mobility and the Limits of International Migration Cooperation', *Journal of Ethnic and Migration Studies*, 42(4), pp. 571–86.

Hansen, R. (2011) 'Making Cooperation Work: Interests, Incentives and Action' in Hansen, R., Koehler, J. and Money, J. (eds.), *Migration, Nation States, and International Cooperation*. London: Routledge.

Herman, E. S. and Chomsky, N. (2010) *Manufacturing Consent: The Political Economy of the Mass Media*. London: Random House.

Hodder, J., Legg, S. and Heffernan, M. (2015) 'Introduction: Historical Geographies of Internationalism, 1900–1950', *Political Geography*, 49, pp. 1–6.

Ince, A. and Barrera de la Torre, G. (2016) 'For Post-Statist Geographies', *Political Geography*, 55, pp. 10–19.

Jeffrey, A. (2013) *The Improvised State: Sovereignty, Performance and Agency in Dayton Bosnia*. Oxford: Wiley-Blackwell.

Jones, R. (2009). 'Categories, Borders and Boundaries', *Progress in Human Geography*, 33(2), 174–89.

Jones, R. (2011) *People – States – Territories: The Political Geographies of British State Transformation*. Oxford: Wiley-Blackwell.

Jones, R. (ed.) (2019a) *Open Borders: In Defense of Free Movement*. Athens, GA: University of Georgia Press.

Jones, R. (2019b) 'Introduction' in Jones, R. (ed.), *Open Borders: In Defense of Free Movement*. Athens, GA: University of Georgia Press.

Koslowski, R. (ed.) (2011) *Global Mobility Regimes*. New York: Palgrave.

Kunz, J. and Leinonen, M. (2007) 'Europe without Borders: Rhetoric, Reality or Utopia?' in Pécoud, A. and Guchteneire, P. D. (eds.), *Migration without Borders: Essays on the Free Movement of People*. New York: Berghahn.

Longman Group (1995) *Longman Dictionary of Contemporary English*. London: Longman.

Maguid, A. (2007) 'Migration Policies and Socioeconomic Boundaries in the South American Cone' in Pécoud, A. and Guchteneire, P. D. (eds.), *Migration without Borders: Essays on the Free Movement of People*. New York: Berghahn.

Martin, D. and Pierce, J. (2013) 'Reconceptualizing Resistance: Residuals of the State and Democratic Radical Pluralism', *Antipode*, 45(1), pp. 61–79.

Martin, P. (2003) *Bordering on Control: Combatting Irregular Migration in North America and Europe*. Geneva: IOM.

Massey, D. (2005) *For Space*. London: Sage.

Mathiesen, T. J. (1974) *The Politics of Abolition*. Michigan: Wiley.

Mitchell, T. (2006) 'Society, Economy, and the State Effect' in Sharma, A. and Gupta, A. (eds.), *The Anthropology of the State*. Oxford: Blackwell.

Nyers, P. (2013) 'Liberating Irregularity: No Borders, Temporality, Citizenship' in Guillaume, X. and Huysmans, J. (eds.), *Citizenship and Security: The Constitution of Political Being*. London: Routledge, pp. 37–52.

Pearsall, J. and Hanks, P. (eds.) (1998) *The New Oxford Dictionary of English*. Oxford: Oxford University Press.

Paasi, A. (1999) 'Boundaries as Social Practice and Discourse: The Finnish–Russian Border', *Regional Studies*, 33(7), pp. 669–80.

Painter, J. (2006) 'Prosaic Geographies of Stateness', *Political Geography*, 25, pp. 752–74.

Peberdy, S. and Crush, J. (2007) 'Histories, Realities and Negotiating Free Movement in Southern Africa' in Pécoud, A. and Guchteneire, P. D. (eds.), *Migration without Borders: Essays on the Free Movement of People*. New York: Berghahn.

Pécoud, A. and Guchteneire, P. D. (eds.) (2007) *Migration without Borders: Essays on the Free Movement of People*. New York: Berghahn.

Robinson, J. (2003) 'Future Subjunctive: Backcasting as Social Learning', *Futures*, 35(8), pp. 839–56.

Salter, M. (2013) 'To Make Move and Let Stop: Mobility and the Assemblage of Circulation', *Mobilities*, 8(1), pp. 7–19.

Samers, M. (2009) *Migration*. London: Routledge.

Sassen, S. (2002) *Global Networks, Linked Cities*. London: Routledge.

Schwarz, C. (1993) *The Chambers Dictionary*. London: Chambers.

Scott, J. C. (1987) *Weapons of the Weak. Everyday Forms of Peasant Resistance*. New Haven, CT: Yale University Press.

Squire, V. and Darling, J. (2013) 'The "Minor" Politics of Rightful Presence: Justice and Relationality in City of Sanctuary', *International Political Sociology*, 7, pp. 58–74.

Turnbull, J., Lea, D., Parkinson, D. et al. (eds.). (2010) *Oxford Advanced Learner's Dictionary*. Oxford: Oxford University Press.

Steinmetz, G. (ed.) (1999) *State/Culture: State Formation after the Cultural Turn*. Ithaca, NY: Cornell University Press.

The Economist (2017) 'A World of Free Movement Would Be $78 Trillion Richer', 13 July. London: The Economist. Available at https://www.economist.com/the-world-if/2017/07/13/a-world-of-free-movement-would-be-78-trillion-richer (accessed 1 May 2019).

Vertovec, S. (2016) *Super-Diversity*. London: Routledge.

Žižek, S. (2006) 'Against Human Rights' [online]. Available at libcom.org (accessed 3 March 2019).

13

REFUSAL FIRST, THEN REIMAGINATION

Presenting the Burn in Flames Post-Patriarchal Archive in Circulation

Sarah Browne and Jesse Jones

We are here to introduce the *Burn in Flames Post-Patriarchal Archive in Circulation*.[1]

This is part of a larger collaborative art project we worked on together, titled *In the Shadow of the State*, from 2014–16. This activist/archival aspect of the project is one of a number of critical feminist tactics we've developed; tactics of resistance and defence against the regulation of the body gendered female under the nation-state and capitalism.[2]

This archive is a tool of feminist pedagogy that exists for a future moment after the fall of patriarchy. It is a way of processing what we see as ideologically obsolete and poisonous material, and labelling it as hazardous for future generations. In the current moment, the archive is designed to highlight and draw attention to these hazardous materials, locations and objects. The material for the archive exists all around us: we do not collect it or try to keep it. Rather than trying to imagine a post-patriarchal future, it presumes this future moment already exists and seeks to reorient ourselves to the present with this in mind.

We begin by identifying and naming physical evidence of patriarchy, whether trivial or profound. Our initial tool in this archiving procedure is a legal stamp (see Figure 13.1), which acts as a way for us to process materials: these stamps are easily

---

1 The name of the archive is inspired by Lizzie Borden's 1984 documentary-style feminist science-fiction film, *Born in Flames*. The film is set in the near future after a successful socialist revolution in the US, and explores the oppression that women of all classes, sexualities and ethnicities continue to struggle with in this context.

2 *In the Shadow of the State* by Sarah Browne and Jesse Jones was a major collaborative project co-commissioned by Artangel and Create (Ireland), supported by ART: 2016, the Arts Council's programme as part of Ireland 2016, the centenary of the Easter Rising in the Republic of Ireland, Dublin City Council, Liverpool Biennial 2016 and Heart of Glass (St. Helens). This project involved close collaboration with women in the fields of law, music, material culture and midwifery, and addressed the regulation of the female body by the nation-state through a series of legal workshops and performances in Derry, Liverpool, Dublin and London.

FIGURE 13.1

made and we encourage you to produce one to use for yourself.[3] Selected objects are identified, stamped, and placed back in circulation to be experienced anew. Therefore, the archive also operates as a collaborative feminist standards organisation.

---

3 If you would like to replicate our design, the font to request is Gill Sans Bold & Gill Sans, and we like to use red ink. You can use one of these photographs as a reference point in the stationer's. At the time of writing, the cost per custom-produced self-inking stamp was c. £20 sterling.

We are conscious, for example, that the language of feminism needs to flex, move and adapt, and we welcome that challenge. The standards in play for the *Burn in Flames* archive are under continuous revision: there is no final cut.

The objects in the archive can fit in the palm of your hand, or they can be architectural, or even larger, in scale. Some of these materials include printed matter, like political leaflets; consumer items; and also non-physical materials like laws and institutions. A selection of these stamped objects is reproduced in the captioned photographs accompanying this chapter. We can also stamp material from the media for recirculation, such as media content or news reporting that is obviously patriarchal in tone and intention. We distribute these stamps to others who want to contribute ideas, which in turn informs the standard. We also share the results online on our twitter account, @pparchive. There, hashtags can be used as a digital stamp also. Examples include #archiveincirculation; #feministadmin; #misogynisttimemachine.

We use the word patriarchy to name the connecting sexist social systems of domination and oppression that also produce homophobia, transphobia, racism and economic injustice. Patriarchal thinking shapes the values of our culture, but rarely do we name it in everyday speech. This silence promotes denial, and we cannot dismantle a system if we are in collective denial that it exists. This archive, as a standards organisation, is an initial effort at naming and locating such hazards. It is a way of seeing where that poisonous material circulates and interrupting that circulation. The challenge for feminists today is how to imagine and create a world without this material in its physical, digital and tactile forms.

Over the last two years, we have presented this archive as an activist tactic with friends, in community settings, through social media and in association with art and cultural events and academic conferences.[4] The archive is activated through a workshop/demonstration format, where workshop participants are encouraged to bring materials to be stamped and discuss why they find this material poisonous, although it is usually self-evident. As the archive has developed in scope, an increasingly thematic focus to the workshop presentations has developed, such as the social construction of 'feminine hygiene' or the nature of patriarchal time itself.[5] We have

---

4 Thanks to those who have hosted presentations to date: *Crisis Aesthetics, Crisis Politics*, National College of Art and Design, Dublin, March 2015; *Still, We Work*, National Women's Council of Ireland touring exhibition at Callan Workhouse, Kilkenny, June 2015 and Hunt Museum, Limerick, October 2015; *Console-ing Passions*, International conference on Television, Video, Audio, New Media and Feminism, Dublin, June 2015; *Idle Women*, Lancashire, October 2015; *Bodies Politic*, symposium of the Casement Project at Maynooth University, February 2016; Ulster Festival of Art and Design, March 2016; Gender Studies outreach programme, UCD/Loreto College Crumlin, May 2016; *Hospitable Bodies*, symposium of the Casement Project at the British Library, London, June 2016; FLaK, 'Mixing Feminism, Legality and Knowledge' seminar, Queen Mary University of London, July 2016. A transcript of the presentation at FLaK was published in feminists@law, vol. 6 no. 1 (2016).

5 In July 2016, we produced *The Truncheon and the Speculum* in partnership with the Liverpool Biennial. This was an online broadcast that explored historic state violence enacted through gynaecological means, and featured two guests – material culture historian Dr. Lisa Godson, and self-identified 'cyborg witch' Klau Kinky of Catalan collective GynePunk. With this event, we proposed a supplanting of the

also given organisers who have invited us a stamp in order to extend and continue the work of the archive themselves. Just as the archive does not behave like a usual archive by holding on to its material, by distributing the stamps we are continually distributing the decision-making and the discussion. We can imagine there might be arguments about what will exist after the fall of patriarchy and what will be definitively obsolete. The stamp is a way of making those antagonisms visible and possible to discuss. It is also fun though, and funny, or we think it is: patriarchy becomes momentarily more defeatable when it can be seen and laughed at in its full, violent absurdity.

The *Burn in Flames* archive shares some affinity with what De Cesari describes in the Palestinian context as anticipatory representation, that is, certain kinds of artistic practice that call institutions into being by 'representing them beforehand' (2012: 82). She uses this framework to analyse a series of artistic practices in Palestine, which tactically perform new state cultural institutions for a nation-state that does not exist – yet. She discusses artist Khalil Rabah's Palestinian Museum of Natural History and Humankind and curator Jack Persekian's Contemporary Art Museum of Palestine (CAMP), as well as the initiation of a Palestinian 'national' art biennial, and the inclusion of a Palestinian 'pavilion' as a collateral event at the 53rd Venice Biennale in 2009. Here, the *Burn in Flames* archive diverges from the projects under discussion by De Cesari, which use the artistic institutions of the museum, and the more recently globalised institution of the biennial form, to represent 'the national identity, [embody] the nation and its aspirations' (Persekian quoted in De Cesari, 2012: 93). The *Burn in Flames* archive, like the examples she describes, but on a more modest and intimate scale, seeks to produce and usher us towards new (post-patriarchal) forms of social arrangement and social relations. Critically, however, unlike those examples, it is not produced under conditions of statelessness and as a result is marked by a more deconstructive impulse. The archive declares aspects of the contemporary world extinct, obsolete, of no value. It suggests refusal first, then reimagination.

At the risk of explaining away all flint from the idea, the *Burn in Flames* archive does not operate like other archives: not like the official archives of the state nor like the unofficial archives of activists or enthusiastic amateurs. We do not hold its material dear. The gloves we sometimes wear to handle the artefacts in the archive are to protect us, not to protect the objects. Participants bring objects to workshops to be stamped, some of which are documented in the photographs reproduced here. The act of stamping objects for the archive is not an act of preservation: it is much closer to an act of destruction. Sometimes the act of stamping constitutes an illegal act of defacement, such as when workshop participants stamped state documents or currency. We have not been permitted to reproduce images of those documents in this publication; however, the documents themselves continue to

---

role of the state-sanctioned broadcast into domestic spaces, inviting the online audience to discuss and challenge the terrestrial illegalities of reproductive rights for women. The broadcast is archived online at https://vimeo.com/176333761.

circulate in the world in their amended form. Stamps from nation-states accumulate beside the post-patriarchal stamped page in the passports, and stains and fingermarks accumulate on the notes that have been stamped, alongside the image of the Queen's face.

The objects that are stamped by participants should not exist, or at the very least are unacceptable in their current form or mode of distribution. These are usually despised objects, or representative of some kind of everyday misery. It may not be feasible to fully destroy the object – if only we were not so dependent on patriarchal capitalism – but the act of stamping it can at least signal a disagreement with the current state of affairs. It is a minimal intervention in a pseudo-official language: feminist graffiti disguised with the politeness of an administration aesthetic.

Figure 13.2 shows a stamped page from *Key Words with Peter and Jane. Book 3c: Let Me Write* (Murray: Ladybird, 2009). This series of best-selling books are highly popular educational aids. Here, the stamp draws attention to a page which further introduces young children to the concepts of separate private and public spheres, and the division of gendered labour along the same lines (daughters help mothers make cakes and sons help their fathers fix cars).

Figures 13.3 and 13.4 show printed material from two recent (defeated) campaigns on constitutional amendments in Ireland, which we critiqued at the time through the intervention of the stamp. Figure 13.3 utilises foetal imagery to advance an anti-choice argument against the repeal of the Eighth Amendment, an article

FIGURE 13.2

FIGURE 13.3

introduced in 1983, which equates the right to life of the 'mother' with that of the 'unborn' (Bunreacht na hÉireann [Constitution of Ireland, enacted 1937], Article 40.3.3°). This effectively produced a constitutional ban on abortion in the Irish state, but also limited all pregnant persons' ability to give informed consent for any medical procedure while pregnant: the National Consent Policy notes that:

> . . . because of the constitutional provisions on the right to life of the 'unborn', there is significant legal uncertainty regarding the extent of a pregnant

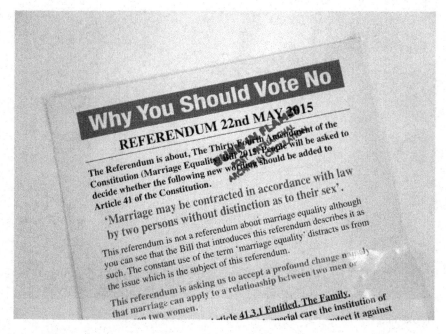

FIGURE 13.4

woman's right to refuse treatment in circumstances in which the refusal would put the life of a viable foetus at serious risk (National Consent Advisory Group, 2016: 41).[6]

Figure 13.4 shows campaign material arguing against the legalisation of same-sex marriage in Ireland: we use the stamp in this case to criticise homophobic rhetoric and the deliberate and disingenuous conflation of the institutions of 'marriage' and 'family'.

Figure 13.5 shows a sanitary towel, which along with tampons, were contributed by participants in a number of workshops who objected to how they are taxed by the (British) state as 'luxury items', thereby imposing a penalty on citizens who menstruate.

Finally, Figure 13.6 is a 'feminine hygiene' spray, designed to 'neutralise and limit the development of odour' from a woman's genitalia. It represents the colonisation of the olfactory sense in order to manufacture yet another artificial beauty requirement, the wearer's purported 'long-lasting feeling of freshness and confidence'. We use the stamp here to criticise the harmful cultivation of feminised shame in order to extract profit from it.

6 On 25 May 2018, a referendum was passed to remove the Eighth Amendment from the Irish Constitution, and after an unsuccessful legal challenge, was signed into law on 18 September 2018. The referendum on same-sex marriage was passed on 22 May 2015 and amended the Constitution to provide that marriage is recognised irrespective of the sex of the partners, signed into law on 29 October 2015.

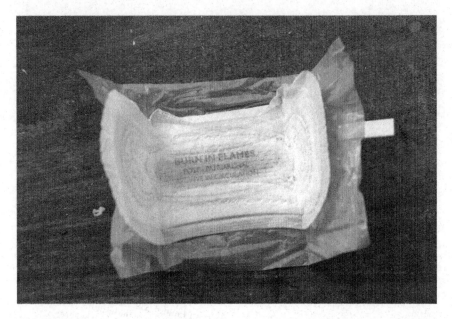

FIGURE 13.5

Mary Douglas describes how our idea of dirt is composed of two things: care for hygiene and respect for conventions (Douglas, 1966). Dirt is defined in relation to what is clean and acceptable, and 'feminine hygiene' is a euphemism we can understand. But what, metaphorically or symbolically, is implied by the need or requirement to enforce feminine hygiene? What about the exclusion of women's bodies in state buildings, and therefore democratic processes? In the Irish state, we can find evidence in our Constitution, where in Article 41.2 women are designated a 'special place' in the home:

> In particular, the State recognises that by her life within the home, woman gives to the State a support without which the common good cannot be achieved . . . The State shall, therefore, endeavour to ensure that mothers shall not be obliged by economic necessity to engage in labour to the neglect of their duties in the home (Bunreacht na hÉireann, 1937).[7]

This legal form of hygiene serves to place women firmly within the zone of the domestic, not to mention conflating the category of 'woman' with 'mother'. We could also think of arguments presented as recently as the 1970s to exclude women's participation in juries on the basis that there were no women's toilets in the Four Courts at the time: Coen (2015) cites the use of this argument in the landmark *de Búrca and Anderson v. Attorney General* case in the Irish Supreme Court, 1975 (the Juries Act in 1976 finally allowed women to sit on juries, and it was after

7 Constitution of Ireland: http://www.irishstatutebook.ie/eli/cons/en/html (accessed 6 March 2019).

FIGURE 13.6

that that a ladies' toilet was established in the basement of the Four Courts in Dublin). All too often, it is women's bodies that are described or understood as being dirty in a given architectural or political order, that is, they cannot belong because there is no allocated space. We locate 'feminine hygiene' as a key tool of violence against women, spatially evident in the assignation of bodies gendered female to interior spaces and the private realm of the domestic.

Historically, the Contagious Diseases Acts of 1864 are significant in Ireland and the UK for the invention and developing ideology of 'feminine hygiene'. This legislation addressed the threat to the health of the male soldiers of the Empire by permitting the compulsory inspection of women suspected to be prostitutes for venereal disease. This legislation was partly responsible for the transformation of physical dirt into social dirt via the body of the prostitute, who could be identified from her unaccompanied movement in public – particularly at night-time, and near military camps. Such women were subjected to arbitrary, compulsory medical examination by specially trained police constables, who were paid an extra allowance for 'the unattractive nature of the duty' (Luddy, 2007: 142). The Contagious Diseases Acts behaved as tools of state-enforced, patriarchal notions of hygiene, and traces of this hygiene campaign remain where bodies assigned female become state sites for the policing of moral character. An alternative, feminist construction of hygiene – another standard – would see not the prostitute, but the forces of the state as being contaminated in this circumstance through the violence of its methods, the truncheon and the speculum forever linked.

In different and unexpected forms, 'feminine hygiene' recurs as a moment of weaponised vulnerability in women's narration of their intertwined experiences of the home and the state in Ireland and the UK. Witness, for example, Patricia Moore's account of being strip-searched in Armagh Gaol in the 1980s:

> There were times when I would have had my period, and I was one of these people who suffered from very heavy periods. There was [sic] times I was left standing with the blood running down the inside of my leg, and formed a puddle. One of the days, one of the screws said to me, 'Look at the mess that you're making' (McLaughlin, n. d.).

Women in the north of Ireland describing their experience of home raids in the 1970s and 1980s also emphasise how such raids were combined with sexual harassment and intimidation, with tampons, sanitary towels and contraceptives routinely being handled and commented on by the raiding soldiers as an active attempt to shame and humiliate them (Harris and Healy, 2001: 19–26). A post-patriarchal state would not weaponise physical vulnerabilities in this way.

The *Burn in Flames* archive is a practice of relational labour, as described by Newman in this volume: 'creating linkages and connections between antagonistic rationalities and practices'. In our case, we move through spaces of art, culture and education to expose harm in objects that may seem innocuous, to challenge and disrupt existing chains of meaning, and to co-create new associations with participants in workshops (Newman, this volume). While we call the archive a 'standards organisation', we are not invested in actually achieving a uniform set of standards that could be replicated across all contexts. That way of thinking about an archive is also patriarchal, and we do not want the form or methodology of the archive to mimic its poisonous contents. We see this question as analogous to older and ongoing debates about the artistic canon (Nochlin, 1971; Parker and Pollock, 1981; Pollock, 1999) and we would argue that the question is not simply to 'diversify' who is included within the canon, but to upend the qualitative standards of the canon altogether. The presentation of the archive as a standards organisation is a provocation towards a discussion about what values, ethics and behaviours we should hold ourselves to in the pursuit of a post-patriarchal state. By stamping everything that will be extinct in this future state, can we work 'backwards' into our present, reorienting ourselves to pathways towards that point? If nearly everything in our present becomes reddened in stamps, what materials are left to help us think through a feminist theory of the state?

De Cesari questions 'the ways in which artists and cultural producers can participate in forging, quite literally, the nation(-state) by staging, by performing its institutions, and by *mocking its operations*' (2012: 82–3, our emphasis). The aspect of mocking, through parody, remains implicit in the remainder of the discussion of the projects in her article, although it is highly relevant, particularly to their status within the symbolic economy of contemporary art. Discussing parody elsewhere, Judith Butler emphasises that it is a function of proximity and investment. She describes how to enter into parody is to enter into a relationship of 'desire and ambivalence' (Butler, 1997: 266). We can also recognise in our parodic, mocking, deliberately contrary and 'incorrect' performance of the *Burn in Flames* archive that a residual desire for a state, a state reimagined, somehow stubbornly seems to remain.

The rules of hygiene change with changes in our state of knowledge. Dirt offends against order. Eliminating it is not entirely a negative movement, but can be a positive effort to organise the environment. Hygiene and dirt are relative concepts: what matters is who has the power to define what is hygienic and acceptable, and what is not. The *Burn in Flames* archive rejects patriarchal notions of hygiene. 'Feminine hygiene' as a concept offers us no protection and it has no value. 'Feminine hygiene' as an idea, a convention, is toxic and dangerous. However, through parody and disobedience, can we hold onto the technique of locating 'dirt' as matter out of place, and as feminists adapt this technique to our own ends? By naming the dirt ourselves through a collective critical process, we can perhaps change the paradigm of classification, thereby re-ordering notions of dirt, place and belonging in the future state.

We invite you to help us locate these hazards, hidden in plain sight, and together to establish a new set of standards.

References

Butler, J. (1997) 'Merely Cultural', *Social Text*, 52/53, pp. 265–77.

Coen, M. (2015) 'Fitting the Jury Box with Mirrors and Hairpins: The Woman Juror Question in Ireland 1919–976', at *Northern/Irish Feminist Judgments Project* drafting workshop, University College Dublin.

De Cesari, C. (2012) 'Anticipatory Representation: Building the Palestinian Nation(-State) through Artistic Performance', *Studies in Ethnicity and Nationalism*, 12(1), pp. 82–100.

Douglas, M. (1966) *Purity and Danger: An Analysis of Concepts of Pollution and Taboo*. London: Routledge.

Harris, H. and Healy, E. (eds.) (2001) *'Strong About it All . . .' Rural and Urban Women's Experiences of the Security Forces in Northern Ireland*. Derry: North West Women's/Human Rights Project.

Luddy, M. (2007) *Prostitution and Irish Society, 1800–1940.* Cambridge: Cambridge University Press.

McLaughlin, C. (n. d.) *Prison Memory Archive* [online]. Available at http://prisonsmemoryarchive.com/armagh-stories/ (accessed 10 May 2015).

National Consent Advisory Group (2016) *National Consent Policy.* Ireland: Health Service Executive.

Nochlin, L. (1971) 'Why Have There Been No Great Women Artists?' in Gornick, V and Moran, B. (eds.), *Woman in Sexist Society: Studies in Power and Powerlessness.* New York: Basic Books.

Parker, R. and Pollock, G. (1981) *Old Mistresses: Women, Art, and Ideology.* London: Pandora Press.

Pollock, G. (1999) *Differencing the Canon: Feminism and the Writing of Art's Histories.* London: Routledge.

CONCLUDING REFLECTIONS

Janet Newman and Nikita Dhawan

This book project has presented diverse responses to the invitation to reimagine the state for progressive politics. Working on it has been exciting, bringing us into conversations beyond our normal constituencies and opening up new personal and political insights. We do not intend here to summarise the contributions, but do want to highlight four features of this volume that we consider to be distinctive. The first is the challenge offered to orthodox theorisations of states, politics and power. In the first section of this final chapter, we highlight how the volume offers resources for 'thinking differently'. Such resources emerge from a range of social and political movements, and from work in different disciplinary perspectives. In particular, we show how insights drawn from feminist, queer, postcolonial and poststructuralist thought enable contributors to think outside and beyond the confines of what Kinna (this volume) terms 'the master's tools' of liberal political theory. A second feature is the ways in which the volume draws on contemporary theoretical work on 'the politics of representation'. Unpacking the dominant spatial and temporal representations of the state is, we suggest, crucial for alternative political projects. Third, the volume draws on a range of political perspectives and experiences from across the globe, as well as from transnational movements. In 'Problematising politics', we trace how these might contribute to progressive, transformative political change. However, change generates contradiction and uncertainty. In the final section of the chapter – 'Living with ambivalence' – we explore the problems of developing progressive reimaginings in the context of dominant tendencies of anti-statism – within the academy, in contemporary social movements and in neoliberal political projects.

Thinking differently

We live in dangerous political times, where populist and authoritarian leaders and politicians are seeking to seize or erode the architecture of states to enhance their personal power and enlarge their sphere of action. With the rise of racism and xenophobia, there is an urgent need to research alternative forms of identity and belonging both within as well as beyond the nation-state as locus of identification and belonging. As proposed by Rai (in this volume), 'an alternative imaginary provides us with a sense of belonging, and of solidarity' that is an antidote to politics of hate, as well as indifference and apathy, while 'multiple imaginings of society and the state require modes of working together towards these new horizons'. These 'necessary utopias' (Panitch and Gindin, 1999), in Rai's view, reassure us that another politics of the state is possible, while challenging the paralysis of pessimism.

But, as stressed in the Introduction, the concepts and approaches through which states are understood have consequences for the kinds of politics that are made possible. In this volume, we have questioned what it means to be a state, in the process challenging dominant ways of thinking that view states as liberal-democratic institutions, as legal entities, as sovereign powers. We have explored the ways in which mainstream state theory tends to legitimate colonial relations of power and oppression, and the hierarchical ordering of 'modern' and 'weak' states. We have traced ways in which contested alignments of religious and secular authority illuminate both historical struggles and contemporary global conflicts. We have explored struggles over territory, sovereignty and borders. And we have suggested ways in which apparently abstract concerns about the law, regulation, coercion, freedom or justice can illuminate contemporary conflicts and the shifting dynamics of state power and legitimacy.

But how does thinking differently happen? Whose ways of seeing (politics of theory), knowing (politics of research) and doing (politics of transformation) are legible and intelligible and whose remains irrelevant? Dominant ways of 'seeing' the state evoke specific strategies of dealing with it. In our view, alternative ways of seeing/theorising states – for example, prefigurative, decentred, emergent – open up possibilities for different imaginaries of the state. The volume has shown the potential of research methods that bring into view the knowledge and experiences of those engaged in transformative politics: for instance, the ethnography of De Cesari, the co-produced research of McDermont, the art practices of Browne and Jones and the activist research of Gill and Newman. The volume has also shown how, by drawing on past experiences and insights from different geographical sites and contexts, progressive policy reforms can be formulated. A continuing thread to the analysis has been attempts to approach the question of the state from different theoretical settings and regional contexts, so as to enable different modes of relationality to the state. Several chapters (e.g. those by Rai, Krämer and Gill) draw on poststructuralist and other forms of critique to highlight the injustices rooted in liberal-democratic conceptions of 'modern' statehood, embedded norms of freedom and justice, and the workings of state power. But we have also shown how empirical and theoretical work that goes beyond critique of the state can enable new forms of experimentation and political learning.

The chapters of this volume suggest a number of ways in which processes of critique and reframing can be provoked. The first is the productive possibilities that emerge from looking beyond and across disciplinary boundaries. The volume offers ways of 'thinking differently' rooted in geography, anthropology, political philosophy, policy studies, cultural studies, socio-legal studies and from the performing arts. These are not, however, discrete categories: many contributors work across theoretical boundaries, and many are at the forefront of attempts to challenge or transform their disciplinary origins. The book was inspired by conversations across disciplinary boundaries: for example, Kinna and Dhawan draw on different theoretical resources to explore the ways in which 'freedom' serves as a framing of legitimate action for state as well as extra state actors, while Dhawan, Clarke and McDermont et al. offer alternative perspectives on the regulatory/coercive practices of states. Our approach was developed through workshops and seminars that further challenged disciplinary orthodoxies and national imaginaries. Approaching the question of reimagining the state from different ideological and geographical perspectives implied that the encounters at the workshops and seminars were at once inspiring as well as challenging. Although there was shared commitment to contest hegemonic discourses and coercive performances of statehood, there was no easy consensus on either what the 'state' symbolised, or about the 'best practice' to reconfigure it. The process itself was instructive in exemplifying how difference and diversity in understanding and approaching the question of the state can support projects of reimagining and transformation.

The second way of enabling 'thinking differently' made visible in this volume is that of bringing alternative perspectives to a (neo)liberal state account to the centre of the analysis, so as to demarginalise them. The representation of queer-feminist, Marxist, anarchist, poststructuralist and postcolonial traditions is particularly strong (see chapters by Dhawan, Rai, Krämer and Herman). Bringing such perspectives into conversation with each other can be productive of new insights. For example, Rai recounts her experience of trying to think feminism and postcolonial theory together in her academic work, and moves questions of social reproduction to the centre, rather than the margins, of analyses of state power. The anarchist-inflected political philosophy of Kinna and the anthropology of De Cesari both enable alternative political formations to be made visible, offering resources for 'thinking differently' and reimagining the possible. One of the expectations of the museum projects described by De Cesari was that they would enable different voices to be heard, mirroring 'the diversity of Palestine and the plural meanings of Palestinianness'.

Subaltern perspectives are also brought into view by contributors who work across the borders of research, policy and activism. Cooper looks back to the transformative possibilities opened up by the municipal radicalism of the 1980s in many British cities, experiments that were designed, in part, to prefigure alternative imaginaries of a future national state. Newman describes the uneasy alignments between social movements of different periods and efforts by state workers to introduce radical reforms. Gill takes his inspiration from his research on political movements addressing the problem of borders, migration and the free movement of populations. By distinguishing between borders and boundaries, he is able to offer alternative imaginaries of how territories may be bounded without the imposition of exclusionary and subjugating borders. There are resonances here with the chapter by McDermont et al. on co-producing new forms of regulation with 'communities at the margins' in two cities in England. Arts practices were one of the methods used to elicit and encourage alternative ways of thinking, and the chapter shows how creative projects can elicit modes of seeing and knowing through a different sense, a 'feeling' for regulatory systems. Likewise, Browne and Jones, in their account of the post-patriarchal archive, retrospect from an imaginary future in which certain materials have been rendered obsolete in order to reflect, but also to act, upon the harms of today.

Finally, we want to highlight the ways in which thinking differently can emerge almost by accident, triggered by events. For example, the Charlie Hebdo massacre in Paris opened up, for Dhawan, issues about how the limits of free speech are defined, leading her to a critical re-engagement with established feminist-poststructuralist standpoints. For Clarke, two different events – the Hillsborough disaster at an English football stadium and protests against police killings by the Black Lives Matter movement in the US – prompted him to revisit ideas about the coercive power of states; while the Grenfell Tower fire in London led Newman to challenge the current political emphasis on de-regulation and to argue for an expanded 'public' role of states. This triggering process resonates with Clarke's understanding of the dynamic of reimagining itself as a temporal practice, 'juxtaposing older resources, current issues and projected possibilities in strained and unsettled ways' (Clarke, this volume).

These contributions offer methodological resources that recognise alternative formations of power/knowledge. They also prompt an understanding of reimagination as a collective practice, itself a potential source of new solidarities – but also one that brings into view the contradictions arising in projects of political transformation (a theme we return to later).

Time, space and the politics of representation

Projects of reimagination cannot begin from a flat historical landscape that erases questions of the historical struggles through which different forms of statehood have been constituted. Rather, they need to acknowledge the historical-spatial specificity of contemporary state forms, and how these represent – or erase – past struggles. Issues of temporality recur across the volume. Of particular interest are the ways in which particular temporal imaginaries – those associated with colonialism, with 'modernity', with liberal thought – become solidified in cultural representations that support would-be hegemonic relations of power. As Castro Varela (this volume) argues: 'Despite decades of postcolonial critique, Western state-theoretical considerations, even feminist approaches, continue to be plagued by Eurocentrism. For instance, the emergence of nation-states, whether European or non-European state formations, are rarely considered against the backdrop of colonial history, even in feminist debates.'

Contributions to this volume were drawn from the Global North and South, from postcolonial nations and neocolonial powers, and from states with more and less settled alignments between religious and secular authority. This range serves to disrupt and decentre representations of the state based on Western imaginaries: representations that offer distorted, Eurocentric temporal and spatial images that are politically consequential. For example, Krämer notes how Africa tends to be treated as a single spatial unit, while Castro Varela argues that postcolonial nation-states cannot be viewed as static entities characterised by a common set of characteristics. Flawed spatial imaginaries are entangled with misrepresentations of history. Krämer shows how the colonial experience is largely written out of hegemonic narratives of African statehood; dominant representations privilege Eurocentric norms, thus perpetuating colonial relationships of dependence and subservience. Herman's analysis of the Israeli state shows how dominant representations – by both the political right and left – ignore the formative role of Christianity in Israeli state formation. Christian Judeophobia and Christian colonialism, she argues, were formative influences, and Protestantism continues to play an important role in support for Israel. It is, then, 'insufficient to . . . consider only 'race' and 'apartheid' or 'Western settler colonialism' minus its Christianity as social processes worth attention' (Herman, this volume). Herman draws on the concept of 'diaspora' to offer an alternative imaginary of a non-nationalist Jewish polity, while De Cesari underscores the importance of diasporic networks in shaping and sustaining prefigurative forms of a national museum of Palestine.

Representations of 'nation', then, offer both negative and positive imaginaries. In colonial powers, the state is often represented through nostalgic images of a past in which sovereignty and authority were unquestioned, while in postcolonial contexts it forms a principal site of struggle for decolonisation to free the nation from the legacies of past – and present – forms of domination. For postcolonial societies, territorial sovereignty and national self-determination were formative principles around which anti-colonial struggles were waged with aspirations for independence and statehood. The failures of economic and political decolonisation have resulted in the erosion of postcolonial sovereignty and the hegemony of international financial organisations and multinational corporations in the post-colony. The postcolonial state is simultaneously an agent and an object of neoliberal globalisation (Dhawan and Randeria, 2013). As outlined compellingly by Rai in this volume, the (postcolonial) state continues to reproduce and re-form the household and social reproduction through law and social policy in order to respond to capitalism's needs and crises. While it must comply with the mandates of transnational capital, as well as international financial and trade organisations, it subalternises large sections of its citizens by excluding them from its protective measures. At the same time, bypassing the state is not always an option for subaltern groups in their quest for equality and justice.

Reading across these different contributions raises questions about the entangled representations of time and space. Representations of the present and future cannot be fully realised without paying attention to the often-invisible pasts out of which they are forged, and in particular the processes of historical erasure on which would-be hegemonic representations rely. Dominant political narratives often rest on depictions of a flawed past and promises of a better future, erasing how the present condenses multiple temporal dynamics that are imperfectly aligned. For example, the dynamic of speeded-up global time serves to represent some nation-states as 'lagging behind', thus legitimating projects of economic retrenchment. And the dynamics of 'slow' political movements (see Gill in this volume) tend to clash with the high-speed imperatives of economic crisis, political regime change or revolutionary struggle.

Gill, Clarke and Newman each draw on Doreen Massey's work on the relational constitution of space and scale. But time, too, is relational. The prefigurative politics discussed in several chapters – a politics based on living in the present as if the desired future already exists – suggests a foreshortening of time. For example, De Cesari shows how present creative practices can be constitutive of *future* imaginings. Each of the experiments she describes are 'cosmopolitan, travelling projects' that offer state-like initiatives instituted by non-state actors who 'playfully engage with' the ambiguities of performing like a state when being a state is impossible. However, prefigurative politics can fail to acknowledge the salience of older forms, not only the dominant form that prefigurative forces seek to escape, but also residual traces of earlier progressive forces from which inspiration – and perhaps difficult political lessons – might be gleaned. Progressive forces may be weakened by charges of either nostalgia (for golden past of radical politics/of social democratic welfare/ of independent sovereignty) or an idealised – and unrealisable – future. They may be set aside by charges that we are living (again!) through times of crisis in which attention to the 'peripheral' concerns of equality or justice movements must be (at least for the present) set aside. Or they may be rendered irrelevant by the seizing of temporality as a site of struggle by the political right and its rendering of past struggles – socialist, feminist, antiracist, queer – as the source of harms that damage the interests of 'ordinary people' and offer a perverted form of democracy. Such a politics is based on a politics of nostalgia: one in which people knew their place, in which nations had unfettered sovereign power, in which colonialism ruled and in which the proper hierarchical ordering – of nations, races, genders and sexes – was unassailed.

But such representations offer a linear view of time that fails to acknowledge the arguments about plurality, ambiguity and paradox that pervade this volume. Political struggles condense multiple temporalities: some may refer to the long durée of colonialism and anti-colonial struggles; some to the fractured and dynamic temporalities of capitalism (punctuated by successive crises); some to the future promises of political projects; others to forms of retro-nostalgia. Filippini draws on this Gramscian conception of time to suggest how temporal multiplicity cannot be incorporated into a single 'harmonious plurality' (2017: 109), but forms the locus of struggle in which one temporality becomes dominant, accepted as normal by subordinating other temporal imaginaries. Such a perspective is helpful in unsettling the representations of Western modernity as an ideal time. But it also underscores the complex narratives of statehood in the chapters on Israel, Palestine, India and 'Africa' in this volume, where authors show how multiple temporal strands of becoming and erasure are inextricably interwoven.

This more complex conception of time also helps illuminate the politics of pre-figuration. Cooper refers to the 'knotted temporalities' in which practices and ideals associated with an imagined future are brought into the present. Such a politics draws on temporal imaginings that condense present and future – living in the present as if the desired future already exists. But the temporal landscape is also littered with what Clarke terms 'exhausted experiments' that haunt the possibility of future imaginings. As Cooper argues, reimagination must work across historical legacies, present constraints and future hopes and possibilities: prefigurative conceptions knowingly take place on a terrain already structured by prior dominant under-standings. In prefigurative feminist projects, then, how might the traces of older feminist politics be represented? How might the future orientation of Gill's border abolition movement deal with the state-centric representations of other progres-sive campaigns? Can the temporality of promise and anticipation described by De Cesari be sustained in the face of more immediate concerns about institutional support and funding or the longer conflicts around Palestinian statehood itself?

Struggles to reimagining the state, then, rest on struggles over representational practices and how ideas and images are articulated (or not) in hegemonic for-mations of power. Unpacking dominant representations is one way of creating a breathing space where thinking otherwise is possible. Much of this volume has been concerned with the conceptual labour of deconstructing dominant repre-sentations, resignifying concepts and asserting alternative meanings. This is because different representations provoke, or close down, the kinds of politics that are pos-sible. For example, notions of a unitary state tend to be associated with hierar-chical, and highly masculine, images of power and control. These elicit outright forms of resistance – for example, the Black Lives Matter movement mentioned by Clarke, or the No Borders campaigns described by Gill. But if we move to a more decentred – and arguably feminist – imaginary, then other forms of politics come into view. For example, Cooper (this volume) contrasts dominant imaginaries of the state as top down, hierarchically ordered with more plural conceptions that might enable open and networked formations. She depicts a 'rhizomatic form of local governance – stretching out, activating and incorporating community projects within a constantly evolving governmental form', a form enabling a flourishing of grass-roots politics and a re-evaluation of the everyday, as well as new forms of state activism on behalf of those they represent. This resonates with McDermont et al.'s projects of reimagining regulation within a fragmentary and dispersed architecture/geometry of power. However, these different imaginaries cannot be mapped onto different systems of governing (centralised/decentralised, plural/unitary); they are, rather, associated with different approaches to politics.

Problematising politics

One tension that runs through the volume is that between a politics that seeks to repair, reclaim, subvert or resignify dominant or hegemonic forms, and a politics oriented towards offering alternatives – although such alternatives are always ambiguously aligned with the hegemonic. This tension is explored by Kinna in her analysis of Mill's attempt to reclaim liberal political theory through a form of 'subversive reframing', despite his acknowledging the ways in which liberal theory is already inscribed with historical forms of injustice, especially racial injustice. Dhawan's chapter also tests the boundaries of liberal thought by drawing on a number of postcolonial, feminist and poststructuralist perspectives on the relationship between speech, power and violence. The right to free speech, she argues, conflicts with the need to regulate forms of hate speech that exert violence on minority groups. Dhawan engages with Butler's analysis of the ways in which the regulation of speech enhances the state's discursive power, limiting the potential for social and cultural struggles over language, including subversive appropriation of hate speech through processes of resignification, recontextualistion and 'speaking back'. But, she asks (in this volume): 'Given the state monopoly on violence and its patriarchal, racist, imperialist proclivities, should feminists, queers, religious and racial minorities be wary of engaging with the state and devote their progressive political labour . . . to extra state initiatives? Given the valid anxieties about the state's coercive powers, can the state be interpellated as a site of redress?'

Kinna contrasts the project of reclaiming liberal theories of the state (the 'master's tools') and an emphasis on prefigurative politics that attempts to align the means and ends of political action. The latter invokes the performative style of politics associated with social movements and locally determined forms of direct action, with transnational movements and embryonic state formations. However, this performative style is never free of wider relations of power and inequality. For example, McDermont et al. describe a number of attempts by subaltern groups to change the power dynamics of their relationships to the state. But they argue that the attempts to co-produce new forms of regulation may create new exclusions, and as McDermont (in this volume) argues: 'Questions of what counts as representation, and expertise and experience, remain unresolved. Inequalities of power and expertise cannot be altered through co-production; politics matters too'. Here, she contrasts the apparently progressive policy discourse of co-production with the structural relations of power that are unlikely to be mitigated, especially in conditions of austerity governance. And prefigurative experiments and emergent forms may get taken up by the state in ways that strip them of the politics that informed them (see Newman on the state's co-option and evisceration of social movements, and Clarke on the practices of refusal, resistance, dilution and diversion that have surrounded equality policies).

Even where it is possible to avoid problems of co-optation and appropriation by the state, prefigurative forms may not be able to engage with basic questions of securing rights (for disenfranchised populations), redistributing resources or regulating corporate or individual behaviour. Clarke debates the fate of struggles to use existing legal agencies and powers to redress inequalities and prevent harms, and highlights the dilemmas of using the law as a means of enforcing desired social change. However, he goes on to argue that some form or forms of social control are needed to regulate social behaviour, whether interpersonal violence or transnational harms. This raises wider questions about the possibility of performing alternative forms of self-governance or self-regulation in non-state spaces. Clarke offers Ostrom's '8 Principles for Managing a Commons', while Kinna draws on Pateman to engage with notions of 'free association', suggesting ways in which rights can be viewed as a matrix of regulatory tools that social groups use to restructure their relations. But both Clarke and Dhawan are ambivalent about such a position. Clarke highlights questions concerning membership of the entities concerned – questions that cannot be resolved within an imagined bounded community or nation – while Dhawan points to the dangers of relying on 'civil society', in effect a composite of family, community and marketplace as alternatives to the state (see also Chatterjee, 2004: 38; Spivak, 2009: 32–3).

This is why the core ambivalence around a focus on state-centric or prefigurative forms of politics discussed here is so significant. The emphasis on re-conceptualisation or actualisation – between thinking differently or performing otherwise – varies across chapters. And, like other binary formulations, it tends to collapse the complexity and ambiguity of lived political experience. However, neither exists in pure form; most movements, whether those of an earlier period described by Newman and Cooper or the radical community projects discussed by McDermont, flow between them (which is perhaps why they are so difficult to sustain).

Living with ambivalence

Reimagining the state is hampered by the widespread ambivalence of progressive movements towards the state. Since the late 1970s, liberal and left critiques of financialisation, securitisation and militarisation have proliferated, particularly in contexts where states have played a negative role in these processes. The causes of distrust and suspicion may vary, from the evisceration of state welfare policies in some nations to the deep memories of the oppressive state apparatus in former communist blocs, or the threatened 'capture' of states by parties of the political right. But all serve to intensify suspicion and distrust, leading both liberals and radicals to turn to forms of activism that seek to bypass, rather than transform, the state. But Foucault cautions against giving in to our fears, anxieties and mistrust of the state: the rise of the neoliberal state in the West is, in Foucault's view, inextricably linked to discourses of state phobia (2008: 75–80, 186–8). An undifferentiated condemnation of the state serves to erase disparate historical processes of state-formation and state-building, as well as diverse strategies of negotiation between states and citizens. In some states, such negotiations have resulted in what were viewed as liberal reforms (equality policies, trade union rights, expansive conceptions of citizenship), although such reforms have often been subordinated to the economic imperatives of neoliberalism.

The ambivalences around the state as the agent of progressive transformation are reflected in this volume. For example, Gill distinguishes between two different political positions on the project of liberalising border control: one state-centric, requiring states to cede some elements of their sovereignty; the second, a more anarchist and performance-based political movement. Cooper highlights tensions between notions of an 'everyday' state (one that reflects and condenses relations of power) and an activist state (that seeks to transform them). Castro Varela points to Judith Butler's ambivalence about the possibility of an 'ethical state', while Clarke (in this volume) wrestles with contradictions, notably the 'problems of trying to "capture" the state for progressive purposes', with its attendant risk of 'being captured by the state and its power'.

It is perhaps this latter risk that underscores the anti-statism of many political movements. Left, feminist and other critiques have led many proponents of radical politics to abandon the state as an agent of equality and social justice and as a focus of participatory politics, looking instead to transnational and local sites of activism. There are parallel moves in some forms of critical work within the academy. Academic work on neoliberal globalisation tends to focus on the loss of state power and sovereignty, rendering the state an unfruitful locus of progressive political transformation; even if they wanted to bring about progressive reforms, it follows, they have very limited capacity to do so (an argument challenged by some contributors to this volume). Poststructuralist theory also offers rich resources for critical engagements with state power, and has informed progressive forms of analysis on which many chapters in this volume have drawn. Governmentality studies, in particular, offer productive ways of understanding the flows of power and knowledge through multiple agents; but in emphasising dispersal and multiplicity, we often ignore the state itself. However, as Foucault acknowledged, 'power relations have been progressively governmentalised, that is to say, elaborated, rationalised and centralised in the form of, or under the auspices of, state institutions' (2000: 345). Academic engagement with questions of power and rule, then, should not reject the state as a locus of analysis.

At the same time, bypassing the state is not always an option for subaltern groups in their quest for equality and justice. Despite strong reservations about postcolonial states, many postcolonial scholars (notably Partha Chatterjee, 2004, and Gayatri Spivak, 2009) point to its indispensability in the quest for rights and justice. The fruits of decolonisation – parliamentary democracy, economic and social justice, civil and political rights – are monopolised by an elite minority, leaving the vast majority disenfranchised in and by their own states as they struggle for survival and dignity. Dhawan and Randeria (2013) argue that, instead of bypassing the postcolonial state, it is urgent to reimagine mechanisms for dispensing justice and claiming rights. Tactics must be developed to negotiate with the contradictory and incoherent organs of the state, a state that must be critiqued, but can also be an inadvertent ally in guaranteeing the rights of vulnerable citizens. Desubalternisation entails the insertion of disenfranchised individuals and groups into the enabling institutional structures of democracy, rights and justice. Despite globalisation of governance and transnationalisation of activism, the state remains the prime addressee for vulnerable citizens, with the national arena being indispensable for those struggling for rights and justice. Drawing on insights from postcolonial scholarship, Dhawan and Randeria propose that instead of a narrow understanding of the state as merely a repressive apparatus, it is important to envisage a different state, one that is capable of articulating the will of excluded subaltern populations. Notwithstanding the widespread disillusionment with postcolonial states (which, of course, are varied in their histories of state formation and state performance) for failing to deliver on their promises, strategies have to be implemented to garner greater answerability of postcolonial states to their citizens, rather than to international financial and trade organisations or international donors.

Anti-statism also rests on a singular, coherent conceptualisation of the state that this volume has challenged. As such, it disregards the dynamic and varied functions embodied by the state and its various institutions and bodies, which sometimes cohere to, but at other times contradict, each other. This plural, dynamic and ambivalent conception of the state offers space for progressive projects of reimagining. As this volume demonstrates, theory and politics are dynamically entangled. The academic focus on critique has perhaps contributed to the shift away from an engagement with the state as a locus of progressive change. Viewing the state as dynamic and ambivalent requires different projects of critique that go beyond state-phobic rhetoric and politics, a complicated and tricky challenge.

But political shifts have also destabilised notions of state radicalism, such that in the late twentieth and early twenty-first centuries, radicalism has tended to be associated with the political right rather than the political left. Neoliberalism, although requiring state activism to expand its spheres of influence, is itself profoundly anti-statist, promoting strategies of state retrenchment, the marketisation of state services and the vilification of state welfare, looking instead to families, communities and enterprises as responsible agents. This intersects with the rise of populist politics in complex ways. While populism is not inherently anti-statist (indeed, it relies on images of a 'strong state'), it is profoundly antithetical to the architecture of state institutions, governance procedures and legal safeguards.

Both neoliberalism and populism draw on, amplify and resignify academic and left critiques of the state. We might follow Dagnino and understand this as a 'perverse confluence' (2007) between different and antagonistic political projects. These originate in different political orientations and point to different political phenomena: the critical engagement with the state by the academy on the one hand, and the assault on the state by neoliberalism on the other. But their alignment – however provisional and incomplete – contributes to the climate of anti-statism that renders projects of reimagining or reclaiming the state problematic. Addressing this perverse confluence requires an ambivalent holding together of critique (of state power and practices) and a more positive orientation to creating new resources, practices and political formations. It means working with contradictions, holding the paradoxes and ambiguities in mind, while getting on with the labour of creating and sustaining new configurations of power. To do so, Gill (in this volume) argues, the progressive academic must move beyond the role of both critic and reformer:

> This is not a space 'between' revolution and reform, but somewhere else, somewhere full of risk and potential. It is to this project that progressive scholarship invites us.

References

Chatterjee, P. (2004) *The Politics of the Governed: Reflections on Popular Politics in Most of the World*. New York: Columbia University Press.

Dagnino, E. (2007) 'Participation, Citizenship and Democracy: Perverse Confluence and Displacement of Meanings' in Neveu, C. (ed.), *Cultures et Practiques Participatives: Perspectives Comparatives*. Paris: L'Harmattan, pp. 353–70.

Dhawan, N. and Randeria, S. (2013) 'Perspectives on Globalization and Subalternity' in Huggan, G. (ed.), *The Oxford Handbook of Postcolonial Studies*. Oxford: Oxford University Press, pp. 559–86.

Filippini, M. (2017) *Using Gramsci: A New Approach*. London: Pluto Press.

Foucault, M. (2008) *The Birth of Biopolitics: Lectures at the Collège de France 1978–1979* (trans. Burchell, G.). New York: Palgrave Macmillan.

Foucault, M. (2000) [1982] 'The Subject and Power' in Fabion, J. D. (ed.), *Power: Essential Works of Foucault 1954–1984*, vol. 3 (trans. Hurley, R. et al.). New York: New York Press.

Panitch, L. and Gindin, S. (1999). 'Transcending Pessimism: Rekindling Socialist Imagination' in Panitch, L. and Gindin, S. (eds.), *Necessary and Unnecessary Utopias*. New York: Monthly Review Press, pp. 1–29.

Spivak, G. C. (2009) 'They the People: Problems of Alter-Globalization', *Radical Philosophy*, 157, pp. 31–6.

INDEX